22.95

W9-CBN-106

CUBS NATION

CUBS NATION

162 GAMES · 162 STORIES
1 ADDICTION

GENE WOJCIECHOWSKI

DOUBLEDAY

New York   London   Toronto   Sydney   Auckland

PUBLISHED BY DOUBLEDAY
a division of Random House, Inc.

DOUBLEDAY and the portrayal of an anchor with a dolphin are registered trademarks
of Random House, Inc.

Copyright © 2005 by Gene Wojciechowski

Library of Congress Cataloging-in-Publication Data

Wojciechowski, Gene.
Cubs nation : 162 games, 162 stories, 1 addiction / by Gene Wojciechowski.—1st ed.
p. cm.
1. Chicago Cubs (Baseball team)—History—21st century. 2. Baseball players—United
States—Anecdotes. 3. Baseball fans—United States—Anecdotes. 4. Sports personnel—
United States—Anecdotes. I. Title.

GV875.C58W64 2005
796.357'64'0977311—dc22

2004065544

ISBN 0-385-51300-3

Book design by Tina Thompson

PRINTED IN THE UNITED STATES OF AMERICA

April 2005

First Edition

10 9 8 7 6 5 4 3 2 1

To Cheryl, Lara, and Taylor

CONTENTS

Acknowledgments   ix

Prologue   1

APRIL   3

MAY   71

JUNE   138

JULY   200

AUGUST   273

SEPTEMBER   340

OCTOBER   405

Epilogue   414

ACKNOWLEDGMENTS

You don't chronicle the life and death of a Cubs season without help. I had plenty, beginning with Doubleday's Bill Thomas and Jason Kaufman. Their address says New York, but their understanding of the operatic qualities of the Cubs says Chicago.

Longtime friend and agent Janet Pawson held this project's hand from the moment an understanding was struck in a Manhattan restaurant with the aforementioned Mr. Thomas. I wasn't there, which is all you need to know about my trust in young Pawson.

As always, I could depend on the advice and help of friends. Rick Reilly comes to mind, though not for his baseball expertise. Reilly thinks the hit-and-run is something you do in a bar fight. And who can forget his gentle, comforting words to me the day the Cubs were officially eliminated from the 2004 playoff chase: "You poor bastard."

Joe Wojciechowski, younger brother and reigning home run leader on his ESPN.com softball team, smoothed out the rough edges of chapters, as well as provided research assistance. He also endured my daily cell calls during the five-block walk from Wrigley to my rental apartment. Those post-defeat rants must have been a treat.

The Gang of Nine—Andy Masur of WGN Radio, Paul Sullivan and Dave Van Dyck of the *Chicago Tribune*, Bruce Miles of the *Daily Herald*, Jeff Vorva of the *Daily Southtown*, Mike Kiley and Toni Ginnetti of the *Chicago Sun-Times*, Nick Pietruszkiewicz of the *Northwest Herald*, and Carrie Muskat of MLB.com—deserves considerable mention for its patience and willingness to accept an outsider of sorts.

Cubs president Andy MacPhail, during a January 2004 lunch meeting at a restaurant near Wrigley, was the first to give his blessings to *Cubs Nation*, which is to say he provided access and support—and required nothing in return. At least a dozen times during this strange, bizarre season, MacPhail would inquire about the progress of the book. "Well, are we giving you enough to write about?" he would say.

Short of a World Series appearance, I can't think of anything.

I remain indebted to MacPhail for his cooperation, as well as to others in the Cubs organization. In particular: Jim Hendry, Scott Nelson, Jimmy Bank, Chuck Wasserstrom, Ed Lynch, Sharon Pannozzo, Samantha Newby, B. R. Koehnemann, Katelyn Thrall, Frank Maloney, John McDonough, Jay Blunk, Joe Rios, Jim Oboikowitch, the Wrigley grounds crew, Pat Hughes, Ron Santo, Steve Stone, Chip Caray, Matt Boltz.

Manager Dusty Baker was extremely generous with his time and insights, and his coaching staff was equally approachable. And with the exception of one player who declined to be interviewed unless he was paid, the Cubs were mostly receptive to my many questions. Michael Barrett, Todd Walker, Paul Bako, LaTroy Hawkins, Mark Prior, Kerry Wood, Matt Clement, Greg Maddux, and Glendon Rusch were especially helpful.

In all, more than 200 different people connected to the Cubs either directly or indirectly were interviewed for this book. I thank each of them for sharing their stories. I also thank O. S. Carr for his considerable assistance, and *ESPN The Magazine* editor-in-chief Gary Hoenig and senior editor J. B. Morris for their support.

And none of this would have been possible without daughters Lara and Taylor, and wife Cheryl, who handled the seven-month, baseball-forced estrangement better than I did. I'll take them to Wrigley in '05, but this time without a notepad. I promise.

CUBS NATION

PROLOGUE

••

I have a friend, Mozartian gifted as a writer, who says baseball suffers from arthritis, that it needs a walker and an AARP card. My friend, of course, is an idiot. He would have never said this had he been sitting where I was sitting the evenings of October 14 and 15, 2003: Aisle 122, Row 13, Seat 3.

Those two nights—Games 6 and 7 of the National League Championship Series—were the birds-and-bees moment for an idea that eventually became this book.

Game 6. The Bartman Game.

Game 7. The Elimination Game.

I took my 20-year-old daughter, Taylor, to Game 7. She was going to witness either history or anguish.

Or drunks. To her left were two of them. But just as Kerry Wood delivered the first pitch of the game, I noticed one of the overserved knuckleheads look toward the sky and mouth the words "Thank you." Even inebriated, he understood the significance of watching his beloved Cubs on this night, and this late in October. And when Moises Alou hit a two-run homer in the third to give the Cubs a 5-3 lead, the other drunk said it was because his dead mother winked at him. I can't make this stuff up.

Behind us were the best kind of Cubs fans: two 40-ish women from New England, thus predisposed to fatalism. When the Florida Marlins moved ahead, 6-5, then 7-5, then 9-5, one of the women yelled, "They're going to stick it up our butts, aren't they?" Meanwhile, the other woman whistled so loud that I'm now being fitted for a Miracle Ear. But she was passionate about all things baseball, and all things Cubs, constantly leaning forward, looking at my scorecard, and asking, "All right, who we got coming up?"

The Marlins won, 9-6. As they celebrated, someone a few rows in front of us yelled, "Get off our field!" The two drunks staggered off into the crowd. The two New Englanders stared at the ancient scoreboard in disbelief.

"There's always next year," said one of the women.

The crowd outside was subdued. "National League Champions" T-shirt boxes stayed unopened under concession tables. No sales there. They would later be destroyed.

Doom. Despair. Despondency. Another Wrigleyville wake.

The Cubs are all too familiar with such solemn gatherings. You know the numbers: no World Series championship since 1908, no World Series appearance since 1945. I'm surprised the anti-Cub, Mayor Richard M. Daley, hasn't ordered the dates posted on all signs entering the city.

Cursed? I don't know. I do know there is a cemetery located just down the street from Wrigley and a cemetery just across the street from the Cubs' spring training facility in Mesa, Arizona. And is it a coincidence that at the O'Hare Airport parking garage, the Cubs' level is located on, sigh, the bottom floor?

This is a book about the 2004 Cubs season, about those who played and those who didn't. And sadly, but almost predictably, it is about those who suffered.

APRIL

••

GAME 1

Monday, April 5, 2004 . . . Cubs 7, Cincinnati Reds 4 . . . Great American Ball Park . . . Cubs NL Central pennant flies: First place (record, 1-0) . . . Stuff: The game sells out in a franchise-record 16 minutes. . . . Disabled list resident Mark Prior does a live, on-field interview with CNBC? What, they want to discuss Prior's portfolio? But the real news is Prior's sideline throwing session, his first since March 22 because of an inflamed right Achilles tendon and inflamed right elbow. . . . Sammy Sosa on the "Lovable Losers" tag: "All the things they say about Chicago is going to be over pretty soon."

Dusty Baker stabs his fork at the postgame salad as if the lettuce leaves and cucumbers are a threat to leap from the bowl. His Cubs are 25 minutes removed from an Opening Day victory against the payroll-challenged and Ken Griffey Jr.–less Reds. Three waves of reporters—TV, then radio, then print—have made their way through the visiting manager's office at the one-year-old Great American Ball Park. Baker, still wearing most of his Cubs gray road uni, is fried.

He didn't sleep well a night earlier. He never does before Opening Day. Too many butterflies spreading their wings in his tummy.

This is Baker's second season as the Cubs' manager, but unlike 2003, when expectations were modest at best, this year's team is the chic choice to go long and far in the postseason. ESPN baseball analyst Peter Gammons, a long-suffering New Englander, has the Cubs beating the equally cursed Boston Red Sox in a seven-game World Series. *Sports Illustrated* also predicts a Cubs World Series title. "Hell Freezes Over," reads the *SI* cover headline. *ESPN The Magazine* goes with the Cubs too.

"I don't read predictions," Baker says. "You can spend time getting ready, or you can *be* ready."

Johnnie B. Baker Jr. is ready. What other manager wears personalized No. 12 wristbands during a game—as if he were *playing*? And who else in the big leagues has on his desk a book entitled *Leadership Secrets of Attila the Hun*?

Baker, 54, is a managerial confluence of Old School and New Age thinking. He hasn't overseen a team with a losing record since 1996. His former Atlanta Braves teammate, the legendary Hank Aaron, used to tell him, "Nervous is good, but just don't be scared." Baker was nervous as he tossed and turned in the wee hours of Monday. But scared? Scared is undergoing a three-hour surgical procedure in 2001 to rid his body of prostate cancer. This was just baseball.

Baker was up by 6 A.M., two hours before his alarm was set to buzz. He said prayers for his family, for his players and staff. He worried and wondered about the new season. By 9:30 he was at the ballpark, nearly a full five hours before the first pitch.

"You get to the park, but you're not really hungry," he says. "You try not to be nervous, but you are. You go around and wish everybody well. Then you have the chaplain come in and say a prayer before we start. Then we go about our day."

There were no pregame speeches today. Baker did that at Sunday's workout at Great American. He detailed what the Cubs had to do to win. The shopping list is short and sweet: no jealousy, no selfishness, pull for each other, make fundamental plays. He emphasized the importance of comeback victories, of getting leads and holding them, of winning one-run games, of winning the first game of a series, of winning getaway games.

End of lecture series.

Baker's pregame preparation includes putting together his statistical cheat sheets, which right now are based on last season's numbers. The pair of sheets are no bigger than a couple slices of French toast, and the key stats and info are highlighted by a green marker (Baker keeps a fistful of different-colored highlighters in a zippered bank pouch). Who hits better against whom? Who hits better against right-handers and left-handers? Who hits well with runners in scoring position? Baker considers an assortment of possible game strategies. Then he waits.

"The best time for me is after they play the National Anthem," he says. That's when he's in his favorite place: in a dugout, with his team, away from the media, a Tea Tree Australian Chewing Stick (flavored toothpick, to you and me) poking from his mouth. It's just Baker and the game.

Monday was different because it was Opening Day, but also because Vice President Dick Cheney—and about 11,000 Secret Service agents packing heat, plus more bomb-sniffing dogs than you could shake a bag of Purina at—was here to throw out the first pitch. Ohio is a Republican stronghold, which explains the GOP-sponsored voter registration trailer located just outside the stadium. Baker is a registered Democrat.

"That's OK," he says. "He's a man you have to respect."

Baker introduced the Veep to everyone in the clubhouse. Cubs traveling secretary Jimmy Bank asked Cheney to autograph a baseball and the back of two business cards. Then Cheney, members of his advance staff, and his security entourage moved on. Afterward, *Daily Herald* beat writer Bruce Miles said, "If Cheney is supposed to be in a secret location, why isn't he at Comiskey Park?"

Hello, IRS audit.

Baker's first managerial decision of the day was when he took pen to lineup card. Players use spring training to prepare for the season; so do managers. Baker tinkered with the Cubs' lineup in Arizona. By the time he arrives in Cincinnati, his batting order is set: Mark Grudzielanek, 2B; Corey Patterson, CF; Sammy Sosa, RF; Moises Alou, LF; Aramis Ramirez, 3B; Derrek Lee, 1B; Alex Gonzalez, SS; Michael Barrett, C; Kerry Wood, SP.

A year ago, the Opening Day lineup was considerably less imposing. Baker had to use the light-hitting Gonzalez in the No. 2 spot. Rookie first baseman Hee Seop Choi was in the five hole. Third baseman Mark Bell-horn batted sixth. Patterson, with only 212 big league games to his credit, batted seventh. Catcher Damian Miller hit eighth.

Now Choi is with the Florida Marlins, Bellhorn with the Boston Red Sox, and Miller with the Oakland Athletics.

During Baker's 15-plus seasons in the big leagues he batted fifth, then third, then seventh, then sixth, then fifth again, then third again. He knows how lineups work.

"The second hitter, generally speaking, should be unselfish and your smartest hitter: take pitches, hit and run, bunt, handle the bat," says Baker. "Your third hitter is generally your best hitter. He's a guy who can get on base, a guy who can run, a guy who's going to score as many as he drives in. Your fourth hitter drives in runs. Your fifth hitter is the clutch man to me. He's basically the foundation man. He's your RBI man. Your sixth hitter is double-leadoff: an RBI guy in case your fourth and fifth guy get on. A real foundation man is your seventh hitter. If he's good, that makes everybody else in between good. Your eighth hitter is a guy who can drive in some key runs and get the pitcher to the plate with two outs. That way I don't have to pinch-hit for him the next inning. Or he has to be a guy who can get on base so the pitcher can bunt him over."

The Cubs made it relatively easy on Baker in the early innings of the season opener. Patterson hit a 1-0 pitch by Reds starter Cory Lidle into the right-field seats for a first-inning, one-run lead. Midway through the third, the Cubs led, 4-0. All was well.

But Wood scuffled in the bottom of the third, thanks to a wild pitch, a walk, an RBI single, an RBI groundout, and a growing pitch count. Baker could read the scoreboard pitch count total too. So when Wood gave up a one-out single in the fifth inning, then a walk, then a two-run double to Sean Casey, Baker had what he now says was the decision of the game: pull Wood with a one-run lead—but only two outs away from qualifying for a decision—or risk a tie or losing the lead altogether by letting him face home run threats Austin Kearns or Adam Dunn?

Kearns, who struggled during the spring while recovering from arthroscopic shoulder surgery, was less of a consideration to Baker. Sure enough, Kearns flied to Patterson. But the left-handed-hitting Dunn, who led the Reds in homers last season and had had an impressive spring, worried Baker. A lot.

Baker had his cheat sheet. Entering the game, Dunn was a career 4-of-20 with one homer against Wood. Baker stayed with his starter and Wood rewarded him by inducing a fly ball to Alou.

"Thank God," says Baker.

With Wood's pitch count at 95, Baker decided to replace the right-hander with Michael Wuertz, who was making his Major League debut after spending his entire six-year career in the Cubs' farm system. Wuertz, 25, was a nonroster invitee to spring training.

"I always say in spring training that I'm looking for a surprise," says Baker.

Wuertz, thanks to a 1.15 ERA in 13 spring appearances, was his surprise.

Nursing a one-run lead—and with Wood's W on the line—is no easy thing. But Baker helped Wuertz by purposely having him face the bottom of the Reds' order. Wuertz, whose parents and brother had driven to Cincinnati from Austin, Minnesota, struck out Jason LaRue and Ryan Freel, then got Juan Castro to ground out to second.

"I knew I only needed him for one inning," says Baker. That's because he used veteran lefty Kent Mercker in the seventh (loved the matchups) and Kyle Farnsworth in the eighth (loved the 100 mph radar readings).

Next decision: Use setup man LaTroy Hawkins?

Baker had some flexibility in his bullpen, thanks to that scheduled off day. He could use four relievers, maybe more if necessary, because of the gameless Tuesday.

"A lot of times people don't understand that you manage to the schedule," he says. "If we didn't have a day off tomorrow—say we were in the middle of 15 days in a row, and that was the first day—then you manage a little different than if you had an off day two or three days from now."

Baker used closer Joe Borowski to get the save, though there were a few perspiration moments.

Afterward, Baker meets the press, shrugs off the questions about Borowski's medium-sized struggles, and then digs into his salad. General manager Jim Hendry sits nearby on a small couch. Gary Hughes, Hendry's special assistant, also takes a seat. They're waiting for Baker.

One day of a season is complete. Baker and the Cubs have survived and conquered. Attila would have been proud.

GAME 2

Wednesday, April 7, 2004 . . . Reds 3, Cubs 1 . . . Great American Ball Park . . . Stat of the game: Greg Maddux, who made his Cubs debut exactly 11 years, 6 months, and 8 days ago—and lost—returns for a second tour—and loses. . . . Stuff: Mark Prior is the subject of a torturously trite "Prior Watch" in the Chicago Tribune *(complete with photo of the pitcher's feet, as well as daily updates of his physical condition).*

His brown hair is still damp from the shower, and his body language all but screams, "Let's get this over with." Greg Maddux is 0-1, thanks mostly to three mistakes: a second-inning cutter to Reds lug Adam Dunn that stayed over the tubby part of the plate and soon found itself in the right-field bleachers ("I don't think he put it where he wanted it," says Dunn, almost apologetically), a third-inning walk to D'Angelo Jimenez, followed shortly thereafter by Ken Griffey Jr.'s homer that traveled farther than some Gemini space flights.

Now Maddux sits unhappily at a small table inside an interview room and tries to explain six innings of decent but flawed pitching (four hits, two walks, three strikeouts, two hit batsmen). His wife, Kathy, and two children, Amanda and Chase, stand at the back of the room near the doors. Kathy knows her husband; this isn't going to take long.

On Opening Day he had sat at this same table, with the same indifferent look, and spoken succinctly about his return to the Cubs.

"I'm doing something I've always done, just wearing a different shirt," he said.

It's a little more complicated than that. Maddux didn't sign with, say, Tampa Bay, but with a franchise born in 1876, the same year, apparently, as Julio Franco. And Maddux and the Cubs have a little history together— six-plus years of wins and, sadly, contract problems followed by a quickie Atlanta divorce. But now, reconciliation . . . plus a three-year, $24-million deal and a team good enough to do some damage.

"I believe in talent," Maddux said on Opening Day. "I think this team has a lot of talent."

What he doesn't believe in is this idea of Maddux as Father Figure. Sure, he's happy to help the younger guys, but the Cubs aren't paying him that kind of coin to show Carlos Zambrano how to grip a two-seamer.

"I'm a player," he said. "I'm a player first, second, third, and fourth. These guys were pretty good before I got here."

I like Maddux because he uses words like "privilege" when talking about starting a game. Tonight's start was the 572nd of his Hall of Fame career, and still he's humble and smart enough to cherish each one. He also knows this season is still in diapers. If he's scuffling in June, then he'll chat.

Maddux has owned the outer edges of the plate for the better part of 20 seasons. Against the Reds he struggled occasionally with the two items that matter most to him: locating his fastball and changing speeds.

Junior's homer was No. 482, so there's no shame in being taken deep by a Hall of Fame candidate. And Dunn, whose thighs weigh more than Maddux, led the Reds in dingers a season ago. Homers happen with these guys.

"I actually had a good time," says Maddux afterward. "It would have been better if we had won."

There are a few more mumbled, halfhearted comments, and then he is gone, making a beeline for his family and those double doors.

GAME 3

Thursday, April 8, 2004 ... Reds 5, Cubs 3 ... Great American Ball Park ... Stat of the game: Matt Clement, who gave the Cubs the heebie-jeebies during spring training (0-3, 8.84 ERA), isn't any better in his first start of '04. ... Why Cincinnati isn't like Wrigleyville: It costs $10 to park 100 feet from the Great American Ball Park. It would take a home equity loan to do the same at Wrigley.

Getaway day.

Stadium workers are already power-spraying the seats. A grounds crew member does stretching exercises near the Cubs' dugout. A tarp, still wet from the previous night's rains, covers the infield.

Inside the Cubs' clubhouse, you can smell breakfast being cooked in the adjacent kitchen. An array of *USA Today*s and Cincinnati *Enquirer*s are carefully laid out on one of the tables in the middle of the room. Someone has made copies of the *USA Today* crossword puzzle and placed them next to the newspapers.

Clubbies quickly fold towels, sani socks, and Ace bandages before the players begin to arrive. MTV is on the main television monitor, but as soon as the first Cub walks into the room the channel is switched to ESPN's *SportsCenter*. And for the Cubs' magazine-reading pleasure are copies of *Celebrity Car*, complete with the automobile excesses of Bill Goldberg, Wycleff, and Cindy Margolis.

Closer Joe Borowski grabs a crossword puzzle and leaves the room. Reliever Kent Mercker comes in just in time to see highlights of Boston Red Sox center fielder Johnny Damon going 5-for-5. Damon, with scraggly long hair and a beard that would have given Sparky Anderson an aneurysm, looks like Tom Hanks in *Castaway*.

"It's Bigfoot!" says Mercker as he watches Damon.

Maddux arrives moments later, changes into his Cubs stuff, and begins distributing sheets for his Masters golf pool. Sammy Sosa won Maddux's Players Championship pool, so there's hope for everyone

"Ever play Augusta National?" I ask Maddux.

"Two rounds," he says.

"And?"

"Shot 80-76."

A handful of players sit at one of the tables. Maddux announces that his birthday is April 14. "And if you'd like to get me something, I could use a dozen Pro-V1s or a tube of toothpaste, the kind that doesn't drip," he says.

Mercker, who also played with Maddux in Atlanta, knows the date well.

"Same birthday (different years) as Pete Rose, and [former Braves pitcher Steve] Avery," says Mercker.

"And it's the same day that Lincoln was shot," says Maddux. "How about that for some useless trivia?"

Dusty Baker is in his office, candle lit on his desk, putting the finishing touches to his baseball cheat sheets. He sips on a cup of Yogi tea as the print reporters file in for their daily pregame session with Baker.

Baker won't say it, but he'd love a little two-hour Cubs win today. That way the team can get on the plane and get to Atlanta in time for Baker to attend the ceremony at Turner Field commemorating the 30th anniversary of Hank Aaron's 715th home run, the one that broke Babe Ruth's record. Baker was in the on-deck circle that April 8, 1974, evening at Atlanta's Fulton County Stadium. You see Los Angeles Dodger Al Downing throw the pitch. You see Aaron laser-beam it over the left-field fence. You see Baker thrust his arm in celebration of one of baseball's most seminal moments.

Baker never tires of reliving that night. During Wednesday's pregame chat, Carrie Muskat lobs a question to him about Aaron. Ten fascinating minutes later, Baker is still talking about a man whose dignified quest of history still affects him. It's also why, one way or another, Baker is going to be at Turner Field tonight—even if he misses the beginning of the ceremony. The way he figures it, he owes Aaron the effort.

After all, it was Aaron who was asked by Baker's mother to take care of her young son. Aaron kept his promise.

"Ralph Garr and myself were always with Hank," says Baker. "Always. Sat next to him on the plane. Ate lunch and dinner with him. Went over to his house. Rode in his cars. I was closer in age to his kids than to him, so I would [hang] with the kids. They were teenagers. I was 19 years old. I was a September call-up.

"Plus, he was on our butt about staying up too late, about not going to church, about not eating breakfast, about not eating right, about seeing too many girls . . . everything. That's because he promised my mom when I signed that he would take care of me as if he were my dad, which he did."

Aaron, says Baker, was a symbol for black America, "a symbol for excellence." He still is, but for the rest of America too.

Baker watched as Aaron withstood the jeers, the death threats, the vicious hate mail. He saw what the quest did to Aaron, but also what it did to others. It brought out the best and worst of America. As had happened with Jackie Robinson several decades earlier, baseball became an accomplice to social change. Aaron's quest helped change it.

Baker remembers a game at Montreal, before the cement nightmare known as Olympic Stadium came to be, when the wind knocked down what should have been a sure Aaron home run.

"Babe Ruth blew it back," Aaron told Baker that day.

And Baker always recalls what Aaron told him before he broke Ruth's record.

"I'm gonna get it over with," he said.

As bat met ball, says Baker now, "I knew it was gone. I'd only seen about 100 or so of them."

Baker thought about rushing toward the plate to greet Aaron, but something kept him at celebration's edge. "It was Hank's moment," he says.

Not that many remember, but Baker followed with a double. It was the least-watched double in the history of baseball.

"When I was hitting, everybody was leaving," he says. "It was cold, man. Everybody's seats were clinking, clinking, clinking. I turned around and said, 'What the hell is going on?' Those wooden seats were clanking as they were leaving. 'Wait a minute, I'm about to hit.' But they were gone."

An oversized photo sits in a protective sheath on his desk. The black-and-white picture is from the 1969 All-Star Game at RFK Stadium. You can see Willie McCovey, Ernie Banks, Roberto Clemente, Felix Milan, Glenn Beckert, and, of course, Aaron.

"I'll get Hammer to sign it," he says.

Too bad he doesn't have two copies.

GAME 4

Friday, April 9, 2004 . . . Cubs 2, Atlanta Braves 1 . . . Turner Field . . . Cubs NL Central pennant flies: Tie-Third (2-2) . . . Stuff: USA Today publishes the salaries of all 833 players on the MLB Opening Day rosters. The Cubs' payroll is $90,560,000, with Sammy Sosa's $16-million salary comprising 18 percent of the total. Rookies Andy Pratt and Michael Wuertz make the $300K minimum. Best bargains: Corey Patterson at $480K and Carlos Zambrano at $450K.

Cubs fans can wax nostalgic all they want, but this is the city where Greg Maddux made his bones. Atlanta. Home of Coke, the 1996 County Fair (otherwise known as the Olympic Games), and enough Peachtree streets, avenues, ways, lanes, and courts to give Rand McNally a cluster headache.

Maddux's return doesn't do much for the drama-o-meter. He pitched in Cincinnati, which means he'll spend most of his three-day stay in Georgia as a spectator.

"Good," says Leo Mazzone, the longtime Braves pitching coach.

Good, because Mazzone misses Maddux like cookies miss a cold glass of milk at bedtime. Sure, Maddux made his debut with the Cubs in September 1986 and spent the next six seasons in blue pinstripes. He won his first Cy Young in a Cubs uni. But when he was "booted" (Maddux's word, not mine) out of Chicago and signed as a free agent with the Braves, it was Mazzone who was waiting with a bear hug and a smile wider than a Varsity chili dog.

"We were thrilled," says Mazzone. "We had already put together a pitching staff in 1992 that had 26 complete games and 24 shutouts. And then to add a pitcher of Maddux's caliber to an already great rotation. It just made you feel like you'd never have a losing streak at all."

Mazzone and Maddux were together longer than a Kia warranty. During those 11 seasons, Maddux won 194 regular-season games, a World Series ring, three Cy Youngs, 10 Gold Gloves, and ensured himself a Cooperstown address. And for what it's worth, Maddux was making $5.875 million when he signed with the Braves, $14.75 million when he left.

"I think the greatest coaching job I've ever done is with Greg Maddux," says Mazzone. "You know why?"

"Why?" I say.

"I didn't mess him up."

And then Mazzone unleashes a belly laugh that lasts for a full five seconds.

This is a strange night for Maddux and the Braves. So much history together. So many memories. So many mixed emotions. It doesn't matter that Maddux is nowhere near the mound. It's just the idea of him being in a different uniform, in a different clubhouse.

Mazzone knew there was little chance Maddux would remain a Brave after the 2003 season. When word came of Maddux's new deal with the Cubs, Mazzone called and congratulated him—not so much for the contract, but for his pitching legacy.

"Thanks for some of the greatest pitching over a period of time we've ever seen in our lives," Mazzone told him.

Corny, but that's Mazzone. He wears his feelings on his jersey sleeve. He lost Tom Glavine to the New York Mets in 2002. Now he loses Maddux.

"It is emotional," he says. "You're not only their coach, but you create a personal friendship over a period of time. You feel like you raised them in a way, but they raised me, too."

Maybe it was just coincidence, but Mazzone always seemed to sway on the bench a little less when Maddux was pitching. There was something comforting and assuring about Maddux. Hall of Fame second baseman Joe Morgan once said Maddux could put a baseball "through a Life Saver if you asked him." But Maddux's gift, says Mazzone, goes beyond a magical right arm.

"I've never been around a pitcher or a coach who knows more about the game than he does in the pitching department," says Mazzone. "He would tell me that if he got a guy out in the first or second inning—and if that guy came up in the seventh inning and the tying run was at second base—that hitter would have no chance.

"He could predict where guys were going to hit the ball. One time we were going to put a runner on first, intentionally walk him with runners on second and third. So [manager] Bobby Cox went out to the mound because he wanted to see what Mad Dog wanted to do. Maddux said, 'Give me two pitches. If I go ball two, I'll put him on. But I think I can get him to pop up to third base.'

"And guess what? He popped up to third base on the second pitch."

Maddux won four consecutive Cy Youngs, his first with the Cubs in 1992 (at which point the Cubs waved good-bye), and then three straight with the Braves. It was during that run with near perfection that Maddux got, well, bored.

"Leo," he would tell Mazzone, "you haven't been out to the mound to see me for a couple of months."

"Well, there's nothing going on," Mazzone would say.

"OK, I'll look in during the sixth inning and you come out and pay me a visit. Sometimes it gets lonely out there. I need somebody to talk to other than the catcher."

Sure enough, Maddux nodded for Mazzone in the sixth inning.

"So I went out," says Mazzone. "Just to visit."

Shortly before the 1996 World Series began against the New York Yankees, Mazzone gathered his pitchers together. One by one he read the Braves' scouting reports on the Yankee hitters. When he was finished with the report on outfielder Bernie Williams, he looked up and there was Maddux with hand raised.

"Can I say something?" Maddux said.

"Sure."

"That report is not correct. I've been watching film of Williams for two weeks and that report is not correct."

Mazzone looked at his pitchers.

"Did everybody hear that?" he said.

"Yeah," they said.

"Well, then the hell with this report. We go with what Mad Dog says."

Williams hit .167 against the Braves that series.

"See, [Maddux] was right," says Mazzone.

He's almost always right. Maddux's last victory for the Braves was September 28 vs. Philadelphia. He won, 5-2. Afterward, he presented the ball to Mazzone.

"Here, Leo, I want you to have this. It's my 300th win."

"Wait a minute," said Mazzone, "that's 289."

"No, that's my 289th *regular*-season win, but I've got 11 postseason wins, too. Eleven and 289 is 300."

Those 11 postseason victories don't count, "but they should," says Mazzone.

Barring injury, Maddux will get his 11 wins—and more—this season. "I think he'll have a tremendous year," says Mazzone, who figures on at least 15 victories, which would mean 17 consecutive years of 15 or more Ws. Of course, Mazzone would prefer that none of those wins come against the Braves.

"The perfect scenario would be for him to pitch well, our starting pitcher to pitch well, we get the win, and he gets a no-decision," he says.

Until Friday, the last time Mazzone saw Maddux was at 2003 season's end in the Braves' clubhouse. It was typical Maddux.

"Leo, I've been around a lot of coaches who have opinions," said Maddux that day. "But there's only a few of them who have beliefs. And you have beliefs."

Mazzone was genuinely touched. "You taught me a hell of a lot more than I taught you," he said.

Maddux paused and said, "Yeah, but you gave me some good tips."

Mazzone will read every Maddux pitching line this season. He'll root for his old friend because he knows his old friend roots for him and the Braves—except three days in April and three days in October. And whenever it happens, Mazzone will be in Cooperstown when Maddux is inducted into the Hall of Fame.

There's only one Mazzone requirement.

"He better have a Braves uniform on."

GAME 5

Saturday, April 10, 2004 . . . Braves 5, Cubs 2 . . . Turner Field . . . Cubs NL Central pennant flies: Tie-Fourth (2-3) . . . Stat of the game: Braves first baseman Julio Franco, older than a clump of Georgia red clay (he's 45), doubles home three runs in a remarkable 13-pitch at-bat against 27-year-old Kyle Farnsworth. Then again, Farnsworth throws only 98 mph.

The Mirage is no longer the finest casino hotel in Vegas, but it does have the three gambling necessities I value most: an underrated race and sports book, cocktail waitresses who understand the importance of delivering frosties (beers, to you) promptly and in rapid succession, and a California Pizza Kitchen. It also has the standard issue of tourist clientele in the 72-seat, 10-big-screen-TVs sports book, which explains the guy in a replica-quality Cubs jersey, long-sleeve T-shirt, khaki shorts, and Arizona State visor.

"I'm telling you, he needs to change his name and transfer," says the 30-something to his 30-something buddy as they swig bottles of free beer and wait for the day's games to begin.

I figure they're talking about the infamous Steve Bartman. They are.

"So I heard the guy took a leave of absence two days after the foul-ball thing," says 30-something No. 1.

"I'd get out of there, too," says his buddy.

I interrupt. Time to put a personal theory to test.

"I couldn't help but notice your jersey," I say to No. 1. "You going to bet the Cubs?"

"Yeah, I'm gonna bet 'em," he says, slouching in one of the school chairs that are lined below the Mirage's huge electronic scoreboard. "What's the odds?"

See? This is the Cubs followers' mentality: Bob Beamon-like leaps of faith, no matter the numbers. This is why Robert Walker, the Mirage race and sports book director, adores these people and yet was nearly burned by them in 2003, when the Cubs were five outs from reaching the World

Series. It is also why he'd comp the infamous Bartman a dinner and hotel suite if he knew where to find him.

I pull a yellow futures sheet from the rack alongside the wall.

Odds to win 2004 National League Championship Series, it reads. The Cubs opened at 3-1. They dropped to 5-2, and then 8-5 when GM Jim Hendry squeezed a little more cash out of Tribune Tower and signed Greg Maddux. Now they're the favorites in the NL.

I turn the sheet over.

Odds to win 2004 World Series.

The Cubs opened at 6-1, then moved down a weight class to 7-2, and then later 4-1 with news of the Maddux deal. The New York Yankees are still the favorites to win it all, followed by the Boston Red Sox and then the Cubs. I repeat, the Cubs.

"We can root for them this year," says Walker, whose windowless office just behind the ticket counters features eight TV monitors, as well as a Sony Vaio that tracks every bet made at the six race and sports book properties he oversees (including the Bellagio and MGM Grand). "This year it was fun to put up the number and bet it."

The 2003 season wasn't so fun for Walker. That's mostly because the Cubs did the unthinkable: they won, and kept winning until they reached Games 6 and 7 of the NLCS.

"We were staring at a *huge*, seven-figure loss if they would have won the NL pennant and the World Series," says Walker. "I thought we were done. I was resigned to it already."

Here's what happened: Thanks to a sparkling 67-95 record in 2002, which included the firing of manager Don Baylor, the one-game "era" of Rene Lachemann (surprise, he went 0-1), and the failed experiment involving Bruce Kimm (33-45), the smart guys in Vegas decided the Cubbies weren't much of a threat in 2003. The opening odds? A meaty 32-1 to win the '03 World Series.

It wasn't Milwaukee Brewers/Detroit Tigers odds, but no one in Vegas was confusing the Cubs with the Yankees. Thirty-two-to-one material is Scott Verplank winning the Masters. It's a pig wearing lipstick—a presentable long shot, but a long shot nonetheless.

"I thought 32-1 was legitimate odds," says Walker. "Then they got Dusty Baker. When they got Baker, which was a significant signing in our mind, the odds went down to about 22-1. Then there was an accumulation of Cub money, an onslaught."

Cubs fans don't care about odds. They bet with their Cubby blue pin-

striped hearts. The more unlikely their chances, the better. To Cubs followers, there's a certain honor in desperation.

Walker loves that about Cubs fans. After all, one component of setting
odds is gauging perception vs. reality. Cubs followers are on their second
100-year plan, so reality isn't much of a concern. Vegas sports books rou-
tinely adjust the Cubs' odds to take full advantage of a loyalty so blind it
needs a Seeing Eye dog.

"The Cubs could put a minor league team out there and [the odds]
would be lower than they should be," Walker says. "You're never going to
get proper value on the Cubs, because we know people want to bet them."

But, hey, what about that Cubs rotation? Kerry Wood, Maddux, Matt
Clement, Carlos Zambrano, and Sergio Mitre/Mark Prior (Prior is sup-
posed to be out until mid-May, or late May, or early June—take your pick).
Those 7-2 odds don't look so bad.

"People would bet them if the Cubs had the worst five starters in baseball," he says. "The thing about Cubs fans is that they're worldwide. They'll
bet 'em. It has a lot to do with losing."

Cubs money poured in. And it kept coming in as Baker continued to
steer his new team to the win column. Walker dropped the odds to 15-1, but
it was still a bargain to Joe Bettor, and especially to the pro gamblers. After
all, you didn't have to be ESPN's Tim Kurkjian to realize the Cubs had a
chance, a real chance, to win the NL Central and who knew what else.

By the time Walker dropped the odds to 8-1, the sports book was on the
hook for low seven figures. This isn't a good thing. When you're booking,
the goal is to minimize your exposure. You don't want too much action on
one team.

Walker was exposed. This was the baseball equivalent of being on the
equator with no sunscreen. This was Underdog Central—the Baltimore
Ravens whupping the New York Giants in Super Bowl XXXV, the Atlanta
Falcons beating the Minnesota Vikings in the 1998 NFC Championship.

"A seven-figure hit is still tough for us," says Walker. "That's a substantial hit."

It isn't a Holyfield-beating-Tyson type of financial hit, when Iron Mike
was a 25-1 favorite and lost ("I walked out of here like Tyson that night,"
says Walker. "I was staggering."), but it's in the same subdivision.

Thing is, Walker says he felt comfortable about the 32-1 opening line for
the Cubs that year, and fairly protected when he dropped the line by 10
when Baker got the job. "But we took too much money at 15-1," he says.

The Cubs won 88 games and the NL Central. They beat the Atlanta

Braves in the NL Division Series. They were up three games to two in the NLCS against the Florida Marlins and had Mark Prior as their starter for Game 6. Walker wanted to weep.

"It was kind of torturous to watch," he says.

Seven figures, baby. Gone.

Walker had a softball game the night of Game 6. When he left, the Cubs were leading and Prior was throwing sunflower seeds. "I saw the score and figured, that's it . . . we're done," he says.

Instead, there was the Bartman Incident, the Alex Gonzalez Glove-of-Stone Incident, the Prior-Suddenly-Throwing-BP Incident. Walker didn't have a clue about any of it as he pulled into his driveway, opened the door, and then glanced at the TV in disbelief.

"I saw the Marlins were up and said, 'I can't believe it. What happened?' "

Does it matter? The Marlins stuck a pitchfork in the Cubs, 9-6, the next night and that was that. No 32-1 payoffs.

"I was relieved," says Walker, who actually likes the Cubs—just not when they're 32-1.

I thank Walker for his time and then take a cab to the Palace Station casino, which is well off The Strip but home of the legendary Art Manteris. Manteris is VP of Race and Sports Operations for Station Casinos and runs 11 sports books for the company. I check the odds sheets. Manteris opened the Cubs at 5-2 to win the 2004 NL pennant, 5-1 to win the 2004 World Series. He later lowers them to 2-1 to win the NL, 4-1 to win the Series. Blame Maddux, as well as the public's perception of the Cubs.

"They are the favorite to win the National League," he says. "Boy, I can't remember ever saying that before, and I've been in this business a while."

A season earlier, he opened them at 35-1 to win it all, but quickly dropped the number as the Cubs kept winning games.

Manteris, 47, has a similar work setup as Walker: Televisions at arm's length and a computer screen to monitor every dollar accepted at all 11 of his company's sports books. He can also monitor the odds and point spreads at most sports books in Nevada and offshore. The only difference between his digs and Walker's is that Manteris has an actual window in his office.

"With the Cubs you get people betting them to win it all every year," says Manteris, a former junior college second baseman who came to Vegas from Pittsburgh in the late 1970s. "I don't know why that is exactly. I suppose WGN has something to do with it . . . especially when Harry Caray was doing the games. It was like a picnic every day in the sports books. In my world he was well known, the Cubs were well known. You watched the Cubs every day. They were very familiar to locals here in Las Vegas."

"And to masochists," I say.

"Masochists . . . that's a possibility," says Manteris. "People do live and die with the Cubs. They do usually acknowledge that they've suffered, but they still like them. And they bet them."

Manteris likes the Cubs' chances in '04, which is why the odds are so low. As was the case at the Mirage, only the Yankees and Red Sox have lower odds. But as always, there is a caveat.

"Let me tell you a story," says Manteris. "There's a guy who comes in here, and he bet the Cubs in '69 to win it all. That was the year they folded down the stretch, the year they blew it. Every year since then, this guy has bet them to win it all.

"In 2003, he got them at 35-1. Bet $100. And it finally looked like they were going to pay off. He figured he would get all his money he bet since '69, plus be 100 bucks ahead. But . . ."

I nod my head. Manteris is offering priceless advice: Don't waste your money, not at 35-1 or 5-1.

So I walk down to the sports book, peel off a Gammons from my small wad of craps money, and make the bet.

"Twenty bucks on 5002," I tell the guy at the window.

"Cubs to win the World Series for $20," he says, handing me my ticket.

What the hell, right? Here's hoping Manteris smiled when he saw it pop up on his computer screen. Here's hoping me and the guy from 1969 finally beat the house.

GAME 6

Sunday, April 11, 2004 . . . Cubs 10, Braves 2 . . . Turner Field . . . Stuff: Your game hero is catcher Michael Barrett, who hits his first Cubs home run. Barrett finishes with four RBI. You can't miss Barrett. He's the one walking around the clubhouse with a smile wider than a cap brim. You'd smile, too, if you didn't have to play for the Montreal Expos anymore.

Asking Eric Karabell a question about fantasy league baseball is like handing Nobel Laureate John Nash a grease pencil and daring him to explain his analysis of equilibria in the theory of noncompetitive games. Before you know it, your dorm windows are a mess and the resident assistant is calling Homeland Security.

Karabell is ESPN.com's fantasy league expert. At last check, there were anywhere between 5 million and 20 million daily page views of ESPN's fantasy sports site, which puts Karabell's Internet popularity somewhere between Google and Paris Hilton's night-vision video. Not bad for a guy who looks likes Harry Potter at 35 and whose own forgettable playing career ended in 2001 when he shattered his elbow while trying to make a catch for ESPN.com's company softball team.

I spoke with Karabell shortly before he made his first-ever trip to Las Vegas, where he would attend the inaugural National Fantasy Baseball Championship draft. The entry fee for the NFBC is an industry-high $1,250, but the overall winner receives a mind-boggling $100,000. In all, more than 250 teams will take part in the three-city draft-day festivities, including 53-year-old Craig Nustadt, who will make the drive that day from the north Chicago suburb of Buffalo Grove to the Rosemont Convention Center. The NFBC will also set up shop in New York.

I want to know what Karabell thinks about the Cubs as fantasy league draftees. There's a difference, you know. In fantasy baseball, a player's worth is generally measured by 10 categories: batting average, steals, homers, runs scored, and RBI for position players; ERA, strikeouts, wins, ratio (or WHIP: walks + hits/innings pitched), and saves for pitchers. You get bupkus for Gold Gloves, sac bunts, hustle plays, quality starts, holds, assists, holding runners, experience, sign stealing, clubhouse presence—all the complementary things that add the necessary third dimension to the game. Thus, fantasy.

Karabell is as cold as Wrigley in April when it comes to player analysis. He is a baseball stockbroker of sorts, and his goals are simple: make money for his clients and for himself (he's in multiple fantasy leagues). To do that, you have to quit with the romantic's view of baseball—the game as some sort of metaphor for life—and instead take the CPA approach and concentrate on statistics, situations, injuries, and projections.

So when cyborg Karabell speaks, we listen.

On Derrek Lee, first base: "I've already done about 10 drafts, and I think he's overrated, because people think he's going to steal a lot of bases. I don't think he's going to run much this year. So unless he hits 40 home runs and knocks in 120 runs, he's not as good as a Richie Sexson or a Carlos Delgado. Is he a top 10 first baseman? Absolutely. I would probably put him in the 6,

7, 8 area. So is he worth $30 in an auction draft or going in the top five rounds? Yes. Is he the kind of guy who suddenly is going to put up Bonds numbers? No, I don't think so. He's durable, so that's nice. He'll probably steal about 10 bases. But he's not a 30-30 first baseman in the making."

On Mark Grudzielanek/Todd Walker, second base: "Grudzielanek was hurt early in spring training, and even when he played all of 2003, he wasn't the most productive guy, at least in fantasy terms. He doesn't knock anybody in. It would be hard to predict him to hit .314 again, based on his career path. He is a forgotten second baseman, especially now that they have Walker. I would rather have Walker than Grudzielanek, but I probably wouldn't be too high on either one of them."

On Alex Gonzalez, shortstop: "He's not really a star, either. He hits a little, but he never hits for average. At a position where fantasy has seen 10 solid guys go in the first five rounds of the draft, Alex Gonzalez will get forgotten. If you need his 20 homers and 60 RBI, he can help you. He never hits for average. I don't have him among the top 20 shortstops, mostly because his batting average outweighs the 20 home runs for me."

On Aramis Ramirez, third base: "The potential is there for him to hit 30 homers and knock in 100 runs, assuming the defense doesn't take him out of the lineup, and I don't think it will. He doesn't get hurt. He's young enough to improve on his numbers. He's a top 10 third baseman. You can make a case he's worth more than Lee. He's a 25-to-30-home-run guy and he should knock in 100 with a better lineup around him. Not a superstar or top five guy, but he's better than Troy Glaus, better than Corey Koskie. I like Ramirez a lot because he's a safe guy, he's durable."

On Moises Alou, Corey Patterson, Sammy Sosa, outfield: "Moises Alou is old. He's older than I am. He's older than you. You have to take that into consideration. He's a guy I avoid. Most people avoid him until the end of drafts. I don't know how he's going to stay healthy. If he knocks in another 91 runs and hits .280, then I guess I'll just be wrong. I have taken him in drafts this year because he was available in the last couple rounds. He's a fifth outfielder. If you think he's going to get back to his 30 [HR]-100 [RBI] days, he's probably not.

"Meanwhile, Patterson has a huge upside here, but you've got to remember—with a torn ACL, will he run again? I don't think Patterson will run as much. He still has the potential to hit 30 homers and knock in 100. I expect he's healthy and ready to go. He probably has the biggest upside of anybody on that offense. I bet he gets close to 30 homers this season, but if he steals more than 15 bases, I'd be surprised. At some point, he'll learn how to take a walk and exercise patience. But it might not be this year. It should be. He should have been able to figure it out by now. Patterson isn't better than Sosa, but he's their second-best fantasy player in terms of upside.

"Sosa has had two straight seasons where he barely had 100 RBI, which isn't really his fault. It's more the fault of a manager who puts guys on top of the batting order with bad on-base percentages. He had 40 home runs in 2003 and he missed some time. He shouldn't miss any time this year, assuming he doesn't cork his bat or doesn't get hurt. I think he's a candidate to lead the league in home runs. I paid $32 for him. He could hit 45 to 50 home runs, and I think he's a safer bet to do that than Bonds in '04. He's kind of a bargain. He can't help but knock in 103 runs, probably 115 to 120. If the Cubs do well, I think Sosa could be an MVP candidate. I haven't seen much drop-off in his game."

On Michael Barrett, catcher: "I don't like their catcher, I can tell you that. Michael Barrett has been an underwhelming player for much of his career. We've been waiting years for this guy to start performing, and he's burned us in the past. He should have been a 20-homer guy for the Expos, and he never was. He's never learned how to hit. He's not in the top 20 of catchers, which, frankly, is hard to do, considering this guy is a veteran. He gets a new start, and certainly Wrigley is a better place to hit than Montreal. I'm not a big fan of Barrett. He's probably a real nice guy, but he's not a really good player. As a late pick, I'd spend a buck on him. He had a good April last year and still managed to hit .208, so that tells you what the rest of his year was like."

On Mark Prior, Kerry Wood, Greg Maddux, Carlos Zambrano, Matt Clement, Sergio Mitre, starting pitchers: "This is probably the best rotation in baseball for fantasy. Not just because all five guys are good and could win 15 games, but also because this is a strikeout staff. There's no reason to think that won't happen again. Prior is the top pitcher in fantasy baseball and he's No. 10 overall in our rankings, though he's hurt right now. He ought to win 18 games annually if he can make 35 starts. He has the potential to strike out 250 guys, maybe a little bit more. He's got to stay healthy. If he does—and he's had problems with that Achilles—I think he could be a monster this year.

"Wood can be a monster, too. The problem with Wood is that he doesn't win enough. He's never been the guy who makes you think he's going to win 18 games. I don't see why that is. I would think Kerry Wood should be a 16-game winner. His career high is 14. If Esteban Loaiza can do it, Wood can too. But he's had five seasons and he still hasn't won more than 14 games.

"Maddux will win his 300th game in 2004. He shouldn't be forgotten in fantasy baseball. However, there has been a disturbing trend in Maddux's pitching the last couple of years. His strikeout totals have dropped every year, to the point he's going to stop being as effective as he is. At some point, he's going to drop off. I don't think it's going to be this year. I think he'll win 15 games.

"Matt Clement is a strikeout pitcher who hasn't taken off yet. He's generally as unhittable as anyone else on that staff, but he does walk a lot of people and he works deep into counts. But he's still a top-30 pitcher. He could be as valuable as Kerry Wood, which sounds crazy. But when you look at Clement's numbers and Wood's numbers, Clement is really just as good as Wood is, except for less strikeouts.

"Zambrano is the one guy that everyone points to as a guy who could develop arm problems. He threw so many pitches in 2003. He's young, and 214 innings is just too many for him. He's still a guy who could strike out 200 batters, though. But he probably can't sustain the success he's had by throwing 110 pitches every outing. If I had my choice of Zambrano or Clement, I would take Clement."

On Joe Borowski/LaTroy Hawkins, closer: "Borowski has earned the chance to stay a closer. I think Borowski will keep the closing job for a while, but LaTroy Hawkins is the better pitcher. He throws harder and is a strikeout guy. If Dusty Baker leaves Borowski as a closer, there's no reason to think he won't get another 30 saves. Right now Borowski can't be considered a top-10 closer, mainly because his setup man is just as good as he is. If he gets those opportunities, he's probably a borderline top-10 reliever."

Patterson is his Cubs sleeper pick. And Karabell wouldn't have any problem passing on Jason Giambi or Delgado in the early rounds and taking Lee later.

Karabell doesn't know it, but this is the exact strategy that Nustadt and Vultures partner Glen Brown have adopted for the NFBC draft in Chicago. They pick last in their 15-team bracket, which means A-Rod will be long gone.

Nustadt is a Cubs fan, but only because his beloved New York Mets traded Lenny Dykstra. That was the day Nustadt, who moved from New York to Chicago in 1980, officially gave up on his boyhood franchise and pledged allegiance to one nation under Cub.

"You go to Wrigley and you fall in love with the ballpark," he says, his New York accent still as thick as a Carnegie Deli sandwich.

Shea Stadium doesn't evoke such emotions. You go to Shea to suffer permanent hearing loss. La Guardia is just down the road, which means the steady roar of Pratt & Whitneys overhead.

The most Nustadt has ever won in a fantasy league is about $500. Nustadt is married, has six-year-old twins, and is starting a new job soon with a signage and displays company. It probably isn't legal, but during his job interview the company interviewer asked, "Are you a Cubs fan?"

The Vultures have targeted Patterson for the seventh round. They want to get two quality pitchers early. Wood is on their short list. This is business, of course, but they'd love to get a Cub or two on their team.

The draft started at noon. Nustadt and Brown sat at a large U-shaped table, and for the next four and a half hours they assembled a 29-man roster. They had one minute per round to make a pick. Not too much was at stake. Only $100K.

With their first-round pick The Vultures took Wood and then used the 16th overall selection on Yankees starter Javier Vazquez. Prior was taken by someone else midway through the first round. In the third round, Nustadt chose Lee. In all, Nustadt gets three Cubs: Wood, Lee, and Hawkins.

Only two questions really matter here: Will Nustadt win $100,000? Is Karabell as smart as we think he is?

GAME 7

Monday, April 12, 2004 . . . Pittsburgh Pirates 13, Cubs 7 . . . Wrigley Field . . . Cubs NL Central pennant flies: Sixth (3-4) . . . Stat of the game: The windchill is 29 degrees. The wind is blowing in from center field at 16 mph, gusting at 25 mph. . . . Stuff: The Newark Star-Ledger, *quoting, well, nobody, reports Mark Prior might undergo Tommy John surgery. Prior stops on his way up the dugout stairs to laugh at the story. . . . Heard in media workroom: Steve Bartman has undergone cosmetic surgery.*

You know it's Opening Day in Chicago when the Budweiser delivery trucks get bigger applause than the famed Budweiser Clydesdales, who clomp around Wrigleyville for a little pregame exercise and, surprise, TV exposure. Meanwhile, a Bud truck pulls up alongside Murphy's and two deliverymen frantically unload cases of brew as if the beer are sandbags and the levee is about to break. Passersby start clapping.

On the Addison side of Wrigley, street vendors sell little stuffed billy goat dolls. "Break the Curse," says the lady. "Only $10." And a new beer bill-board on Sheffield reads, "Curse Quenching."

Failure sells.

This is the 89th Cubs opener at Wrigley and, as usual, you need some-thing from your winter collection (or a flask) to stay warm. The team pen-nants on the center-field scoreboard flagpoles are doing a Viagra, compliments of that stiff breeze off Lake Michigan. The sun is out, but not the ivy. Too cold. Too early in April.

The press box is in overflow condition, and the media dining room, temporarily turned into a media workroom, is SRO. So I bum a small space in the cramped but friendly confines of the WGN Radio booth, Pat Hughes and Ron Santo presiding.

This is Hughes's ninth season as WGN's radio play-by-play man. Before that, he spent 12 seasons as Bob Uecker's partner on the Milwaukee Brew-ers Radio Network. First Uecker, now Santo. God bless him.

A confession: When I first met Hughes in 1996 (his first year with the Cubs), I thought he was the newest inductee into the Urkel Hall of Fame. He wore chemical engineer glasses. He dressed straight out of a Sheboygan Kohl's. And I nearly doubled over in laughter when, during a road trip that season to Houston, he asked if I wanted to shoot hoops with him at a nearby health club.

Then he started stroking jumpers from the baseline, foul line, three-point line, halfcourt line, parking lot line. He waxed and buffed me. The geek, who never quite mentioned he played briefly at San Jose State, had serious game.

Since then Hughes has ditched the Coke bottles for Lasik surgery, and apparently went clothes shopping with the *Queer Eye* guys. *Hip* isn't the right word for the 49-year-old Hughes, but at least now he doesn't look as if he ordered his shirts from *Reader's Digest*. And he can still shoot the rock.

Hughes, one of the nicest guys you'll ever meet, doesn't treat games like the Battle of Dunkirk. He doesn't show off. He doesn't pummel you with stats. Instead, he invites you to the back porch, hands you a cold one, and then tells you a story. He plays the straight man, but with a twist. Hughes is funny, but he picks his spots. He understands the game is the star of the show, not him.

Then there's Santo, whose life is so compelling that his son, Jeff, made a movie about it: *This Old Cub*, which has received boffo reviews and is one of the most successful documentary films of 2004.

Here's why: Santo played 14 seasons with the Cubs, put up Hall of

Fame-quality numbers (perhaps one day the freeze-dried Veterans Committee will do the right thing and vote him in), lost both parents to a car accident in 1973, became a member of the 'GN radio team in 1990, underwent nearly 20 diabetes-related surgeries that cost him both legs (amputated) and his bladder (removed because of cancerous tumors), survived two heart attacks and a bypass operation (doctors had to restart his failed heart), has helped raise millions of dollars for the Juvenile Diabetes Foundation, and had his number retired by the Cubs. And if he's not careful, he might end up in the broadcasters' wing of Cooperstown.

Santo, 64, is a homer, but in a good way. He wants the Cubs to win more than some of the actual Cubs. He understands Cubs pain. After all, he was part of that 1969 team.

Most of all, Santo is beloved. During the 2003 NLCS, the Cubs kept his No. 10 jersey in the dugout. And you should see him with Cubs fans. They don't know whether to shake his hand or hug him.

Santo's thick wooden cane, big enough to line a double to the gap, leans against the first-row desk in the 'GN booth. Santo sips on a cup of coffee and glances at the lineup. He goes on the air in less than a few minutes, but you'd never know it. Of course, back in 1990 when he made his radio debut, Santo wasn't so relaxed. Thom Brennaman was the play-by-play man then. Just as Brennaman began the opening segment that day, a gust of wind blew through the booth, spilling Santo's cup of coffee onto his scorebook. Santo let loose with a collection of four-letter words not approved by the FCC— *on the air*. Brennaman stared at his new partner in disbelief.

But Santo turned out to be a natural. He says what he sees, and he doesn't hide the joy or the hurt when he sees it.

Today the booth window is cracked open only a few inches, just enough room for some crowd noise and fresh air to sneak in. As the seconds tick down to showtime, Hughes playfully turns to Santo and says, "Who are we playing today?" Santo ignores him.

Jeff Santo has brought some *This Old Cub* baseball hats into the booth. "Great," says Ron. "I want to give one to Bill Murray when he comes by."

Murray, a longtime pal, is throwing out the ceremonial first pitch and later is singing "Take Me Out to the Ballgame." At least, that's what the Cubs hope he'll do.

Down on the field, children from the nearby Lemoyne Elementary School recite the Pledge of Allegiance. Then Wayne Messmer steps to the field microphone and sings "The Star-Spangled Banner" the way it's meant to be sung. Santo stands, and when Messmer hits "and the home of the brave," the former Cubs star can't help himself. He whistles and pumps his right fist. Santo is psyched.

The Cubs' 2003 Central Division banner is raised on the left-field foul pole. The sellout crowd is going nuts. And then a cue is given by engineer Matt Boltz, and suddenly Hughes and his perfect radio voice come to life. "Chicago Cubs baseball is on the air!" he says, and off we go.

Hughes looks as if he's working on a science project. He has his over-sized scorebook. He has reference materials (media guides, daily notes, stats) and a green apple to his left, and a small plastic pouch filled with pens, Wite-Out, tape, and so on to his right. And he has his trusty Electra Voice RE 20 studio microphone. Santo prefers a Sennheiser headset mic, but Hughes is sweet on the old-fashioned Electra, which Boltz even brings on the road.

As Hughes does his intro, Murray appears on the mound for the first pitch. Catcher Michael Barrett crouches behind the plate. Here's the windup . . . and Murray heaves the ball over the backstop. Then he shakes Barrett's hand, stomps on home plate, and disappears into the dugout.

The 'GN booth isn't much. Santo and Hughes work on the first level. On the floor between them sits an unused space heater in an open box. A fax machine placed under the desk spits out letters from fans. Three steps up is Andy Masur, who does pregame reporting and a brief relief appearance for Hughes during each broadcast. Boltz sits to the right of Masur and a soundboard. They each have laptop computers hooked up to the Internet (they'll feed Santo and Hughes pitch counts and factoids during the game). In a carpeted closet to the right of Boltz is an 8 × 10 glossy photo of television star Jane Seymour. "To Ron, With Love," it reads. Figures. Chicks dig the long ball, and Santo hit 342 of them in his career.

During the first inning, Hughes mentions the three retired jersey numbers that hang from the right-field foul pole: Ernie Banks's No. 14 (Murray wore a No. 14 throwback jersey on the mound), Billy Williams's No. 26, and Santo's No. 10. Santo, who cries at the drop of a rosin bag, gets emotional.

"That's my Hall of Fame," he says.

Between pitches, Santo glances at the faxes. There's one from the goat doll makers.

"Oh, Gawd," says Santo before flipping the paper into the wastebasket.

Santo has predicted a low-scoring game. It's cold. The wind is blowing in. Greg Maddux is pitching. A no-brainer, right?

Pirates shaggy-haired first baseman Craig Wilson steps to the plate in the second inning. Hughes asks Santo about Wilson's shoulder-length do.

"Well, when you can grow it, why not?" says Santo, who wears hair not of the same family tree as his scalp.

Wilson singles. So does Jose Castillo. Then Maddux, in a rarity, walks pitcher Kris Benson.

"Oh, gosh," mutters Santo.

A sacrifice fly by Tike Redman gives Pittsburgh a 1-0 lead, followed by an RBI double by Jack Wilson, followed by a two-run RBI double by Jason Kendall. Pittsburgh leaves the top half of the inning with a 5-0 lead.

"Boy, oh, boy, you didn't expect this," says Santo.

The Cubs score a pair of runs in the bottom half of the second and Santo is feeling better about things. In between innings, Santo mentions that his Tuesday off day was interrupted by a call from a marketing consultant.

"That's why I have caller ID," says Hughes, stretching his legs as Boltz monitors the commercials.

"Caller ID?" says Santo. "Pat, you don't even answer it when it's *me*. [Santo lowers his voice, as if he were Hughes.] 'Hi, it's Pat, Janell, Amber [his two daughters] and Trish [his wife]. We're not home right now . . . and don't call me back!'"

Boltz summons Hughes and Santo back to their microphones. It isn't pretty. Maddux hits Rob Mackowiak. Then Craig Wilson lines a double to left.

"This is the most I've seen Maddux off," says Santo.

It gets worse. In the fourth, Maddux loads the bases and then walks Craig Wilson to force in another run. Dusty Baker emerges from the dugout, taps his right arm for reliever Michael Wurtz. Maddux is through and, as it turns out, so are the Cubs.

The rest of the game is spent killing time, as the Pirates keep adding to their lead and the Cubs keep adding to their futility. Hughes and Santo make their guesses for the daily attendance contest. A few friends stop by to get baseballs autographed. A Cubs official sticks his head in the door and asks Masur if Hughes and Santo want to chat with Illinois governor Rod Blagojevich. Masur asks Hughes.

"He wants to be on the air?" says Hughes. Pause, before pretending to interview the Guv. "Now, Governor, about that state income tax . . ."

Former Cub and Santo teammate Randy Hundley walks into the booth during the fifth inning and takes a spot on the second stair. Blagojevich, a huge Cubs honk, arrives seconds later, sees Hundley, and is so thrilled that he blurts out, "God!" The governor puts on a headset and immediately starts quizzing Santo.

"What happened to Maddux?" he says.

Blagojevich starts talking about Cubs fever, about how he was recently in Florida and everybody wanted to talk about the North Siders.

"I know I'm going to get in trouble for saying this, but I think it is our patriotic duty to root for the Cubs," says Blagojevich.

It's obvious the governor loves the Cubs. When Sosa hits a long fly ball to left, Blagojevich nearly leaps out of his seat. "Oh, yeah!" Raul Mondesi makes the catch well short of the warning track. Blagojevich tells Santo that he's taking his seven-year-old daughter to see *This Old Cub* the following week. And at inning's end, Santo and the governor discuss some sort of education initiative involving preschoolers. So *this* is how policy is formed.

The governor wants to stick around for another inning, so Boltz presses a switch and whispers into Hughes's earphones, "The governor is still here." Then, in one of those surreal broadcast moments, Santo tells his listening audience, "The governor has a great head of hair."

Blagojevich quickly changes the subject. Hair debate averted.

At mid-inning, Murray walks into the crowded booth, sees Blagojevich, and shakes his head in mock anger.

"He's everywhere," Murray says. Then he tells Masur, "We'll come back in an hour."

But he's kidding, of course. Murray, wearing a Cubs cap, Cubs shirt, Cubs warm-up jacket, and a pair of overalls, shakes hands with Hundley (they've known each other for years) and waves to Santo.

"Hey, my man," says Santo. "Congratulations. I was hoping."

Santo is talking about Murray's Academy Award nomination for best actor in *Lost in Translation*.

"Oh, we'll hope for each other," says Murray.

Murray appeared in *This Old Cub*. It's clear he has a genuine fondness for Santo and for the Cubs. Why else would he imitate Santo's swing in the movie?

"You had my swing down," says Santo.

"Did you see it?" Murray says to Hundley. "Did you think I had it?"

Blagojevich stands to leave. Murray issues an order.

"Iowa—do something about it," Murray says.

"We're annexing Iowa," says the governor.

"No, we're *moving* Iowa," says Murray, rolling his eyes.

Murray puts on the headset and immediately cracks wise about the governor's "patriotic duty" line.

"I am still crying over what the governor said," he says. "Not a dry eye in the booth."

Hughes asks him about the ceremonial first pitch.

"I was in the training room and the guy said, 'You're not ready to go,' so he gave me a shot. Unfortunately, it was for horses. So I had a little more arm strength than usual."

Like all Cubs fans, Murray suffered through the 2003 NLCS. He was in Italy making a movie at the time, but he paid for a satellite dish so he could watch the games.

"It cost me a lot of money," he says. "Fortunately, it was in euros, so I had no idea what it meant."

Asked about the lingering effects of the loss to the Marlins, Murray says, "Cubs fans can take it. We're men and women. We are not like the others."

Murray isn't through. He demands a raise for Cubs general manager Jim Hendry. He talks about his reaction when he didn't win an Oscar. "I stood up and said, 'Let's go, let's get out of here. Get the programs and get out of here.'"

At inning's end, he turns to Santo. "This is tough," he says, nodding at the scoreboard. "It's like caddying for somebody who can't make birdies."

Then he leaves for a half-inning's work on WGN-TV with Chip Caray and Steve Stone. Before he enters the TV booth, he sees Caray's wife, Susan, and asks, "Is that gel in his hair?"

Murray reverts to Nick the Lounge Singer during his Seventh-Inning Stretch stint, first doing a commendable bridge from Sinatra's "My Kind of Town" ("Now this could only happen to a guy like me. . . . And only happen in a town like this. . . . And so I say to each of you most gratefully . . . As I blow each one of you a kiss"), and then belts out, "Take Me Out to the Ballgame."

By the bottom of the eighth inning, Santo and Hundley are telling stories from way back when, and Masur is showing off digital photos of him and Shania Twain. Impressive—Shania, not the Hundley/Santo stories.

In the ninth, Santo asks Hundley on the air, "When you were catching, did you ever get hit in the back of the head with the bat?"

"Yeah, I did," says Hundley.

Hughes waits a beat. "That would explain a lot of things," he says.

The game is mercifully over a few minutes later (thank you, Paul Bako, for the grounder to short). Pirates 13, Cubs 2.

After the brief, final wrap-up ("We'll just look forward to Wednesday," sighs Santo), Hughes packs his things and readies himself for the hour drive home to his north suburban home.

"Ronnie, you did a good job today," says Hughes.

"Thanks, Patrick," Santo says.

But you can hear the hurt in his voice. Good job. Bad loss.

GAME 8

Wednesday, April 14, 2004 . . . Cubs 8, Pirates 3 . . . Wrigley Field . . . Cubs NL Central pennant flies: Tie-Fourth (4-4) . . . Stuff: Ocean's Twelve cast members Matt Damon and Andy Garcia have primo seats two rows behind the on-deck circle. They gut it out until the bottom of the eighth. . . . Mark Grudzielanek goes on the disabled list, infielder Jose Macias is activated from the DL, reliever Andy Pratt and his 21.60 ERA is sent to Triple-A Iowa.

Todd Walker hit .283 last season, drove in 85 runs, and became the first player in Boston Red Sox history to hit five homers during the postseason. The Red Sox were so thrilled with Walker that they fired him.

Now the Cubs have Walker for a Wal-Mart-reasonable $1.75 million (Wal-Mart-reasonable by baseball standards) and the Red Sox have former Cub Mark Bellhorn, as well as Pokey Reese.

Bellhorn, a career .229 hitter, is off to a teensy-weensy slow start (.174). Meanwhile, Walker just finished a 3-for-5 afternoon with three RBI and is now at the .300 mark, which is exactly what he hit in two-plus National League seasons with Colorado and Cincinnati. In six-plus big league seasons, Walker is batting .290. He's what Cubs coach Gary Matthews calls "a professional hitter."

Walker was signed in December 2003 as a backup for Grudzielanek. But then Grudzielanek suffered a slight tear in his right Achilles tendon and was put on the 15-day disabled list, and suddenly Walker was no longer a backup.

"I certainly don't wish injuries on anyone," says Walker, meaning it. "But I didn't have any fear of rotting on the bench, so to speak."

Walker isn't going to win a Gold Glove anytime soon, but he's better than the defensive adventure he was in Boston. Anyway, the Cubs didn't sign him to make the world forget Ryne Sandberg. And they didn't sign him just because, like the Cubs, he and the Red Sox were five outs away from a World Series appearance last year. The Cubs needed versatility (you can stick him in the outfield, even at first, in a pinch), a left-handed hitting option, experience, insurance, a moderate price tag, and a team player.

An introduction to the guy who can shave at 9 A.M. and have a 5 o'clock shadow by 9:05:

Walker on why he joined Cubdom: "There used to be 15 teams that could say they had a chance to win the World Series. Now it's down to about five. The Cubs were one of those teams, and I just wanted to be part of that. I've been on losing teams before, and it's just not a lot of fun.

"You have to realize there's different parts of a player's career. There is a time when you want to play every day and establish yourself, and then there's a time when hopefully you have both: where you have a chance to play every day and win. But you want to be on a winner. I didn't have that option this year, so I had to go where I knew the team had the best chance to win and where we could have the most fun.

"There were people who said I signed too early, but I had a chance to be a part of a team that had a chance at a World Series, so I jumped at it. Winning is a big part of it. I just stepped out of that playoff situation last year, then became a free agent. It was so exciting to be a part of the playoffs, so I didn't want to go somewhere where I put up numbers and went home in October. I just didn't want to do that."

On what opposing players were saying about the Cubs, pre-2003: "The way I've always described it, based on my situation in the past couple of years, is that people like to talk about the differences between Boston and Chicago. The ballparks are similar, both fun to play in, but when you went to Boston, well, Boston's always won. They haven't won the World Series since 1918, but they've always won. And the Cubs have always been the Lovable Losers, the team that everybody came in and beat up on. In the last couple years, that's changed.

"Let's put it this way: It was different going into Wrigley than it probably would have been going into Yankee Stadium, because the Yankees have always been the powerhouse.

"I think this year a lot of people know that when they come into Wrigley they're going to have their hands full. I know when we go on the road—not that they're afraid of us—but I think they know we're going to bring it when we come in, and we've got a great team."

On "The Curse of the Bambino" and other Boston quirks: "They talk about the negativity all year long. We were four games up in the wild card in the middle of September, and all they could talk about was how we weren't going to make the playoffs. Papers. Fans. That's what they thought.

"You've got to battle negativity in Boston more than anywhere else. I don't think it's so bad in Chicago. I think they're just now getting to the idea . . . that the only reason you get disappointed is if you expect to win and you lose. I don't know if in Chicago they've expected to win during the last 20 years. But they should start to expect it now.

"As a player, you don't think about curses or that stuff. Last year was the best year of my life, but everybody who had been following the Red Sox for a long time would say it was 'The Curse' coming out again, especially the way it ended. That's just things you have to put up with. I didn't grow up in Boston. For me, I don't think twice about that stuff. And I don't think anybody in the clubhouse thinks about it either. We didn't feel like because we had this curse hanging over our head we were going to lose. We fully expected to win."

On watching Steve Bartman in Game 6 of the 2003 NLCS: "I think if I would have had headphones on, sitting in the front row, I probably would have done the same thing. Probably everybody else would. Unfortunately, that poor guy was in the wrong place at the wrong time. I think if you associate yourself with the Red Sox or the Cubs, either as a player or as a fan, you put yourself in jeopardy of something like that happening, fair or unfair. Was it [Bill] Buckner's fault the Red Sox didn't win the World Series in 1986? Of course not. He made an error, like everybody else has in their life. But when you associate yourself with the Red Sox or the Cubs, you put yourself up for that type of scrutiny if something bad happens.

"I think the city of Boston would have reacted the same way [toward Bartman] as the city of Chicago did, which is to the extreme. As players, you wouldn't want the fans to be any other way. You want them to be extreme, because if you do well they'll love you forever."

GAME 9

Thursday, April 15, 2004 . . . Cubs 10, Pirates 5 . . . Wrigley Field . . . Cubs NL Central pennant flies: Third (5-4) . . . Stuff: The Sun-Times *reports that buddies Sammy Sosa and Donald Trump occasionally trade phone calls. At call's end, Sosa tells Trump, "You're fired."*

Nobody sings Francis Scott Key's little number better than Wayne Messmer. The 53-year-old Messmer has belted out the "The Star-Spangled Banner" almost 4,000 times and is a regular pregame fixture at Wrigley Field.

You've heard what The Anthem can do to singers: forgotten words, notes never reached, interpretative renditions that last longer than an at-bat by Nomar Garciaparra. But Messmer is a perfectionist, and a gamer, too. He sings despite a scar on the left side of his neck (the result of a gunshot wound received as a victim of a 1994 robbery), and he sings no matter the Wrigley temperature, even if it means wrapping heating pads around his waist and keeping heat packets in his pockets.

Nine things you should know about Messmer and his favorite song:

I sing it in B-flat. That's the standard key for a baritone. The original John Philip Sousa arrangement, I believe, was in A-flat.

The first time I sang it publicly, I was in graduate school at Loyola, 1974. I had buddies on the hockey team and they had nobody doing the public address announcements, so I thought I would do it just for fun. The tape recorder broke, so I said, "What the hell, I'll sing The Anthem." Nobody knew I could sing [he was a music major], so I just went out there and let it rip and they were looking at me like, "What the hell is that?" These guys are banging their sticks and screaming at me, "Boy, that was good."

I've never forgotten the words. I always talk it through. I always warm up. However, I have swallowed a fly out here one time in the middle of singing. I saw him buzzing around, but I didn't want to look like a nut. He flew closer and I'm thinking, "Aw, crap," when all of a sudden I took one big breath and . . . click, he was in. But I just kept singing. What do you do?

People say it's the most difficult song to sing. Not for me, though you let people think it is. For me, my voice falls in that range. It's an octave and a fifth, which is way more than the average singing voice can do. That means eight notes, a long stretch. For me, that's a low B-flat to a high F. The average person sings in a five-note range. So if you're sitting next to someone here trying to sing The Anthem, they'll either miss on the bottom or the top.

I still don't feel I've hit exactly as I want it. But in 2001, we were the last team to return home after the 9/11 attacks. We had been out on the road, and then we rescheduled a 10-game homestand. Then I walked out to the pitcher's mound and really let it go. That was a pretty amazing experience. And that was having sung earlier in the day out at O'Hare, and doing so standing next to President Bush. It was pretty emotional.

That night when we got back home, I turned to my wife and said, "That was not your typical day."

I've done recordings of the National Anthem, the Canadian national anthem, "God Bless America," and "America the Beautiful."
At O'Hare Airport, I'm on the sixth floor of the parking garage. [The elevator banks on each floor feature music from each Chicago professional team—the Cubs, Bears, Sox, Blackhawks, Bulls, and Wolves.] For a guy who was born in Chicago—and I'm thinking of the old phrase, "To bloom where you're planted"—that's really kind of a fun thing. Relatives come in and I'll park on the sixth floor. We'll get off the elevator, there's me singing The Anthem for the Wolves, and I'll go, "Oh, what a coincidence."

If you're going to sing The Anthem publicly, do it with sincerity, conviction, and *lead* the crowd singing the song. It's not a time for, "Hey, look at me . . . time to show off."
I think recording artists—and it's really a hot button with me—think if they sing one style, that you can use that style to sing the National Anthem properly. Sing it the way it was written. I put an ending on it for flair, but I'm a stickler for doing it right.

The song should last a minute and a half, tops. I've seen them last over four minutes, and then it starts to get painful.

I'm blessed. What a great thing to be known for: "The Guy Who Sings The Anthem."

GAME 10

Friday, April 16, 2004 . . . Cubs 11, Pirates 10 . . . Wrigley Field . . . Stat of the game: Sammy Sosa ties the game in the bottom of the ninth with his 512th Cubs career home run (hello, Ernie Banks) . . . Stuff: Dusty Baker botches a seventh-inning double switch and then gets booted for arguing about it. He sheepishly calls his wife. "Did Darren see it?" he says. Nope. Dusty's five-year-old son, Darren, was in the bathtub, but later compares him to blowtorch-tempered Tampa Bay manager Lou Piniella.

I'm standing near the corner of Waveland and Kenmore, which is where any Ballhawk worth his beer gut positions himself during a Cubs game.

Ballhawks chase baseballs. That's what we do. We're a sad, pathetic people living lives of quiet desperation. You've seen us on TV. A $5 Rawlings wearing a coat of rubbed mud from the Delaware River basin sails out of Wrigley and we sprint, jump, lunge, even dive for the silly thing.

Some Ballhawks have been doing this for 10, 20 years. Others (me) have been doing this for, oh, 10, 20 minutes.

Right now, only me, fellow Ballhawk Terry Macchia, a handful of tourists, and a member of CPD's finest are at Waveland and Kenmore, which sits about 50 feet behind the left-field bleachers. According to the Wrigley center-field scoreboard clock, which you can see from the street if you lean forward, the game will start any moment now.

"I don't see the regulars," says Macchia. "But don't worry. They'll be here."

Macchia, 40, drives a garbage truck for the city. He lives near Taylor Street and comes from a Chicago family tree filled with cops and Cubs fans, but prides himself on being the lone White Sox follower. He has yet to set foot inside Wrigley.

"Hell, no," he says. "Why jinx it? I like it out here. Where else can you get a suntan like this?"

Macchia lights a cigarette. He's wearing sandals, Calvin Kleins, a wide leather belt, no shirt, a backward baseball cap from the 2003 All-Star Game, an earring in his left lobe, and sunglasses. Earphones from his Sony pocket radio hang from his neck. In his right hand is a tee ball.

"What you do is throw this back if you catch a real ball," he says.

Ah, tradition. It is customary for all home runs hit by the opposition to be tossed back onto the field. To keep such a ball is bad form—unless you happen to have a spare.

"In 11 years I've got about 200 balls, but that includes batting practice," Macchia says. "My uncle, he almost got Ernie Banks's 500th home run, but it bounced off his hands. If only he'd had a mitt."

Macchia doesn't use a glove. "I let it bounce," he says, "then I try to get it. But I'm telling you, it's all luck. No matter what anyone tells you, it's all luck."

There were thousands of people lining Waveland during the 2003 playoffs. And in 1998, when Sammy Sosa and Mark McGwire were chasing home run history, there were hundreds of fans waiting here. Now there are about a dozen fans at the corner.

"You got to know when Sosa, [Aramis] Ramirez, and [Moises] Alou are coming up," he says. "Those are the big three for the Cubs. And you gotta—"

He stops to admire two women beautiful enough to do Victoria's Secret ads.

"See that?" he says. "Stand out here five minutes and you'll see those kind of women. They're everywhere, especially in the summer. I take my chances with them. Sometimes it works, sometime it doesn't. Watch."

Macchia waits until the women are directly across the street from him.

"Hey, you want tickets?" he yells.

The women continue walking, but two other women—holding hands, by the way—turn around. Macchia rolls his eyes.

"Not *you!*" he tells the hand-holders.

Macchia was here Wednesday when Alou homered in the third.

"I came close to that one," he says. "I jumped on the ball over at that dirt patch there. Then I got elbowed in the ear, got my hat thrown in the street, had dirt all over me. And I didn't get the ball."

The game begins and Macchia darts down Waveland toward the left-field line. I count the crowd. Our numbers have grown to 46.

Moments later, a tall, sandy-haired guy wearing a Blackhawks cap, Cubs shorts, white sneakers, and a "Hit Me Sammy" T-shirt walks by. He has a batting glove and a worn, battered Fila outfielder's mitt on his left hand.

"How many balls you got now," says the cop. The cop knows this nerd?

"Uh, 3,699," says the guy.

This guy is no nerd. He is legend.

"All I know he's the guy with the orange van and all the baseballs," says Macchia. "I think his name is Dave something."

His name is Dave Davison and he has no Ballhawk peer. At last count, he has 19 Sosa street-caught game balls, including Sammy's 12th homer of that historic 1998 season.

"May 27, 1998," says Davison. "I was the only one out here."

He caught Doug Glanville's first home run as a Cub.

"Gave it back to him for nothing," he says.

On Thursday, he caught Pirates rookie Humberto Cota's first big league homer.

"I waited for 20 minutes, but nobody from the Pirates came out," he says. "I betcha they just gave him another ball."

Davison, 35, works at the Home Depot on North Avenue. If the Cubs are in town, he's done with his shift by 11. If the Cubs are in town and the wind is blowing out, he's on Waveland by 11.

Listen to the master for Ballhawking tips:

"Stand away from anybody with a glove. . . . Don't follow the crowd. . . . Pay attention. . . . Seventy-five percent of everything you catch is on the fly. . . . Kenmore and Waveland is the best spot. . . . Listen to the crowd."

You don't have much choice. From Kenmore and Waveland you stare at the spot where Wrigley's brick and cement outer walls come together. Glance upward and you see the backs of Bleacher Bums. In the distance is the top of the grandstands.

Davison steers me toward Moe Mullins, who is leaning against the hood of a rusting minivan parked on Kenmore. "Tell him about No. 62, Moe," says Davison, before returing to Waveland for the bottom of the second inning.

No. 62 is what Sosa hit September 13, 1998, off Milwaukee reliever Eric Plunk. The homer broke Roger Maris's record, set in 1961. Mullins had the ball. Then he didn't.

"The ball landed in front of the Kelly fence and then bounced toward the alley," he says of the black iron fence protecting the house on Waveland and Kenmore. "I got the ball, took two steps, and then everybody grabbed. My thumb was pulled all the way back. Tore the ligaments. There were people on top of me. I couldn't breathe. I believe I actually passed out for a few seconds. I remember thinking, 'Moe, let the ball go. It's not worth dying over.'"

Mullins went to court to regain custody of the ball. He never got it back.

There was a time when Mullins, 53, was the master of the Ballhawk domain. He has been coming to Wrigley since 1958. He pulls out a Cubs pocket schedule and recites some handwritten numbers.

"I caught two balls today, six yesterday," he says. "I'm up to 4,356 now. I've got 228 game-ball homers, four career grand slam balls."

Alou is up. Mullins, who carries a mitt and wears a black knee brace, doesn't budge from his place against the minivan. You hear a roar and then a tiny white speck appears from the grandstand backdrop. It moves closer . . . closer, clears the fence, then the sidewalk, then lands directly into the sweet spot of Davison's Fila. He catches it while holding a can of Pepsi he bought minutes ago at the nearby Engine Co. 78 fire station.

Other Ballhawks trade high fives with Davison. Mullins looks on with admiration.

"I told you," says Mullins. "Dave Davison is like the best Ballhawk out here now. When I was his age . . ."

When he was Davison's age there was a code of ethics out here. You didn't cut in front of somebody to make a catch. You sure as hell didn't tear their thumb ligaments.

Mullins was here the day Dave Kingman hit a ball to 3705 Kenmore, which is three houses down the street. Legend has it the ball hit the house porch. "Nah, it one-hopped the oak tree, but the ball never hit the porch," says Mullins.

He walks me down to the house. "See this?"

He points to a patch of street where someone has spray-painted something: *HR 508, 536'.*

"Sammy hit that," Mullins says of the June 24, 2003, home run blast. "Sammy's ball went six feet further than Kingman's."

The fourth inning comes and Mullins is through chatting. "We got three lefties coming up for the Reds," he says. "I gotta go." So off he goes for Sheffield.

I'm left standing next to longtime Ballhawk Ken Vangeloff, who runs a website called ballhawk.com/wc2004. Vangeloff moved here from Cleveland in 1990. He lives three blocks away from Wrigley.

His Ballhawk claim to fame is getting McGwire's No. 48 in 1998, as well as the Sosa bomb in 2003. He caught a break on the Sosa homer because the crowd surged forward as the ball appeared against the night sky. Vangeloff was on the crosswalk of Kenmore and Waveland and saw the ball coming directly toward him, and then, incredibly enough, *over* him.

"I just turned and started running back," he says. "I mean, it cleared the tree. When I got there, the ball was just sitting on the grass. I dove on it."

Vangeloff checks weather.com before coming to the park, or he simply looks out his apartment window to assess the wind conditions. He works for Accenture but can do most of his computer work at home and after the games. Ask him his age and he says, "Paul Warfield."

Warfield played for the Cleveland Browns. Good ol' No. 42.

"Next year is Mike Pruitt. Then Leroy Kelly. Uh-oh."

Vangeloff tells stories for the next couple of innings. In 1993, he caught a home run by Florida Marlins rookie catcher Mitch Lyden. It was also Lyden's first big league at-bat. Someone from the Marlins' clubhouse found Vangeloff and invited him inside. It was time to trade.

"I went in there—and I'll never forget this—[pitcher] Charlie Hough is on an exercise bike, smoking a cigarette and eating a donut," says Vangeloff.

The Marlins gave him a Jeff Conine bat, wristbands, and a few other trinkets. Then-Marlins reliever Trevor Hoffman threw in a golf shirt.

Vangeloff starts another story when the Wrigley crowd erupts. Ken Griffey Jr. sends a homer over the left-center fence. It bounces on Waveland, against the Kelly fence, and rolls toward the feet of a businessman walking home from the L stop on Addison. The businessman picks up the ball, takes a few steps, and then heaves the thing back onto the field. The Cubs fans roar with approval. The Ballhawks are mortified.

"Did you see what that guy did?" says one of the Ballhawks. "He threw it back. He threw a Hall of Famer's ball back. For chrissakes!"

In the eighth inning, the Reds' Wily Mo Pena homers to left. This time it clears the fence, hits the roof of a parked Pioneer Coach Lines bus, and bounces into a yard, where, once again, a passing businessman picks it up and throws the ball back. The Reds lead, 10-7.

The Cubs score two runs in the bottom of the eighth, thanks to Todd Hollandsworth's pinch-hit homer onto Sheffield. Then the Cubs hold the Reds to zilch in the top of the ninth. Drama time.

Sosa arrives at the plate. That's what the scoreboard says. Vangeloff finds a spot on Waveland. Davison is about 10 yards away. He spits in his glove, as if he's actually playing left field for the Reds. I move to the east side of Kenmore. Danny Graves is pitching for the Reds.

The count goes 0-1, then 1-1, then 1-2, then 2-2, then 3-2, then . . . crack of the bat, roar of the crowd . . . and then bedlam as Sosa ties the game, and ties Ernie Banks with his 512th career homer as a Cub. But, sigh, the ball stays in the park.

Moises Alou is next. I don't move from my spot.

This time the roar is even louder. I can't see a thing until the last moment, when, incredibly enough, the ball is coming frickin' right . . . at . . . me! The ball hits the pavement, bounces a few feet in front of me, caroms to the left, bounces back toward the right, eludes the cop, goes through the hands of a half dozen fans, caroms back toward the charter buses, where a dozen or so people dive headfirst onto the road. Think mini-riot. Fifteen seconds later, a bloodied man emerges from the horde with the ball and sprints immediately onto a charter bus, presumably to tend to his compound fractures.

A few of the Ballhawks linger after the game. They stay because some of the Cubs players will drive by after games and visit for a few minutes. Alou has done it in the past. He'll toot his car horn, and the Ballhawks will hold up their catches of the day as if the balls are rainbow trout. Sometimes Alou will stop and sign the baseballs.

If so, Davison is waiting.

GAME 11

Saturday, April 17, 2004 . . . Reds 3, Cubs 2 . . . Wrigley Field . . . Stat of the game: Kerry Wood loses a 2-1 lead—and his temper—in the ninth inning when he thinks he's getting squeezed by home plate umpire Eric Cooper. Dusty Baker comes out to pull him after 131 pitches, but it's too late. Wood goes postal on Cooper, gets tossed, then throws a helmet out of the dugout. Fines to follow.

Illinois governor Rod Blagojevich sits in Aisle 19, Row 7, Seat 3. Blagojevich adores the Cubs. There are those who say he spends more time in Wrigley Field than in Springfield.

Mudslingers.

The temperature has dropped nearly 20 degrees since the first pitch, but Blagojevich doesn't seem to mind. He has on a black polo shirt and a pair of slacks. His seven-year-old daughter, Amy, sits on his lap. Deputy Governor Bradley Tusk is in Seat 1, boyhood friend Lou Nova sits in Seat 4. Nearby is a security man wearing a gray suit, an earpiece, and a firearm. Two other bodyguards are also assigned to his detail.

Two and a half innings with the Guv:

The Seventh Inning

"First time we saw the Cubs, it was my older brother and me . . . 1965 against the Houston Colt 45s. The second game I ever went to was Lou's first game—Cubs and Giants—with Jesus Alou, Moises's uncle. We've been coming here ever since, mostly during the lean years, there's been so many.

"Baseball is a metaphor for life, and it's very much a metaphor for politics. Politics is very competitive. The campaigns are long, just like baseball seasons. Like innings in a ballgame, you have a certain game plan. You have tactics and strategies.

"Being a governor, and governing, sort of puts you in a position where you're like the manager of a team, versus when you're a candidate for the office, where you're more like an active participant. But the ups and downs, the struggles, the competition, the strategy, the mental toughness that it takes to pick yourself up from a bad inning, a bad event, get up the next day and go after it. . . they're similar to baseball.

"If you're asking me would I prefer singing the Seventh-Inning Stretch song as governor of Illinois, or actually play center field for the Cubs—another strikeout by Kerry Wood!—hands down, center field."

"Last year I was a first-year governor, and you're sort of like the manager of state government, the executive branch, anyway. I was very interested in watching how Dusty Baker manages the Cubs, how he deals with the ups and downs. So I had a chance to meet him in early September. He was very gracious with his time. We came here at noon for a 3 o'clock game. It was a fascinating meeting.

"Dusty's a real student of the game. He reads Sun Tzu and *The Art of War*, studies George Patton, military history, leaders—the same things I've been interested in and have read about. The Cubs had just played the Expos in Puerto Rico a few days earlier. They had had a big lead going into the eighth inning, and then a ball fell between Alex Gonzalez and Moises Alou. It cost them the game, and in a tight pennant race every game matters. I watched Dusty's reaction, and it was very stoic. So when I met with him I asked, 'How do you deal with something like that?' I told him I had watched the game.

"What's he gonna throw here, Bradley?

"So I asked him if he talked to them after the game. He said they feel bad enough as it is, so you leave them alone for 24 hours, then privately you see each one of them. In that case, Gonzalez had talked to the press and rightfully said it was the left-fielder's ball, but he wrongfully talked about it in the press. So Baker sort of suggested he go apologize to Alou, which he did. Very *esprit de corps*. You take into account different players, different personalities. Interesting insights."

The Eighth Inning

"Last year, I don't know, I probably went to 10 to 15 regular-season games, to Busch Stadium, Dodger Stadium, the All-Star Game, the playoff games at home. I took Amy to an extra-inning game once, got home at 11:20, and my wife wasn't very happy. She said, 'A mother's a mother, but a father's an uncle.'

"Strike three!" (Cooper doesn't give a close pitch to Wood. Blagojevich is annoyed.)

"When I was at Busch, I got to call a few innings: one inning with Joe Buck on TV, two innings of radio with Mike Shannon. I've done radio here and for the Sox."

"For the most part, you're either a die-hard Cubs fan and you don't like the Sox, or you're a die-hard Sox fan and you *hate* the Cubs.

"That's a strike!

"Cubs fans don't like the Sox, but Sox fans hate the Cubs. There is a difference. And there are those who like both teams but have a preference. Growing up, I was a Cubs fan and didn't like the Sox. Now that I'm governor I know [Sox owner] Jerry Reinsdorf, but my preference is strongly the Cubs. But I root for the Sox. I think they're going to do really well. But when the Cubs play the Sox, I'm for the Cubs, that's a given."

"I have not [granted executive clemency to Steve Bartman]. I got into trouble for refusing to do that. No pardon. But I've got to be careful, because I got into a little bit of trouble. I was messing around a little too much. I sure was [joking], but I had no idea of what he was up against."

(Wood walks D'Angelo Jimenez with one out.)

"What I said was, if he ever commits a crime he'll never get a pardon out of me. Then I was accused of being an insensitive governor. A lot of people were angry at [Bartman], he needed security to leave the ballpark. I compounded the problem by saying, 'I know what we'll do for him—we'll help him get into a witness protection program.' It was all in fun.

"It's such an extraordinary situation, but Alou could have had that ball. All those fans reaching for that ball, they shouldn't have been doing it. The Cubs were five outs from having a chance to go to the World Series. I mean, I was counting outs."

"I played Little League. I tried out for the high school baseball team. But I learned early in life that as much as you may want to be something, as much as you like something, if God didn't give you the skills to do it, you may want to go into politics.

"There's danger here, *chérie*. How 'bout the bullpen here?"

(Jimenez moves to third on Barry Larkin's grounder back to the mound.)

"OK, two outs, man on third."

"Here's one for you: I run. I've done some marathons. I'm pretty serious about it when I have time. Last September—uh-oh . . . this is a big play, this is it right here. Man on third, two outs, baby! The great Ken Griffey Jr. up. Kerry Wood pitching.

"OK, about three miles into my run—it's about a seven-, eight-mile run—I feel a real sharp pain in my left hamstring. I run about another three blocks, but the pain is unbearable. The long and the short of it is I had a slight tear in my hamstring.

"Nobody in the pen? It's ball two."

(Griffey hits a knuckling, sinking liner toward left field.)

"He caught the ball! Moises caught the ball! What a play!

"So someone says, 'Why don't you call the Cubs?' Good idea. I'm in the office. . . I get a phone call. It's the Cubs' trainer, who was Dave Tumbas at the time.

"I say, 'I really appreciate you calling me back, but shouldn't you be putting ice on Kerry Wood's arm?'

"He says, 'I am. He's sitting right next to me talking to the press.'

"I tell him, 'You don't have to call me now. You're busy.'

"He says, 'Aw, man, you're the governor.'

"So anyway, I come in the next morning at 8 o'clock. I get to go into the Cubs' locker room [it's "clubhouse," Guv] and into the training room. I told [Cubs VP of Marketing and Broadcasting] John McDonough that this is more thrilling than being in the Oval Office for me, and I've been in the Oval Office."

"Another story: In 1967, my cousin had leukemia. The medical bills bankrupted his family. He was very sick and died in October. My cousin's favorite player was Ron Santo. Santo went to the hospital and visited my cousin. He signed a birthday card. You were asking about mementos? That's the one memento I kept. I was 10 years old.

"OK, here's Sammy. Let's get some more runs."

The Ninth Inning

"OK, Amy, 2-1, top of the ninth inning.

"Kerry!"

(Wood is the Guv's favorite current player.)

"Bradley, whattya thinking here?"

(Sean Casey singles to center. Then Wood walks Dunn on a close pitch.)

"Looked like a strike to me."

(Ryan Freel sac-bunts the runners to second and third. Jason LaRue is up.)

"Here's an opportunity to suck it up, show the world how tough you are!"

(LaRue hits a sacrifice fly to left. Tie score. Wily Mo Pena is up.)

"Whattaya throwing here, Bradley?"

(Pena doubles home Dunn. Out comes Baker. Wood throws his fit and gets tossed by Cooper.)

"Oh, well. Right, Amy?"

(Amy scrunches her nose. "I don't like umpires!" she says. That's OK. Neither does Wood.)

GAME 12

Sunday, April 18, 2004 . . . Reds 11, Cubs 10 . . . Wrigley Field . . . Stuff: Seven home runs are hit, including a first-inning dinger by Sammy Sosa. Sosa becomes the all-time Cubs leader in homers.

I find Dan Miller, a 20-year-old Northern Illinois University student from Park Ridge, seated on the front row of the left-field bleachers. The record-breaking Sosa ball is in a zippered compartment on the side of his cargo shorts. Miller is waiting for a Cubs official to arrive. Then the negotiations for the ball can officially begin.

I bought the tickets on the Internet for $26. I came here at 10 A.M., waited for an hour and a half for the gates to open, then ran to the seats.

My dad is retired, and before I came here I told him I wanted Sosa's home run ball. I told him I'd get it for him. The ball's hit, I jump up, it goes in the basket, my buddy blocks everybody, and I get it. You had to be an idiot to miss it.

I don't know about giving it to my dad. [The Cubs]. . . we have to start some negotiations. It depends on what they offer. C'mon, how much was the Bartman ball worth? Maybe I'll take season tickets. I'm a big Cubs fan, but I need money. I'm a college student.

[I check on Miller later on his cell phone. No one from the Cubs ever came to his seat. "I couldn't believe it," he says. The ball is now in a safety-deposit box.]

GAME 13

Monday, April 19, 2004 . . . Cubs 8, Reds 1 . . . Wrigley Field . . . Cubs NL Central pennant flies: Fourth (7-6) . . . Stuff: Why spring training is weird: Matt Clement wins, again, and has given up one run in his last 12⅓ innings.

Two hours before the first pitch. Veteran Reds reliever Todd Jones, who won a day earlier against the Cubs, can be found in his usual pregame spot at Wrigley: sitting on the brick backstop just to the right of home plate. The former Astros, Tigers, Twins, Rockies, and Red Sox pitcher leans against the black netting, soaks in the rare April sun, and waxes poetic about the dream World Series, Wrigley Field, Todd Walker, Sammy Sosa, and heat.

If these guys [nodding toward the Cubs, who are taking BP] and the Red Sox go to the World Series, it'd be the ultimate cherry, the ultimate game. These seats in back of me, they'd go for over $10,000 apiece. At the end of that Series, half the rosters would retire, because as a player, you couldn't do any better than Chicago-Boston.

They love their baseball in both places. It's intense. Last season [with the Red Sox] there were a couple of guys who didn't want to be Bill Buckner. But you've got to get over it.

[Red Sox pitcher John] Burkett and I were out having dinner, shooting pool 'til about midnight [near Fenway Park], and a guy tapped on the window. We look up and he says, "You guys got a day game tomorrow. You got to get to bed."

It's so neat to be at a place like that, where they care like that. It's got to be the same thing here.

This is one of the best parks in the big leagues for me. When you're a little kid you're not dreaming about Kansas City, or 16-degree weather, or artificial turf. You're thinking about the fresh-cut grass, the beautiful sun. What you're dreaming about is Wrigley, that's what you're dreaming about.

That's why I had to come to Cincinnati. You can't go from a playoffs with the Red Sox to a place that can't win. Look at Todd Walker. He had a two-year deal with Cleveland. But how can you go from Boston to Cleveland?

In this game, you try to make enough money to take care of your family, and then you try to get back on the fun train. You want to win. I got lucky enough last year that I got out of Colorado and got to Boston. The fun train. In Walker's case, he went from Boston to here.

The Cubs' lineup? I think it all starts with Sammy. You're always conscious of where he is in the lineup. You're not going to let him beat you. This team will be carried by Sammy. No offense to Moises Alou or anybody else, but they're not Sammy.

Hot today, isn't it? We were just talking about that. This is the first time we've sweated here in April.

GAME 14

Tuesday, April 20, 2004 . . . Cubs 8, Pirates 1 . . . PNC Park . . . Stuff: The announced crowd is 11,746. WGN's Steve Stone isn't so sure. He says the Cubs had bigger crowds in Mesa.

Billy Corgan knows songwriting, rock, and the Chicago Cubs. Put a pair of red seams on the sides of his shaved head and he'd look like a Rawlings baseball.

Corgan was born in Chicago, grew up in west suburban Glen Ellyn, and, thanks to his grandmother Connie, spent most of his preteen and teenage years wanting to wear Cubby blue. When that didn't happen he became a rock star, which is nice, but it's not quite the same as taking the mound at Wrigley or rearranging your cup on WGN.

Of course, Corgan has done just fine, and done it on his own terms. Not many gigs like that. His Smashing Pumpkins stuff is legendary. His Zwan phase had its moments. And the solo thing is a no-brainer.

But one of my favorite cover songs done by Corgan is "Take Me Out to the Ballgame." He sang it in 1998, and again in 2003, to a Wrigley crowd numbed by a Florida Marlins 9-5 seventh-inning lead in Game 7 of the NLCS. The Cubs lost that game and the series, but Corgan did his best to rally a clinically depressed crowd off the mezzanine-level ledge. He spoke first from the heart. Then he sang from the heart. Nothing new there, but it's why there's a certain purity to the way he supports the Cubs.

Corgan isn't a late-arriving Cubs celeb fan. He's been there through thick and dental floss thin. He TiVos almost every Cubs game. He attends at least 10 games a season, more if his road schedule allows. His favorite single is "Sleepwalk," by Santo and Johnny. Santo? That can't be a coincidence. He's even written a song about the Cubs. And go ahead, ask Corgan about the Cubs' Lovable Losers tag and he'll glare at you as if you'd just requested him to play something from the Donny and Marie collection.

"I don't buy into all this loser shit," he says.

Corgan will talk ball with you until you're so geeked that you want to buy a fungo bat.

His Cubs thoughts:

I can tell you one small story that always sticks in my mind of how crazy a fan my grandmother was. We would go hours before the game and we would stay until we were literally the last people out of the park. It was like an all-day thing to go. We stayed so long we were watching people clean the seats. They would literally have to throw us out. She didn't want to leave.

We saw Randy Hundley—this was probably in the mid-'70s—and she says, "Oh, my God, it's Randy Hundley." She broke down crying—and my grandmother is not an extremely emotional person. I remember thinking, "God, how intense."

Randy Hundley is looking at her like, "OK . . . great." He was kind of distant, not really sure how to deal with it. People cry in front of me all the time, and I usually hug them.

Some of the earliest memories of my life are sitting on the couch with my grandmother watching the Cubs. When the Cubs game was on, that was it. We didn't go outside, we didn't do anything. We just sat there. It was very intense and visceral.

And certainly, growing up a Cubs fan in the '70s . . . it wasn't the yuppie, boomer institution it is now. In fact, when I went to school my friends used to make fun of me for being a Cubs fan. They were just seen as, well, they suck.

This was the era of the Dallas Cowboys, and glamor, and big names. It was Pete Rose, superstars, larger-than-life personalities. We had Jose Cardenal. We didn't have Charlie Hustle. We had Jose Cardenal with the Afro who hides the ball. We had Dave Kingman, who hits .220, but, my God, he hits really far home runs.

I do remember Ernie Banks hitting his 500th home run. That's my earliest Cub memory. I didn't really enter into full consciousness with the Cubs until I was probably eight or nine, and then it was baseball cards, and I wanted to be a baseball player.

Yeah, I did *The Simpsons.* Homer? I wouldn't take him for a Cubs fan. He's not enough of a masochist. Though his boss could work for the Tribune Company.

Everybody talks about Ryne Sandberg when they talk about that '84 team. But to me the guy who made that '84 team was Gary Matthews. He was like the difference maker on that team. I watched, like, 140 of those games. Gary Matthews was the man of that season. He was the one who got the big hits. He was the one who brought them together in the clubhouse. Now who's going to be that guy this year?

On this team, Kerry Wood is probably the closest I could relate to. Kerry Wood plays like I played, which is like a hardass. I was a pitcher, too, and I would put you right on your ass. I think that's the way baseball should be played. That's what I like about Kerry Wood.

The great story of my career is that I didn't make the baseball team in high school [Glenbard North], so I started playing guitar. If I would have made that team, I'd probably be working at 7-Eleven.

I had written about 12 songs about Chicago. I was sitting around one day and I thought, "Well, I've got to write a Cubs song." What I like about the song is that it both praises the Cubs and at the same time kind of kicks the Sox down, which is perfect. That's the way it should be.

I go to Sox games. But I was very disappointed [in 2003] when the Cubs got on a roll—and I listen to a lot of sports talk radio—and Sox fans really had a piss-poor attitude. They were calling up going, "I hope the Cubs lose . . . I hope the Yankees beat them in the Series." C'mon. When the Sox win, I'm rooting for them.

I went to the All-Star Game in [2003] at Cellular . . . whatever it's called now, and they were booing the Cubs. To me that made the Sox organization look like a minor league organization. If your fan base at a special event like the All-Star Game is going to boo Cubs pitchers . . . I mean, c'mon. That's embarrassing. That's how you want to portray your organization: the beer-swilling idiot? We've got our own beer-swilling idiots on the North Side, but at least they drive BMWs.

Some of the guys I work with, some of the engineers, they give me shit when the Cubs are playing bad. That's the way it's supposed to be. It's no different than when you see a Cardinals fan.

I've been in hostile environments. Even [in 2003] when I went to Florida [for the NLCS], those people were hostile, hostile people. I just don't understand the hostility. People were getting ready to get in fistfights. A guy from New York tried to pick a fight with me.

One of my favorite memories is after the Cubs won Game 4, and they're up in the series, 3-1. Me and my dad were walking down the ramp to get to the car, and the Marlins fans were shouting, "You're going to lose to the Yankees anyway." That was their last retort.

But we all know what happened after that.

I sang at Game 7 [in the 2003 NLCS]. They called here the afternoon before Game 6 and said, "OK, if it goes to a Game 7 do you want to do this?" I thought, "Yeah, right, it's not gonna go to a Game 7. There's nothing to worry about, so, sure, I'll do it." I figured at the worst, I'd have tickets for Game 7.

But that was like singing for a funeral. That was one of the most depressing things. It really was like a wake. It's a weird thing to be part of something you've seen so many times. Usually, there's a good amount of energy, but this time nobody was singing. It was like, "Oh, my God." But like one of my friends said, "You're the perfect person for that. You were the perfect person at that moment to do that, because nobody else would have handled it like you did." It was hard. It was really hard.

The whole country was sort of having their Cubs moment. Everybody can make it as quaint as they want. I mean, we really do love our team. I know it's become a yuppie, boomer thing. But people who really love the Cubs really do love the Cubs. It's not about the stuff everybody talks about. There really is a passion for the team.

Lovable Losers? I think that's bullshit. The fact that the ballpark is populated by a bunch of people who view it as another stop on their tourist destination is not my problem. I really do love my team. I loved my team when there were only 7,000 people in the stands.

Everybody seems very focused on getting the Cubs to the World Series or winning a World Series. But to me, I'd like to see them win three in a row.

If you're a Cubs *fan*, you're going to be here no matter what happens. That's the true definition of what being a fan is. It's what I ask of my fans, that if you're a fan stick with me through thick and thin.

There's been some really noble seasons with shitty Cubs teams, where guys gave a level of effort that inspired me. Guys were playing out of their depth. I saw some Andre Dawson seasons that were unbelievable, and he did it on some unbelievably shitty Cubs teams. But Andre Dawson played with a level of pride and dignity that still inspires me.

Even Ryno, he played on some pretty bad teams, but he busted ass every day. You've got to watch 100-something games to know if a guy is faking it.

I've been around a lot of people in my life. Pretty much anybody you've seen on TV I've met, especially in the entertainment world. There's very few people I'm impressed with. But when I saw Andre Dawson at an All-Star Game, I was like, "Wow!" because I know the nobility of that man. I went up and got an autograph from him, which is something I never do. He wasn't the friendliest guy, but I'm telling you, that guy played his ass off. Now, that's what being a fan is. He didn't give me what I wanted when I said hello to him. I certainly didn't tell him who I was. I was just standing there like any ol' fan. But that doesn't change the fact that that guy gave me something intangible.

I've gone online a few times, looked at a few auctions to find sort of the right Cubs stuff. There are two things that I really treasure. One, which I bought on eBay, is a team picture sponsored by Jewel [grocery store] or somebody of the '77-'78 Cubs, with Mick Kelleher, Cardenal, Joe Wallis, and these guys. That was sort of my boyhood-era team.

The other thing I have is a ball signed by Ernie Banks, which in and of itself is not that distinguished, but I've actually gotten to meet Ernie a few times. I actually had dinner with Ernie and sat and talked with him. He's just an incredible human being. He's such an intelligent, learned man. I always had a perception of him from a public persona. But actually being able to talk to him about politics and everything under the sun, I understand why that guy was so successful. Not only does he have a baseball body—he's got the baseball butt and the hands—but his intellect is so supreme. Now I understand how he went out and did what he did every day and for so long. That's the kind of thing that really inspires me, where it translates into my work. I really treasure that.

GAME 15

Wednesday, April 21, 2004 . . . Cubs 12, Pirates 1 . . . PNC Park . . . Cubs NL Central pennant flies: Tie-First (9-6) . . . Stuff: So much for NBC's claim that tonight's lame-o Law & Order *episode was "ripped from today's headlines." Apparently, NBC gets its newspapers delivered a little late, because the episode features a baseball fan who costs his team a title when he reaches for a foul ball and—gasp!—is later murdered. Game 6 of the NLCS was October 14, 2003. And Bartman, we think, is very much alive.*

Rookie Sergio Mitre, who is the next-to-lowest-paid player on the Cubs roster ($305,000), won his first big league game tonight. It took him parts of two seasons and five starts, but he now has his very own W. Before that, his main claim to fame was recording his first career hit off a no-name pitcher named Greg Maddux.

Mitre, 23, was drafted in the same Class of 2001 as Mark Prior, but Prior was the No. 2 overall pick, whereas Mitre was taken six long rounds later. In fact, the only reason Mitre is in the rotation, or perhaps on the big club at all, is that Prior is nursing a sore elbow and Achilles tendon. Who knows what will happen when Prior returns.

Until then, Mitre will always have Pittsburgh.

Afterward, during the postgame interviews, Mitre received the traditional shaving cream pie from LaTroy Hawkins, then Francis Beltran, then Carlos Zambrano. Mitre didn't mind.

Dusty gave me the lineup card and the baseball. He said, "Congratulations and keep it up."

I just went back to my hotel room and spoke to my family [in San Diego]. That's how I celebrated: stayed in, told them all about it. Every time I pitch, after being done for about an hour, it usually gets to me and I don't feel like doing anything. You're tired.

I had the big lead, but it could have gone either way. I sat for about a half hour before I got out there [to pitch]. I was trying to stay loose, keep my concentration. With such a big lead, you just go out there and try to pitch solidly.

I'll keep the ball and put it next to the other two: one for my debut, and one for my first big league hit. I'm saving those. The hit [off Maddux] was a line drive. I've got the tape, too. Or my family does. They're the ones saving everything.

So far, so good. I wanted to make the team out of spring, and I did, but unfortunately it's because Prior's hurt. That's not good for the team, but I'm doing what I can right now to help the team. I'll keep doing that, and hopefully everything works out.

GAME 16

Friday, April 23, 2004 . . . Cubs 3, New York Mets 1 . . . Wrigley Field . . . Cubs NL Central pennant flies: Tie-First (10-6) . . . Stat of the game: Greg Maddux wins his first game as a Cub since September 30, 1992.

Sandwiched between Maddux's long-awaited first win of 2004 and Joe Borowski's first drama-free save of the season is an underrated eighth inning that makes both possible. For this the Cubs can thank Kyle Farnsworth, who makes radar guns cry.

The eighth inning, Dusty Baker says regularly, "can be a lot more important than the ninth."

"That was huge," says catcher Paul Bako of Farnsworth's 21-pitch appearance in the eighth.

Wins and saves get the headlines, but this game was likely won or lost in two places: in the third, when Maddux squeezed out of a bases-loaded situation, and in the eighth, when Farnsworth, whose thighs make women swoon, arrived on the mound.

Four batters later, the Cubs still had their all-important two-run lead and some wiggle room for Borowski in the ninth.

Anatomy of a hold:

Baker and pitching coach Larry Rothschild know the seventh inning will be Maddux's last of the day. Maddux has given up just one walk and six hits, including a home run by Mike Cameron, but his pitch count is beginning to reach "Danger, Will Robinson" status, and nobody wants to see Maddux start the season 0-3. So when third baseman Todd Zeile singles to right to start the Mets' seventh, Farnsworth is told to get ready.

Bullpen catcher Benny Cadahia: "When Zeile got on, Farnsworth got up in case of a double play. That way he'd have enough time to get warmed up again. He has a routine: He throws about 15 pitches, takes a little water break, and then he throws a couple of more and he's ready to go. That's all he needs."

Maddux strikes out second baseman Joe McEwing, then faces pinch hitter Joe Valent, who flies to left field for the second out. Zeile is forced out at second on a grounder by Kazuo Matsui.

Meanwhile, Farnsworth begins to reach ramming speed.

Cadahia: "Farnsworth usually warms up really good all the time. But this time he really had the ball going where he wanted it. He just doesn't like the long innings. He likes to get warmed up, get ready to go, and get in the game. He got ready to go and then he had to sit down for a while."

That's because Ramon Martinez leads off the Cubs' eighth with a walk. Bako strikes out, but Maddux reaches on a fielder's choice. Then Todd Walker lines a ball to left to end the inning. Enter Farnsworth, all fast-twitch muscles, scowl, and triple-digit radar readings.

Cadahia: "I always love to see him pitch. I've never seen somebody throw it so damn hard—99 to 100 mph, all the time pretty much—and have such command of his pitches. His slider looks like it's there . . . and then it's gone.

"Now sometimes when he's throwing the ball that hard and he gets it up just a little bit, about thigh high, that's when he gets hit a little bit. But when he's dialed in, he's pretty much untouchable.

"This time he's facing the heart of their order."

The Mets' heart:

No. 2 hitter Shane Spencer, who enters the game with a .310 average. Spencer already has singled twice off Maddux.

No. 3 hitter Karim Garcia begins the day hitting .283 with two homers and six RBI.

No. 4 hitter Mike Piazza, who has power to all fields, as well as to all streets surrounding Wrigley. Perhaps the greatest-hitting catcher of all time, Piazza, batting .328 at game's start, scares the bejabbers out of the Cubs.

No. 5 hitter Mike Cameron, who already has one home run in the game.

To really understand the nuances of the situation, I duck into the Cubs' video room near the dugout. Ed Cohen, the ponytailed Cubs video coordinator, cues up the eighth inning on his computer system.

You see Spencer take his place in the batter's box and then . . .

Fastball, 97 mph—strike one . . . Slider, 84—ball one . . . Fastball, 95—swing, strike two . . . Fastball, 96—foul . . . Fastball, 96—foul . . . Slider, 84—ball two . . . Fastball, 93—ground-ball single to short.

Bako on Spencer: "We know he's a pretty good fastball hitter, so we're trying to get the ball down and away from him. But the fastball we threw—and Kyle didn't have his good slider with him yet—was up and over the middle of the plate, and Shane did a good job of hitting that."

Man on first, no outs. Garcia is up.

Cohen: "I got a gray hair on this pitch."

Fastball, 97—fly ball deep to right-center field, just short of the warning track. One out.

Bako: "We were lucky he kind of got that off the end of the bat a little bit. But after that, Farnsy really beared down on Piazza and Cameron. He really dialed it up a notch when they came up."

Piazza steps to the plate.

Fastball, 99—strike one called . . . Slider, 83—strike two swinging . . . Slider, 83—foul . . . Fastball, 99—ball one . . . Slider, 82—strike three swinging.

Cohen: "Look at that. The bottom just dropped out."

Bako: "[Piazza] is the guy in the whole lineup, on any given day, you don't want him to beat you if you can help it. With Farnsy's fastball, you kind of got to get started early to hit that type of velocity. So on that third strike, with Farnsy throwing his good slider, it looks like a fastball to begin with. I'm sure that's what got Mike out in front on it."

Two outs. Cameron is up.

Fastball, 99—strike one swinging . . . Fastball, 96—ball one . . . Fastball, 99—ball two . . . Fastball, 98—strike two . . . Fastball, 99—foul . . . Slider, 83—ball three . . . Slider, 84—foul . . . Slider, 83—strike three swinging. End of inning.

Bako: "When you go out there in the top and middle of their order, it's probably tougher than getting the last three outs in the ballgame. Where Joe had kind of the bottom of the order, Farnsy had the two-three-four and five to go through. That's awfully tough, man. He did a hell of a job to get through it."

GAME 17

Saturday, April 24, 2004 . . . Cubs 3, Mets 0 . . . Wrigley Field . . . Stuff: Lee Jenkins of the New York Times *reports that one Mets player pumped his fist when told earlier in the week that Wood wouldn't pitch in the series. Oops. The rainout in Pittsburgh bumps Wood to the Mets series. . . . Wood on the 2004 Cubs: "I thought in spring training we were a better team than last year."*

Alex Gonzalez is in mourning. He recently lost his best friend to old age: his glove.

The Cubs shortstop and the black Wilson A2000 model had been buddies for more than five years. They went everywhere together: from the

American to National League, to the left side of the infield, to second base, to the dugout, on charter flights and charter buses, to the clubhouse. They led the AL in total chances and double plays in 2001. And in 2003, Gonzalez and Mr. Wilson led the NL in fielding percentage, committing only 10 errors in 625 total chances.

They were pals through the tough times, too. Those 21 errors in 2002 weren't much fun. And don't even mention the eighth inning of Game 6 of the 2003 NLCS.

But gloves can't live forever. Gonzalez's gamer had cracks in the leather. The stitching that held together the glove's pocket gave way. So Gonzalez sent it to the people at Wilson in hopes it could be saved by reconstructive surgery. The results of the initial operation weren't encouraging, and a second surgery has been scheduled.

"I always felt my other glove was a part of me," he says, sitting in front of his locker about 70 minutes before the day's game. "It's a little bit unusual not to have that glove that I've used for the last five years. So I'm trying to adjust."

He's been using an A2000 since 1994. Back then, you could tighten or loosen the finger pressure in the glove with a turn of a small dial on the wrist strap. Gonzalez is a glove purist, so he had them take the dial off. Now he has a new gamer, as well as another A2000 he uses to take pregame grounders.

"Really, if you put them next to each other they look exactly the same," he says. "But they have a little different feel. I'm still trying to get that same feel that I had with the other one."

A glove's "feel" is almost an esoteric, ethereal condition. It's a relationship. Eric Clapton has one with his favorite guitar. Yo-Yo Ma has the equivalent of a gamer cello. Something just feels right.

"It's the way the glove kind of molds to your hand, the way you close it, the way the ball enters the glove," says the 31-year-old Gonzalez. "A lot of times you don't really squeeze your glove when the ball hits. It kind of closes on its own. When you're catching a lot of ground balls, your hand learns the glove too, the way the ball enters the glove and sticks."

I understand. Sort of.

"Here," he says, handing me his gamer and a baseball. "Now throw the ball in there, throw it in the pocket. Do it about five times."

One, two, three, four, five.

"Now do it with this one," he says, handing me his pregame glove.

This time the ball sinks deeper into the pocket. The glove seems to want to wrap itself tighter around the Rawlings.

"Feel the difference?" he says.

"Absolutely," I say. Same glove, different feels.

"Every glove closes differently and every glove receives the ball differently," he says. "See how much deeper that pocket is compared to this one, which is shallower? As an infielder, you want to get that ball and get it out. But the more ground balls you take with a glove, the deeper that pocket is going to get."

Gonzalez started breaking in his new gamer at the end of the 2003 season. He doesn't break in a glove by tying string around it with a ball in the pocket, or sitting on it, or doing one of a dozen other methods favored by players to get the stiffness out of it. Instead, he breaks it in the same way he plans to use it: by taking grounders, catching line drives and pop-ups.

He pulls out a plastic bottle of something called Lexol. "It's for saddles," he says. "It doesn't soften the leather. It gives it a little firmness. Good stuff."

Before each game, Gonzalez squirts a dab of the lotion onto the upper heel of the glove pocket and rubs it in. "Now feel the pocket," he says.

The surface is ever so slightly sticky. Not Velcro-sticky, but definitely not slick anymore.

"That helps the ball not to spin, so when it hits there it will stick there," says Gonzalez. "You can even hear it spin [in the pocket] sometimes. So if you put something a little more tacky in there, it will help stop the spinning and you can find the seams faster."

Gonzalez regards playing shortstop not simply a profession but a craft. Otherwise, you don't consider such things as spin rates on baseballs. Or glove sizes.

Gonzalez places his gamer back into his locker. He wants to like it, he really does. But best friends are hard to replace.

GAME 18

Sunday, April 25, 2004 . . . Cubs 4, Mets 2 . . . Wrigley Field . . . Cubs NL Central pennant flies: First (12-6) . . . Stat of the game: Matt Clement strikes out a career-high 13 as the Cubs win their sixth consecutive game.

Edwin Caraballo's Sunday congregation isn't large, but he does have the only church where you can get your clothes washed and your ankles taped.

We knew Wrigley Field was a cathedral for baseball, but who knew it also could double as the real thing? Then again, God works in mysterious ways, which is why Caraballo just finished delivering his morning sermon to the Mets in the cramped laundry room of the visitors' clubhouse and now awaits his 12:05 religious tee-off time in the Cubs' training room, followed by a visit to the dinky umpires' room.

Today's topic: a toughie—Acts, Chapter 2 . . . Repent, or else.

"When I saw the subject list we use and it said, 'Repent,' I was like, 'Uh-oh,'" says Caraballo, sitting in the dugout during BP. "We have that image in our mind of John the Baptist, of a minister telling them to change their lives. I try to be sensitive to that."

Caraballo, 38, is an ordained evangelist from the Grace and Peace Church on the northwest side of Chicago. This is his second season as a chapel leader in the Baseball Chapel program, which spreads The Word from the big leagues to the minor leagues. He's out here during every Sunday homestand by 10 o'clock, knapsack slung across his blue denim Baseball Chapel shirt, his precious clubhouse pass dangling from his neck.

As ministries go, this one has some quirks. Caraballo, a social worker by trade for the Chicago Board of Education, must find a common ground with millionaire ballplayers and managers, whose lives are often insulated by baseball's cocoon. The common ground, it turns out, is faith and frailties.

"Everybody thinks that because these players have money they don't have problems," he says. "But they go through what we go through: anxiety, dread, fear."

Pitchers Clement and Carlos Zambrano are the Cubs' chapel reps. Pitcher David Weathers is the same for the Mets. They set the chapel times with Caraballo. Today he had the Mets from 11 to 11:30, and now is killing time before his noon-ish visit to the Cubs.

"I start chapel with a prayer, then I read a scripture basically related to the topic at hand," says Caraballo. "Once that's done, there's like a 10-minute sermon, and then we pray. The guys on the Cubs, our relationship is strong, so they'll tell me specific prayers: for people in their family, themselves, for struggles that they're having. I honor their confidentiality. But our trust is growing, it's growing. As men, we're not used to that. We're not used to being honest and open."

Attendance is voluntary, of course, but Caraballo can usually count on an audience of about 15 or so players and staff members. One of his Cubs regulars is none other than the spiritual Baker.

"He always says, 'Don't start without me,'" says Caraballo. "A great guy."

Caraballo, who along his wife, Luz, also ministers to the wives of players and staff before Tuesday-evening home games, never prays for victories but for the integrity of their work. Self-satisfaction has its own rewards.

"If they don't get that, then they've missed the boat," he says. "It's like if they win the World Series, that's not the important thing. It's just doing your best."

Memo to Caraballo: Keep the World Series-not-being-important thing to yourself.

GAME 19

Monday, April 26, 2004 . . . Arizona Diamondbacks 9, Cubs 0 . . . Bank One Ballpark . . . Stat of the game: Randy Johnson improves his career record against the Cubs to 12-0—in just 13 starts. . . . Stuff: Cubs reliever Francis Beltran makes history—the not-so-good kind. He gives up the longest homer in The BOB history, a 503-foot physics lesson by Richie Sexson that knocks out several lights in the Sony Jumbotron located high above the center-field wall. . . . Cubs traveling secretary Jimmy Bank goes to the local Nordstrom to do some shopping. A salesperson approaches him. Turns out it's Fred Goldman, whose son Ronald was killed with O. J. Simpson's wife, Nicole Brown Simpson, in 1994.

As farewells go, Mark Grace deserved better than the one he received from the Cubs after the 2000 season, which was no farewell at all. Grace might not have been a management or Sammy Sosa favorite, but he was certainly a fan favorite, as well as a media favorite. His departure felt clunky, less than artfully handled. One day he was a Cub—all he had known since being drafted in the 24th round in 1985—then a free agent, then an Arizona Diamondback, wearing those hideous uniforms.

Grace's departure remains a tender subject with both Grace and the Cubs' front office. But there are simple truths involved here. The Cubs wanted a younger, more prototypical, and cheaper first baseman than Grace. Also, Grace and Sosa were the India-Pakistan of the Cubs' clubhouse. It was Grace who good-naturedly mocked (but mocked, nonetheless) Sosa during a D-Backs BP last season by carrying a bat with a wine cork taped to the end of the barrel. Sosa seethed, and later told WSCR's Bruce Levine, "He never liked me and I never liked him."

But sometimes a player becomes more than just a player. He becomes part of the franchise itself. Ernie Banks is the best example of that, but Grace, a three-time All-Star and four-time Gold Glove winner, was in the neighborhood. He was no icon, but he seemed as familiar as ivy. In even a less-than-perfect world, Grace should have retired a Cub.

Instead, he won a world championship ring as the Diamondbacks' starting first baseman in 2001 (17 homers, 78 RBI, 142 hits, .298 BA, .386 OBP) but was phased out of the lineup by 2003. He retired at 2003 season's end, is married and has two young children, and now does color for the Diamondbacks' TV broadcasts.

Meanwhile, the Cubs are on their fourth starting first baseman in four years. Matt Stairs wasn't exactly an heir apparent in 2001, which is why the Cubs paid big money to acquire "Crime Dog" Fred McGriff—or, in this case, just dog. By 2003 McGriff was gone, replaced by Hee Seop Choi, the protypical first baseman the Cubs craved. Now he plays for the Florida Marlins, and Derrek Lee is at first.

That's baseball. That's business. But for all his supposed deficiencies and the clumsily handled non-negotiations after the 2000 season, Grace's Cubs legacy shouldn't be one of burned bridges and hard feelings. For years he was one of the few reasons to watch the Cubs. That shouldn't be easily forgotten.

Grace on the early years, the departure, Cubs president Andy MacPhail, his TV career, teammates, retirement, tributes to Bill Murray, regrets:

My signing bonus was $25,000. I think I got a car. I got an old Pontiac Fiero. That got me to and from spring training in Arizona with the Cubs.

[Cubs traveling secretary] Jimmy Bank was always in charge of the aliases on the road. Right now, my hotel alias is Wells Fargo this year.

I would say the best alias I ever had was Carl Spackler. That's Bill Murray's character from *Caddyshack*. Murray's a friend of mine, so that's the one I used.

Leaving the Cubs, it was kind of disappointing.
The whole time, Andy MacPhail was saying, "Hey, we're going to redo you, we're going to redo you, we're going to redo you." That thought of [a farewell] never came to mind in 2000, because I just assumed I'd be back.

I was a free agent. My agent was in contact constantly with Andy

MacPhail. He told my agent [Barry Axelrod], "Well, we don't want to do anything with you now because we're in the [Mike] Hampton Sweepstakes and we're in the A-Rod [Alex Rodriguez] Sweepstakes." Those were the two big free agents that year. They said, "We'll put you on the back burner until we figure out where we are with A-Rod and Hampton. As soon as we find that out, then we'll get you worked out."

OK, no problem. We understand that. Another couple of weeks go by and it's, "All right, don't worry about it. Everything's cool." And finally, at the zero hour, with no time left on the clock, they're not going to tender me a contract. That's what pissed me off, that he lied, that he was saying all this and all that. That's what really pissed me off about Andy MacPhail. To this day I'll always think, hell, if he'd just told me that a month or two prior, I could have been out looking for job. Instead, now I'm sitting here jobless and damn near everybody has their team intact.

No farewells. MacPhail didn't have the decency to call me. He didn't have the decency to do any of that. Thirteen years of your life with a club . . . I felt like if he had just called me and said, "Hey, we think Hee Seop Choi is ready, we're gonna go in a different direction," I would have understood. I would have said, "Hey, that's great." But don't sit there and tell me, "Yeah, we'll get it done, we'll get it done, we'll get it done," and then not do it. That's just an out-and-out lie, and I thought it was bullshit.

Those three years in Arizona were the best of times and the least of times. For me, obviously winning the World Series is something that wouldn't have happened in my career had I remained with the Cubs. So obviously that was a blessing. That's also where it ended, too. It's where I became a lesser player, so to speak.

Eventually, I'd like to manage, but right now this is a stepping-stone to do that. But I just felt like I needed to get out of the game to save face a little bit. I think I got two starts in the second half last year. The most games I started in a row last year was two, and that was against Kevin Brown and Hideo Nomo—hey, go get 'em, kid.

I wasn't a very good pinch hitter. And because of that I knew I wasn't going to get an everyday job this year. I was a lousy pinch hitter, and I didn't enjoy pinch-hitting. So did I really want to go to, say, Toronto, and come off the bench pinch-hitting? No, so I decided this is it, get in the booth, hang around the game a little bit, still be around the guys, still be around the organization that has taken real good care of me.

My last hit came on my last at-bat in the last game of my career—against Sterling Hitchcock. I got a base hit, got a pinch runner, and walked off the field to a standing ovation.

I didn't cry or anything. I knew last year at the All-Star break I was going to retire. I announced it the last week of the season, but I had told my teammates, my wife, most of my friends that, "Hey, this is it. If you want to come out and watch, you need to do it now, because the free tickets are all up, because I'm retiring."

We called the press conference, and pretty much everybody knew what it was about when I came in there with my suit and everything. I said, "I want to thank everybody for coming. I just wanted to let everybody know I've signed a two-year extension." [GM Joe] Garagiola and [owner Jerry] Colangelo were sitting next to me and they're looking at me like, "What the hell are you talking about?" I looked back at them and said, "Oh, you mean you didn't tell them yet?"

Broadcasting . . . it's certainly not what I was born to do, but I'm learning a lot. Obviously, I don't get the same rush I used to every day. You're not competing. But I also was very much at peace with the decision I made to retire. I wasn't any good anymore. I wasn't getting to play anymore. And that was embarrassing. I always said when the game's not fun for me anymore I'm gonna get out, and not playing was no fun. So I got out and I moved on to this, and I'm enjoying it so far. I'm getting better at it, and maybe eventually I'll get good at it.

GAME 20

Tuesday, April 27, 2004 . . . Diamondbacks 10, Cubs 1 . . . Bank One Ballpark . . . Stat of the game: Todd Hollandsworth replaces an injured Derrek Lee (foot) and homers. . . . Noted baseball author and Washington Post *columnist Thomas Boswell writes: "By September, there will be serious discussion of whether the current Chicago rotation—yes, the Cubs—is the best five-man assemblage in history."*

Steve Gold says his AU Sports store in Skokie has the largest collection of Cubs memorabilia available in Chicagoland. After stopping by to see the place, I think he might be right. About the only thing missing is a billy goat and a signed stick of Doublemint from P. K. Wrigley.

"People can get lost in here for days," says Gold, who began selling sports collectibles—cards, programs, and so on—at card shows in 1973 and opened the Skokie store in 1980. Even the fellas at the Dallas-based *Becket Baseball Collector*, the price guide bible of baseball card owners, know and vouch for Gold.

The store, which is about 25 minutes from the Wrigley entrance, does have more Cubs stuff than Dusty Baker has toothpicks. There's a reason for that: "The Cubs are going to be hot sellers regardless of what they do [on the field]," says Gold. "When they lost 90-something games and the White Sox were in first place, the Cubs were still outselling them in my store."

Even though he has yet to pitch this season because of injuries, Mark Prior remains Gold's No. 1 seller. The sales volume isn't quite what it was before spring training began, but Prior stuff still brings premium prices. In just two seasons he's become the book equivalent of Harry Potter.

"I just sold a Prior card for $50," Gold says. "It lasted a day. The next one I get I'll put it at $60. I'll keep raising the price until people start balking."

Same goes for the so-called jersey cards, where a card maker attaches a tiny strand of jersey material to a card. Prior's jersey cards, when Gold can find one online, rarely make it to closing time. "I usually double my money on those, or pretty close to it," he says.

Of course, Prior's 2001 rookie cards are the real keepers, especially the autographed Ultimate Collection card produced by Upper Deck. Sitting down? It starts at $600.

OK, so Prior is a hot seller. And then Sammy Sosa, right?

"Nah, Woody is No. 2," he says of Kerry Wood merchandise. "Sosa, he's kind of dropped off since the corked bat incident. His stuff is not as desired."

Harry Caray stuff sells. An autographed menu from his restaurant goes for at least $150. Ryne Sandberg remains popular, as does Ron Santo, Ernie Banks, Billy Williams, and even Jody Davis. Mark Grace . . . not so much.

"He used to be a very popular ballplayer with the Cubs, but then he started bad-mouthing the team," Gold says. "I still have Grace stuff. I can't sell it for 50 percent of what I got before."

Grace deserves a better legacy than the 50-percent-off rack, but those pesky laws of supply and demand aren't very forgiving. Grace suffers from the collectibles triple play: retired, didn't retire as a Cub, didn't get a post-retirement job with the Cubs.

There are no discount racks for the Tobacco Era baseball cards of Cubs legends Joe Tinker, Johnny Evers, and Frank Chance. That's where the real money is. Tinker, Evers, or Chance cards go for $1,500 (and climbing) if you want the best. The asking price for any nineteenth-century-issued Cap Anson cards starts at $1,000. Ditto for Anson's almost-impossible-to-find book published in 1900.

Not so bullish on Cubs memorabilia—at least from a national perspective—is Ed Jaster, director of the acquisitions/pop culture department for Heritage, which does about $200 million of business each year and bills itself as the largest dealer and auctioneer of collectibles in the world. Jaster's domain includes comic books (he oversaw the sale of Nicolas Cage's massive collection), movie posters, and, among other things, sports collectibles. The Cubs? Yawn.

"The Cubs aren't all that different from baseball in general, in terms of what's valuable," says Jaster, who was born and raised in Highland Park and spent nearly 50 years in Chicago before relocating to Heritage's headquarters in Dallas. "You don't have a Gehrig, a Mantle, a Ruth. You don't have any of the big-money guys. Chicago is more a place of charm collectibles. Chicago collectors make their own mini-market."

Jaster would happily return your phone call if you had Hartnett-, Rogers Hornsby-, or Hack Wilson-related items, especially game-used materials. But Chicago's most marketable player wore a White Sox uni: Joe Jackson. "A Jackson bat went for $250,000 about two years ago," Jaster says.

Baseball cards? Don't bother.

"Sosa cards, they're almost a reverse investment," he says. "It's almost a sucker market for anybody who buys them."

But this is Sammy, I tell him.

"I don't care if he hits 10,000 home runs," he scoffs. "Anything contemporary has virtually no value in the long term."

How about the balls from the Mark McGwire/Sosa HR Chase of 1998?

"That stuff is worth a mere fraction of what it [sold for], a mere fraction," he says.

The Bartman Ball? This one gives Jaster pause.

"It was like catching your prom date making out with your best friend one more time," he says. "If anything epitomizes being a Cubs fan, it's that ball. But from a national view, that's a piece that can only be supported by a regional market. Guys in New York, Boston, Los Angeles . . . they don't care."

In a perfect collectibles world, only a handful of truly priceless Cubs memorabilia remains unaccounted for. AU Sports's Klein has already prepared his wish list.

"Maybe some people would say the Bartman Ball would be the Holy Grail," he says. "But if anybody has the ball—and the documentation—from the final out of the 1908 Cubs World Series, that would be the Holy Grail right now. And can anybody verify they have the ball that Gabby Hartnett hit for the Homer in the Gloamin'?"

Meanwhile, Steve Gold needs exactly a half-second to make his pick for most-wanted Cubs item.

"You mean, besides the Steve Bartman Ball?" he says. "Otherwise, I would like to have a program from the 1908 World Series. That's one thing I'd love to get my hands on."

And the price tag on that puppy?

"Nah," he says, "I'd keep that one for myself."

GAME 21

Wednesday, April 28, 2004 . . . Cubs 4, Diamondbacks 3 . . . Bank One Ballpark . . . Stat of the game: Dick Pole becomes the all-time-winningest manager (by percentage, 1.000) in Cubs history. He's 1-0. . . . Stuff: Word arrives from the Major League Baseball disciplinary office: Kerry Wood gets a five-game suspension for going postal on home plate umpire Eric Cooper during the April 17 game against the Reds. Dusty Baker gets a one-game suspension for throwing a fit after the infamous April 18 double-switch screwup against the Reds. Five-year-old son Darren tells him it's a "time-out." . . . The Cubs take sole possession of first.

A longtime National League scout (on the condition of anonymity) assesses the Cubs:

I'll tell you what, they're really good. It's a son of a bitch when you play them.

With Zambrano and Clement, the ball's moving all over the place and the hitters are extremely uncomfortable against them. Wood and Prior—he'll be back—are classic No. 1 starters on any staff. But Zambrano is as good as any of them.

Then you get to their bullpen, Hawkins and Farnsworth—they throw so hard they're an extension of Wood and Prior.

Offensively, they've got a heck of a lineup there. The thing I like about their club, they're built for power and pitching. Alou, Sosa, Ramirez, Lee, even their shortstop Gonzalez—he can hit you 20 when he's healthy—can hit the ball out of the park. When you send that many sluggers up there—and they get four, five at-bats a game—somebody's going to hit a home run. So they've got starting pitching that can hold you down, combined with home run hitters.

The most important thing when you put together a team is starting pitching. Their starters on a daily basis. . . put it this way: If you're comparing who's pitching for the Cubs and who's pitching for you, the Cubs guy is better. And not many clubs are going to hit many more home runs than them. It's just a great formula for wins there.

Sosa doesn't seem to be aging. Yeah, he has the back thing, but he'll be OK. He's a tough guy to keep out of the lineup. He looks better than ever, really. Plus, you've got a few athletic guys running around there. So it's just really a nice formula there for success.

Right now they're just OK defensively. And because of injuries, they haven't exhibited a strong left-handed side of their bullpen yet. But these are very minor weaknesses.

I know about all their injuries. But I don't think they're unhappy about putting Walker out there instead of Grudzielanek. And Martinez does a fine job at shortstop.

Patterson is interesting. He's a little bit like Sosa when he was a younger player. Sosa's philosophy was "I'm going up there 600 times, so I'm up there hacking and I'm going to hit 30 home runs." That's Patterson.

Truthfully, I just don't see the Cardinals' pitching staff matching up with them. I think Houston is getting a little old on the field. So I really don't see how over the course of 162 games anybody in that division is going to overtake the Cubs.

GAME 22

Friday, April 30 . . . St. Louis Cardinals 4, Cubs 3 . . . Busch Stadium . . . Cubs pennant flies: Tie-First (13-9) . . . Stat of the game: Ahead 0-2 in the count, LaTroy Hawkins walks Mike Matheny, forcing in the winning run with two out in the bottom of the ninth. "You f——ing want to talk to me?" he says to reporters afterward. And then Hawkins talks. . . . Rookie reliever Michael Wuertz is sent down, and veteran left-hander Glendon Rusch is brought up.

Mike Royko spun in exactly seven years and a day ago. Brain aneurysm. He was 64. He died not liking many things, including hypocrites, yuppies, Louis Farrakhan, the New York Mets, softball with gloves, crooked politicians, injustice, sloppy reporting, self-important editors, light beer, bureaucrats, dim-witted readers, and the St. Louis Cardinals.

This being the season's first series between the Cubs and the Cardinals, it seemed like the proper time to remember Royko. That's because Royko was a Cubs fan. He was also a Pulitzer Prize–winning Chicago columnist whose work was syndicated in more than 600 newspapers. Cubs fan . . . Pulitzer Prize winner. Probably in that order.

Royko Heaven would feature the Billy Goat's Tavern (and dearly departed owner William Sianis presiding behind the bar), an inexhaustible supply of Pall Malls, Beck's on tap and Jameson chasers, as well as a clear view of the Cubs game on the tube in the corner. He would root for the Cubs—and root against the Cardinals—because that's what he always did.

If you haven't read Royko's stuff, you need to Google immediately or make a beeline for the nearest bookstore. Either that or ask the Daley family about him.

But some of his better columns were written about the Cubs. After all, Royko was born and raised in Chicago, saw his first Cubs game in 1939 (it was always "Cubs Park," not Wrigley Field, to Royko), was there for Jackie Robinson's Chicago debut in 1947 (you'll get misty reading his account), was forever bitter about the Cubs' collapses in 1969 and 1984, tried and failed to convince Marshall Field to buy the Cubs (Royko wanted to buy a half of 1 percent interest), attended the first night game at Wrigley (and hated it), threw out the first pitch in an August 6, 1984, Cubs game, and even made an appearance in the WGN booth when Harry Caray was recovering from a stroke. And as fate would have it, Royko's final column, written March 21, 1997, was about the Cubs.

Royko was the guy who said former owner P. K. Wrigley was the reason for the Cubs' championship free fall. Wrigley didn't OK the debut of the team's first black players (Ernie Banks and Gene Baker) until late 1953, which was like showing up for a movie just in time for the final credits. "So what might have been, wasn't," Royko wrote.

He would write an annual Cubs quiz. Q: "Which of these three players pitched a one-hitter in the 1945 World Series: Eddie (Curly) Cronin, Greg Czag, or the immortal Dicky Gongola?" A: "None. They were all my relatives and enjoy seeing their names in the paper."

He would assess the effect of lights at Wrigley. "Yes, it is a new era.

The only thing that remains the same is that the team stunk then and it stinks now."

And he would reduce Cubdom philosophy to three sentences: "I always believed that being a Cub fan built strong character. It taught a person that if you try hard enough and long enough, you'll still lose. And that's the story of life."

Paul Sullivan, who has covered the Cubs for the *Chicago Tribune* for five seasons and baseball for much longer, knows a little something about Royko. Sullivan spent two years at the *Trib* as Royko's legman, meaning he was part gofer, investigative reporter, phone answerer, researcher, fact-checker, whipping boy, and anything else the famed columnist required. Covering baseball (generally considered the most difficult beat in any sports department) is nothing compared to working for Royko.

"Yeah, he loved the Cubs," Sullivan says. "He watched the games, had a TV in his office, and watched every game. He'd torture me by turning it up just enough so I could hear Harry [Caray] always going, 'Aaaaaagggggghh-hhh!' I'd say, 'What happened?' He'd say, 'Get in here.' Then he'd tell me what happened, and I'd stand there and watch it and he'd go, 'All right, get back to work.'"

Royko, hooked by the Cubs' playoff run in 1984 (they blew a 2-0 series lead against the San Diego Padres), bought a season-ticket package for 1985. The Cubs finished 77-84 that year, 23½ games out of first.

"In '85 they sucked," Sullivan says. "They were out of it real early, so he wouldn't want to go to the games and I'd have to get rid of his tickets. I'd go through the newsroom peddling his tickets. If I couldn't sell them, he'd just say, 'Ah, give 'em to somebody.' But most days I sold them. I was like a scalper, a Royko scalper."

One of Royko's favorite players was outfielder Jose Cardenal. Cardenal is the Cub who missed time at spring training because one of his eyelids wouldn't open. He is also the same Cub who was tortured by a chirping cricket. You can't make this stuff up.

Royko would have loved writing about 2003.

"I thought about that every day," Sullivan says. "There was the corked-bat thing with Sammy, the Steve Bartman thing, the Antonio Alfonseca belly-bumping incident, where Dusty Baker said it was assault with a deadly belly. Royko would have been all over that.

"And yeah, he would have ripped the yuppie bandwagon jumpers. I think he would have been all over Bartman too, actually. Why? Because everyone was on Bartman's side after he got harassed in the papers. I felt sorry for him, but I can see Royko taking the other side. He'd say, 'Take your earphones off and pay attention to the game!'"

Sullivan says Royko, a longtime regular in the 16-inch softball leagues, would have gotten along famously with Baker and would have absolutely adored Kerry Wood.

"He would have loved Kerry because Kerry threw at the Cardinals," Sullivan said.

Not long after Royko died, there was a memorial service at Wrigley Field. Sullivan was there. He and other Royko faithful sat in the sun behind the Cubs' dugout as family and friends, such as Studs Terkel, took turns telling their favorite story about the great columnist.

And when the memorial service was finished, some of the attendees couldn't help themselves. They made their way onto the field and began playing like schoolchildren. They ran the bases. They wandered out to the ivy.

Royko didn't like many things. But here's guessing he would have liked that.

MAY

• •

GAME 23

Saturday, May 1 . . . Cubs 4, Cardinals 2 . . . Busch Stadium . . . Cubs pennant flies: Tie-First (14-9) . . . Stat of the game: Matt Clement wins his fourth straight game. . . . Stuff: Game-time temp is 49 degrees and dropping. Rainwater begins to drip into the press box, which is about as cozy as Dantès's dungeon at Château d'If.

The first pitch is three and a half hours away, but Cubs hitting coach Gary Matthews is already in uniform and staring at the TV monitor in the middle of the near-empty clubhouse. The team bus hasn't arrived, which means Matthews can watch cut-ups—edited video of Cardinal Jeff Suppan's recent start against Houston—in relative peace.

Kerry Wood crouches on the floor and plays a board game with Greg Maddux's young son, Chase. LaTroy Hawkins smiles at Chase.

"You having fun?" says Hawkins.

Chase says nothing. Instead, he pinches the bill of his Cubs cap.

"You see that?" says Hawkins to the room. "He tipped his cap."

Matthews doesn't look up. He sits on the edge of a coffee table, hands on knees, and looks for Suppan's weaknesses. This is what hitters do, and for 16 big league seasons Matthews was a hitter to be feared. He retired with a career .281 average, 2,011 hits, an All-Star Game appearance, a World Series appearance, and a 1984 Cubs season to remember (101 runs, 82 RBI). Without Sarge, there is no Cubs NLCS that year.

Now he teaches hitting, if there is such a thing. He did it on the big league level for Toronto, for Milwaukee, and since 2003, for the Cubs.

The cut-ups aren't new. Every team has them. But Matthews makes sure the tape of Suppan will run from now until game time. He wants his hitters to compare the reports prepared by Cubs advance scouts with the video. He wants to see if Suppan tips his pitches, or if the Cardinals' infielders tip the pitches by their movement (if shortstop Edgar Renteria cheats toward the hole on a right-handed hitter . . . breaking ball).

"Look at last night," says Matthews. "[Cards starter] Woody Williams didn't have his best stuff, but look at how he gutted it out. You look for character from guys."

You also look for trends. How did Suppan pitch to the Astros' Jeff Kent, or Craig Biggio, or Jeff Bagwell, or Richard Hidalgo, or Lance Berkman? Bagwell is a right-handed power guy. Will Suppan pitch Sammy Sosa, another right-handed power guy, a similar way? Maybe. Probably.

Suppan is a 29-year-old right-hander who enters the game with 2-2 record and a 3.65 ERA. He was 13-11 a season earlier, and 9-16 in 2002. He chews up innings, too—200-plus in each of the last two seasons. But radar guns rarely work up a sweat when Suppan pitches.

"If a guy cannot throw the ball by you, then you don't have to cheat," says Matthews. "In other words, the only way a guy can get you out is by tricking you. A Kerry Wood can throw it by you, so you're thinking, 'All right, I'm going to look for that fastball.' That's why you saw so many guys swing at that slider of his in the dirt, because it looked like a fastball. A guy who can't throw it by you, you can actually look at the ball a little bit longer. This is what separates Bonds from everybody."

Bonds. Barry Bonds. Matthews loves to talk about Bonds.

"It's not even a debate. You pitch to this guy and he could have 100 home runs."

The Cubs' lineup isn't without its share of accomplished hitters. Todd Walker is a near-career .300 hitter. Corey Patterson shows flashes of brilliance. Sosa is a Hall of Famer. Moises Alou is a 20-90 guy. Aramis Ramirez is in the No. 5 spot, the RBI spot, for a reason. Derrek Lee is averaging 25-plus homers over the last four seasons. Alex Gonzalez has 20-homer power but also 100-plus strikeouts. Michael Barrett appears to be thriving in a post-Montreal enviroment.

"In terms of being a pure hitter, there's several in that category," says Matthews. "Mo, Ramirez. Mo is also a clutch hitter. Now, for pure power, you're looking at Sammy. If you ask pitchers who they'd rather face with two outs and a man on third, they'd rather face Sammy first. But if you're down two with two guys on, my guy's Sammy. Sammy will try to drive it out."

Today, Matthews wants his hitters to understand Suppan's limitations and tendencies. He wants them to step into the batter's box with a plan, and adjust the plan as the game evolves. His philosophy is simple: If you have reliable mechanics, can hit a fastball, and know the strike zone, you're going to be cashing some nice seven-figure checks. "But the fact of the matter is they're the ones doing it," says Matthews.

A postscript:

Suppan pitches well, going eight innings and giving up three runs and seven hits. Matthews stands in front of his locker and assesses the performance of his Cubs hitters. Nutshell version: He isn't happy with with Walker and Patterson (a combined 0-for-9). . . . Ramirez, who hit a three-run dinger off Suppan, was a mini-Bonds of sorts, taking advantage of a rare Suppan mistake. "That was the only bad pitch he made," says Matthews. . . . Lee is coming around, what with a single and double. "Lee's been coming off the ball. Then he took that [double] to right field. I'm happy to see that." . . . Overall performance: "We worked the count and made some adjustments."

GAME 24

Sunday, May 2 . . . Cardinals 1, Cubs 0 . . . Busch Stadium . . . Stat of the game: Reliever Kyle Farnsworth can't find the plate. He walks three to load the bases in the bottom of the 10th, and then gives up a game-winning single to Scott Rolen. Farnsworth's explanation: No comment. . . . Stuff: The priest at Old Cathedral, the oldest Catholic church west of the Mississippi (and only a few blocks away from Busch), welcomes visiting Cubs Nation residents with this greeting during the homily: "To the Cubs fans here today, we find it our duty to pray for those lost souls."

A St. Louis perspective . . .

"Look at Tony," says a St. Louis TV cameraman as Cardinals manager Tony LaRussa mingles with reporters in the Cardinals' clubhouse after the 1-0 extra-innings victory. "Today he's in here laughing, talking to us. Must have been a big one."

LaRussa's 702nd career win with the Cardinals isn't going in a time capsule, but it did have its share of goose-bump moments. Starters Carlos Zambrano and Matt Morris were virtually unhittable. The game was scoreless through regulation. A sellout crowd of 47,757 didn't budge.

"It was no fun being a hitter today," says LaRussa.

Unless you're Scott Rolen.

Rolen doubled in the second, singled in the fourth, and then arrived at the plate with bases loaded and Farnsworth on the mound in the 10th.

It has been a difficult few days for Rolen, the 29-year-old All-Star third baseman. Rolen's young nephew is suffering from health problems. He has been on the phone throughout the day, checking on his nephew's condition.

"A real emotional day for him" is the way LaRussa explains it.

Rolen entered the game hitless in his last nine at-bats. But his plan was simple against the hard-throwing Farnsworth: "Look fastball," he says. "No great strategy."

And still, even with bases loaded and Rolen walking toward the batter's box, LaRussa wasn't overly confident about the Cards' chances.

"Anytime Farnsworth comes in the game, you know you have your hands full," he says. "The guy has such a damn good arm."

Rolen, who had a career-high 27 RBI in April, had everything to his advantage. The Cubs' infield and outfield were in. And Farnsworth had no choice but to throw something over the plate. No way did the Cubs want a repeat of Friday evening's game, when they walked in the winning run in the bottom of the ninth.

"I went up there to hit," says Rolen. "With Farnsworth throwing so hard, I was in there hitting all the way through the count."

Farnsworth's first pitch was a slider. Ball one. Then he missed again. Ball two.

Rolen is smart enough to know what's coming next. Fastball. Rolen puts it on the meaty part of the bat and drives the ball to the left-field wall. Moises Alou barely bothers to move as the ball whistles over his head.

The base hit, says LaRussa, was dedicated to Rolen's ill nephew. Afterward, Rolen stands in front of his locker and politely answers questions, except one.

"Tony mentioned that your nephew was having health issues?" says a reporter.

Rolen shakes his head, waves off the inquiry, and then walks away. He's done for the day.

So are the Cubs.

GAME 25

Monday, May 3, 2004 . . . Cubs 7, Cardinals 3 . . . Busch Stadium . . . Cubs pennant flies: Tie-First (15-10) . . . Stuff: Little-known fact: Cubs pitchers pick the jersey tops worn for the game. Maddux chooses the grays with CHICAGO on the front.

Rick Hummel has covered about 4,000 Cardinals game during his last 31 years with the *St. Louis Post-Dispatch*. About 500 of those games were against the Cubs.

Hummel is known as "The Commish" by his peers. I have no idea why. I do know there are about 800 members of the Baseball Writers Association of America. BBWAA card numbers are issued on the basis of seniority, and Hummel is No. 61 (Dave Anderson of the *New York Times* is No. 1).

Hummel on The Rivalry*:*

The difference in this rivalry, as opposed to Yankees-Red Sox and Dodgers-Giants, is that the other teams' fans aren't in Yankee Stadium. You get a few Red Sox fans in Yankee Stadium, but you have almost no Dodger fans in San Francisco, and vice versa. But you have half and half here. I know this is a little closer than San Francisco and Los Angeles, but not much closer than Boston and New York geographically.

There's a lot more camaraderie among these fans. You would never see Red Sox and Yankees fans go across the street for a beer, unless one was trying to rob the other guy. And you don't see Dodgers and Giants fans hanging out together. But in this rivalry, especially at Wrigley Field, you'll see guys walking across the street with their arms around each other, falling-down drunk, sitting down on a stoop, one of them wearing a Cardinals hat, one wearing a Cubs hat. The game's over. That's just the way they are.

My favorite memories of this rivalry: Ryne Sandberg hitting two home runs off Bruce Sutter in that [June 23] game in '84. The Cardinals led almost the whole game. Sandberg homered to tie it twice [he finished with five hits and seven RBI]. But neither home run won the game. That was the great part about it. They got a bloop single by Dave Owen in the 11th to win it. So how many times do you see a short reliever allow two homers to the same guy, and neither homer is the game winner? Anyway, it defined the Cubs that year.

The five-game series in 2003. That was an electric series. The Cardinals just kind of folded up their tent that day, even though they had three and a half weeks to go. That series just drained them emotionally. They should have been able to overcome that, but they didn't.

Keith Hernandez realized the importance of this series. Bruce Sutter, having been a star on both teams, understood. Lee Smith, too.

Matt Morris would be one who comes to mind off this team. Some of these other guys, I'm not sure they do. Scott Rolen is just starting to appreciate it.

I don't like anything about Wrigley. I don't care about the ivy. I care that the fans are having a good time, but I hate it. I do like the scoreboard. But that's about it.

GAME 26

Tuesday, May 4, 2004 . . . Diamondbacks 6, Cubs 3 . . . Wrigley Field . . . Stuff: Bartman for a day: Corey Patterson gets booed for not running out a dropped ball on a third strike. . . . Urinegate: Moises Alou tells ESPN's Gary Miller he sometimes urinates in his hands to toughen them up for batting.

Today is George Will's birthday. Will was born May 4, 1941, in Champaign, Illinois, and spent his childhood with ear cocked toward the living room radio as Cubs broadcasts crackled through the speaker. After interviewing him, I'm surprised he didn't actually *invent* radio.

Covering sports for a living doesn't often lend itself to interaction with many intellectuals. Will is an intellectual. His ear wax is smarter than any part of my brain. I'm used to talking to athletes who think the Helsinki Accord is a Honda sold in Finland. I'm used to Sosa, in a moment of earnestness and religious fervor, blurting, "I just thank God for the opportunity to thank God."

Will was educated at Trinity College in Hartford, Connecticut, as well as

Oxford and Princeton. He won a Pulitzer Prize in 1977 for commentary, is syndicated in more than 450 newpapers, and is a regular contributor on ABC. He is a political conservative who has forgotten more about politics than Rush Limbaugh will ever know.

Will does have a weak spot. He adores the Cubs. He was at Wrigley Field for Games 6 and 7 of the 2003 NLCS. After those two Cubs losses, he didn't know whether to laugh or become a Democrat.

"It was surreal," I say of those games.

"No," he says, "it was all too real."

Ten minutes talking to Will about the Cubs is about all this land-grant university graduate could handle. I felt more overmatched than Dan Quayle on *Jeopardy*. ("Alex, I'll take potatoe for $1,000.") Those 10 minutes . . .

Q: *You once wrote, "From [former Cubs shortstop Roy] Smalley I learned the truth about the word* Overdue.*" What is that truth?*
Will: That truth, as my father explained to me, is that Stan Musial batting .242 is "overdue." Roy Smalley batting .242 is having a career year. Overdue is a way of not taking seriously the strong probabilities of baseball.

Q: *And how does that relate to the Cubs?*
Will: The Cubs' problem isn't a billy goat. And it isn't a fan in the front row along the left-field line. The Cubs' problem has been a long history of in-adequate front-office management. Don't blame the billy goat for Brock for Broglio. Don't blame the billy goat for getting Ralph Kiner too late. Don't blame the billy goat for getting [Greg] Maddux twice with 250 or so victories in between.

Baseball is a serious business, and the Cubs have not always been well run. Proof of this point is that now that they are well run, they bestride the National League Central like a colossus.

Q: *Do you see any similarities between managing a Cubs team and managing government?*
Will: No, no, because the Cubs have talent. Managing the Cubs is closer to a priestly duty. [Government] is bureaucratic muddling through.

What's the governmental equivalent of Mark Prior? Abraham Lincoln, I suppose, and they don't come along that often.

Q: *Do you think there's a certain nobility in being a true Cubs fan?*
Will: No. It seems to me . . . God, I suppose there's a certain nobility in

being a Tampa Bay Devil Rays fan. Loyalty is kind of noble, and steadfastness is noble. But any team can produce fans who have that kind of nobility. There is a kind of Cubs fan who seems to rather relish the fact that there's been so much losing and futility. They need to get out of the house more and get a life.

The fact is that losing and the decades of futility is not admirable and it's not funny, and it's over. That episode in Cubs history is behind us. And people who luxuriate in it need to see an analyst.

Q: *You'll get to Wrigley, what, a handful of games a season?*
Will: At most, a handful at Wrigley, until October, and I expect to spend a lot of days until about the 28th of October at Wrigley Field. [October 28 is the day after Game 4 of the Series. In other words, Will has the whisk broom out.]

Q: *What is it about Wrigley that soothes the soul?*
Will: It's a venue made just for baseball, a blazing sunburst of insight that took the twentieth century eight decades to get back to, with Camden Yards and all the rest. Baseball is the most observable of team games, nine people thinly scattered on a pleasing green background. And therefore, a ballpark should take advantage of the observable nature of it. Get people close to it, but not too many people. Wrigley Field does that.

The three most important things to happen in baseball since the Second World War were Jackie Robinson, free agency, and Camden Yards. And all Camden Yards did was get back to an old truth.

Q: *Will the Cubs win the World Series during the Arnold Schwarzenegger tenure?*
Will: The Cubs will win the Series this year.

Look, being serious, you can't say that. You get into a seven-game shootout with teams at that level in the postseason and anything can happen. But pitching is, what, 85 percent of baseball until the postseason—and then it's 90 percent. And the Cubs have the best pitching in baseball.

So if I had to bet my house on one of these teams, I'd bet it on the Cubs.

Q: *What would you rather see: a Republican president in office, or the Cubs winning the World Series?*
Will: Win the World Series.

Let's see, the Cubs won the World Series [1907, 1908] during a Republican administration—Teddy Roosevelt. Since then, how many Republican presidents have there been? Taft, Harding, Coolidge, Hoover, Eisenhower, Nixon, Ford, Reagan, Bush, Bush. So there have been 10 Republican presidents since the Cubs won the World Series.

It's time for the Cubs.

GAME 27

Wednesday, May 5, 2004 . . . Diamondbacks 2, Cubs 0 . . . Wrigley Field . . . Stuff: The Curse lives: Alex Gonzalez is out 6 to 8 weeks with a broken wrist bone. . . . Urinegate—The Aftermath: Dusty Baker says when he played in Latin America it wasn't uncommon for players to tinkle in their hands to toughen up the skin. Moises Alou does it here and guess what? "Nobody's shaking his hand," says Baker. "Everybody's just giving him the fist."

John Tait, signed by the Chicago Bears during the off-season, throws out the first pitch. According to the Cubs, the 6-6, 323-pound offensive tackle becomes the biggest person ever to take the mound at Wrigley. His terrifying tale:

Let me preface this by saying there's a story behind the horrible pitch and one of the most embarrassing moments of my life. Glen Kozlowski—he's a BYU guy like me—calls and says, "Do you want to come to a Cubs game? There's a charity thing I got going on one of the rooftops." I tell him I'll do it.

On the way over there . . . he says to me, "There's a little bit of a change of plans. I got you throwing out the first pitch."

I tell him, "Hold up here, buddy. Glen, I haven't practiced. I need to throw a ball 60 feet."

"No, you'll be fine," he says.

Glen works for WGN, so I guess he arranged it. But I never really played baseball my whole life. Throwing out the first pitch, that's a big deal.

I started thinking—and this is where I went wrong—that it's not that far from the mound to home plate. It's 60 feet. I'll just lob it up there. Plus, how many people get the chance to throw out the first pitch? And at Wrigley Field?

I tried to stay loose. But I was more nervous throwing out that first pitch than I've been in NFL games. It's such a big crowd. And I can't even tell you the last time I threw a baseball. And offensive linemen . . . our shoulders are not too limber.

The funniest part was sitting in the dugout. Dusty Baker came up to me. Sammy Sosa gives you a pound. The players tell you, "You'll do fine and, by the way, just get it across the plate." They just add that in there at the end— *just get it across the plate.*

All of a sudden someone says, "Get out there and throw it." So I go out there and, well, I wish I could have that one back. As soon as the ball left my hand, I knew it was horrible. The thing is, I've gone to games where somebody throws out the first pitch and it doesn't make it to the plate. I've booed several people who threw badly. So the karma came back, I guess.

First you hear the laughing. Then you hear the booing. Glenn kept telling me they weren't booing. He said they were "ooooing." I said, "Are you sure?"

The worst part was I had to walk back up through the stands. I start hearing, "Nice throw, Tait." Or, "I hope you can block better than you can throw." But at least I made it to the dirt. I even got the scuff mark on it. And they give you a jersey, though I was such a last-minute deal I didn't get my name on the back.

Ask my wife, I was pretty upset about [the pitch] for a week. But at least I can laugh about it now.

GAME 28

Thursday, May 6, 2004 . . . Cubs 11, Diamondbacks 3 . . . Wrigley Field . . . Stuff: Matt Clement wins his fifth consecutive game. . . . News of a fatal shooting just outside the Cubby Bear Lounge reaches the Wrigley press box about two hours after the game. The initial details are sketchy, but one report says the shooting was a result of a traffic altercation between a pedestrian and a passenger in a passing SUV.

Two cases of beer stacked atop each other in a red plastic mini-tub weigh about 48 pounds. Now put a strap around the back of your neck, attach the clips to each side of the tub, and start climbing those steep Wrigley Field stairs for five hours.

Congratulations, you're David Mariotti, who has been lugging beers up and down those stairs since 1983.

Mariotti is a teacher by day, beer vendor by night, weekends, and holidays. He was born on the South Side (61st and Pulaski) but now lives in Oak Lawn. It takes him 40 minutes to get to Wrigley, nearly double that to get home. If the Cubs are out of town, he'll work the White Sox games.

The drill is always the same: Check in when the gates open two hours before the game. Buy your ticket vouchers, get your loads of beer, sell. Beer vendors make their money on commissions and tips.

The wisdom of a beer man:

You average 10 loads a game, but you're hoping for about a dozen. The cutoff time has been shortened. In the old days, in the '80s, you could sell even after the game was over. People would park outside the bathrooms waiting for you.

Now I can't get any beer once the seventh inning begins. Society and the neighborhood have changed the way beer sales have gone. If the game goes into extra innings, doesn't matter. We're done. I'm on Lake Shore Drive listening to the game on the radio.

The older guys take single loads because of their backs. I've got a strong back, weak mind.

At Wrigley, beer goes for $5.25. When I started at Sox Park, beer was $1.50. Now they're at $5.50. The Cubs were below $2.00.

You get tips here, but tips are a '90s phenomenon. When we first started here in the '80s, there was no such thing as tips. If you got $4 on 10 cases, you were lucky. The best thing that happened here was one year when they made beer $2.40. Why they picked that odd amount, I think it's because three beers was $7.20—WGN's call numbers. Nobody wanted all those dimes, so they'd tell you to keep the change.

And five and a quarter is a great price, too.

Best tip I ever got? What you want, clean or dirty?

Dirty? OK, Cubs-Cardinals game. I had Old Style that day and the crowds, they were just happy to see a beer person. They were just happy to get their beer. I had these guys and girls, big group. They were tipping. At the end, they ran out of money. Nothing left for tips. So three of the girls came up and flashed me, and that was the tip. Excellent-looking girls.

Sold a beer to Tom Hanks. I should have gotten an autograph.

Oh, and sold beer to Studs Terkel and Mike Royko. I got exact change on that one. Studs and Mike did not tip me. That was back in the '80s. They were both sitting together. Can't remember who bought.

I used to sell Old Style. Old Style used to be the best-selling beer here. Then Harry [Caray] became Cub Fan/Bud Man and that was the end of Old Style. Harry did something that Jack [Brickhouse] never did. Harry came up in '84 and says, "I'm a Bud Man."

So I get Bud. All the cases are 3-1: 18 Bud Lights and six Buds. Light is a better seller than regular Buds. Old Style just doesn't do as well as the Lights. When you get seniority you get first pick of the beer, and Bud always goes first.

Four things:

You have to have an understanding wife. I know two years ago if you did it right you could work every single game at both ballparks.

You have to be consistent. You're going to have good days, you're going to have lousy days. When you take a day off, you have to make a smart decision. I always look at the schedule. There are days you highlight that you know you have to be there: Cubs-Sox series, Cardinals-Cubs, Opening Day, the Houston series, the Sox-Yankees.

It's all competition. It's looking where your fellow vendors are and aren't. You have to look to go where they haven't been. You just can't follow.

If you can get a regular clientele, that helps.

Best day: Friday afternoon. The guy who invented the Friday-afternoon, 3:05 start—before they made them 2:20—was the beer man's idol. With a 3:05 start you got the businessman who doesn't have to go back to work. A 2:20 start is sort of the same.

I'll be honest with you: The numbers here are consistent, which means when you walk in here today you pretty much know you can do 10 loads. But when Sox Park is packed, there's no better place to sell beer than a packed Sox Park. But you don't get that. Those days are few and far between there. But Opening Day at the Sox is always tremendous.

I used to be left field, now I'm right field. You get the sun late in the afternoon, which is April, May, September—that's good. You'll see a migration of people moving to the warmer section if they can. June, July, August, those seats are unbearably hot, the sun is really shining. That's good for the water guys. Those are the days a beer man gets killed by a guy selling water.

The need for a job is why I did this. I said this was only going to be a short trip. But it's like that old line from *Saturday Night Live*: "Baseball's been very, very good to me."

GAME 29

Friday, May 7, 2004 . . . Cubs 11, Colorado Rockies 0 . . . Wrigley Field . . . Cubs NL Central Pennant flies: Second (17-12).

The Associated Press
Chicago—A 22-year-old man was charged with murder Friday in the fatal shooting of a man outside a popular bar across the street from Wrigley Field after a Chicago Cubs game.

Police said Rodrigo Caballero of Chicago shot 26-year-old Frank Hernandez on Thursday night after an altercation between Hernandez, his friends, and the occupants of the sports utility vehicle in which Caballero was riding.

The incident started because of a traffic dispute between the pedestrians and the driver of the SUV, police Cmdr. Michael Chasen said.

Hernandez was a Chicago White Sox fan who decided to join friends watching the Cubs play the Arizona Diamondbacks on Thursday.

Frank Angelo Hernandez Jr. was 26, the same age as Kerry Wood. He'll be buried at Resurrection Cemetery and his gravestone will read, *Loving Son, Brother, Always In Our Hearts.*

His absence has already been noticed by his three-year-old niece, who keeps asking, "Where's Frank?" Rather than try to explain the unexplainable, she is told softly, "Sweetheart, Frank went away."

Frank's grandmother doesn't know either. She's still recovering from a stroke so severe that doctors informed the family there was virtually no hope for recovery. Then, on Good Friday, only a few days before Frank Sr. was going to have his mother taken off life support, Susie Hernandez told the hospital attendant not to turn on the TV in her room. Doctors were summoned. They still can't believe it.

"It was like a miracle," says Frank Sr.

But Frank Jr. was Susie's favorite. Frank Jr. was everybody's favorite. It was Frankie—that's what almost everybody called him—who would come to the hospital and introduce his longtime girlfriend, Liz Martinez, to his then-nearly comatose grandmother.

"This is my girlfriend," he would say cheerfully. "We're all praying for you."

So rather than have another heart broken, the Hernandez family is waiting until she's fully recovered. They've even instructed hospital personnel to keep the TV off during the afternoon and evening news programs. No need for Channel 2's Diann Burns to be the first to tell her about those 9mm bullets that killed Frankie.

Not that it really matters, but Frankie was a Cubs fan too. During the 2003 playoffs, he bought Cubs hats and T-shirts for himself and his old man, Frank Sr. And he was enough of a Cubs fan that with only two innings remaining in Game 6 of the NLCS against the Florida Marlins, he turned to his dad and said, "I'm going down there."

So he bolted from the family's second-floor apartment near Midway Airport, where it sounds as if the planes are going to do a touch-and-go on the building's roof, and took the Orange Line to the Loop, then the Red Line to Wrigley. The Cubs led, 3-0, when he left. By the time he stepped onto the L platform at Addison, the Marlins were ahead, 8-3.

Frankie called home. "Dad, what happened?"

Bartman happened. A Gonzalez error happened. An eight-run eighth happened.

Not a morning passed without Frankie checking the Cubs' box score in the sports section. He knew their roster. He knew that Corey Patterson was scuffling in the No. 2 spot. He knew the countdown on Mark Prior's return. Two weeks from now, he was supposed to go to a game against the Cardinals. He already had tickets.

Frankie worked at a downtown architecture firm, where he oversaw the company's archives and assisted in administrative matters. He did his job so well that the firm's cofounder had planned to call in the Daley College graduate and give him a 20 percent raise.

But Frankie had requested Thursday off. He was going to the Cubs game with his younger brother Vince. Liz, who attends Harold Washington College, drove them to Wrigley.

As they made their way north on Lake Shore Drive, Frankie gestured toward a freshly cut patch of grass. He leaned his head slightly out the window and then said to his girlfriend of six years, "Take a deep breath. You smell that, Liz? Smell the grass. Isn't it great?"

Liz dropped Frankie and Vince off at Wrigley and began to drive away. That's when the phone rang. It was Frankie. He just wanted to hear her voice again.

The game was a blowout. The Cubs scored five runs in the fifth, two in the sixth, and three more in the eighth. By then a friend had taken a snapshot of Frankie and Vince mugging for the camera as they sat happily in the bleachers. That was the same afternoon Frankie and Vince talked about life, about their future.

About 90 minutes after the game, Frankie and Vince were crossing Clark Street when a Chevy Suburban brushed past. Vince swore at the driver. The car stopped and the driver confronted Vince. That's when Frankie became protector and peacekeeper. He pulled the driver away from Vince, but by then Caballero allegedly was making his way out of the SUV, his handgun drawn.

Lynn Hernandez, Frankie's mom, heard the phone ring a few minutes later. It was one of Frankie's friends.

"Frank was just shot," said the friend.

Lynn handed the phone to Frank Sr. The old man kept asking, "Is he alive? Is he alive?"

Alice Hernandez, Frankie's older sister, was the first to arrive at the Illinois Masonic Hospital. A doctor took her aside and said, "It's not your brother's fault."

In shock, in tears, Alice asked, "How's my brother? Is he in surgery?"

"No," said the doctor.

Alice's mind raced. Maybe they needed permission from a family member before they could operate. But then the doctor began to speak again. She recalls only bits and pieces of what he said: "The wound was fatal." . . . "We couldn't save him." . . . "He was gone in an instant."

Liz arrived shortly thereafter. As she walked from the parking lot to the hospital entrance, she kept telling herself that the doctors would take care of Frankie, that Frank Sr. and Lynn could go to work tomorrow, that she'd look after Frankie as he recovered.

And then a hospital security man asked her to follow him. That's when she knew.

Meanwhile, Frank Sr. and Lynn tried to make their way through the maddening rush-hour traffic. Frank Sr. kept telling his wife, "He's a strong boy. He's going to make it."

When Lynn walked into the hospital room, she saw her oldest son with eyes closed. "He looked like he was sleeping," she says. "He was so beautiful. I kept saying, 'Frank, Mom's here. Mom's here.' I just wanted him to wake up."

In an hour or so there were nearly 30 friends and family at the hospital. They took turns going into the room to see Frankie.

"I just wanted him to say, 'Mom, I'm OK. It's beautiful where I'm at now,'" says Lynn. "But we don't get that. There were no good-byes."

"That's the hardest part," says Alice, holding an 8 × 10 photo of Frankie and Vince in the Wrigley bleachers. "I just want to take him out of this picture and hug him."

Alice would like you to know that Frankie was as sweet as a Hershey Kiss. A week before his death, he called to remind her to be careful about walking home by herself at night.

Liz would like you to know that Frankie valued family above all else, that he was generous and caring, that he kept a journal containing his life's goals: passion, marriage, family, Liz, the ability to offer respect and receive it.

Frankie and Liz first met on an Orange Line train. In fact, he walked her home from the L stop that very first day. He liked writing. She liked writing (Frankie bought her a diary). He liked music. She liked music. He liked sports, especially fishing, baseball, and basketball. She liked writing and music.

"I knew that was the man I wanted to marry," she says. "He was everything I wanted out of a man. He was so passionate about life."

Lynn would like you to know that Frankie loved homemade mashed potatoes, and spaghetti and meatballs, but only if it was Frank Sr.'s recipe. He had decided to pursue a career in real estate, which explains the nearly 50 books he had read recently on the subject.

Of course, Lynn isn't cooking now. She can't. The memories are too fresh.

"I imagine he's still here," she says. "I breathe in so deeply. . . . I try to breathe for him. If there are miracles in the world, our miracle would be Frank coming in through that door."

Frank Sr. would like you to know that his son's laugh was as contagious as the flu, that he once treated his friends to a fishing trip on Lake Michigan, that "he was never in trouble a day of his life." He listened to R&B albums. His favorite shows were *The Sopranos*, *The Simpsons*, and *Seinfeld*.

"Parents should not outlive their kids," he says. "Frank should have lived to be an old man."

Frank Sr. paws at a poster board filled with photos of his son. There's Frankie at his high school graduation ceremony. There's Frankie and Liz at prom. There's Frankie, no more than seven or eight years old, wearing an Easter suit.

Lynn stands near the couch and dabs at her tears. Soon her son's accused killer will appear in bond court. The Hernandez family will be there.

"Does he realize what he's done?" Lynn says. "I would tell him, 'If you would have known my son, you would have loved him too.'"

GAME 30

Saturday, May 8, 2004 . . . Rockies 4, Cubs 3 . . . Wrigley Field . . . Stuff: Hey, isn't that Colorado reliever (and former Cubs kook) Turk Wendell riding a bike around Wrigleyville about four hours before the game? . . . Former Cubs GM Dallas Green sings "Take Me Out to the Ballgame." He sounds like a frayed fan belt.

Three hours after the Cubs loss, a pair of cars pull into the parking lot next to the administrative offices at Wrigley. Out spills the wedding party of newlyweds Dan Felten and his bride Cherina Cyborski, as well as Felten's best man and younger brother, Brett, the maid of honor, assorted parents, and a photographer. The men look like Gingiss ads, Cherina looks heavenly, and the maid of honor isn't so bad herself.

Across the street you can see a couple of overserved knuckleheads shoving each other over who gets to climb first into a waiting taxi. And then there's the drama-queen girlfriend knocking the St. Louis Cardinals cap off her boyfriend's head before she storms off in a drunken huff. Sirens squeal in the backround. Horns honk. But none of this matters to Dan and Cherina, who are mesmerized by the moment, by their love, by a building built in 1914.

"My brother and I grew up in Evanston," says Brett, who lives just two blocks from Wrigley and works for Dell as an account manager. "Growing up, we used to take the L down from Evanston. We lived and died with the Cubs. We'd come home from school, watch the game, listen to Harry, grab our bats, and swing like we were Mark Grace. We had a neighbor, her name was Alice. Huge Cubs fan. She used to dress her beagle in Cubs clothes."

OK, so this is beginning to make sense.

The wedding party assembles under the famed red marquee. The photographer, also wearing a tuxedo, drops to the sidewalk, practically with his back on the cement, and begins clicking away. Say "Lee" (as in Derrek).

Dan and Cherina have had a teensy-weensy bit too much time on their hands leading up to the wedding. They're both doctors, with Cherina set to begin work at the Rehab Institute of Chicago, and Dan going to Rush to practice pediatrics. But that's after the honeymoon ("We're going to Disney World!"). Leading up to the ceremony, they had five weeks to put their own touches on the big weekend.

The rehearsal dinner, which was held at Dan's parents' house, was interesting. Rather than give his best man a traditional gift, such as a flask or piece of jewelry, Dan gave Brett a baseball bat.

"Thirty-two ounces," says Brett. "Made by George & George. It's engraved: 'Best Man—Brett Felten.' The funny part is that Cherina's aunt gave them a bat with their names on it."

Dessert at the rehearsal dinner featured cake. Except this cake was shaped and decorated like Wrigley, complete with a candy center-field scoreboard and candy stands. No word if Sears purchased signage rights for the cake.

The wedding ceremony was perfect. Sun shining. A cool but pleasant early-May afternoon at the Lincoln Park Conservatory. And, of course, the family pastor making numerous references to the Cubs.

Afterward, there were the traditional photos of the happy couple, followed by the nontraditional request to stop at Wrigley on the way to the reception at Wilmette Harbor.

So here they are, beaming as if Corey Patterson didn't really whiff three hours ago in the bottom of the ninth with two outs and Cubs runners on first and third. The photo session doesn't take long. Dan and Cherina pose in front of the marquee. Then they pose in front of the giant Cubs logo on the nearby stadium wall. Then it's off to the reception, where they are introduced to the 130 guests as husband and wife. Applause and then . . . everyone begins serenading them with "Take Me Out to the Ballgame."

"I'm embarrassed for them," says Brett, who is two years younger than Dan.

It gets worse. Or better, depending on your degree of Cubs allegiance. Instead of individual seating placards on the tables, each guest finds his or her face superimposed on a Cubs baseball card, which is attached to a baseball signed by Dan and Cherina. Like I said, they had a little too much time on their hands.

Brett's face is Photoshopped over Mark Prior's body. Brett would prefer Prior's paycheck superimposed over the one he gets from Dell.

On the back of the baseball cards are Dan and Cherina's "statistics." Yeah, it's queer, but that's what couples do. Years from now they'll shriek in horror.

First meeting location: John Barleycorn's (after a Cubs game, of course).

Proposal date: May 20, 2003.

Wedding date: May 8, 2004.

Brett looks over the rest of the card.

"First kiss . . . First date location . . . New home . . . First kiss . . . First time I said I love you," he says, reciting the categories. "I can't believe my brother put this on there."

This is what true love can do. This is what the Cubs can do.

GAME 31

Sunday, May 9, 2004 . . . Cubs 5, Rockies 4 . . . Wrigley Field . . . Stuff: The Cubs release former 1999 first-round pick Ben Christensen. Christensen is best known for beaning an Evansville player in the on-deck area. . . . Guess who's at the game? Brett Felten. Beats going to Disneyworld.

Richie Terrile and about 10 other autograph-seeking regulars have been staked out here at the Harry Caray statue since about 8 A.M. This is the Wrigley location of choice if you want an autograph from visiting players—in this case, the Colorado Rockies.

The routine is fairly simple: A taxi pulls up just past the corner of Addison and Sheffield; a player gets out, then walks the 20 or so yards from the curb to the iron entrance gate. If you're Terrile, you've got about 30 seconds to recognize the player, thumb to the exact place in your three-ring binder where that player's card or photo is located, pull out the card or photo, uncap your blue Sharpie (blue shows up better than black), and somehow convince the player to pause long enough to sign.

"If you don't recognize them, you might give the player a different card," says the 35-year-old Terrile, who lives only a few blocks away from Sox Park. "Somebody did that the other day when the Diamondbacks were in. Somebody gave Luis Gonzalez a Steve Finley card to sign." Terrile rolls his eyes. Rookies.

Terrile's three-ring binder, complete with the Rockies' roster on the back for easy reference, sits on a nearby concrete ledge. For now he carries a clipboard with two Denny Hocking cards attached. The cards are from Hocking's days with the Minnesota Twins.

And then . . .

"Excuse me," says Terrile, who bolts as he spots a cab as it slows to a stop.

It's Rockies All-Star first baseman Todd Helton. The pack descends on Helton, who barely breaks stride as he signs a few autographs. Terrile has his binder open, but it doesn't matter. His late start (my bad) costs him.

"Helton . . . I would have liked to have gotten him," says Terrile, back at his spot next to Harry's statue. "Oh, well, I ain't going to call it a day."

Terrile began collecting autographs about five years ago. He has about 2,000 signatures, some on baseball cards, some on photos and baseballs. He isn't a pro. He says his autographs don't end up on eBay.

"Some guys hunt and fish," he says. "I do this."

Helton is the prime autograph target when the Rockies are in town. The Terrile scouting report on him is simple: "He'll sign, but he'll only sign a couple."

Barry Bonds? "I got Bonds," Terrile says. "That was a good catch for me. He was all right. He signed coming in Comiskey.'"

Sammy Sosa? "I haven't gotten Sosa yet," he says. "He's tough. And I don't have Kerry Wood yet. A lot of them are good, though. If you catch them at a good time, they're nice."

The whole time Terrile is talking, he's scanning the corner and sidewalks for players. Bingo.

"There's Hocking."

The Rockies utility man walks up holding a cup of Starbucks and wearing a bemused smile.

"Jesus Christ, I signed for you guys yesterday," says Hocking as the autograph hawks move toward him, cards, photos, and pens outstretched.

A woman in her thirties hands Hocking several items to sign. This time he glances suspiciously at the woman. "I know mothers don't collect cards," he says.

Hocking happily signs for several minutes. He tells the remaining autographer seekers, "You want me to sign Helton's, too?"

There are about 10 autograph regulars out here, including Ballhawk legend Ken Vangeloff. They're here by 8 o'clock or so, because that's when the coaches and manager usually arrive. The players begin trickling in later.

Meanwhile, the pros have already come and gone. They left after their No. 1 target/moneymaker—Helton—did the fast walk into Wrigley. The collectors don't care much for the pros who hawk signatures.

"It's rough when they bring a little kid out here to get an autograph for them," says Terrile. "Or they'll just run or push past you so they can get their stuff in there. There's one lady who brings both her kids here to have players sign. Then she'll ask us, 'Who's that? Who's that?' We don't tell her."

A white Escalade drives past. One of the regulars—a kid no older than 12 or 13—sprints down Addison toward Clark. He catches the Escalade at the stoplight.

"Who's that?" I ask.

"Aramis Ramirez," says Terrile.

"He won't sign," says one of the regulars.

The Escalade takes a right onto Clark and moves toward the Cubs players' parking lot. The kid, out of breath from the run, returns a few minutes later.

"Well?" I say.

He smiles. "Got it."

GAME 32

Tuesday, May 11, 2004 . . . Los Angeles Dodgers 7, Cubs 3 . . . Dodger Stadium . . . Cubs NL Central pennant flies: Second (18-14) . . . Stat of the game: Thirty-eight. That's how many pitches Kerry Wood throws before leaving the game with tightness in his right triceps. Team president Andy MacPhail, who's making the West Coast trip, leaves Dodger Stadium with tightness in his throat.

The three best baseball movies, in reverse order, are:

Major League

First of all—and I mean this in the most professional way possible—I'd clean home plate with my tongue to watch Rene Russo do anything. Then you have Bob Uecker doing the play-by-play, Charlie Sheen as relief pitcher "Wild Thing" (and looking as if he really knows how to throw a heater, as opposed to Gary Busey's spaz delivery in *Rookie of the Year*), and pre-24 Dennis Haysbert as Pedro Cerrano. Best of all, you have former big league pitcher Pete Vukovich as a New York Yankees slugger named Haywood. Sneers Vuke to catcher Tom Berenger as he steps into the batter's box: "How's your wife and my kids?"

The Natural

A soundtrack from heaven. An old-time feel as realistic as the wool New York Knights unis. And did I mention Kim Basinger in pouting splendor?

Bull Durham

This is baseball's *Casablanca*. As perfect as an ivy leaf. Costner's Crash Davis delivers lines to remember. ("I believe . . . in the hanging curveball, high fiber, good Scotch, that the novels of Susan Sontag are self-indulgent, overrated crap.") I can even overlook Tim Robbins's goofy-ass pitching delivery (Susan Sarandon throws better), because he absolutely nailed his bonus-baby character. ("Why's he calling me 'Meat?' I'm the one driving a Porsche.")

Bull Durham was released in 1988 and it still holds up like breast implants. I've only seen it about 1,100 times, so I'm still picking up the nuances. In fact, I tried to convince writer/director Ron Shelton to do a sequel to his 108-minute classic, but all I got was a polite smile and a pause for awkward silence.

I had flown from Chicago to John Wayne Airport in Orange County earlier in the day, then made the delightful rush-hour drive from the OC to Santa Monica in a little under 16 hours. A mutual friend had helped arrange the interview, which would center around a simple question: If you were to do a movie on the Cubs, what would it be?

Shelton didn't have too much on his plate. Only a script to finish (tentatively titled "Jones"), a company to run (Bordertown Pictures), a schedule to keep, and a family to tend to. Otherwise, he had plenty of time for some pasty-white yahoo from Chicago asking make-believe movie questions about the Cubs.

The Bordertown offices are in a neat little bungalow complex, and his office is ski-lodge cool. I didn't know whether to sit down or wax my Rossignols.

"C'mon in," he says, gracious, hand extended, his face lit by only a few soft office lights and the glow from the desktop computer screen. "Just finishing up something."

Shelton was a hell of a minor league ballplayer, and had fate's smile lingered on him just a bit more, he could have been a respectable Major Leaguer. All he's left with now is a boffo film career, a loving, five-alarm-gorgeous, cardsharp wife/actress, Lolita Davidovich, and an armful of wonderful children. Poor sap.

In his office, among other items, is an Eddie Mathews baseball card and bat. There's a photo of Jackie Robinson, as well as assorted boxing memorabilia.

The phone rings. Shelton takes the call. His voices rises. I can't help but him hear him say, "Keanu, if you were any more wooden of an actor, they'd name a silver maple after you."

No, not really. But that's what I'll tell my kids when I get home.

Shelton does inform me that his dinner date has canceled and would I want to grab a bite to eat? Does Nuke LaLoosh wear garters?

I follow him and his Audi convertible to a restaurant on Wilshire Boulevard called the Pacific Dining Car. The maître d' greets Shelton by name and eases us into a booth. Miguel, our waiter, is so happy to see Shelton that I'm worried he might ask him to the prom. I glance at the menu. The T-bone steak is more expensive than the entire left side of a Quizno's menu, my neighborhood restaurant of choice.

Shelton orders a Scotch—of course, a man's drink. Meanwhile, my Corona with a lime mocks me.

Shelton played against Dusty Baker in the minors. Baker was working his way through the Atlanta Braves farm system, this time at Triple-A Richmond. Shelton was in his first season as a second baseman for Rochester, part of the Baltimore Orioles organization.

The abridged version of Shelton's baseball career is easy enough: born and raised in southern California, he signed his contract at LAX, flew all night to Bluefield, West Virginia, and woke up that morning in the Appalachians, now a member of the Rookie League there. Then he spent time in the California League, where he led the league in seven hitting and fielding categories. He played winter ball, was later promoted to Triple-A, got dropped to Double-A, and suffered what he called the first major depression of his life. He returned to Triple-A, kicked butt in spring training, but suffered a bladder infection and began the season on the disabled list. He scuffled, eventually regained his hitting stroke, and ended up batting .260. This was 1971. The next year, with one kid to feed and another one on the way, Shelton had to make a decision.

"I hung 'em up and went back to school," he says. "Because honestly, I didn't want to turn into Crash Davis. I didn't want to be a guy in his thirties and still in Triple-A ball.

"Anyway, no regrets. I love this."

Miguel appears again. Rack of lamb for Shelton. T-bone for me (what the hell, I'll take out a small home-equity loan).

Shelton has been to Wrigley Field a few times. His daughter lived in Chicago a few years ago, so he'd catch a game or two. When he does go to a ballgame, he likes to sit right behind home plate. "I like to call the pitches," he says. "I like to talk about the infield and the outfield, although the infield is more important."

The salads and soups make an appearance. Shelton, bless his heart, makes an attempt at the Cubs movie concept.

"So, a story about a team who you love more because they lose, not because they win," he says. "And how do you reduce that to a two-hour story that summarizes that sort of bittersweet joy of failure in a way that I think—unfortunately for my friend Bill Buckner—encapsulates the grief of a franchise? It's another subject you can talk about—and it's wrong for your book—but you can make the case that a franchise is so caught up in its own mythology that the incidents get blown out of proportion."

Great. This guy is talking off the top of his head, and he's already six times as profound as I'll ever be. I jot furiously.

"Grady Little gets fired by the Red Sox because he makes all the right moves all year and makes one wrong move: He leaves the best pitcher in baseball in one batter too long. And that batter gets a broken-bat hit and Grady Little, who won 94 games on average the last few years, is out. So would Grady Little have been out anywhere except Boston? No, because he serves the mythology of Boston."

I stare at my soup spoon. I thought I would come to L.A., meet the great writer/director, and get a Hollywood pitch phrase for my imaginary Cubs movie. You know, it's *Titanic*-meets-*Bad News Bears* kind of stuff. Instead, I'm hanging on for dear life.

Then I hear something recognizable:

"...but that poor fan who reached up for the ball has had more hung on him, and he didn't even do anything wrong," Shelton is saying. "He did what any other human being on the planet would do. He reached up for a foul ball. Isn't that what you're supposed to do? This is a city where they throw the ball back, for chrissakes. And guess what? He cost an out for the Cubs. How come he is the guy we remember?"

"Exactly," I say.

"How about the pitcher who gave up line shot after line shot after line shot?" he says. "How about the ground ball to short, and they're out of the inning?"

I suddenly understand.

"So that feeds the mythology," I say.

"Same things," says Shelton. "Grady Little and Buckner. They are convicted by the mythology more than their actions. Not only did Bill Buckner not lose the World Series, but he didn't even lose that game."

All right, now we're getting somewhere. I feel like I'm in film school.

"We love the nonlogical endings," says Shelton. "There's a great line from *The Man Who Shot Liberty Valance.* You can look it up, but it's something like, 'When the legend becomes fact, print the legend.'

"The legend is better than the fact with Buckner."

I tell Shelton I was at Games 6 and 7 of the 2003 NLCS against the Florida Marlins, that Cubs fans were expecting the worst.

"Yeah, that's it," he says. "History has convinced them: We're going to find somebody to blame. You'd expect it would be somebody on the team, somebody whose ass we've been kissing all year, somebody we love and we brag about at the workplace and around the water cooler. We didn't think it would be this poor fan, but we'll take him. I mean, who was it who couldn't catch the ball—Moises Alou? The next day, he apologized for his body language. In my opinion, we can all act impulsively."

Shelton gets lots of money to write movie scripts. I'm paying him with a measly rack of lamb. But you throw in the broccoli, the two glasses of wine, and the espresso, well, he owes me, right?

"So if you were to write a scene . . ." I say clumsily.

"You could make a movie about the guy who fucked up but didn't really fuck up," he says. "That's the story. I don't tell the Cubs story, but I tell about that guy, the whole season. You know, him buying his season tickets or whatever. Him going to work in his Cubs hat. The guy had a Cubs hat and a Cubs jacket on, or whatever. My heart went out to this guy."

"And he was a Little League coach," I offer.

"Ah, these are the kind of guys that this country needs," Shelton says.

"So you tell ..."

"You tell his story. And the joy, and the reaching up, and the glory . . . and then the feelings, the assault, the locking of doors, the changing of numbers, the reporters."

Geez, I can't write fast enough. "What's the third act?" I blurt out.

Shelton glances up.

"I didn't come to dinner tonight with a three-act pitch," he says. "The third act is always spring training of the next year. Sort of forgiveness, a resolution. There has to be resolution. Maybe there's not forgiveness, but there has to be a redemptive act, even if the redemption is only in the heart and soul of one guy that did that one thing."

Shelton has a certain empathy for people who are casually demeaned. He wrote and directed *Cobb*, an underrated 1994 film (Davidovich was in it) that got panned in the States but embraced abroad. It still annoys him. That's why he remains intrigued by our fan along the left-field wall.

"What's the guy's name who fucked up the foul ball?" he says.

"Steve Bartman."

"What's his job?"

"Consulting."

"Perfect. Some job we can't even describe. Wouldn't even know what the fuck he does. He speaks a language you don't. The way he connects with us is he loves baseball, he loves the Cubs. See, that's even better than him being a bus driver, because we know what bus drivers do. Consultant guys are the guys I call and say, 'Fix this because I don't want to deal with it. I'm going up to the bar. Call Bartman. Fix it.'"

I've barely made a dent in my T-bone. "Eat, eat," Shelton says.

By now, the thing is room temperature, and anyway it was cooked too rare. But that's fine. I've got a Corona buzz, and the guy who wrote and directed the best baseball movie ever made just hand-delivered me three hours' worth of expertise for (get over here with that check, Miguel) . . . $168.06, plus tip. Talk about your bargains.

But there's one last thing to discuss.

"About that sequel," I say. "When we last saw Crash, he was getting ready to drive to Visalia in that Shelby 500 of his. He was going to manage the minor league team. What about a sequel where he's working his way to the majors as a manager?"

I might as well have said, "Would you like to see my niece's photos from band camp?"

Shelton nixes *Bull Durham II*. If he does anything, he'll do a sequel to

Tin Cup. This time Costner goes through Q-School. Fine. The more Russo, the better.

GAME 33

Wednesday, May 12, 2004 . . . Dodgers 4, Cubs 0 . . . Dodger Stadium . . . Stat of the game: Alex Cora fouls off 14 Matt Clement pitches before homering to right field and giving L.A. a 4-0 lead. The epic at-bat lasts 13 minutes, 13 seconds. He gets a standing ovation during the at-bat. . . . Stuff: Former Gold Glove shortstop Rey Ordonez signs a minor league deal and will report to Single-A Daytona.

Wrigley Field didn't need lights when Ernie Banks played because his personality illuminated the place. He could make a Buckingham Palace guard smile. And in his day, he could make opposing National League pitchers want to find a quiet place in the corner of a dugout and assume the fetal position.

Banks lives in Los Angeles now. In fact, he was at the game tonight. But from 1953 to 1971, his home was usually at shortstop or first base at the Friendly Confines (more on that later). You can find Mr. Cub's mug on a plaque in Cooperstown, and his retired No. 14 jersey number on a flag that flies from the Wrigley left-field foul pole.

I've interviewed Banks several times in the past few years. By the time I close my notebook, I want to join the Peace Corps or sing a show tune. The best I can figure it, the *C* on Banks's Cubs cap must have stood for Cheerful.

Banks was born January 31, 1931, in Dallas, but he's so New Age you half expect to hear Enya in the backround. We were two minutes into our chat when he started dropping Dr. Phil on me:

"Quit worrying about the past, concentrate on the present, plan for the future . . . Recognize that you deserve the very best in life and can have it."

I try to interrupt. Banks ignores me.

"Visualize your dreams coming true . . . Yank yourself from negative situations and then know the steps needed to reach your goals. What are your goals, Gene?"

"Huh?"

"Your goals, Gene. What are your goals?"

"You want to know what are my goals today?" I say.

"Yeah, I'm talking about today."

"Well, I need to make up with my wife."

"Make up? She left you, didn't she?"

"Well, she went grocery shopping, if that's what you mean."

Banks knows a thing or two about women. And baseball. And just about anything else you want to discuss.

Ask him who are the most influential people in his life and he says the late Cubs owner Philip K. (P. K.) Wrigley, Banks's father, Negro Leagues legend and former Cubs coach Buck O'Neil, former NBC broadcaster Linda Ellerbee, women's activists Gloria Steinem and Betty Friedan, and Oprah Winfrey.

"So," I say, "this relates to the Cubs in what way?"

"You mean, what am I saying?"

"Right."

There's a long pause, and suddenly Banks isn't so cheerful.

"You have to learn to overcome pain. You're gonna have it, it's there. You have to look at the positive side of life, put it in your mind. There was a saying in a movie on Sherlock Holmes: 'It's all elementary, my dear Watson.' This pain is all elementary."

Banks played 2,528 games for the Cubs. Not one of them took place after the regular season. And yet he concentrates on the elementary positives? This is quintessential Banks.

The first time Banks walked onto the Wrigley Field grass, he was 21. Most rookies would need to be treated for nervous tics. What did Banks think?

"That I belong here, that this is my home," he says. "When I was 12 years old, my dad used to go to work, and it was dark when he left and dark when he came home. I used to sit and think to myself: 'I hope someday I have a job where I can work in the daytime.' That was in my mind when I signed with the Cubs, and the Cubs played all day games. So what you wish for sometimes can come true."

Banks's father was a porter. He made beds, fixed things, cleaned whatever needed cleaning. From that came a saying for the ages: "Let's play two."

"Whenever I played an extra-inning affair with the Cubs or a double-header, I would say to myself that my father used to do this all the time, so it's not going to bother me," Banks says. "Play two. That's what you got to do in life—play two. Ain't got no time to rest. If you rest, you rot."

And did you know that Banks, with a major assist from a teammate named Jerry Kindall, came up with Wrigley Field's nickname, "The Friendly Confines"? Banks still gets all mushy when talking about the place.

"Disneyland is a happy place for people to go," he says. "The families go on rides. There's games, and all that. Wrigley Field, to me, is the second-most-happiest place in America. Because everybody really loves each other.

"Comradery and love are the park itself. Closeness . . . it's beautiful, it's pure . . . the building's pure because it's one with the community. It's love, it really is. Nothing better than that. It's love and it should be a love's nest. That's what I would change Wrigley Field's name to: A Love's Nest."

Banks is on a streak. And you never mess with a streak.

"It was a very environmentally friendly park," he says. "I think that's why Mr. Wrigley didn't have lights. It was the only park that played all its home games in the daytime. Isn't that marvelous? We had baseball in the afternoon and love at night."

"Uh, Ernie, I thought we had love during baseball."

"That's right," he says. "We have love both ways now. Mr. Wrigley—when they asked about playing night games—used to say that the moon and stars are for love, that baseball is meant to be played in the daytime."

I don't know what Mr. Wrigley was chewing back then, but it wasn't Doublemint.

It would be nice if the Cubs reached a World Series while Banks is still in a good mood. I'd let him throw out the first pitch. Hell, I'd let him play shortstop. He'd hit for a higher average than Gonzo.

Banks will be fine either way. He got most of his wishes answered: day games, a Hall of Fame career, the respect of a city. Especially the respect of a city.

"It makes me feel bigger than an owner," he says. "I feel like, wow! I'm not an owner. I don't play. I don't know how to explain it. I'm feeling like Mother Teresa, or the Pope, or some great leader of the world that deals with human nature, human kindness."

Pope or no Pope, no way are we renaming Wrigley "The Friendly Love Nest."

GAME 34

Thursday, May 13, 2004 . . . Cubs 7, Dodgers 3 . . . Dodger Stadium . . . Tom Hanks, sporting an L.A. Dodgers cap, is at the game. So is Loni Anderson, sporting her signature set of WKRPs. . . . Dodger Stadium has lots of things going for it, but my new favorite is this: Stadium ushers shoo away cell phone morons who mug for the camera behind home plate. MLB should immediately make this standard policy for all teams. . . . Zambrano "accidentally" hits Alex Cora with a pitch. Payback, baby, for flipping the bat after Wednesday night's homer off Matt Clement.

Paul Rathje (pronounced "Rath-jay") has the look of someone in need of two more hours' sleep. His plain burgundy tie is slightly crooked, his shirtsleeves are a tiny bit wrinkled, his shoes a little scuffed.

You can find the Cubs' director of stadium operations in a windowless office just off the main concourse of Wrigley. His digs are like the stadium itself: old, quaint, lacking in modern conveniences.

The walls are straight out of your grandparents' wood-paneled basement. The desktop computer, apparently a 1980s Compaq prototype, is bigger than a set of Samsonite luggage. There are a handful of Cubs-related photos, a first-aid kit, and a couple of cartons of Rawlings baseballs.

Even with the Cubs on the West Coast, Rathje has a to-do list as long as the first-base foul line. Wrigley is 90 years old, so it needs its share of daily TLC. Welders are upstairs working on a ramp fence. Two White Way Sign trucks are parked on Waveland, their crews attending to the stadium boards. The *B* in the giant neon CUBS light behind the center-field scoreboard needs to be fixed.

Rathje's job is to make sure Wrigley ages gracefully. He oversees a full-time staff of eight, a part-time staff of 400 to 500, and an auxiliary staff of another 400 to 500. That's ushers, security, grounds crew, medical personnel, plumbers, carpenters, concessionaires, vendors, parking patrols, cleaning crews, maintenance crews, and electricians.

"It pretty much involves anything related to the stadium," he says.

He became a Cubs employee 22 years ago after getting his undergrad degree at Northern Illinois, his master's at Ohio State, and his practical experience with the Columbus Clippers, the New York Yankees' Triple-A team. In 1998, he was placed in charge of stadium operations.

On occasion, usually the night before the Cubs' home opener, you can find Rathje sitting by himself in the empty stands or simply walking along the aisles of the stadium.

"It's a feeling of everything is finally ready to go," he says. "And it's kind of a different place when there's nobody in the building. I like the history of it. If you're walking in for the first time, and you want to sit and watch a ballgame, there's not a better place to do it."

Rathje has never been to the oldest ballyard in the big leagues, Fenway Park, but he's aware of the similarities. Charm out the wazoo. Integrated into the neighborhood. Tiny clubhouses. Hardly any spare space for offices and storage areas.

"You learn over time what a challenge it is on an operational level," he says.

There are no underground service tunnels like in the newer ballparks. Rathje couldn't even replace the urinal troughs in the men's restrooms if he wanted to. City code calls for individual urinals, which would be a pee disaster at restroom-challenged Wrigley.

His workday begins at 8 A.M., but only after making the 52-mile drive from Peotone. Today he reads the comment and suggestion forms left by fans. He'll reply to each response.

On game days, he'll walk around the inside and outside of the stadium and make sure the overnight cleaning crews have done their jobs. He'll visit the handful of Cubs parking lots. He'll answer e-mails, review parking lists, meet with his security and crowd management personnel. He'll speak with police, traffic details, and CTA officials. His radio and cell phone are never out of reach.

Some things you can never prepare for.

"Game 6," he says.

The Bartman Incident.

"I was down in the [Cubs'] clubhouse," he says. "We were all starting to map out the postgame setup. I was with the MLB people discussing the ceremony for the postgame. That's when one of our security personnel made a radio call to me."

By then Steve Bartman had fumbled away the infamous foul ball, been escorted out of his seat and away from an angry crowd, and taken to the Cubs' offices.

"I think they were looking for some type of guidance, but they handled the situation the right way," says Rathje. "Now it's just another piece of the folklore."

Rathje is 49, and you sense by his wry, sad smiles and his beleagured look that the job has taken its toll. He has one daughter at Illinois and a son in construction. During the season he works nights, weekends, whatever the old broad requires. His one regret is missing some of those family moments, but there's a way for Cubs fans to thank him.

Just drop a little note in the comment box.

GAME 35

May 14, 2004 . . . Cubs 6, San Diego Padres 1 . . . PETCO Park . . . Cubs NL Central pennant flies: Second (20-15) . . . Mark Prior receives his business degree from USC. . . . Padres wear throwback Burger King unis.

Denise Gawrych guns her Jeep Cherokee through the last legal wisps of a yellow light, maneuvers through the heavy afternoon Wrigleyville traffic as if she's Dale Earnhardt Jr. at Daytona, and then parks alongside a yellow street curb that prohibits this very thing.

"We're not going to be here long," she says, happily ignoring the parking sign as she makes her way to a three-flat brownstone that has a bottom floor for rent. Asking price: $1,550, plus another $75 for parking. The windows haven't been cleaned since Windex was invented, and the kitchen appliances were last used by Mamie Eisenhower. Otherwise, it's perfect.

Gawrych, a real estate agent who sells and rents properties in the Wrigleyville area, doesn't linger long. Her scouting mission is done in less than 10 minutes.

"If you're looking for a studio in the area, it's probably going to start at $800," she says. "Two bedrooms in new construction can go up to $3,100. You can have super-nice or kind of dumpy."

Whatever you want, it costs more during baseball season. Landlords jack up rents because of Cubs fever, though sometimes they'll throw in a pair of rooftop game tickets as a rental perk. Gawrych, who worked as a

Wrigley Field usher during her junior and senior years of high school, marvels at the Friendly Confines' powers.

Her favorite Wrigley rental story:

There was a guy who came into my office looking for an apartment. He was an architect on assignment in Chicago just for the year and he wanted to live near Wrigley Field. He had a nice-size budget to work with, so I showed him some really nice apartments.

The last place I showed him—and I knew it was going to be one of the dingier places on the list—was embarrassing. We go in there and the floors are all warped, the appliances are brown and yellow, and everything is old and run down. Terrible. And he *loved* it because we were on the corner of Waveland and Addison, on the third floor, and you could look into right field.

He said, "Oh, my God, I'll take it. This is probably the worst place I'll ever live in, but I've always watched the Cubs on TV and I'm only here a year."

And I kept saying, "Are you sure? Are you sure?"

For what he spent on it he could have gotten something a lot nicer. I was embarrassed. The only windows in the place were at the front of the building, and as you walked toward the back it just got darker. The walls probably had 400 coats of paint. The floors were so bad, you could be standing next to the person and he's below you because everything was so warped. I asked for a new stove for him, because the one in there was made in the '20s or something.

I was nervous, because I thought he'd move in and then freak out on me. But I never heard from him or saw him again. I'm glad, because I didn't want to hear how bad the apartment was.

GAME 36

Saturday, May 15, 2004 . . . Cubs 7, Padres 5 . . . PETCO Park . . . Cubs NL Central pennant flies: Second (21-15) . . . Stat of the game: Sammy Sosa hits one so far that the ball has a NASA logo on it. His 549th career home run moves Sosa past Mike Schmidt and into sole possession of ninth place on the all-time homer list.

I don't know much about horse racing. I thought a filly was someone who got yelled at by Larry Bowa. But this being Preakness Stakes day at Pimlico, the second jewel of the Triple Crown, it's best to consult with experts. Moises Alou is an expert. If he were any more into thoroughbreds, he'd have hay and oats in his locker.

Alou is becoming someone to watch, thanks to the all-important contract year. I'll say this for the guy: He prepares hard, plays hard, wins hard, loses hard, and sometimes whines hard.

I think Alou overreacted on the Bartman play, thus empowering the fragile Wrigley crowd to turn fatalistic and help unnerve a young Mark Prior. But it was also Alou who quickly said Bartman wasn't to blame for the NLCS loss. And when this silly urine-on-the-hands story came out, Alou didn't hide behind the usual excuse of "I was taken out of context."

Of course, that doesn't make him the most approachable player on the team. Introduce yourself to Alou for an interview and you'll usually get a wary look and a series of reasons why now is not the best time to talk. But ask him if he has a few minutes to discuss the ponies and he treats you like a winning Pick Six ticket. He pulls a chair from a nearby table and invites you to sit down. You can't help but notice the *Daily Racing Form* at the foot of his locker.

I went to the track one day—it was in 1996, in the Dominican—and it was love at first sight. My wife and uncle had a horse. He was racing that day and my uncle invited me to see the horse race. Watching them train, watching them walk in the paddock area . . . I fell in love right away. They were beautiful. Then I saw real races for the first time and it was unbelievable.

I thought to myself, "I might buy me a horse one day." And I bought me one. Then I bought me two. Then I bought me four. I have, like, 80 now. I have a farm in the Dominican. I'm breeding some horses. As a matter of fact, this year my first five horses that I bred are going to start racing as two-year-olds.

It really keeps me busy. During the season, I'll be in the hotel room with nothing to do and I'll get on the computer and start reading about horses. I'll read the *Racing Form*, read pedigrees and stuff. I love it.

The only bad thing about horses is that they can't talk. Whenever they're going to race you don't know if they have a toothache, or a stomach pain, or whatever. Sometimes, with myself being an athlete and knowing what it takes, I even give my trainers some tips. "You should do this with the horse, do that."

One thing I'll tell you, whenever one of my horses is the favorite to win the race, I get really nervous when I'm watching the race. I've faced Randy Johnson in the bottom of the ninth with the go-ahead run on second base, and I don't get nervous at all.

I always wanted to get a tattoo. I wanted to have something that really meant a lot to me. I felt like a horse was the thing I really loved. So I have a horse tattoo on my left arm.

I've followed the history of horse racing. I love Mr. Prospector [one of the sport's greatest sires], but Real Quiet is my favorite horse. He won the Derby and the Preakness in 1998.

I really loved that horse. I followed that horse. I went to see that horse in Kentucky one time. We were in Cincinnati and had an off day, so I got to go see him.

In April, I went to the Claiborne Farm in Kentucky. I met Mr. [Seth] Hancock [president of Claiborne Farm] and he showed me around. They have a cemetery there. I got to go to the grave of Secretariat.

There are about 10 to 12 horses buried at Claiborne. Usually they bury the heart and the head. With Secretariat, they buried the whole horse. That's how they honored him.

My first horse was a filly called "Hey, Listen," because my father-in-law used to say those words a lot. I've named horses after teammates. I named a horse after [Houston Astro Jeff] Bagwell. I named him "Baggy." I named one after [the Astros' Craig] Biggio—"Biggio7." [Astros reliever] Octavio Dotel is "Sargento."

No Cubs yet.

GAME 37

Sunday, May 16, 2004 . . . Cubs 4, Padres 2 . . . PETCO Park . . . Stuff: The Curse lives: Sammy Sosa sneezes so hard in the clubhouse that he suffers a series of back spasms and is scratched from the lineup.

There are 5,721 Cubs-related items on eBay, most of which you wouldn't buy at a neighborhood garage sale. But a few collectibles are worth a double click of the mouse.

An autographed photo of former Cubs bat babe (and Playboy model) Marla Collins goes for $2.95. Zero bids . . . A Cubs ear radio "still in original package" goes for $4.95. Original ear wax is extra. . . . A Leon Durham signed baseball goes for $9.99. A ground ball actually caught by Durham is unavailable. . . . A Mark Grace 8 × 10 photo goes for 1 cent. A penny. It will cost more to ship it than buy it. Just out of respect to Grace's 1,910 games as a Cub, I bid it up to $5. . . . Cubs press-on tattoos go for $2.99. Just what you want: Jose Macias on your buttock.

A Robert Machado game-used uncracked bat goes for $24.99. You mean *the* Robert Machado? . . . A Harry Caray Restaurant cookbook goes for $9.00. Every recipe begins with these instructions: "Marinate with Bud for 3-4 hours." . . . A set of 1935 Cubs commemorative World Series feathers goes for $35. Tar is extra. The Cubs had a 1-0 lead in that Series against the Tigers, but then lost four of the next five. . . . A Chip Carey (*sic*) signed game-used bat goes for $24.99. Caray used it to beat the hell out of Ozzy Osbourne after Double O slurred his way through "Take Me Out to the Ballgame." . . . A 1990 All-Star Game Kleenex box (unopened) goes for $3.99. Kleenex goes for $3.99, Gracie goes for a penny? Madness . . . A Cubs Grateful Dead T-shirt goes for $10.50. Jerry Garcia could sing "Take Me Out to the Ballgame" better than Osbourne *now*.

GAME 38

Tuesday, May 18, 2004 . . . San Francisco Giants 1, Cubs 0 . . . Wrigley Field . . . Sammy Sosa's sneeze attack in San Diego caused a sprained ligament in his lower back. The DL is a certainty. . . . Record since Sosa sneeze: 1-1.

Harold Rothstein, managing partner of Hi-Tops bar at Sheffield and Addison, is a businessman first, Cubs fan second. That's why the bottled beers cost $5 (you'd give up drinking if you knew how little those beers cost wholesale), why the Ugly Waitress truck never makes any deliveries here, and why his other Hi-Tops in Pittsburgh is also in the shadows of PNC Park (location, location, location).

Rothstein was born and raised on the North Side, used to sneak into Wrigley as a kid, but quickly adds, "We root for the Sox, too. We're not Sox haters." Like I said, he's a businessman first.

We sit at a table on the second floor of the bar. From here you have a perfect view of the Harry Caray statue and the growing crowd at Wrigley. The game starts in about 90 minutes, plenty of time for Rothstein to tell you exactly what he thinks about the Wrigleyville bar business and all things Cubs.

This neighborhood . . . it didn't have the vibe it has now. In '96, we still had the poststrike blahs. Things started to turn in '98 with the Sosa-McGwire home run thing.

The reality is that Wrigleyville is the biggest beer garden in the world. And if you turned the seats the other way in Wrigley Field, it'd still sell out.

As crazy as it sounds, it's better for the bar when the Sox are over here and win. Down there they really don't have anyplace to celebrate. Here they do.

We hold 500 [people] at a time, and about 2,000 will come through. We keep it within occupancy. We stay to code. After all, you want it so people can get to the bar. We're charging $5 for a bottled beer, $8 to $12 for liquor. We give people the best, and we charge them.

On average we'll sell about 9,000 [bottled beers], plus drafts and liquor drinks. We've sold 60,000 bottles of beer in one weekend. And we encourage bottles over drafts. You can open six bottles of beer in the time you can draw a draft. See what I mean?

We've had the whole Cardinal team up here. When the Cubs won the division, the whole team came up here. We had the Pirates up here, too.

We try to separate the yahoos, the jock-sniffers. That way the players can enjoy themselves. And you don't see any pictures of us with our arms around the ballplayers. I think it's a respect thing.

We have good music, a good-looking staff. But it's no secret what makes a successful bar: cold beer, hot women.

The playoffs [in 2003], business was off the hook. The Friday-night game against Atlanta was our best playoff game. And we lost that one, too.

Counting the series against Atlanta and Florida, we had four wakes. The Cubs went 2-4 at home in the playoffs. That didn't help business. Plus, everybody thinks it's better to be the home team. But for us, in reality it's better to be the road team. That way you get the Friday, Saturday, Sunday games.

Farnsworth has pulled back. I saw a guy who drank all the time. Now he's cut back. He should be The Guy.

[Joe] Borowski, man, he's terrible. The visiting players who come in here, they say they can't wait to see Borowski.

I was there for Game 6 [of the 2003 NLCS]. Front-row seats, right in back of the Cubs' bullpen. I left in the seventh inning. I'm thinking this place is going to be up for grabs.

Then a lifelong Sox fan, Bernie Mac, sings the Seventh-Inning Stretch? How sad is that? You want Bernie Mac to bring the Cubs in? You talk about a curse. Bartman wasn't the fault. That was the fault.

Where's Bill Murray? Where's Jimmy Buffett? These are lifelong Cubs fans. Instead, we get Bernie Mac. I'm sure it was a Fox thing. He has a show there.

The Cardinals? They feel they can win it all. That's how they are.

But the Cubs . . . they have a swagger. They didn't have it before. In the 13 years I've been here, that's the first time it's been that way. The Cardinals *always* think they're going to win.

GAME 39

Wednesday, May 19, 2004 . . . Cubs 4, Giants 3 . . . Wrigley Field . . . Stuff: Moises Alou directs a generous supply of four-letter words toward ESPN's Gary Miller during BP. Miller, here as a reporter for the ESPN broadcast, is the guy who reported the urine thing about Alou. Miller's worst nightmare: Alou hits the game-winner. Surprise! Miller doesn't get a postgame interview. . . . In a pregame news conference, the Tribune's Paul Sullivan innocently asks Sosa if he's going to stay for the game. Sosa has a small hissy fit. "You should be in my body one day," he says to Sullivan.

To reach the umpires' room at Wrigley, you walk down the Cubs' dugout steps, down a short tunnel, hang a left, and then take a quick right. This is where you'll find what looks like a small Army barracks, what with the old-time lockers, the plain white interior, and the shoes and uniforms arranged just so.

This is also where you'll find former Army sergeant Jimmy Farrell, who served three years under Gen. George Patton during WWII, then worked in the blood and muck of the killing floor of Agars meatpacking in the Chicago stockyards. Then he spent 25 years as an engineer/custodian for the Chicago School Board.

Retired and bored stiff, Farrell was told that he ought to apply for a part-time job at Wrigley. So Farrell went to Wrigley in the winter of 1981, was handed a 3 × 5 card, wrote his name, number, address, and then mentioned that he was retired. A few days later, the phone rang. The Cubs were looking for an umpires' room attendant, someone with a little mileage.

"It was the strangest thing," he says. "It was almost like a gift from God. That's the way I looked at it."

He started in 1982 and has become as much of a Wrigley fixture as kelly-green paint. Farrell, who was born and raised on the South Side (Canaryville), starred on the Leo High School and Loras College basketball teams, and was later inducted into the Chicago Catholic Hall of Fame, is 83 now.

You've seen him. He's the guy standing near the bottom steps of the Cubs' dugout, dressed much like an umpire himself: dark slacks, blue shirt, dark cap.

I find him in his wood-paneled office next to the umpires' dressing room at 9 A.M. There's a desk, a leather couch, a couple of chairs, a Stair-Master, a couple of exercise and stretching balls, a television and VCR. There are also dozens of photographs of Farrell and his umpires. "I'm almost like a father figure to all of the guys," he says.

The sons take care of their old man.

A few months ago, when Farrell and his wife, Eleanor, were nearing their 60th wedding anniversary, umpire crew chief Charlie Reliford called Cubs GM Jim Hendry. Would it be OK if Farrell and Eleanor accompanied Reliford's crew to home plate that day?

OK? Hendry arranged for a photographer and a public address announcement of the event. Farrell was dressed in his usual umpire's garb, while Eleanor arrived at home plate holding a bouquet of roses.

"His 50th anniversary, I was there for that also," says Reliford. "I have that picture. You have to understand that Jimmy's been in the big leagues longer than I have. Not only does he work with us, he's been a friend to everybody. There's not a nicer man alive than that guy."

The Cubs players want to give him a group hug. The umpires like him so much that he gets invited for dinners and even fishing trips. Dusty Baker calls him "Sweet Jimmy." If Baker catches Farrell waving to Eleanor before a game, he'll turn to the players and say, "Hey, there's Jimmy waving to the ladies again."

The guy is a sweetheart. I ask to visit for 15 minutes. He lets me stay for nearly an hour. I wish I could have stayed for two.

I never met a bad umpire since I've been here. I get along with them all. They're all great.

I guess my favorite has always been Doug Harvey. God himself. Always a great guy. He always helped the young umpires out. Minor leaguers would come down here, knock on the door. He'd invite them in and help them with the strike zone. He'd take time. He'd say, "Now listen, meet me at the hotel after the game and we'll go over some other stuff." He'd spend time with these kids. He was very good with those kids.

All these guys—Eddie Montague, John McSherry, Charlie, Eric Gregg, you name it—wonderful people. Eric Gregg, he always liked to have cheeseburgers. He loved his cheeseburgers. One time he went to a fat farm and he calls me up at home and says, "Jimmy, send me some cheeseburg-ers. They're killing me here. They won't let me have anything."

He got out and he went back to the same old ways. He just loved to eat. It almost killed him.

I've got a story about Greg Maddux. He was young, maybe a rookie or so at the time. He hadn't gotten a hit on the road yet. So when he was going on the road, I said to him, "Greg, when you get your first hit out there, when you get to first base, wiggle your ear like this on the television."

He says, "OK, I will, Jimmy."

Me and Eleanor are watching at home. So he gets a hit, gets to first base, and she says, "He's not gonna do it, Jimmy." I say, "You watch."

All of a sudden, like something hit him, he tugs at his ear, wiggles it. We just about fell off the couch laughing.

I get along with the ballplayers. I like them all. Billy Buckner has always been a great friend of mine. Greg Maddux. Mark Grace. I could just go on and on. But my favorite on this team is definitely Woody—Kerry Wood. He'd do anything for me.

He always kids around with me. If we're in the dugout and I'm talking to somebody on the side, he'll say, "Hey, Jimmy, the game's out there, not in here." And if I catch him talking, I'll say, "Woody, the game's out there."

I put the ball and the rosin bag on the mound. For Game 7 of the [2003] NLCS, I wrote a *W* on the ball. I did it for Kerry. That was a special game. He was under a lot of pressure—it was for a chance to go to the World Series.

When he picked that ball up, he kind of laughed a little bit. He looked at me in the dugout, kind of tipped his hat to me. He noticed it right away. But he still lost.

[I ask Wood about it later. "That wasn't the first time. He'd do it if I had a few bad games in a row. The first time I saw it, I thought, 'What is this *M* on the ball for?' It was upside down. But Jimmy is a great guy. He's seen us all come and go."]

Rick Sutcliffe was having a tough time one time. So I brought a rabbit's foot. When I put the ball on the mound, I put the rabbit's foot right next to the mound. He goes out there, picks the rabbit's foot up with the ball, looks at me, and puts the rabbit's foot in his back pocket. He won that game, too.

And yeah, he looked over. He laughed.

One time Eleanor and I were having our anniversary. It was our 40th. I was in the dugout and Billy Buckner was there. I said, "Billy, we're having a party tonight. It's our anniversary. Why don't you come by?"

He said, "Where's it gonna be at, Jimmy?"

I told him the address. It was all the way in Lisle, Illinois. Never in a million years is he going to find Lisle, Illinois, and then find the address. No way. All of the sudden, at 8 o'clock, Billy Buckner is knocking at the door wanting to be at the party. He came by himself. I thought that was very, very nice of Billy. Usually, guys don't do that. That always stuck in my mind.

Mark Grace was always very nice. He'd come in here, meet your family, put his arm around them, meet the umpires' families and stuff.

I remember Harry Wendelstedt, a great umpire, tell me a story about Grace. Harry and his crew were out at a restaurant and Grace came through. Grace sent a $300 bottle of wine to the umpires.

I guess Harry knew his wine, because he knew this was really a good bottle. But he told his umpires, "We'll drink this wine, but we've got to send the same bottle of wine back to Mark—same price, same bottle. Never let the players do something for you that you don't do for them."

Ryne Sandberg invited me to his wedding when he married Margaret in Arizona. Oh, sure, we went.

He's a changed man. Ryne Sandberg, when he first started with the Cubs, he was very shy. If you took a picture with him and the umpires' wives, he wouldn't put his arm around them. He was a shy guy. He married Margaret and, man, she changed him around. He'll sit in the skybox now, make paper airplanes, and put his name on them, and toss them down. She changed him around 100 percent. I didn't think someone could change someone around that fast and that good. Now he's just an outgoing guy. Great guy.

I get here at 9 o'clock, clean the room up, get it ready, and then I'll make sure all the uniforms are hung up properly. I'll do the wash, then I'll clean and shine their shoes. After that I'll get the baseballs—six dozen for the game, three dozen for the office as reserves. I rub those up.

After that I'll go to the office and see if there's any mail for the umpires. And after that I'll go get the towels for the showers, get the room ready, and get the tape ready to tape the game on the VCR. They like to see the game afterward, especially for the younger umpires. They'll do it more than the old-timers do. The young umpires take the tape back to the hotel, look at it, see if they made any mistakes. That's a must now, to tape the game.

When the umpires come in, usually about an hour, an hour and a half before the game, I make sure I get the food for them. Then I'll take their ticket list out. Sometimes they want me to make sure their friends or family get the tickets.

Once the game begins, I'm in the dugout. I make sure they have water or whatever else they need. Maybe they forget their sunglasses, or a pen, or their slicks if it rains. So I'll go get it for them.

I usually go in the room at the eighth inning. So after the game, they come in and I've got the food ready for them. There's no beer allowed now, no more alcohol. That stopped. And there's no more autographed balls between the players and umpires.

I was home this past November [of 2003], right before Thanksgiving. That's when I got a letter from Jim Hendry. He sent me a check for $2,000. He said the players voted me a share of their playoff money. I don't think in the history of baseball a clubhouse guy for the umpires got playoff money from the players. The umpires take care of me. The players don't have to take care of Jimmy.

I was never expecting that. I thought that was unbelievable.

I've had it great here. Everybody's been so nice. If God should take me tomorrow, I don't think I've missed anything. I've seen it all.

GAME 40

Thursday, May 20, 2004 . . . Giants 5, Cubs 3 . . . Wrigley Field . . . Stat of the game: Giants second baseman Neifi Perez, who hits a home run every third Ice Age, hits a home run—the game-winner against Joe Borowski in the top of the 10th. It is his first homer from the left-hand side in 596 at-bats. . . . Stuff: The Curse lives: Kerry Wood goes on the disabled list. . . . The season reaches the quarter point of the schedule.

The phones began ringing three days ago, when the Cubs confirmed what the team's Single-A affiliate was hoping, almost praying, would be true:

Mark Prior would make his first rehab start Thursday evening—tonight—in the Lansing Lugnuts' very own Olds Park.

By early Monday morning, the Lugnuts' Web site already had 300 ticket orders, some from as far away as Texas and Florida. Media credential requests quadrupled, from the usual 20 to 80. Commemorative T-shirts were rushed into production: "I Saw Mark Prior Pitch At Olds Park 2004." The *Lansing State-Journal* printed 5,000 Prior posters.

In short, the team was following its own advice. Call the franchise's front office and the last thing you hear on the message machine is "Go, Nuts."

The Lugnuts have seen their share of accomplished players and prospects. Corey Patterson played here. So did Sergio Mitre, Todd Wellemeyer, Francis Beltran—all Cubs big leaguers. When the team was a Kansas City Royals affiliate, veteran pitcher Kevin Appier made a 2001 rehab appearance in Lansing.

But this was different. Nothing against Appier, but Prior is pitching royalty.

"If the World Series were ever to come to Lansing, I would imagine it would be like this," says Darla Bowen, the Lugnuts' vice president of marketing.

First they had to get Prior a uniform. The pants weren't a problem, but the jerseys would have to be custom made by Russell Athletic at its headquarters in Alexander, Alabama. Lugnuts jerseys are fairly work intensive, and Russell had only about 36 hours to turn around the order.

Prior's No. 22 already belongs to Lugnuts first baseman Brian Dopirak, so the team issued the Cubs pitcher No. 32. O. J. Simpson, another USC alum, wore No. 32, right?

Hotel arrangements were made. Transportation was provided. Team officials even made sure his fruit plate of strawberries and blueberries was arranged in the shape of a Cubs logo.

The plan is simple: Prior will start the game, throw about 45 pitches, and retire to the clubhouse for an appointment with an ice wrap. He'll throw mostly fastballs. But who will catch him?

Jake Fox, who played at Michigan, arrives at the ballpark thinking he'll be in his usual spot behind the plate. A couple of days earlier, when he learned of Prior's rehab assignment, Fox called his folks in Indianapolis and told them to make the drive to Lansing for tonight's game.

But when Fox, 21, looks at the Lugnuts' lineup card, his name isn't on it. In fact, no Lansing catcher is listed. Instead, Cubs backup catcher Paul Bako is scheduled to catch Prior.

Lugnuts pitching coach Mike Anderson approaches Fox.

"Jake, I'm really sorry," he says. "I know you wanted to catch this game. If I were you, I'd walk in [manager Julio] Garcia's office and ask why you're not getting the chance."

"No, that's OK," says Fox.

"I mean it," says Anderson. "You ought to walk in there and let him know how you feel."

"It's all right."

"Jake, get in there."

So Fox walks into Garcia's office.

"I guess I just wanted to say I'm a little disappointed not to be catching tonight," Fox says.

"Well," says Garcia, "I just talked to Jim Hendry and let him know I didn't think you were ready to catch Major League pitching."

This isn't going well for Fox.

"Uh, I have to disagree with you on that," Fox says.

"Get out of my office," says Garcia. "And take this with you."

It is the official lineup card. Fox's name is on it.

Minor league game. Major league prank.

Prior throws exactly 45 pitches. His last pitch is a called third strike to end the third inning. Fox makes a beeline to the Cubs star.

"I had a great time tonight," says Fox, holding the ball. "It was an honor catching you. Could I get this autographed later?"

"Bring it up the tunnel and I'll sign it," says Prior.

And he does, too. It will go nicely with his memories of warming up Kerry Wood during spring training.

Afterward, Prior says he's a little disappointed with his consistency. This is news to Fox.

"Every pitch hit the glove," says Fox. "You always wonder what the difference is between minor league pitching and Major League pitching. Now I know the difference. If he said he was a little disappointed with his control, well, I'd take lack of control like that any night."

Garcia keeps the two MLB-authenticated lineup cards. The Lugnuts ask Prior for his white jersey and then, with an MLB authenticator on hand, he autographs it. The jersey will be framed and the No. 32 might be retired.

The hat? Prior wants to keep the hat.

"He looked good in [the uniform], didn't he?" says Bowen. "That's a total girl thing to say, isn't it?"

As is the custom when a big leaguer makes a rehab appearance, Prior bought the postgame dinner for the Lugnuts. Steaks for everyone. He also made a $500 contribution to the team's charity.

"Isn't that neat?" says Bowen.

Prior could be back next week. "We have no confirmation of that," Bowen says.

Doesn't matter. Ticket orders are already coming in.

GAME 41

Friday, May 21, 2004 . . . Cardinals 7, Cubs 6 . . . Wrigley Field . . . Stuff: Attendance for Prior's appearance in Lansing: 9,823. Attendance tonight without Prior: 5,826 . . . A first: No Cub goes on the disabled list today.

You don't have to be Rudy Martzke to know Bob Costas is on a fortune-cookie-sized list of all-time greatest broadcasters. Costas could make stocking Wonder Bread at the local Piggly-Wiggly compelling television. He is Boy Scout–prepared, funny, and able to recognize the drama of any event.

Costas was born and raised in New York but has had a home in St. Louis for the last 30 years. He worked for St. Louis radio giant KMOX and did the play-by-play for NBC's *Game of the Week* for years. He remains NBC's cleanup hitter.

I think one of the things that distinguishes the Cardinals-Cubs from other rivalries, like let's say Yankees-Red Sox, is that it's almost entirely good-natured. It's passionate, but it's mostly good-natured. The really hard edge isn't there. The best example of that was the weekend that Mark McGwire moved past Roger Maris, and the Cardinal fans spontaneously give Sammy Sosa a standing ovation every time he bats.

Someone said of St. Louis, some out-of-town writer . . . wrote he had never seen the combination of passion and civility at a ballpark that he found at St. Louis.

But the whole tone of the rivalry itself is appealing. Plenty of passion, plenty of excitement, but nothing dark about it.

For a long, long time, I guess St. Louis was the closest National League city to Chicago, and vice versa. You have lots of people, hundreds of thousands, if not millions of people, who live roughly equidistant between them. You have those towns in Illinois where it's almost like the dividing country, where Cardinal country is south and Cub country is north. And because of their respective radio stations, being big, powerful outlets—WGN and KMOX—for all those decades, before cable television, you could listen to the games of both. You have the geographic proximity, at a time when people didn't think that much of hopping into the car for a weekend and traveling hundreds of miles. Possible for Cardinal fans to go to Wrigley. Possible for Cub fans to come to St. Louis. You see that every time they play, especially if it's a weekend. The red shirts at Wrigley, the blue shirts and caps at Busch.

I came to St. Louis out of college almost 30 years ago, in 1974. So I've witnessed the rivalry firsthand ever since then.

Right now, I think that most Cardinal fans take a clear-eyed view. They don't view the Cubs as these sort of cuddly losers. They look at them as having better personnel right now than the Cardinals, and as a team that's likely to beat them in the division. I think that 10 years ago, 20 years ago, for the most part, they would have viewed the Cubs as their National League Central neighbors, but we'll beat them most of the time. Now I think it's more of a competitive rivalry.

One memory that I can speak to individually, because I was involved in it, is The Sandberg Game in '84. People still call it The Sandberg Game.

I think it was June 23 or 24 [the 23rd]. It was the game that stamped him as the MVP, which he ultimately did win. It happened to be the *Game of the Week* on NBC. I remember saying to [NBC broadcast partner] Tony Kubek—the game was 9-9 and we were going into extra innings—this is the kind of game that if you were sitting in Wrigley Field today, you couldn't tell if it was 1984 or 1954, and you wouldn't care.

What made it good was that the Cardinals were good—they didn't win the pennant that year, but they were a contender throughout the mid-'80s—and the Cubs, lo and behold, were getting good. And then you had this incredible game that had every element: just a beautiful Saturday afternoon, the Cardinal red in the stands, the Cubs fans there.

In the first five, 10 years after that game, guaranteed anytime I was in

Chicago, 10 people a day would come up to me and talk about it. Even now I could be standing on the corner waiting for the light to change so I could cross Michigan Avenue and a cabdriver will roll down his window and say, "Hey, Bob, The Sandberg Game."

The last pitch that [Bob] Gibson ever threw in the Major Leagues, late September 1975. The last pitch he ever threw was hit by Pete LaCock for a grand slam home run at Busch Stadium. LaCock was with the Cubs. [Manager Red] Schoendienst comes and gets Gibson, and Gibson doesn't pitch the last 10 days of the season and then he retires.

Now, the way I've got the story, it's 10 years later or so, and there's an old-timers game. LaCock comes up against Gibson, and Gibson hits him in the ass. Isn't that great? He waited that long for the retribution and he got it.

GAME 42

Saturday, May 22, 2004 . . . Cubs 7, Cardinals 1 . . . Wrigley Field . . . Stuff: The Curse lives: Reliever Kent Mercker goes on the disabled list with a bad back. Eight Cubs have spent time on the DL since spring training (three this week).

He sprinted from the Cubs' dugout as if his jockstrap were on fire, and he didn't stop running until he had completed an arc in front of the right-field Bleacher Bums, all the time cupping his hand to his ear in an "I-can't-hear-you" gesture, and then pumping his arm in the moist afternoon air. Three innings later, he hit the home run that turned an undecided game into a rout.

Meanwhile, the guy in the No. 1 spot of the rotation was busy putting the collar on a Cardinals lineup Cubs manager Dusty Baker calls "one of the best-hitting clubs in the world." Nine strikeouts, one earned run, and 110 pitches later, he left the mound to a standing ovation.

Thank goodness for Sammy Sosa and Kerry Wood.

Check that. Thank goodness for their Cubs subs, Todd Hollandsworth and Glendon Rusch.

Baseball is often criticized for being too slow, but you should have checked the pulses of Hollandsworth and Rusch today as they helped nudge the Cubs into first place. Think Keith Moon drum solo.

This is Hollandsworth's 10th season in the Major Leagues. He was the National League Rookie of the Year in 1996 and owns one of those dough-nut-sized 2003 World Series rings. He's seen some stuff.

Now he is a Cub, and usually a backup Cub at that. But with Sosa out because of a sneeze-induced back sprain, Hollandsworth is getting quality playing time in right field.

"I'm nervous as ever," he says. "Ten years in the big leagues and I still don't relax. I think every game to me is a World Series game. Dusty tells me to relax, but . . . It's probably how I'm made up, I guess. You play in front of 40,000 and you don't want to let them down."

Hollandsworth is among the first to arrive at the Cubs' clubhouse, home or away. He is among the first to spend time in the batting cage located under the Wrigley right-field bleachers. He is hitting .346 with five homers, eight RBI, and 12 runs in only 52 at-bats. And yet nobody in Cubs Nation circled December 12, 2003, on their calendar—the day Hollandsworth signed a one-year free agent contract—and said, "We've now won the 2004 NL pennant."

Hollandsworth, 31, lost his starting job in Florida to a hitting prodigy named Miguel Cabrera. Hollandsworth wasn't thrilled about the demotion, but at least the Marlins were honest about it. So he adapted.

"I kind of refocused on being a clutch pinch hitter," he says.

Hollandsworth is 6-for-12 with two homers and three RBI as a pinch hitter. But who figured Hollandsworth could do a Sosa? First the pregame Sosa-like sprint to right ("My teammates told me I had to do it."), then the two-run dinger in the third inning that gave the Cubs a 6-1 lead (Hollandsworth owns Cards starter Woody Williams: seven hits in 16 at-bats for 3 homers and 6 RBI).

"I am not going to fill Sammy Sosa's shoes," he says. "He's really gifted and he's done things in this game that kids dream about doing. I'm trying to hold down the fort until he gets better, do my part."

This is what "Lemons" do. That's what the Cubs subs call themselves, "The Lemons."

Rusch is a Lemon. He was 1-12 with the Milwaukee Brewers in 2003 and couldn't even earn a 2004 roster spot on the pitching-challenged Texas Rangers. Four days before the season opener, the Cubs signed him to a minor league contract.

"We knew," says Hollandsworth of the signing. "This is a bona fide big league starter."

The bona fide big league starter couldn't keep his starting job on the losingest team in the NL Central in 2003 and couldn't earn a job on the losingest 2003 team in the AL West. These aren't items you highlight on the résumé.

But Rusch is a left-hander, and he is a six-plus-year big league veteran and, well, stranger things have happened. For example, today's victory against the Cardinals, and with the wind blowing out, too.

"It's been a little bit of a long road, starting with what I went through last year," he says. "As soon as [the opportunity] became available to sign here when spring training was over, I jumped on it. It took about 10 minutes to think about it, and I did it."

This isn't a permanent gig. Wood, on the DL with sore triceps, is expected back for his May 28 start. But whatever happens, Rusch will always have today's standing O.

"That will give you some chills," he says.

The feeling, it turns out, was mutual.

GAME 43

Sunday, May 23, 2004 . . . Cubs 4, Cardinals 3 . . . Wrigley Field . . . Stuff: The Curse lives: Kerry Wood throws exactly eight pitches in a simulated game before walking abruptly off the mound and back into the clubhouse. A bone scan for his right arm is scheduled for Monday. . . . Thick storm clouds stay just out of reach of Wrigley. According to a grounds crew member, you know it's going to rain at Wrigley if birds start appearing on the field. Why? The incoming wet weather prompts insect movement, so the birds come in to dine. For what it's worth, no birds . . . Record since Sosa sneeze: 4-3.

Sports Illustrated photographer Damien Strohmeier is here not only for the Cubs-Cardinals series, but because *SI* knows a potential cash cow when it sees one.

Strohmeier, whose work is consistently among the finest found in the magazine, has already taken about 1,600 digital images of the first two games of the series. Several of those photographs might make it in this week's *SI*, but Strohmeier figures the rest of the images will go into the magazine's files for use in a commemorative issue should the Cubs win the World Series. Remember, *SI* predicted a Cubs title.

A commemorative issue on the then-national champion Nebraska Cornhuskers did the most business for *SI*, but a Cubs or Boston Red Sox World Series championship "would double, triple, maybe do even more than that," says Strohmeier, who lives in Boston. "The Cubs and the Red Sox are so much more compelling."

About 20 years ago, Strohmeier and I worked together at the *Denver Post*. Dedicated? He has a scar in the middle of his forehead, thanks to an errant NHL puck and 54 stiches. And his roommate in Denver was a no-talent hack named Rick Reilly, who is now running out of fingers for all his National Sportswriter of the Year rings. Anyway, those were two rent checks worth saving.

Strohmeier has been to Wrigley lots of times. For this series, he and his two Canon EOS-1Ds are positioned in the photographers' well on the first-base side of the field. He likes that side of Wrigley because of the way the field opens up.

"I love the lack of commercialization here," he says. "You're not constantly trying to frame out a computer ad. Here you have the green backround. You have the ivy on the wall. If someone makes a catch against the ivy, it looks like a scene from *Field of Dreams*."

From his place at field's edge, Strohmeier observes things that go unnoticed on TV or high above in the Wrigley press box. From a photographic perspective, he sees a stadium of clean, clear lines. But what Strohmeier hears from the crowd is especially telling.

"The fans here have taken on more of a hard edge," he says. "I'm always listening to how people react. Now they expect to win here. It used to be they'd come here to root for the Cubs, and winning was a bonus."

Of course, Cubs fans are kittens compared to the terminally caustic and cynical Red Sox fans.

"That guy who tried to catch the foul ball?" says Strohmeier of Chicago treasure Steve Bartman. "That guy would have been in *danger* had that happened in Boston."

Not so in Chicago. Here, he's only in hiding.

GAME 44

Tuesday, May 25, 2004 . . . Houston Astros 5, Cubs 0 . . . Minute Maid Park . . . Record since Sosa sneeze: 4-4 . . . Mark Prior bumps up to 62 pitches in Lansing. He's likely to make one or two more starts at Triple-A Iowa. . . . A bone scan of Kerry Wood's right arm reveals no structural damage, but he'll miss two and a half to three weeks.

Steve Stone and Chip Caray are finishing up their lunches in the media dining room. I pull up a seat and ask about their legendary practical jokes on Ron Santo.

Like two proud fathers, they tell their stories. The conversation:

Stone: Just as various countries have their national sport—soccer is a European national sport, baseball is the Japanese national sport—for Chip and I, our national sport is to pick on Ron Santo on a daily basis because it eliminates the pressure of a long season.

Me: So this is a service you're providing.

Stone: I believe it's a public service. He's become one of the great characters in our broadcast.

Me: In what way?

Stone: There's nothing quite as funny as stealing his jacket from the booth, issuing a ransom note, and then, on the air, narrate in the backround exactly what's going to happen. [Stone breaks out the official broadcast voice.] "Here's Ron Santo. He's just been given the ransom note. He does not believe his jacket is missing, so let's see what happens." And then Ronnie will start looking under the counter of the booth, all around, and then he'll realize the jacket is not there. He'll read the note and look over to our booth and make some sort of gesture, if not obscene, certainly uncouth. Meanwhile, he doesn't realize that he's on the air.

Caray: We're at the Rainwater Steakhouse in San Diego. Ronnie and I take turns when we're on the road and buy each other dinner and stuff. This time it was his turn, and he invited three or four people. We had some nice steaks, some wine. A very nice dinner.

Well, Ronnie goes to the bathroom, so while he's gone we tell the waiter, "No matter what happens, when [Santo] asks for the check, bring the biggest check you got in the house."

So Ronnie gets up and goes to the bathroom. The check comes. Ronnie comes back, and because I'm sitting right next to him and he can't see that well in the restaurant, I say, "Ronnie, you want me to sign this for you?"

He says, "Yeah, sure."

I say, "What do you want me to tip?"

"Twenty percent," he says.

"Ronnie, 20 percent is pretty good. It's a pretty big check. You sure about this?"

"Yeah, 20 percent," he says.

Then he looks at the check and the tab is $1,400.

"Jesus Christ," he says, "how much wine did you drink? Oh my God, I said a couple glasses, but this is ridiculous!"

I tell him we're kidding. His face is all flushed, so the waiter brings him a glass of wine. Then the real check comes—about $200 for five people. Ronnie pulls out his corporate American Express card—green, not gold—and the waiter says, "What's this?"

Ronnie says, "It's my credit card."

The waiter says, "I'm sorry, sir, we only take cash."

Ronnie can't believe it. "What the hell kind of place is this?"

Me: So they only took cash?

Caray: No, the waiter was in on it.

Me: Tell me the memo story.

Stone: It was my idea, and then [Senior VP Marketing/Broadcasting] John McDonough implemented it. It happened during the first year I was gone [Stone left WGN and the Cubs for the 2001 and 2002 seasons]. I came back to throw out the first pitch, and I said to John, "To really piss off Ronnie, use the official Cubs logo and an official memo and announce a three-man radio team, with me as the newest member of the booth."

John came up with the language, and it was a wonderful Cubs memo extolling my virtues, describing what a wonderful analyst I am, calling me the best in baseball, detailing Pat Hughes's desire to have me in the booth. At the end of the memo, in the last sentence, as if it were an afterthought, it says, "And Ron Santo will also be in the booth."

So [McDonough] gives this to Ron and says, "We want you to review this because we're going to announce it before the game today."

Ronnie went crazy. He started crumpling up the thing and says, "I quit. I'm going home."

John had to run almost full bore to get to Ronnie before he could get to the stairs. He looks at him and says, "I quit. I'm not putting up with this. They don't even tell me about this? I quit."

John tells him the true story and Ronnie goes, "Why do they keep doing this to me? Why?"

It was a classic.

Me: What's the story about the spaghetti photo?

Stone: He hates that picture more than life itself. It was a spaghetti ad he did years ago. The guys at Fox [TV] had that picture on a split screen, so we'll be talking about Ronnie and they show him on one side, and the ad picture on the other. It might as well be a nude of him. He looks like a combination of Alf and Don Knotts. And what pisses him off the most is that it was in *Reader's Digest*.

Caray: My dad [Atlanta Braves announcer Skip Caray] was here at the ballpark and there was a Xerox machine, so we Xeroxed about 75 of the pictures.

Stone: This is just something we do every day. It's one thing or another.

Caray: The reason is, as you know, you don't screw around with people unless you really love them. And he gives it back to us in other ways. I think he has fun with it. It keeps him loose.

Stone: In this age of reality television, you could make one of the funniest bits of reality TV if you just had a camera following Ronnie around on a daily basis. After all, guys don't have their hair catch on fire in a Shea Stadium press box on Opening Day [Santo's toupee caught fire on a camera light].

Caray: That was—[He can't continue because he's laughing too hard.]

Stone: His hair is smoking, so he starts pouring coffee and water on his head. He had to go the rest of the game looking like a bad Rod Stewart imitation.

GAME 45

Wednesday, May 26, 2004 . . . Astros 7, Cubs 3 . . . Minute Maid Park . . . Cubs NL Central pennant flies: Third (25-20) . . . Stat of the game: Greg Maddux gives up three more home runs, bringing his season total to 14 in 10 starts. Not good.

Sixth inning. Two outs. Michael Barrett on second. The Cubs trail, 5-3.

Jason Dubois hits a one-hopper to Astros right-fielder Richard Hidalgo, who scoops up the ball and throws a one-hopper back to home plate. Barrett hasn't even rounded third base by the time Hidalgo has the ball in his glove. Doesn't matter. "Wavin'" Wendell Kim sends him home, despite Hidalgo having the best arm in the Houston outfield. Barrett is out by the length of the Cubs' DL list.

Afterward, Dusty Baker defends his third-base coach by saying Kim was following Baker baseball doctrine: Be aggressive. Kim, who has spent 32 years in professional baseball, appreciates Baker having his back, but this isn't the first time he's been second-guessed for waving someone around. And it won't be the last.

Kim on Kim:

I'm not perfect. I think I screwed up twice last year and a couple times this year.

Dusty knows me, he's seen my percentages are pretty good. He still wants me to be aggressive. But I know when I screw up. I know it in my head. I hate screwing up.

I'm going to make some bad moves, just like anybody else. But I try to keep it down and not gamble unnecessarily with certain players, because I know they're hurt. That's why I go to the trainers, even the strength coach, and ask them if anybody's injured that I don't know about from the game before, or in batting practice. I always update that, because sometimes [the players will] lie to me and that's when I get in trouble. They'll say they're OK, but they're not. It hasn't really happened very much with the Cubs, but with a lot of different teams it has. Maybe they're going for another year on their contract, I don't know.

Most of the time, unless it's a new player, I know exactly what they can do.

Last year, [St. Louis Cardinal Albert] Pujols was playing first base. But before that, when he would play left field, I used to watch him throw with [Jim] Edmonds in center field. He had to get 50 feet away. Usually they're throwing more like 100 feet away. So I knew something was wrong. And then, when they put him at first base, I knew something was definitely wrong. So when he played left field, I would run on him.

That's what I try to do on every team. I chart and I do the defensive alignment on the infielders. [Cubs coach] Gene Clines has the outfielders.

In my computer for the past 13 years now I have a lot of alignments, and a lot of them are still true. There might be some changes—a guy's not pulling as much because he's gotten older, things like that.

I've got all the pitchers and all their velocities, too. I have a chart at my locker with all the arm strengths of the outfielders and infielders. I know all their arms. I watch between innings how they throw. That gives me an idea, and I can make a more logical decision whether to send him or not.

I've been a third-base coach, first-base coach, bench coach, infield coach, baserunning coach, sliding coach.

When I break down a player as a third-base coach, I look for foot speed, and also the way they break on the ball in the outfield. Let me give you an example: A long time ago, Manny Ramirez, when he was with Cleveland and played the outfield, if he caught a ground ball to the outfield, I don't run on him. But if he goes for a fly ball, I will send the runner every time. His footwork was different on fly balls than on grounders.

When somebody is on second base, say Moises Alou or Todd Walker, and I see them kind of slow up at second base on a double, I'll be like this: [he slaps his hips, then does a thumbs-up]. If they say no, thumbs down, then I know they can't run the same speed I know they can run. That way I won't take a chance sending them.

Jim Edmonds. He gets rid of the ball fast. He may be the best center fielder I've seen around. He has arm strength, and he gets rid of it, and he can hit.

The field [at Wrigley] is crowned, banked along first and third base. It used to be the worst. The players would slip, especially if they didn't make a tight turn around third base. Since then, the grounds crew has leveled it a little more.

I've been hit at third. I got hit last year. I was watching second base so my runner doesn't get picked off. Alou hits a line drive and it hits me right on the knee. I just threw it back. Didn't do anything.

GAMES 46, 47

Friday, May 28, 2004 . . . Pirates 9, Cubs 5/Pirates 5, Cubs 4 . . . PNC Park . . . Stat of the doubleheader: The Cubs' bullpen blows not one, but two games in less than six hours. . . . Stuff: Record since Sosa sneeze: 4-7 . . . Tom Goodwin and Todd Wellemeyer go on the DL. That's nine. The Cubs now qualify for federal emergency relief funds. . . . Cubs honk Governor Rod Blagojevich's job-approval rating does a Nestea plunge, from 54 percent to 40 percent. More good news: The Guv is quoted in a Sporting News *ghostwritten guest column (aides approved the final draft) as saying he wouldn't wear a White Sox cap "even if they made the World Series." . . . Even with the injuries, the Cubs remain an 8-5 bet at Mandalay Bay in Vegas to win the NL pennant. And incredibly, they've gone from a 4-1 bet to a 7-2 bet to win the World Series.*

Kiljoong Kim emigrated to the United States from Seoul, South Korea, in 1984. He was 13, and didn't speak a word of English except for a heavily accented "Thank you" or "You're welcome."

The way Kim looks at it, at least his parents had the decency to move to Chicago, a city where he could have his choice of baseball teams. Kim loved baseball then. Kim loves baseball now. It remains a universal dialect.

"Yes, 1984, which incidentally was the year the Cubs were magical," he says. "That's the year I cried in front of the TV with my sister."

Welcome to Cubs Nation, Kiljoong.

He cried because his adopted Cubs blew a 2-0 lead in the five-game series against the San Diego Padres. Just think what he would have done had he been a Cubs lifer, or been in Houston and Pittsburgh this week during The Road Trip That Wins Forgot.

Magical 1984 was the first time the Cubs had advanced to the playoffs since 1945. Then-manager Jim Frey says he still has nightmares about the lost series. He isn't the only one. Kim says if he calls his own sister and simply mentions two words—*Leon Durham*—"she is going to start crying. I know that for a fact."

Twenty years have passed and yet Frey, Kim's sister, and countless other Cubs fans still haven't unloaded the emotional baggage at curbside check-in. This intrigues Kim not only because he remains a loyal Cubs follower himself, but because he is a professor of sociology at DePaul University (just a few L stops from Wrigley), as well as research director of the school's Egan Urban Center. Kim got his undergrad degree at the University of Wisconsin in Madison, his master's degree from DePaul, and his baseball degree from Heartbreak College, located at the corner of Clark and Addison.

He didn't cry in 2003, when the Cubs blew the 3-1 lead to the Florida Marlins in the NLCS. Instead, he inadvertently helped others to find their inner emotions.

"I live up in Rogers Park," he says. "A half hour after the game [Game 7 at Wrigley], I was walking home near campus and this guy was sitting outside a bar, just totally devastated—you could just tell. He had a Cubs jersey and he was just completely out of it. So I put my hand on his shoulder and said, 'You know, next spring, we do this over again.'

"And he just started crying."

Kim became a Cubs fan because of television and timing. He would return from school each day and there would be his new friends the Cubs on WGN, along with a man named Harry on WGN Radio, who wore large glasses and occasionally spoke of sacred dairy animals. On especially sun-kissed school days, Kim and his sister would do a Ferris Bueller and skip classes for a Cubs game. Five bucks would buy a bleacher seat.

Since high school, Kim has tried to attend at least 10 to 15 Cubs game a season, as well as make one road trip to a different stadium each year. He took a Greyhound to St. Louis once and unknowingly rented a room at a hookers' hotel. In '94, he drove to the Metrodome for a Minnesota Twins-Cleveland Indians game. It lasted 22 innings and didn't finish until 2:30 A.M. "Terrible stadium, by the way," he says.

Kim remember his first Cubs game (July 6, 1984, against the Houston Astros). He remembers Jerome Walton's fielding percentage in 1989 (.998). He remembers getting engaged to Heather Smith and actually thinking, "Do I raise my kid as a Cubs fan or a Sox fan?" (His wife was raised in the Sox denomination.)

In short, Kim is more than qualified to give a thumbnail sociological sketch of Cubs Nation. He teaches a class at DePaul called The Sociology of Sports, which uses baseball as a tool to examine economics, labor, gender and race, and globalization, to name a few. He's given some thought to the microcosm that is the Cubs community.

First of all, Kim says the Cubs are blessed with Wrigley Field, which isn't exactly a news flash. It's old (1914), cozy, and attracts a diverse clientele. That's the trick, says Kim. The Cubs get the baseball purists, the generational fans, the out-of-towner raised on the WGN superstation, the locals, the Bleacher Bums, the "Whooeee, let's get wasted!" lunkheads, the corporate types with mezzanine-level suites, the suburbanites, the casual fans, and the bandwagoners.

"Wrigley," he says, "provides this fantastic opportunity to get them all together."

Most Cubs fans are generational—that is, they grow up on ivy, Sammy's home run hop, a manual scoreboard. And most Cubs fans get a perverse pleasure from the Lovable Loser label. They romanticize it to the point, says Kim, where it creates a sense of belonging, a shared grief or joy.

"I don't think people go to Wrigley to have their hearts broken," says Kim. "I don't think that is the anticipation. It's almost like dating. You don't go into a relationship thinking, 'Well, is this going to end in a horrible way?'"

But there is a certain Cubs fatalism, right?

"Well, sure," he says. "I can't be the only one who has this hope that wouldn't it be cool if they won it all in my lifetime. And this has only been effectively the third generation of people that have that eternal hope in a way. There's something about witnessing victory [as a Cubs fan] that contains a different element than witnessing it as a Yankees fan. Twenty-six Yankees titles—a lot of people have seen that. But how many Cubs fans, how many people in general do you know that have witnessed a Cubs championship? There's something about that type of novelty.

"I think the biggest characteristic about the Cubs fans is that they tend to really romanticize the team a lot more than other people I have talked to."

Not long ago, someone posed a question in one of Kim's classes: What happens if the Cubs win a World Series? It was met with mixed feelings. After all, we've been dealing with Cubs futility since 1909.

Kim can handle the breakup. Streaks, not hearts, were made to be broken.

GAME 48

Saturday, May 29, 2004 . . . Pirates 10, Cubs 7 . . . PNC Park . . . Stuff: Rob Mackowiak, otherwise known by Cubs fans as "Satan," hits another home run. He has three dingers and 11 RBI in two days. . . . Record since Sosa sneeze: 4-8.

Eddie Vedder and his wife are expecting a daughter any day now. And yet, when the Evanston-born and Cubs-raised Vedder is asked to discuss his Cubs Nation residency, he finds time during the big countdown to e-mail his answers. In fact, the Pearl Jam lead singer ends one of the e-mails with "Peace. Go Cubs." Vedder gets it.

Q: *Someone from, say, Oklahoma . . . Belgium, wherever, sits next to you in the Wrigley bleachers. They've never seen a game at the Friendly Confines. If asked, how would you explain the Cubs to them? How would you articulate the importance of Wrigley?*

Vedder: First things first: they can't miss batting practice. Some of the best heckling takes place during warm-ups, when the opposing teams are in the outfield, unprotected. To struggling alcoholic Dickie Knowles: "Hey, Dickie, keg party at my place!" Or "Hey, Dickie, does the third-base line remind you of something you may have done last night?"

Even the Cubs were not immune. I remember a guy blustered up enough to shout at Milt Pappas [whose wife had gone missing for over a year at the time], "Hey, Milt, your wife's been over at my house." Even weathered, afternoon-drunk bleacherites couldn't approve of that one. Just groans and embarrassed laughter.

By the time the game starts and the sun comes out—if this Belgianite, or whoever, has been drinking like the rest—it will all become clear. If a great play happens before him and he hears the grass crunch under the diving catch . . . If a rally happens to score a guy from third with two outs and the crowd stands, unified in Chicago summer sweat . . . If a home run lands two rows behind him and he lands on top of a guy in a wheelchair while going for the ball . . . Wrigley will articulate it for him.

Win or lose, he'll be exiting with a wobble out the back gate, past a couple of cops and into Murphy's. The evening will continue with new friends, and at some point, will end up with him either puking, going to jail, or stumbling into his hotel room. Either way, he'll wake up having been to Wrigley Field.

Q: *What kind of gig is it to sing during the Seventh-Inning Stretch?*

Vedder: It's a great invitation, 'cause of course Harry still lives at Wrigley. You sing it for him. And your gramma who's watching 'GN. It ain't pitching the seventh game, but it's a nice way to contribute to the energy of the ballpark.

It would be great to do it from the bleachers. Harry used to do one game a year from out there.

Q: *Remember your first game at Wrigley? And do you ever have flashbacks when you walk into the place?*
Vedder: It starts just inside the bleacher turnstile. It's the same concrete and metal as when I was zipper tall. It's dark, echoey, and that smell of yesterday's spilled beer and urinal tablet is pervasive. Walk round the ramp going up . . . look down on the street, someone's banging a plastic drum or playing sax with his case out for coin. Then the sounds of the park organ take over as you keep moving up. Then you hear the cracks and pops of bats and mitts. That's when it gets me.

My grandfather took me the first time. I remember that sound. And you turn the corner and there it is in full glory: the green, the white . . . the blue pinstripes. It works every time.

Q: *Billy Corgan says he relates to two players: Jose Cardenal and Kerry Wood. Who are your guys, and why?*
Vedder: Billy should get his own favorite players, 'cause he knows these are mine. Of course, Jose was the coolest Cub to ever take the field, but I know Billy related more to "Fat" Pat Bourque. Actually, Corgan used to tell me how he had fantasies of getting his head squeezed between the powerful thighs of their jockstraps. The only reason I can see Billy, Tyrannical Ex-King of the Pumpkins, liking Cardenal is that Jose wore No. 1, and that's what Billy wants to be.

Q: *Most memorable Cubs moment? And where were you?*
Vedder: I'd have to say the doubleheader in 2003, second-to-last day of the season, against Pittsburgh.

With three games left, they had to win at least two and Houston had to lose one to clinch the division. The Cubs looked strong, and people with radios were screaming the Milwaukee-Houston score into the bleacher air. The Brewers were fucking doing it.

When the numbers went up on the manual scoreboard, you could see the scorer's arms sticking out of the antique structure, clapping. It was as good as it gets. Sexson hits a homer or something to seal the Astros' demise, and the Cubs rallied big with the momentum. They take Game 1.

Between games, I've never seen such glee and apprehension combined in the faces of the fans. The roar in right field was off the scale when we took the lead in Game 2. And on defense, each pitch got a reaction, with cliques of men decked out in fake Clement chin beards. It seemed unfathomable that a win could clinch it. Didn't seem possible. But it was happening.

It was dark by the time the final out approached. I think it was a fly to Lofton in center. It was total release. Everyone within 100 feet of each other became family. Men, 20 to 60 years old, with beer guts and stubble, were weeping onto their crooked smiles.

The next day, in the cold of early winter, Santo's number was retired before the game. The exact MOMENT they finished the speeches, the sun magically shone. Everybody looked up. Ernie Banks lifted his arms up and beamed back at the sky. Fergie Jenkins shook his head. The crowd looked at each other in disbelief. It was eerie. Joyful. God-fearing. You don't choreograph nature.

Ron, standing up with the help of his cane, looked into the sun, then at his wife, who was crying. The crowd erupted and people were embracing as his number was hoisted. I remember thinking, "Fuckin' Wrigley." (I should mention there were only two minutes of sunshine that day.)

Q: The Tribune Company calls and says it will sell you the Cubs for market price. You buying? And if so, your first act as new Cubs owner?
Vedder: Yes, I would, and my first act would be to take batting practice with the team in full uni. Then I would make the superstars go to couples therapy. Either they would work it out, or they'll keep their shit together so they won't have to go back.

Q: Do you have a prized Cubs memento—something from your childhood, something given to you by a player, that sort of thing?
Vedder: I've been blessed with opportunities to obtain pieces of Cub history. The complete set of game-used mitts from the '60s and '70s Cubs. The bloody hat that [Kyle] Farnsworth was wearing when he kicked that Reds guy's ass [author's note: the Reds guy—Paul Wilson, June 2003]. Kerry Wood set me up with that one. Adds a bit of violence to the collection. The full Kerry Wood uniform with mitt and spikes on a MOVING mannequin (the dogs go ape-shit). Four large binders of signed Cubs 8 × 10s (spanning time at 500 something, and counting) that were originally Johnny Ramone's collection passed on to me. Charlie Root's cap from the '20s. The giant W and L flags from the scoreboard. Programs, all in order since 1927. Great artwork.

But then there's the Jose Cardenal shrine. His mitt from '72. His custom bats [Jose was the first ever to use the hollowed end on his bat]. His rookie jersey. Signed photos of every team he's played on.

But the best item of all must be the original photo of a 10-year-old Jose playing Little League in Cuba, circa 1953. He sent that to me, and I am moved by it to this day.

GAME 49

Sunday, May 30, 2004 . . . Cubs 12, Pirates 1 . . . PNC Park . . . Cubs NL Central pennant flies: Tie-Third (26-23) . . . Stuff: Clubhouse consensus—today's victory might have been the most important of the young season. Instead of a winless six-game road trip and sole possession of last place in the division, the Cubs pound the Pirates on getaway day. . . . Record since Sosa sneeze: 5-8 . . . The Reverse Curse: Florida's Josh Beckett goes on the DL.

First-year Cub Michael Barrett (he's the one walking around with the I-Can't-Believe-I'm-Here smile on his face) receives 10 to 15 fan letters each day. As a Montreal/San Juan Expo, he got half that.

Cubs fans are nutty this way. They'd write to the rosin bag if they thought they'd get a response. The Big Three—Sammy Sosa, Kerry Wood, and Mark Prior—get the big numbers when it comes to fan mail, but Barrett isn't complaining about his nearly 100-letters-per-week pace. That matches some crowds at Olympic Stadium.

"I try to read them all," says the perpetually pleasant Barrett. "You never know what you might come across."

Barrett knows what it's like to get stiffed by the pros. He's still waiting for a response from Nolan Ryan, who never returned the two photos Barrett and a friend sent years ago for autographs.

Barrett also knows he doesn't get superstar-mail volume. Former Expos teammate Vladimir Guerrero does. Even in the baseball wasteland that is Montreal, Guerrero received at least two industrial-sized plastic containers full of fan mail every week. And as you might expect, the somewhat reclusive Guerrero, now an Anaheim Angel, told a clubbie to dump them, right?

Nope. "He would sit down and read all the mail in those tubs," says Barrett.

Presenting four randomly picked letters from Barrett's mail bag:

To Michael Barrett,

I wanted to let you know that I am a big fan of yours and the Chicago Cubs. Plain and simple you are an awesome catcher and I enjoy watching you play in the majors. I have been following your career since your rookie season in the Montreal Expos organization. I admire how you give 110% day in, day out, which shows your dedication to baseball and your team. You are very talented and play the game with a lot of heart and emotion on the diamond. Best of luck to you and the Chicago Cubs, plus continued success.

If it's not too much trouble could you sign this card?

Thanks.

Dear Mr. Barrett,

My name is Greg. I am 16 years old and have been a fan of yours ever since you first came up with the Expos. I have enjoyed watching you play over the years and hope to see you find a home in Chicago.

Could you please sign my cards. I realize that you are busy, but an autograph from you would mean a lot to me.

Thank you for reading my letter and good luck this season. Go Cubbies!

Thanks.

Hi, Michael:

I am finally getting most of the Cubs 40-man roster cards signed. Please take a moment and sign yours for my Cubs team book. Thanks, and hope to see you at spring training in Arizona.

Regards (a fan from Arizona Fall League Days).

Michael,

I have been watching you on TV. You just hit a foul home run. You got a double. I cut an article out of the paper about you.

I hit a home run Saturday. It went over their heads and rolled to the fence. I hope I am as good as you are one day. You are the best!

I love you.

I ask Barrett about the last letter, which is scrawled in the large, unsure handwriting of a child.

"I'd like that one back," says Barrett.

Turns out the letter belongs to a little boy who continues to defy a serious disease (Barrett politely declines to provide specifics). Barrett knows this because he opened the envelope, answered the pencil-printed note, and later contacted the boy's family.

See, you never know what you might come across. Now Barrett is the one sending fan mail.

GAME 50

Monday, May 31, 2004 . . . Cubs 3, Astros 1 . . . Wrigley Field . . . Cubs NL Central pennant flies: Tie-Second (27-23) . . . Stuff: The two happiest men in America are Mark Prior and Tribune *reporter Paul Sullivan. Prior will make his first start of the season Friday. Sullivan no longer has to write the editor-mandated "Prior Watch."*

What is it about Wrigley Field that causes an outbreak of goose bumps? How can a dinky stadium older than the Versailles Treaty render jaw muscles useless? Why can't anyone go one minute at the place without blubbering the words "baseball's cathedral"?

It's a stadium, right? There's cement, steel, uncomfortable seats. Big whoop.

And then you get to the corner of Clark and Addison . . .

Do you remember your first time? Mine was in 1990, at the All-Star Game. It rained. It was colder than a just-poured Bud. And my seat was behind a girder. Baseball's cathedral, my butt.

But Wrigley and I made up. You can't help but fall hard for the place.

I never thought I'd go chick-flick teary-eyed over a 90-year-old broad, but that's what happened. She puts her hand on your knee, nibbles at your earlobe, and before you know it you've got a motel room under the name of Mr. and Mrs. Wrigley.

By happy accident I covered the Cubs for the *Chicago Tribune* from November 1995 through mid-June 1996. It wasn't much of a tenure: about 30 spring training games, just 71 regular-season games. But I'll remember sitting in the press box on a sun-smooched day and thinking, "This is my office. Not even The Donald has this view."

I'm not the only one who feels this way about Wrigley. Joe Spear has been courting and sweet-talking the Friendly Confines for years.

Spear is a senior principal and one of seven design directors for famed HOK Sports + Venue + Event. Spear's work can be seen at the modern era's Wrigley, otherwise known as Oriole Park at Camden Yards in Baltimore. He also was the lead guy on Coors Field in Denver, Jacobs Field in Cleveland, and whatever they're calling the drop-dead-gorgeous place where the San Francisco Giants play these days. Put it this way: When Spear gets done with a stadium, someone should frame the blueprints.

His first visit to Wrigley came in the winter of 1983. The Tribune Company had purchased the Cubs in 1981 and the new team executives wanted to improve the Wrigley experience. They asked a question Spear loves to hear: "Help us understand why this park is a meeting place that fans enjoy coming to." Spear knew what to tell them. It's the same speech he would give to any Architecture 101 class.

"You look at an aerial photograph of the park and you're struck by how integral it is to the neighborhood," he says. "It's not a park like those built in the '60s and '70s, when they were building multipurpose stadiums. No. 1, most of those were built in cornfields out of town. And the ones that were built downtown had enough land to build whatever they wanted. But that didn't happen with Wrigley. The architects had to fit the ballpark into what was really kind of a strange site, and it lends to the intimacy, if you will."

No duh. This odd little piece of property is bordered by the four horsemen of street names: Clark, Addison, Sheffield, and Waveland. That's one of the first things Spear looks for in a stadium project: Is it part of the community, part of the neighborhood? In many ways, Wrigley *is* the neighborhood.

"In terms of an experience going to a game, it's a pretty rich experience," he says. "It's why baseball should be in urban areas, downtown areas, because it just means a lot more than living out in the cornfields."

Wrigley Field was built in 1914 (only Fenway Park is older, by two years) for about $250,000. Sammy Sosa earns $250K in less than three games.

If Spear did a Zachary Taylor Davis (the chief architect of the original stadium) and wanted to build a new Wrigley, he says it'd cost about $200 million or so. The infield would go for about $1 million—the dirt, not the players. Stadium seats would run you another $4 million. You get the idea.

You could build a replica, but it would never truly be the same. Wrigley Stadium grew up, much like the city around it. In essence, Wrigley is a homemade recipe—a pinch of this, a pinch of that. The tinkering will—and should—continue, says Spear.

"I think that ballparks need to live and evolve," he says. "If you say to a ballclub that you can't modify the architecture, or the seating, or make changes, then the thing is going to die."

Wrigley won't need CPR anytime soon. It remains a head-turner, an ivy-and-brick photo op. When Spear first met with the Giants' owners about building a new park, they said they wanted a combination of Wrigley Field and Camden Yards.

"I thought it was actually a very sophisticated and efficient way to have a conversation about architecture and ballpark design," Spear says. "I think it's wrong for an architect to say, 'I'm not going to re-create Wrigley Field.'"

Re-create all you want. After all, you know what they say about imitation.

JUNE

• •

GAME 51

Tuesday, June 1, 2004 . . . Astros 5, Cubs 3 . . . Wrigley Field . . . Cubs NL Central pennant flies: Fourth (27-24) . . . Stat of the game: Corey Patterson, whose strike zone is from the bottom of his cleats to the top of his armpits, Ks not once, but twice with bases loaded. Boos follow. . . . Stuff: You should have seen hitting coach Sarge Matthews's face when Patterson whiffed. Derrek Lee and Ramon Martinez also failed to deliver with bases loaded. . . . Record since Sosa sneeze: 6-9.

Bob Rosenberg is one of several regular scorekeepers at Wrigley. He does 30 games for the Cubs, 51 for the White Sox. He's a regular scorer at Bulls games, too.

You can find Rosenberg, 63, near the end of the second row of the Wrigley press box. He has his own homemade scorebook. ("I took a sheet from the Phillies PR guy, had copies made, then had books made.") His notations on the scoresheets are also his own creation. If Melville were alive, Rosenberg would be his Bartleby the Scrivener.

I looked at the rules once. That was it. If a new one comes in, it's at the front of the rule book. Then I'll look at it.

I get $125 by the game. That's what every scorer in Major League Baseball gets. It used to be $50. Perks? You get free meals, parking right up front, but no gas money. If there's a rainout, the game has to start or else you don't get paid.

There was a game when Shawon Dunston had a 3-2 count and the ump signals that he's been hit by a pitch. So I score it hit by pitch.

Later, he says, "I think it was a walk."

I say, "Shawon, I checked with the ump; he said you were hit by the pitch."

"No, no, he's wrong."

You know, I think he might have needed a certain number of walks to get something in his contract.

The toughest to score is whether it's a wild pitch or a passed ball. That's why I always wait to watch the replay first. The second-toughest call is if the ball hits the lip of the grass and then goes under the fielder's glove. Hit or error?

In my opinion, if a player loses the ball in the sun or lights, I will not give him an error. It's a hit in my book. A lot of scorers will give him an error. A lot of scorers will also say it has to be a clean hit for the first hit. But what happens if it's in the ninth inning and the same thing happens? You've got to give him a hit. That's what I think.

If a PR guy asks me, "Would you please look at that play again?" I will. If I'm wrong, I change it.

I did the two All-Star Games here, '90 at Wrigley and '03 at Comiskey. I got [an All-Star] ring each time, just like the players. I've got other rings. I got championship rings with the Bulls. I got all six rings. I never expected that. The other guys at the [scorer's] table got watches.

GAME 52

Wednesday, June 2, 2004 . . . Astros 5, Cubs 1 . . . Wrigley Field . . . Stat of the game: Someone needs to test Roger Clemens for anti-aging drugs. The 91-year-old Clemens (OK, 41), whose thighs would give Kyle Farnsworth's a run for the money, improves to 8-0. . . . Record since Sosa sneeze: 6-10.

The future of the Cubs, or at least part of it, is being decided today beginning at 10 o'clock in a dumpy little building that Wrigley old-timers will remember as a doughnut shop, and then later as a greasy spoon. Look hard enough and you can still see the weather-worn sign on the roof advertising hot dogs and beef sandwiches.

This is where Cubs scouting director John Stockstill, who looks like a member of the Marine Corps surfing team, and assorted staff members will hole up during the next seven days. The annual first-year amateur player draft begins Monday, which means it's time to put together the Cubs' big board.

It isn't much of a war room. Then again, it wasn't much of a greasy spoon, either. The Cubs don't have much office space in Wrigley, so they bought the small, one-story restaurant next to the stadium parking lot, gutted it, and now refer to the building as The Annex.

Stockstill, 44, knows all about Cubs drafts. He was their 10th-round selection in 1978, received about a $20,000 signing bonus, and never made it out of the farm system. Billy Williams was his first hitting coach.

"I was about fourth in line of 15 or 20 who stood in line to succeed [Ron] Santo," says Stockstill, who was signed as a shortstop but moved to third, then catcher, then every other position except pitcher before calling it quits in 1981.

In 1987, he returned to the Cubs as an associate scout and eventually was promoted to scouting director in August 2000. There wasn't too much pressure. All he had to do was to organize and oversee what one day might be considered the most important draft in team history, or at the very least, the most important one since 1982, when the Cubs selected Shawon Dunston as the No. 1 overall pick.

There were three players who mattered in the 2001 draft: a high school catcher from St. Paul, Minnesota, named Joe Mauer; a third baseman from Georgia Tech named Mark Teixeira; and a right-handed pitcher from USC named Mark Prior. The Minnesota Twins had the No. 1 pick. The Cubs had the No. 2 pick, their highest selection since choosing Dunston 20 years earlier. Screw this one up and you're wearing a blue vest with a smiley face pin as you greet folks at the Wichita Wal-Mart.

"I was a little [nervous]," Stockstill says of his first draft. "I knew about 10 days before the draft I was going to get one of the guys I wanted."

But Stockstill wanted Prior the most. It was Prior who was listed No. 1 on the Cubs' draft board, followed by Mauer, then Teixeira. The Twins loved Prior, too (who didn't?), but were debating if they could afford to sign him. A half hour before the draft, Stockstill got the news: The Twins were taking Mauer.

"I weighed about 40 pounds more then, but I'm sure I tried a backflip," he says.

Mauer signed for a $5.15-million bonus, while Prior agreed to a five-year, then-unprecedented $10.5-million guaranteed deal. Nine minor league starts later, Prior was in the big leagues.

"I found the guy I don't think anybody else knew about," he says, laughing. "Hey, when you're good, you're good."

Stockstill is still sweet on Mauer, and had Prior gone first the Cubs would have happily taken the catcher. But pitching is what gets you a ring-fitting session with a jeweler.

"I don't know if there will ever be another pitcher who was that ready," says Stockstill. "A lot of times you'll hear people say, 'This guy can pitch in the big leagues.' But Mark could have pitched in the big leagues the day we signed him."

This time the Cubs don't choose a player until the 66th pick of the draft, thanks to the LaTroy Hawkins deal that sent their first-round selection (No. 25 overall) to the Twins as compensation. And since MLB rules prevent trading up in the draft, the Cubs have zero chance at the most prominent prospects.

Even without a first-round pick, the Cubs still have to rank all the players for their big board. The appraisal process started nearly a year ago, when player names were compiled and scouting assignments were made. The Cubs employ 17 area scouts, as well as three cross-checkers who assess a player after a Cubs scout has already submitted a report. There are also about a dozen special-assignment and freelance scouts at the team's disposal. Stockstill also serves as a national cross-checker.

If you love baseball, Marriott points, and never seeing your family, this is your kind of career. Otherwise, you might want to consider a different employment path.

"The job is a lot of nights in hotels," says Stockstill, who has been married for 10 years and has a two-and-a-half-year-old son. "A lot of miles. You're going to drive 50,000 miles and you're going to be away from home all the time. It is not a glamour job at all. In many places, you're never known. Scouts are judged on their results."

Stockstill is a big believer in drafting the best player available, regardless of if the Cubs are already loaded at the position on the big league level.

"Corey Patterson is someone I always use as an example," he says. "Great player, we love him, but it still took four, five years to get him ready. So if you go by that timetable, we would have to draft this year based on what we need in 2009. But how do we know what we need in 2009? So we take the best available and hope for the best."

Stockstill and his scouts have already rated all the players for rounds 8 through 50. That's the easy part. Beginning this morning, they'll start ranking their top 80 players for the big board.

There's an outside chance one of the top 43 players (that's the number of elite prospects this year) could fall into the Cubs' lap. Stockstill says there are seven teams that will draft only college players, meaning a boffo, high school player in that top 43 might drop all the way to 66. Might, but don't count on it.

Next Monday, there will be more Cubs officials (20) in The Annex than the Cubs have actual draft picks on the first day (17). GM Jim Hendry will be in there. So will team president Andy MacPhail. So will the Cubs' cross-checkers and five selected scouts. In the end, though, Stockstill will make the selections.

I ask him who he thinks the Cubs will take at No. 66. The response? Put it this way: He doesn't do a backflip.

GAME 53

Friday, June 4, 2004 . . . Pirates 2, Cubs 1 . . . Wrigley Field . . . Stat of the game: In his first start of the season, Mark Prior goes six innings, gives up two singles and zero runs, strikes out eight, and walks zilch.

Pirates shortstop Jack Wilson enters the game among the league leaders in batting average, hits, road batting average, and batting average against right-handers. None of it means bupkus against Prior.

"He's the best pitcher I've ever faced, by far," says Wilson, who has been in the bigs for four seasons and has exactly one hit against Prior. "Second best? [Roger] Clemens. And [Matt] Clement owns me . . . just carves me up. But it's not the same thing, you know what I mean?"

Wilson could tell the difference on a May evening in 2002, when Prior made his big league debut. "I was the second Major League batter he faced," says Wilson. That was the night Prior struck out 10 in just six innings and the Cubs got the win.

These days Wilson doesn't even bother watching game tape of Prior or reviewing the detailed scouting reports. "No point," says Wilson. "You don't forget the last time you faced Prior."

So I ask him about Thursday's three at-bats against Prior. No way he forgets those.

First inning. Wilson is up second. One out.

"You don't really know what to expect from him, this being his first time back. He's a right-hander with a fastball and curveball, and both are A-plus pitches for him. With a guy like him, he has so much power. Then to have the hammer like he does? And his delivery is outstanding, very smooth.

"The first pitch was a ball away, fastball. Anytime you can get ahead of Prior, that's a good thing. The second pitch was a fastball right down the middle. I was looking fastball. Maybe I was a little anxious. I popped up to third. But when you're ahead in the count, you're looking dead red. You're basically trying to hit one off the ivy."

Fourth inning. Wilson is up second. One out.

"I got ahead, 2-0. Both were fastballs. A hitter's count is 1-0, 2-0, 3-1, 3-0, so with a 2-0 count I was looking fastball. His third pitch was a fastball. Fouled it off. The next pitch was a fastball and I swung right through it. Then he threw me an unbelievable curveball. At 2-2, I'm not looking for any one pitch—you can't with him. When he throws the curveball, it looks like it's coming at you. I bailed. I didn't pick up the spin until it was halfway there. So I just kind of threw my bat out there and hit it to third."

Sixth inning. Wilson is up fourth. Two outs, man on first.

"Fastball. Ball. Then a fastball for a strike. I foul it off. Then a curveball for a strike. Now it's 1-2. Then a ball. It's 2-2. Then he struck me out with a fastball away. The ball was a little up, but it was a good pitch."

Wilson slides off the equipment trunk he's been using as a seat in the laundry room. If he's annoyed about those three at-bats, he doesn't show it.

"Hey, it's good to see him healthy," he says.

GAME 54

Saturday, June 5, 2004 . . . Cubs 6, Pirates 1 . . . Wrigley Field . . . Stat of the game: A crowd of 40,024 puts the Cubs over the 1 million mark in a team-record 26 home dates. Cubs president Andy MacPhail is seen shirtless and popping bubbly in his private stadium suite (no, not really).

Former U.S. president Ronald Reagan dies today. He was 93.

One September afternoon in 1988, Reagan visited the WGN broadcast booth.

Steve Stone remembers.
I really didn't know he was coming. Harry [Caray] certainly did, because Harry wore a jacket and tie. I remember saying to Harry, "You going to a funeral or something?"

He said, "No, no."

I said, "Well, then why are you wearing a jacket and tie?"

He said, "Uh, there's something going on." But he didn't elaborate on it.

I remember walking up the stairs and seeing all the tarps placed over the fence openings in the stadium. You usually can see through to the street. But this time they had obscured the view, because they obviously didn't want anybody getting a look at which ramp the President was walking up.

We started the show, and Harry and I are talking. That's when I felt a tail in my lap. I was looking at the camera and there was a tail in my lap. I'm thinking, "Wow, a squirrel jumped down from the rafters." It's an old booth and an old park, and I'm thinking, "This squirrel is going to bite me and I'm going to get rabies here." But I couldn't look down, because I was in the middle of a soliloquy and [producer] Arne [Harris] wanted us to keep on going.

So I finally reach down with my left hand. All of a sudden, I felt a very wet nose and a muzzle. I realized then it was a dog. Because [President Jimmy] Carter had been in our locker room in 1979 when I played for the Orioles in the World Series, and they had brought explosive-sniffing dogs, I thought, "The president's going to be here." That was the first time I realized Reagan was going to be here.

He walked up to the booth wearing a very heavy bulletproof vest under his Cubs jacket, and he was out of breath. In those days it was a long walk, even in the old booth. At that point I think he was 77, and he's wearing a very heavy bulletproof vest.

Harry wisely watched him and said, "You know, Mr. President, we'll give you a chance to get acclimated up here. You just sit back and relax a little bit, and we'll do the second inning together."

Harry did a half inning with him, and he did a half of play-by-play where I was his color man. At one point he said to me, "I'm having a hard time seeing the pitches. It must be the glass up here."

I said, "With all due respect, Mr. President, there is no glass up here."

He said, "Well, there was when I was last here with Pat Piper."

I said, "Yeah, but that was in the '30s. Things have changed a little bit. I'll tell you what I'll do: I'll mark two pieces of paper and when it's a ball I'll point to it, and if it's a strike I'll point to it. Then you can call the pitches."

He said, "Thanks."

So that's what we did.

GAME 55

Sunday, June 6, 2004 . . . Cubs 4, Pirates 1 . . . Wrigley Field . . . Stuff: Corey Patterson strikes out on a shoulder-high pitch. More boos. Patterson now has 47 Ks in 201 at-bats. . . . Why ballplayers are different from you and me (but in an amusing, creative way): A Pirates player—one of the most accessible and quotable in the NL—wears a T-shirt that reads, "Do I Look Like A F——ing People Person?" It doesn't work; reporters still hit him up for interviews in the clubhouse. This same player has a protective cup with a drawing of "Wilson" of Tom Hanks/Castaway fame.

The Major League's busiest trainer arrived at Wrigley at about 7:30 this morning. When you have eight different players on the disabled list—Joe Borowski (right shoulder strain) becomes the latest member of the DL—you tend to crank up the whirlpools and crack open the ice bags a little earlier these days.

"We've had nine guys on the DL at one time," says first-year Cubs trainer Dave Groeschner. "That's a lot for one year."

Groeschner is here mostly because he has a history with Dusty Baker

(Groeschner spent eight seasons in the San Francisco Giants organization, Baker's former employer) and partly because the previous trainer, Dave Tumbas, had the misfortune of having Mark Prior get hurt on his watch. So the Cubs made a change and hired Groeschner two months after the 2003 NLCS belly flop.

What happened next is the stuff of Cubs medical lore: Prior (elbow, Achilles), Mark Grudzielanek (Achilles), Alex Gonzalez (wrist), Kerry Wood (triceps), Sammy Sosa (uh, sneeze), Todd Wellemeyer (shoulder), Kent Mercker (back), Tom Goodwin (groin), and now Borowski have been sidelined this season.

Of course, no one is blaming Groeschner for any of this—at least, not yet (if it can happen to Tumbas . . .).

Trainers are a big deal in professional sports, especially in baseball, where a team is together from February until the first week of October, or even longer if you make it into the playoffs. It isn't just about wearing polyester pants, a golf shirt, and carrying a pair of surgical scissors and a roll of tape. Relationships are formed. Trust is formed. At least, that's the plan.

Groeschner, 33, was hired by the Cubs in mid-December of 2003. He didn't have time to prepare individual off-season workouts for the players, but he could pick up a phone.

"I started calling the players and introduced myself," he says.

Groeschner began studying the medical history of every Cub on the 40-man roster. Some computer and paper files were thicker than others. He wanted to know each injury, each test (MRI? X-ray? CAT scan?), each surgery, each rehab, each DL stay, each notation by the attending doctor.

"You just got to get in the trenches with the players and work," he says. "You help them get through the injuries. You talk to guys on the plane, on the buses, in the clubhouse. The biggest thing is building that trust. I'm still working on it."

For a 1:20 start, Groeschner and assistant trainer Sandy Krum usually have the training room up and running by 8 A.M. Groeschner will review his injury reports and also surf the Net for new injuries around the league. And he always knows the DL situation of other teams. After all, you never know when someone might want to make a trade due to injuries.

Thanks to the Achilles-related injuries of Prior and Grudzielanek, Groeschner has closely followed the rehab progress of Boston Red Sox shortstop Nomar Garciaparra. Garciaparra is finally making some rehab starts in the minors. The recovery time has been similar for Grudzielanek.

"You try to get 25 guys ready every day, plus the eight rehab guys," Groeschner says. "It's tough. You never get to breathe sometimes."

Groeschner isn't complaining, but it's hard to remember a first-year head trainer stuck with an injury list this long. Borowski, the latest DL member, is an interesting case study because he'd rather have a knitting needle rammed under his toenail than visit the trainer's room. But as Borowski's velocity decreased, concerns about his health increased.

"It got to a point where we started asking questions," Groeschner says.

Borowski didn't want to go on the DL, but he recently admitted that he had felt a little something—not pain, but tenderness—in his throwing shoulder. Groeschner now has another patient, but that's OK.

"It goes back to building trust," he says. "Sometimes our job is to protect the players from themselves."

And sometimes his job is to savor the sight of the franchise phenom making his long-awaited 2004 debut. That's what Groeschner did Friday as Prior delivered six near-perfect and pain-free innings.

When Prior walked off the mound and into the dugout after the sixth inning, he told Groeschner, "I'm tired, but I feel pretty good."

"Tired . . . I can live with," said Groeschner.

See? One happy ending. Only eight more DL endings to go.

GAME 56

Monday, June 7, 2004 . . . Cardinals 4, Cubs 3 . . . Wrigley Field . . . Cubs NL Central pennant flies: Fourth (29-27) . . . Stuff: In a semibizarre pregame interview with reporters, new closer LaTroy Hawkins announces, well, no more interviews with reporters. "I just want to do my job and go home," he says.

It wasn't exactly a dream come true, but a night earlier Grant Johnson went to bed thinking he might be a Chicago Cub today. That was the rumor on the eve of Major League Baseball's first-year player draft.

"I had heard there was some word that the Cubs would like to select me with their first pick in the second round," he says. "I thought it might happen, but it wasn't definite."

It is now. With the 66th overall pick in the draft, the Cubs use their first se-lection on the Notre Dame right-hander. Johnson is local (Lyons Township), is Carlos Zambrano-like exuberant on the mound, and is only a season re-moved from shoulder surgery. As far as the Cubs are concerned, none of these are bad things, including the surgical scar on Johnson's throwing shoulder.

A few days ago, he beat UC Irvine in the NCAA Regionals to improve his record to 6-0. The Irish season ended shortly thereafter, but nobody could blame Johnson, who finished with a 1.87 ERA. He did this despite facing metal bats and not throwing a breaking ball until after his sixth start of the season.

"From what I hear, the [radar] guns put on me show my velocity was close as my freshman year," he says in a teleconference call.

His freshman year is why the Cubs think they might have stolen one here. Johnson led ND to the College World Series in 2002. Then came the shoulder problems, but also a 2004 recovery.

Johnson still has two years of eligibility remaining, which is why he makes a halfhearted attempt to sound coy about his future. "I'd like to sign," he says one moment. "But there's no harm in going back [to Notre Dame]," he says the next moment.

Somewhere his IMG "advisor" is wincing at the bad acting job.

After Johnson finishes with the beat reporters, I ask him about his day. Turns out he's fresh from a final team meeting at Notre Dame. It was dur-ing that meeting that the cell phone of Irish coach Paul Mainieri began to ring. Mainieri took the call. Moments later, he turned to the team and told them that Cubs GM Jim Hendry just called; Johnson had been drafted by the Cubbies.

"Everybody was cheering and laughing," says Johnson, who chatted with Hendry. "The rest of the meeting was more of a somber mood. We said good-bye to the seniors. It was kind of an emotional roller coaster."

For negotiating purposes, Johnson has to pretend he might play the Notre Dame card in 2005. But it's obvious he's thrilled about being a Cub.

"It's going to be really nice to be able to play for a team like the Cubs, in an organization like they have, and be close to home," says Johnson, noting that Single-A Lansing (Michigan) and Triple-A Iowa are within easy driv-ing distance for his family.

But the real clincher is when I ask him how he'll spend his evening tonight. Nothing much, he says, just have some dinner with his parents. Long pause.

"And I'll have a celebratory cigar."

The Ballhawks wait at THE corner for catching home runs, Waveland and Kenmore.

Dave Davison (standing under the stop sign), considered the greatest Ballhawk ever.

See the Harry Caray caricature on the rooftop house? Dusty Baker calls on it for divine baseball.

Dale Wheeler, keeper of the pitcher's mound at Wrigley. Here he smooths out the third-base area between innings.

TOP: *Moises Alou led the Cubs in home runs, RBI, baserunning blunders, and helmet tossing.*
BELOW LEFT: *No Cub played in more games than Derrek Lee, and it showed as he wore down in September.*
BELOW RIGHT: *Third-base coach "Wavin'" Wendell Kim was a victim of the post-2004 purge.*

Sammy Sosa, the self-proclaimed Gladiator, watched his health, playing skills, and credibility deteriorate.

Carlos Zambrano, the All-Star pitcher whose on-field antics angered teammates and opponents alike.

The pro's pro, Greg Maddux (with former Atlanta Braves teammate John Smoltz), won No. 300 but was "embarrassed" by the Cubs' late-season swoon.

Nomar Garciaparra's arrival at the trading deadline energized the Cubs, but injuries reduced his effectiveness.

Cubs GM Jim Hendry (center) put together the team to beat in the NL Central, until injuries and an inexplicable September/October collapse arrived.
BELOW: *The Wrigley faithful.*
BOTTOM: *Even the scouts noticed Aramis Ramirez's improved defense at third. They already knew about his offense.*

Trainer Dave Groeschner's (center) first season with the Cubs was also his last.
BELOW: *Hi-Tops bar, part of the Wrigleyville beer garden.*
BOTTOM: *Tony Cooney (center) has yet to ding a car in baseball's tiniest players' parking lot.*

TOP: *Note the Billy Goat and the message.*

LEFT: *A Wrigley postgame ritual: Fans take turns sitting in the infamous Steve Bartman seat.*

BOTTOM: *The Steve Bartman seat (113).*

GAME 57

Tuesday, June 8, 2004 . . . Cubs 7, Cardinals 3 . . . Wrigley Field . . . Stuff: Sammy Sosa takes his first public batting practice since the sneeze.

Right field at Wrigley is like Cindy Crawford's birthmark; you won't find it anywhere else.

Look at it (right field, not Cindy): 353 feet down the line . . . mere inches between the foul line and the padded brick wall to the side . . . a 15-foot-high wall at the farthest corner, a 10-foot-high wall at the bleachers . . . screen baskets . . . brick hiding behind ivy . . . a quirky swelling of space under the thinnest part of the bleachers . . . a bullpen at field's edge. Now add the unpredictable winds that tickle fly balls, or a noon sun that dares you to look up, and you've got baseball's version of Punk'd.

Todd Hollandsworth introduced himself to Wrigley's right field on Opening Day. Game-time temperature: 41 degrees with 16 mph winds. Since then he has played 14 more games there as Sosa recovers from Sneezeapolooza.

I'm still getting the knack. You check the wind every day. I'm always out there picking up grass, throwing it in the air, seeing what's going on out there. The funny thing about that wind is it changes all the time. A lot of times, early in the game, the wind is blowing out, howling. Later in the game, the wind is blowing in a little bit. You take batting practice and you're thinking, "Boy, the ball's really jumping." Then the game comes and it's not jumping. What's that saying around here: "Wait five minutes and the weather will change"? You almost kind of believe it. It does change.

The one place where right field really kind of forgives you is at that elbow [where it bulges near the corner]. You kind of know where you're at there. Where it kind of hurts is that gap out there between right and center field because it gets real big. I know it says 400 on the wall, but that's not actually dead center field. It's right of center field. It's not dimensionally correct. That 400 marker is off about 15 feet to the right, so it's actually a little bit longer out there.

You've got the short foul line and no foul territory down the right-field line where that pad is at. You've got the big well.

You have to be alert. You're playing balls off the wall down the line. Somebody hits a line drive down the line, you're going to get a ricochet off the pad. You have to play aggressively cautious. And you have to be real careful about how hard you go into that wall over there. So you kind of have to be ready for everything.

Day games? [He laughs.] I can't wait until August, because I've gotta believe the sun's going to move. A day game here means the sun is just parked right over your head. It's right there. You just got to play the ball off to the side.

Early in the game, that sun crosses over almost from the right-field foul line to the left, and it crosses from behind you.

My first time playing it was Opening Day. I got to go out there. It was freezing cold, and the wind was blowing straight in. Like I said, you never know. Wait five minutes, right?

GAME 58

Wednesday, June 9, 2004 . . . Cardinals 12, Cubs 4 . . . Wrigley Field . . . Cubs NL Central pennant flies: Tie-Fourth (30-28) . . . Stat of the game: Mark Prior's second start of the season is a clunker: 3⅔ innings, five ernies, five walks. . . . Stuff: Welcome to the Brushback Festival. Prior and rookie Jon Leicester send a couple of Cardinals to the dirt. Cards pitcher Matt Morris throws one at Derrek Lee's ear flap. Lee says some naughty words to St. Louis manager Tony LaRussa. Benches clear.

Peter Gammons sits at a desk in the far corner of the ESPN newsroom. You know it's America's baseball god because his silver hair occasionally pops above the partition as he completes a phone call with who knows who. Bud Selig? Jim Hendry? Pizza Hut?

Gammons, 59, is a scoop machine. If there were a Mt. Rushmore of baseball journalists, he might get two of the four spots. But more important, he still sees the beauty of the game despite decades of watching base-ball's owners and players try to drag a razor across the sport's wrist.

About a drag bunt away from Gammons's desk is the glass-enclosed ESPN News studio, where the top story of the 8 P.M. show appears to be Larry Bird's comments about the NBA not having enough white players. Gammons isn't watching. Instead, the Sony Trinitron monitor on his desk is tuned to the San Diego Padres-Red Sox game at Fenway.

Across from Gammons is *Baseball Tonight* producer John Totten. Next to Totten is host Dave Revsine, who is filling in for Karl Ravech tonight. Revsine is a Northwestern grad who is a Chicago anomaly: "A North Sider who loves the White Sox," he says. Nearby is Harold Reynolds, the former big leaguer who now teams with Gammons on the show. With the exception of a quick handshake and hello, Reynolds spends every minute I'm there with one, sometimes two phones cradled next to his ears.

The *Baseball Tonight* staff met late this afternoon to plan the one-hour show. Totten hands me a rundown sheet. They're going to lead with Nomar Garciaparra's return to the Red Sox lineup, followed by Padres-Red Sox highlights, followed by Gammons talking about No-mah, followed by Philadelphia Phillies-White Sox highlights. Then America will see San Francisco Giants-Tampa Bay Devil Rays highlights (whooeee!), then Reynolds talking about Jason Schmidt, then a series of teases for the next segment. The Cubs-Cardinals game highlights won't roll until nearly 20 minutes into the show.

"If Prior had had another great game, that might have been in the A-block," says Jay Levy, the show's senior coordinating producer. "A-block" is TV-ese for the first segment. Instead, Prior gets lit up like a church candle, which explains why Reynolds will do an analysis of pitchers (Prior and Florida Marlin A. J. Burnett) making their second rehab starts.

Levy is the first to admit that the Cubs carry national viewing clout. ESPN loves doing their games, but a Cubs blowout—in the afternoon, no less—means B-block for the loss at Wrigley.

The show is scheduled for 10 P.M., but it's beginning to rain in Boston. A rain delay could mean ESPN junks its Red Sox telecast and bumps up the broadcast time of *Baseball Tonight*. "We may have to do some talking," says Totten, suddenly faced with the prospect of having to stretch the contents of an hour show to perhaps 90 minutes.

It is now 9:16. Reynolds holds a cell phone to one ear and an office phone to the other. Meanwhile, Gammons casually glances at a notecard dropped on his desk by an ESPN researcher. And somewhere in a stack of stat sheets are the latest numbers for Cubs minor league pitcher Bobby Brownlie, the franchise's first-round pick of 2002. I know this because Gammons has already recited Brownlie's stats from his last start and then double-checked the right-hander's ERA.

Gammons has done a billion of these shows. He's already made his calls to sources, monitored the Web for tidbits and game updates, and completed his research. So now he watches as the rain drowns Fenway.

"My wife says it's not raining on the Cape," says Gammons, who has a place on Cape Cod as well as a home in Brookline, which isn't far from Fenway. "But this is good for the garden in Brookline."

You've got to like a guy who doesn't wear socks. Gammons wears loafers, no socks, khakis, a striped shirt, and understated tie. Sixty minutes . . . 90 minutes, Gammons doesn't seem too concerned about the late change in program time.

"I'm the human fill," he says.

So Gammons waits. And talks baseball and the Cubs. After all, Gammons is the one who picked the Cubs to win it all in 2004.

I still think they have a great chance to win it. That could mean trading Corey Patterson and getting [Kansas City Royals star outfielder Carlos] Beltran to try to win right now. Or you get a guy who can get on base and run out of the leadoff spot. But I do think they need an on-base guy at the top of the order. My guess is that they will.

Someone brought it up to me today: Will they take the [New York] Yankees' problem, which is Kenny Lofton, if the Yankees paid him? I don't think Jim [Hendry, Cubs GM] would do that, because he likes Corey so much.

There really is something about Dusty. I really like Dusty. I know if I played for him I'd trust him. I'm a great believer that players have to trust managers. Whether he's technically a great manager, a great game manager, I don't know . . . whatever. I don't get wrapped up in that. I get wrapped up in who wins. He's got a thing about him that's extraordinary. And I think [pitching coach Larry] Rothschild is the best in the business.

I also kind of staked a lot on the idea that this was going to be the year that Kerry Wood absolutely took off. I'm sorry he got hurt. He said to me last year in spring training, "You know, don't be talking to me. I've never won more than 13 games."

That shows me that now he's really grown up. I was really surprised at that line. [Wood would finish with 14 victories in 2003.] There's just something about him. I think there's a meanness about him, where he's going to rise to the occasion. He's hurt now, but it wouldn't surprise me at all if he were the World Series MVP.

[The NL Central is] not as good as I thought it was at the top, but it's obviously much deeper. I think Cincinnati, Pittsburgh, Milwaukee will fade. But the Cardinals are still very dangerous. And there's a lot of unrest in Houston over Jimy Williams's eccentricities.

I don't think there's pressure on Dusty, although Dusty thinks there's pressure on him. I'm sure Dusty mentioned the whole thing between him and [former ESPN and big league manager Bobby] Valentine. Bobby didn't like any other manager, but he just killed Dusty [on the air], just *killed* him.

When Dusty came to the 2003 World Series—for some special award or something—I saw him and shook his hand. I said, "Congratulations, that was a great year." He said, "Oh, I thought everybody at ESPN thought I had blown it or something."

But he had a great year. He went from 95 losses to the playoffs. If you don't blow a 4-nothing lead in Game 1 of the Florida series, you probably win the World Series.

I don't mind this being written about, but this is the way Dusty is as a person: A story came out on ESPN about his tax problems in San Francisco. Now, I never read about the tax problems. But the first day of spring training [in 2003], he asked me if I'd come into his office alone with him.

He said, "I have to ask you about this and I have to do it one-on-one. That whole tax thing—a couple of writers in San Francisco told me [Giants managing general partner] Peter Magowan leaked it to you and you gave it to ESPN."

I did start to get pissed, and I started to get out of the chair. He said, "OK, all right, I see right away. But I had to ask you."

So the next two days he spent a lot of time with me explaining a lot of stuff. I took it as a great compliment. I liked him so much more because of how he handled that situation. He couldn't think something about someone without first confronting them about it. Remember, the story came out in October, I think. He had been told about this over the winter, but he wanted to wait until he saw me in February.

The great advantage the Cubs have is that they have so much pitching in their organization. They can trade one or two guys and not touch the favorite son, Mr. Carlos Guzman.

Wrigley and Fenway. Wrigley is more comfortable than Fenway. I think the difference between the two is the fans. Boston fans are so intense. I think there's more of an edge at Fenway. But that's the nature of the East Coast.

I think there are similarities between the two teams. I think the fans of both teams get a little self-absorbed there. In Boston there's a thing on [all-sports radio station] WEEI where you hear a voice say, "They ruined my summah."

Sometimes I get tired of it. I think the difference is that the Red Sox have been closer more often, that they've absolutely snatched defeat from victory so many times. But last year was the worst.

But I know all along that [Cubs president] Andy MacPhail can't stand it. I can hear him: "I don't want to be a Lovable Loser. I want to change the Cubs to being just lovable."

If they can keep him healthy, I think there's a lot of dramatic moments in Moises [Alou].

I stick with my pick. I keep being told there's more to the Andy Pettitte injury than we're being told. Houston's good. They're very good, but I wouldn't underestimate St. Louis. They've got the best stars in the division with [Scott] Rolen and [Albert] Pujols. They're very, very good.

I always thought that maybe a great book about Greg Maddux was to write one where you just let everybody else tell the stories.

[Catcher] Eddie Perez told me a great story about Maddux. They're at a pregame meeting and they're going to face Houston in the Dome. Greg says, "I don't have enough to pitch on the inner half of the plate against Jeff Bagwell. I just can't do it. I don't have enough to get him there."

So he's got a one-hitter in the eighth inning and he's winning by, like, eight runs. Maddux always calls the pitches, and this time Bagwell comes up, Maddux throws a fastball in, and Bagwell hits it out. After the inning, Eddie says to him, "You've got a one-hit shutout. What are you doing? You told me you didn't want to come in there to Bagwell."

Maddux says, "My next start is against them. What do I care about shutouts? Stats like that are meaningless."

Sure enough, next game, seventh inning, bases loaded, two outs, he strikes out Bagwell on three straight changeups. Maddux told Eddie, "Hitters only remember what they hit, not what they didn't hit."

Maddux, he's the best.

GAME 59

Thursday, June 10, 2004 . . . Cubs 12, Cardinals 3 . . . Wrigley Field . . . Stuff: Dusty Baker and Tony LaRussa are the oil and water of the big leagues. It isn't much of a secret that they can't stand each other. So what does LaRussa do today? Waits until 30 minutes before the first pitch to inform the Cubs that Danny Haren, called up from the Triple-A club, would replace Jason Marquis as the Cards' starting pitcher. The breach of etiquette isn't anything new. LaRussa has done this to Baker in previous games. . . . Sammy Sosa changes his mind and now says he'll make three rehab appearances before returning to the active roster. His Samminess also tells reporters: "They need me, no question about it. You don't know what you got until you lose it." Just what his teammates need to hear these days.

So here now is the never-before-told story of how Frank Maloney became the most successful ticket salesman in Cubs history:

Luck.

Wait a second. Before the first Wrigley turnstile even budged in 2004 the Cubs had sold about 2.8 million tickets. In three days alone, they sold 737,000 single-game tickets, which nearly tripled the previous Major League record—held, surprise, by the Cubs. Subtract the comp tickets the team supplies to players, coaching staffs, scouts, umpires, sponsors, and the assorted celeb, and you're looking at an average of about 2,500 seats available for any given home game. Of course, if the Cardinals, Milwaukee Brewers, White Sox, or Astros are in town, forget it. That 2,500 drops to zero.

So luck? Please. It's not like Maloney was, say, a career football coach who applied for a commercial paper industry job and instead became the Cubs' director of ticket operations, even though he had no experience in the business.

Oh, wait, that's exactly what happened.

Maloney, who is as South Side Irish as a rendition of "Danny Boy," played football at Michigan, was head coach at Mt. Carmel High School for five seasons, spent six years on Bo Schembechler's staff in Ann Arbor, and then in 1974 became head coach at Syracuse, where he won 32 games in seven seasons. His Syracuse staff included Nick Saban, owner of a national championship at LSU; Jerry Angelo, general manager of the Chicago

Bears; Tom Coughlin, head coach of the New York Giants; and George O'Leary, head coach of Central Florida.

"I did a better job of getting coaches than players," says Maloney.

Maloney is modest that way. I looked it up: He beat Bobby Bowden, Howard Schnellenberger, Don James, Don Nehlen, Larry Smith, and George Welsh, among others. By the way, the Carrier Dome wasn't available until his final season at Syracuse, which means he didn't have much to sell to recruits, other than one of the worst facilities in the country (weary Archbold Stadium) and snow up to your chinstrap. Still, he and his staff discovered hidden gems such as Art Monk, Gary Anderson, and Joe Morris.

Syracuse thanked him with a pink slip after a 5-6 record in 1980. He was 40 years old, burned out on football, and had a young family to support.

Gil Brandt gave him a scouting job with the Dallas Cowboys, but Maloney was trolling for something else. A friend suggested he interview for a job with a commercial paper business run by Chicagoan Andrew McKenna. Near the end of the interview, McKenna asked, "How would you like to work for the Chicago Cubs?"

"Gee," said Maloney, "that would be interesting."

Yes, it would be, especially since McKenna didn't own the Cubs. The Wrigley family did.

"I'll tell you what," said McKenna. "Think about it for a couple of days and then give me a call."

That afternoon, the announcement was made: The Tribune Company had purchased the Cubs. McKenna would be the CEO.

Maloney was hired as director of group sales in 1981, was promoted to director of ticket sales in 1984, and bumped to director of ticket operations in 1987.

"A one-in-a-billion shot," he says.

Relatively speaking, the Cubs couldn't draw green flies in 1982—1.24 million. The year before, they sold only about 2,000 season tickets. It wasn't unusual for the upper deck to be closed.

"Then 1984 came and this world changed forever," Maloney says.

The Cubs won the NL East. Attendance climbed to 2.1 million. But there was more to it than that. WGN became a powerful sales tool. So did Harry Caray. So did a revitalized Wrigleyville area. Cubs tickets soon became hotter than a swig of Tabasco sauce.

Maloney could have tried coaching again. Then-Green Bay Packers coach Bart Starr called Maloney at his mother-in-law's house in 1983 and offered an assistant's job. Maloney was flattered but turned it down. He was a Cubs man, so much so that he often wears the red-jeweled ring given to him when the Cubs hosted the 1990 All-Star Game. He rotates it with his four Big Ten championship rings won at Michigan.

For a 1:20 start such as the one against the Cardinals, Maloney pulls his Ford Taurus into the Wrigley lot by 7 A.M. The ticket windows open at 8, so he checks the game status and what tickets are available (fat chance for the Cards), including obstructed-view seats.

The Cardinals start arriving soon thereafter, so Maloney arranges their comps. Generally speaking, 250 prime tickets are given to a visiting team. If the players want more (they usually get six apiece), they'll have to settle for standing-room-only space.

Maloney is constantly on his office computer monitoring the ticket sales and phone orders. His phone is ringing more than Westminster Abbey. Maloney lets the calls go to voice mail and listens to them then. About 50 percent of the calls are problems or complaints. Typical.

Did you know the ticket window personnel are union? Maloney didn't, until he had to start managing that workforce.

"They do every event in town," says Maloney. "They can do us during the day, and then might be at the Shubert Theatre selling tickets that night."

Did you know absolutely no one has asked Maloney to sell them a ticket for the infamous Steve Bartman seat? Maloney doesn't even know the exact location of the seat, other than to say it's in Aisle 4, and that the Cubs organization is trying to move forward Bartman-wise.

Maloney doesn't see an inning of the game live. It's on the office TV, but that's it for sights and sounds. In fact, except for the playoffs in 2003, Maloney hasn't seen more than four or so innings live during an entire season. Too busy, especially today.

The Cardinals are box-office gold. "I wish we played them in the middle of the week every time," he says.

Brewers fans also make a Cheesehead Express for Wrigley. The Astros draw a nice crowd, as do the Los Angeles Dodgers and the San Francicso Giants. "Bonds," says Maloney of Barry.

On occasion, Maloney will get the celeb call for tickets. Comedian Tom Dreesen has been a regular, as has Tom Bosley of *Happy Days* fame. Bill Murray used to call himself, but that was more than 10 years ago. Former Notre Dame coach Ara Parseghian has visited with Maloney. The same goes for former Ohio State coach John Cooper, Syracuse hoops coach Jim Boeheim, and Northern Illinois football coach Joe Novak, whom Maloney tried to hire when he was at the 'Cuse. Novak said no.

There's bookeeping to be done, so Maloney "reconciles" the day's take. Everything has to be accounted for: group sales, walk-up sales at the windows. In 2003, that meant somewhere between $200,000 and $300,000 at a home game. That number has dropped in '04, simply because there are fewer daily tickets available.

Maloney is in the leased Taurus by 5 P.M. Before he leaves, he goes George Bailey on me.

"I've got zero regrets," he says of his career choice. "I've had a wonderful life."

GAME 60

Friday, June 11, 2004 . . . Anaheim Angels 3, Cubs 2 . . . Angel Stadium . . . Stuff: The Cubs announce that Joe Borowski has a tear in his right rotator cuff and won't be back until at least August. . . . Kansas City GM Allard Baird says star outfielder Carlos Beltran is available—for the right price. Will the Cubs make an offer?

Robert Haddad was born and raised in New York, adores the Yankees, and now lives in Jersey City, New Jersey. So, of course, New York-based Major League Baseball Productions assigned him to film and produce a DVD on the *Cubs'* 2004 season?

I've seen the bearded Haddad, 27, and his crew of one or two freelancers skulking about since Opening Day in Cincinnati. They do so with the blessings of John McDonough, the team's newly promoted senior VP of marketing and broadcasting. If all goes well, Haddad has until November 15 to deliver an hourlong DVD. If the Cubs are in trouble by the All-Star break, McDonough can pull the plug on the project. So injuries galore and a record only two games over .500 isn't exactly what Haddad was hoping for.

In the meantime, Haddad is shooting enough digital video and high-def footage on his $3,000 camera to fill a cargo plane. He doesn't have it easy. That blue MLB Productions golf shirt and clubhouse pass he wears buys only so much credibility. He wants access and candid moments. The players, always suspicious of outsiders, aren't sure if he'll embarrass them. Ballplayers hate to be embarrassed. It's in their DNA. And even though the project was greenlighted by the powerful McDonough, Haddad still finds himself negotiating/semi-begging for a chance to bring his camera onto the team charter plane or bus (a polite no, so far).

"To be able to trust someone that they're only going to show what's relevant, that they're going to use good judgment, that's difficult," Haddad says. "It's hard to put trust into one person. Honestly, there have been people in the past who have been burned, not necessarily by Major League Baseball, but it's happened. You know, someone put a live wire on them and then caught them cursing on TV."

Haddad doesn't have a *Lord of the Rings* budget. Sometimes he and his sometimes crew look like they are a straight-out-of-junior-college audiovisual class. Or maybe that's part of Haddad's plan: the more nonthreatening, the better. He has a little more than 50 hours of tape in the can right now. If the project makes it past the All-Star break, he'll finish the regular season with another 150 hours of footage, and another 100 hours if they reach the playoffs. That's about 300 hours of tape . . . for a one-hour DVD.

During Haddad's lifetime, the Yankees have won six World Series and nine pennants. The Cubs have won zilch and bupkus. So how in the name of Leon Durham can Haddad understand the mentality of this franchise?

"I don't know if I have a theme to this season, but I think there's an idea," he says. "I guess the story line right now would be building on the success of last year. And how do you build on the success of last year when you were five outs away from the World Series? That's my outlook: This is a team with potential. Some people call them the Lovable Losers, but there's more to it than that."

OK, the New Yorker gets it. And now I know why.

"Ryne Sandberg was one of my favorite players growing up," Haddad says. "Every time the Cubs played the Mets, I'd watch some of the game. Just to watch him."

Ah, another victim of 1984. He understands.

GAME 61

Saturday, June 12, 2004 . . . Cubs 10, Angels 5 . . . Angel Stadium . . . Stat of the game: The Cubs pick on the portly Bartolo Colon, who left the White Sox for a four-year, $51-million deal with Anaheim. Colon now hasn't won since April 22. . . .

Stuff: Glendon Rusch, a small lifesaver during Kerry Wood's absence, improves to 3-1.

You probably don't remember Scott McClain. He was just a nonroster invitee, spring training filler (jersey No. 71), a 31-year-old long shot with just 20 career big league at-bats.

And then he started hitting.

As March inched toward Opening Day, McClain started to give GM Jim Hendry and Dusty Baker something to think about. In 48 at-bats he had six home runs, 16 RBI, five doubles, 11 runs, and a .333 average. He wasn't going to start ahead of Derrek Lee or Aramis Ramirez, but McClain could come off the bench and hit with power.

It doesn't happen often, but even Cubs front-office types were pulling for the likable McClain to make the final 25-man roster. What a nice story: former 22nd-round pick who spent almost his entire career in the minors or Japan makes the Cubs' big club.

Instead, there was a line of agate in your April 2 newspaper: *P Bryan Corey and IF Scott McClain returned to minor league camp.*

Turns out McClain was the next-to-last cut. Soon thereafter, he and his wife, Jennifer, made the long flight to Tokyo. McClain was a Seibu Tiger again.

We e-mail each other for a few weeks and finally set a date: June 12. Sure enough, my phone rings this morning at 8:30 Chicago time, 10:30 P.M. Tokyo time. McClain is calling from his four-bedroom apartment.

I Google the latest information I can find on the Seibu Tigers. They're 37-23-1 (yes, ties). You can buy an authentic Seibu cap for $150, a game uni for $380, and a Kazuo Matsui (a former Tigers star now with the New York Mets) for $42. And now the bad news: McClain was recently sent to Seibu's minor league team.

Not quite sure what to say, I manage a "How's it going?"

"It's not going," he says. "It's kind of a funny thing. It's like they needed me over here in such a rush. Then I couldn't play for two weeks because I didn't have a visa. I sat around for two weeks. Finally, I got in there about three weeks later. I felt like I kept my swing, was getting some hits, was starting to get hot—and then they started sitting me. They had some young guys doing really well. So I started pinch-hitting every four, five days, but I never really got it going. Then they sent me to the minor league."

There is no anger in his voice. McClain, jersey No. 00 with Seibu, knows the Japanese pro leagues are a riddle wrapped in cowhide. This is his fourth season in Japan, and while the money is good (with incentives he could earn as much as $600,000), the baseball logic is sometimes incomprehensible.

Only four foreigners (*gaijin*) are allowed on each team. McClain, the only American on the roster, was replaced by Venezuelan Alex Cabrera.

"Nothing over here amazes me," he says. "I had agreed I would go down once Cabrera had gotten back [from the States]. I would kind of be an insurance policy, or what have you. But they sent me down before he's even back. They're winning right now with Japanese guys, so there's not much I can say. But anything they do over here doesn't surprise me. It's not for everyone. It's not just seeing the ball, hitting the ball."

There is no laughing in the clubhouse. You practice constantly. There is no margin for error, especially if you're a foreign player.

McClain was sent down after only 49 at-bats (he was hitting .204 with two homers, five RBI, six walks, eight runs, 15 strikeouts).

"Jen, how many times do you think I started this year?" he asks his wife. Pause. "She says maybe six, seven times. It was really kind of weird. I started the first two games, hit the ball all right: 0-for-3 the first game, 1-for-3 the second game, but they pinch-hit for me. Then I sat for a game or two, then they started me and I hit a home run. So then they sat me the next day. Then I got in and hit a home run—went 2-for-4—then the next day I'm sitting again. Then I go 0-for-3. Then I didn't play for a long time after that.

"You bite your lip, roll with the punches. What I tell foreigners is to erase the word *why* from your vocabulary. Some things will amaze you and nobody will have an answer about it. I'd ask, 'Why wouldn't you do it this way?' And they'd say, 'I don't really know. This is the way we do it.'"

McClain didn't want to return to Japan in 2004, but he didn't have much of a choice. He could accept Seibu's attractive money offer, or try to get by on Iowa Cubs wages and hope for a break with the big league club. He chose the semi-sure thing in Japan.

Of course, who knew position players Sammy Sosa, Alex Gonzalez, and Mark Grudzielanek would get injured and the Cubs eventually would pull guys from Triple-A?

"I read the newspapers a little bit and know what [the Cubs] do every couple games," McClain says. "I know if they're winning, where they are in the standings. I know they've had injuries. But I don't ever sit there and say, 'If I'd stayed, that would have been me.' The thing is, I don't have the time to hit in Triple-A and wait for an opportunity that may never come."

McClain roots for the Cubs, for Baker, and for his Tucson-trip busmates Michael Barrett, Paul Bako, Todd Hollandsworth, and Todd Walker. Baker is the guy who gave him an actual chance, rather than the usual garbage time for a nonroster invitee.

"He kept running me out there, let me get hot," says McClain. "He told me, 'Keep swinging the bat. Keep the fans on your side. Make it difficult.'"

McClain made it difficult. In the end, the Cubs couldn't find a place on the 25-man roster, and McClain couldn't wait for a better offer.

"The way things were going, I was enjoying American baseball," he says. "Yeah, I wanted to be on the Cubs. I wanted to help them be in the World Series. That was the ultimate plan: to get some sort of call-up and play in the World Series."

Their Tokyo apartment has satellite TV, so the McClains can watch Fox News and ESPN. They e-mail, or simply call friends and family back in the States. The Japanese League playoffs begin in October, but who knows if McClain will be with the Seibu big club by then.

Earlier today, the Tigers' minor league team won, 8-7, in the ninth inning. McClain went 0-for-2 with a sacrifice fly. He probably won't be asked back to Seibu in 2005.

That's OK. He'll be 32 come the next spring training camp. He has just one favor to ask of big league GMs.

Remember him.

GAME 62

Sunday, June 13, 2004 . . . Cubs 6, Angels 5 . . . Angel Stadium . . . Stat of the game: The Cubs play their longest game of the season: 5 hours, 8 minutes. Stuff: Jon Leicester, recently promoted from the minors because he could chew up innings in relief, earns his first big league win by holding the Angels scoreless in the 13th, 14th, and decisive 15th inning. He gets the traditional shaving cream pie in the face during a postgame interview. . . . Cubs and Angels starters and relievers combine for 499 pitches. . . . Ron Santo, who isn't on the Anaheim part of the road trip, watches the game at home with his wife. When the Cubs win in the 15th, he tells his wife, Vicki, to expect a long win streak, maybe even a sweep in Houston. . . . Record since Sosa sneeze: 12-14.

Lemon Tom Goodwin, 35, pinch-hits for shortstop Rey Ordonez in the 11th inning. He grounds out. That's his one at-bat in a five-hour, eight-minute game. Such is life as a backup.

I'm a bench player. I became a bench player in the second half of 2001.

In this job, you plan on *not* knowing when you're going in the game. Actually, Dusty does a good job of letting us know two, three days before the game that we're going to [start]. That way you're just not guessing when you'll go in. But pinch-hitting is different.

The difficult part of pinch-hitting late is this: We don't have too much tape of relievers. Basically, you go by scouting reports: what they've thrown the last couple of times out, what you've done against certain guys who might be similar to who you might be facing tonight. Things like that. After that, it's still about going up there and getting a pitch to hit. You shorten it down and keep it as simple as you can.

What I do, you can't worry about "Well, the next time I'll do better." The next time might never come, so you've got to be ready to go that one time. You really have to focus on that one at-bat and simplify things as much as you can.

Honestly, the good thing and the fun thing about this team is that—and I don't want to jinx this [he knocks on his wooden locker]—but with our pitching staff we're usually in every game. So there's not a lot of blowout games, or a lot of games where you're going to face a long reliever. It's usually going to be a setup man, a specialty reliever: a left-handed specialty, or closer. So we have to come in prepared.

Most of us on this bench used to play all the time at some time. [Todd] Hollandsworth. Myself. Ordonez. Ramon is probably the only one who hadn't played every day, but he has a lot of time in. The guy who hadn't played the most every day is now the guy playing the most every day.

I really didn't have that much interest going on as far as offers [he was signed as a minor league free agent in January 2003]. Honestly, once you find a manager like Dusty. . . you trust him, he trusts you. He's only after it for one thing. He doesn't care about accolades. He doesn't care about Manager of the Year, Manager of the Week. He wants to win as bad as anybody.

GAME 63

Monday, June 14, 2004 . . . Cubs 7, Astros 2 . . . Minute Maid Park . . . NL Central pennant flies: Tie-Second (34-29) . . . Stuff: Twelve-year-old Michael McHugh of nearby Friendswood Junior High is the best bargain in sports journalism. The stone-faced McHugh, who gets $15 a story for the nearby Friendswood Reporter News, *has already scored a one-on-one interview with the media-distant Barry Bonds. Today he gets a bemused Greg Maddux to answer his list of typed questions (Maddux says Bonds is the toughest batter he's faced). . . . Sammy Sosa injury update: He'll be back Friday (he goes 1-for-4 in his second rehab start). . . . Only at Minute Maid Park can you get the latest natural gas, crude oil, unleaded gas, and heating oil prices on the stadium scoreboard.*

Maybe it means something, maybe it doesn't, but nearly two and a half hours before tonight's game you could find Mark Prior and Maddux sitting together in the corner of the visitors' clubhouse watching a DVD of Astros hitters on a laptop. Matt Clement crouched down to watch a few minutes of the footage, but this was mostly a viewing audience of the 23-year-old Prior and the 38-year-old Maddux.

They didn't say much. They didn't have to; the hitters do most of the talking without knowing it. Prior, who started tonight, and Maddux, who starts Tuesday evening, were looking for Astros tendencies on certain pitch counts, for holes in their swings, for subtle strengths and weaknesses. It is more art than science, which probably explains why Prior pulled up one of those wooden director's chairs and sat next to Maddux, the master artist.

And perhaps it's time to buy into the premonitions of Baker, who told reporters in a pregame interview session to expect the best when Prior faced Clemens in front of the 10th Astros sellout of the season. "You got a young lion versus an experienced lion," Baker said. "Mark's going to rise to the occasion, I think. I'm not worried about Mark."

Young lion went five-plus innings, struck out eight, gave up five hits and zilcho runs. Experienced lion took it in the compression shorts (six innings, five runs, 10 hits, first loss).

"Tonight for me was more personal," Prior says afterward as Staind's appropriately titled "It's Been Awhile" plays on the clubhouse sound system. "I wanted to really make some improvements off my last outing [a dreadful 83-pitch appearance against the Cardinals]. It was more determination, kind of a personal battle with myself."

Prior vs. Prior. Now, there's a ticket worth scalping.

"He definitely threw the ball better tonight," says catcher Paul Bako. "[He threw] as well as he threw during the second half of last year."

That could be some well-meaning Bako hyperbole. We'll see. After all, Prior went 10-1 with a 1.52 ERA after a stay on the disabled list during the second half of the 2003 season. Then again . . .

"I think it was pretty close, as good as I felt since last year," says Prior.

Meanwhile, pitching coach Larry Rothschild grabs a roll and a plate of salad from the postgame spread and takes a seat in front of the VCR/TV unit. As he does after every game, he fast-forwards to each Cubs pitch.

Maddux, whose locker is near the monitor, starts watching too. Prior stops by minutes later.

Maybe it means something, maybe it doesn't.

GAME 64

Tuesday, June 15, 2004 . . . Cubs 4, Astros 2 . . . Minute Maid Park . . . Stat of the game: Dusty Baker turns 55. The Cubs give him a come-from-behind victory as a birthday present. . . . Stuff: The emotional Carlos Zambrano throws a major hissy fit when Todd Walker fails to double up Jason Lane at second. The knucklehead moment by Zambrano doesn't go unnoticed by the other Cubs players.

Ramon Martinez made his 32nd start of the season at shortstop tonight, which isn't exactly what the Cubs had in mind for 2004. Of course, they also didn't figure on Alex Gonzalez breaking a wrist bone or Mark Grudzielanek injuring his Achilles tendon.

So here is Martinez—so coveted by the Kansas City Royals in 1993 that they gave him tip money ($4,000) as a signing bonus—starting half the games for a Cubs team picked by many to win the World Series. Not only that, but he cranks his first home run in more than a year and then delivers a game-winning, bases-loaded, two-out, two-run single in the ninth against the stunned Astros. And then he ends the game by going deep in the hole and throwing out Morgan Ensberg.

Afterward, Martinez provides a detailed explanation of his first homer since June 8, 2003, and his .404 average at Minute Maid Park: "That's baseball. That's something I cannot explain."

OK, how about that career batting average in the high .300s with the bases loaded?

"That's something that I cannot explain," he says.

All anyone knows for sure is that the Cubs have won four consecutive games, all of them on the road. There are assorted reasons for the streak, but no list is complete without mentioning the 31-year-old Martinez, who played for Baker in San Francisco and came to Chicago in 2003 as a reserve.

Martinez is a Baker favorite because he's versatile, his hands are as soft as pizza dough, he doesn't bitch about playing time, and he isn't scared of big moments. Nor is it an accident that Martinez spends a lot of time with young Aramis Ramirez, and that Ramirez is becoming a pro's pro.

"A lot of people would love to have [Martinez]," says Baker. "A lot of people."

Martinez is here for one reason.

"Because of Dusty," he says. "He just told me to give Chicago a chance to match whatever offer I had out there [in 1993]."

Martinez is as flamboyant as a white, button-down shirt. He is a worker bee. He loves his pug named Buca, his Puerto Rico, his family, his girlfriend, and baseball. Chicago is earning a spot in his heart too.

"Great fans," he says. "I think all players should play one year in Chicago."

Reporters don't often visit his locker, but tonight they did. The laidback Martinez could only shrug his shoulders and say, "You just got to react. See the ball and hit it."

A few feet away is Gonzalez's locker. Gonzalez, who recently had his cast removed, is taking ground balls again. It won't be long before he replaces Martinez in the lineup.

"I'll go back to a utility role," Martinez says. "I'll prepare myself mentally."

He isn't in a hurry to give up his starting spot, but he'll do as Baker asks. For Martinez, it is always team first. And if you have to ask why, you're in for a long wait.

That's something he cannot explain.

GAME 65

Wednesday, June 16, 2004 ... Cubs 4, Astros 1 ... Minute Maid Park ... Stuff: About an hour after the game, someone emerges from the Cubs' dugout in street clothes (jeans, Hawaiian print shirt) and walks in the semidarkness to the tarp-covered pitcher's mound. "Who is that?" says someone in the press box. I squint. "It's Maddux," I say. And here's what he's doing after winning career No. 295: He has a cell phone to one ear, a plastic drink cup in his hand, and while talking on the phone he begins to simulate the beginnings of a windup. Typical Maddux. What a perfectionist.

Corey Patterson goes 2-for-4, including a bunt single that leads to the tying run in the seventh inning. He also triples and scores in the eighth inning, and makes a marvelous, inning-ending catch on a ball hit by Astros third baseman Morgan Ensberg.

Patterson is hitting only .267, but it beats the .246 batting average of 10 games ago. The strikeouts and the boos are coming less regularly at home now, but they still come. So do the wisecracks from beat reporters, columnists, and authors (guilty).

I ask Patterson if he has a few minutes. The former No. 3 overall pick in 1998 disappears into the players' lounge, pours himself a cup of coffee, and leads me outside the clubhouse.

"Go ahead," he says.

Q: *I take it you never got booed in Little League, high school, or the minors. So what's it like the first time you got booed as a Cub?*
Patterson: Honestly, it didn't really bother me because—obviously, you hear it, but you don't. You're putting pressure on yourself and thinking about what you're doing rather than focusing on what's going on in your environment. You put attention on something else. To be honest, the crowd really has no effect on how I'm feeling or how I'm doing. Anybody who plays sports, you're your own worst enemy, your own worst critic. What I try to do is divert my attention to something else.

Q: *For whatever reason—and perhaps it's your demeanor on the field—Cubs fans don't seem to be able to wrap their arms around you. Have you sensed that?*

Patterson: Just because I don't show a lot of emotion, nobody knows what's going on inside. You can try to show physically, "Hey, I'm this way" [he makes an intense face], but deep down inside you're not going to fool yourself. It's about knowing yourself, the kind of player you are, and learning how to be on an even keel. You've got to act the same whether you're going good or bad. That's what I try to do. A lot of times my physical appearance might be the same, but mentally I'm not thinking the same thing. And no one knows that but me.

Q: *Does it matter if fans know you, like you?*
Patterson: I know there's some fans out there who are pulling for me, and I really appreciate that. Whatever they want to do—boo, cheer—it doesn't really matter.

I play for my teammates. Of course, the fans, too, the ones who care and really know what's going on. I think there are some people who don't have a grasp of it and don't know what's really going on. They're just reacting to what they see. They don't know why it happened. They don't know what that person is feeling.

Q: *Don't you think the strikeouts are the main reason for the boos?*
Patterson: It [strikeouts] happened a couple times to other players, too, during the course of a few years, and I haven't really heard them boo anybody. That's why I don't understand sometimes why.

Q: *You've been bunting the ball more. Why?*
Patterson: Before, I'd bunt the ball and the pitcher or third baseman would make a pretty decent play on a bunt. I'd get pissed off and I wouldn't want to do it again. A wasted at-bat. Really, now that's not my attitude. I really do it to see the ball. And I'm thinking about the right things, instead of thinking about "Oh, what am I doing wrong?"

Q: *Even with the knee injury, the surgery, and the rehab of 2003, has this season been more difficult?*
Patterson: I think so, more from a mental standpoint. Of course, I had that little stretch where things weren't going so well for me. So you're going to try so hard, you're going to fight your way out of it. Sometimes the harder you try, the worse it makes things.

But everything that has happened in my career so far, I wouldn't change a thing. When it's all said and done, you can say, "I've been booed. I've been cheered. I've struck out with the game-winning run on third base. I got the game-winning hit. I went through, I don't know, salary arbitration. I went through trade talks." It's just one thing after another. When it's all said and done, I wouldn't change one thing.

GAME 66

Thursday, June 17, 2004 . . . Cubs 5, Astros 4 . . . Minute Maid Park . . . Cubs NL Central pennant flies: Tie-Second (37-29) . . . Stat of the game: Glendon Rusch, professional godsend, improves to 4-1. This from a guy who went 1-12 last season. . . . Stuff: The Cubs tie their longest win streak of the season (six) and finish with their best road victory streak since 1991. By the way, the Astros kind of suck right now. . . . Record since Sosa sneeze: 16-14. Sosa returns to the lineup Friday and will soon discover this isn't his team anymore. It now belongs to the pitching staff. . . . It's only mid-June, but the Cubs are scoreboard watching. They gather around the clubhouse TV to watch Oakland gag away a ninth-inning lead against the NL Central-leading Cardinals.

LaTroy Hawkins has barely talked to the media since his nutty press conference (arranged, oddly enough, by the Cubs) to announce he was lowering the cone of silence. Meanwhile, the earth continues to spin on its axis, Baker still chews on toothpicks, and Paris Hilton remains famous for reasons unknown. In other words, life goes on, which was Hawkins's point in the first place.

Hawkins has one of the great scowls in baseball, but he also has one of the great smiles—when he shows it. Somewhere in between is a personality that doesn't care what you think, and absolutely doesn't care if he sees another Minicam or tape recorder anytime soon.

About a month earlier, I had spoken to him about an interview. I wanted to know who taught him how to be a pro. Not a ballplayer, but a big leaguer. There's a difference.

So I approach his locker and remind him of the previous interview request. Will I be done in by the cone?

"Yeah, I remember," he says. "OK, let's do it."

Hawkins unplugged:

As a kid, I learned about baseball by watching the Cubs on TV. That got me in the game. Growing up in Indiana, we always loved watching them on television. We couldn't get the Sox games. If they'd been on TV as much as the Cubs, I'd probably been a White Sox fan. But they weren't, so I was a Cubs fan big time.

My brother and me, we'd go outside and play as kids. I was always Leon Durham. His nickname was "The Bull," and I liked it when he hit a home run.

I liked to be Fergie Jenkins when I pitched. I had to be Fergie. In fact, we talked at spring training this year. I'm a big-time Jenkins fan. When I pitched, I was Fergie Jenkins. When I was a position player, I was Leon the Bull.

I went to one Cubs game. It was when my Little League went. I was eight. It was the only time I'd been to a Major League stadium before I played in one.

I was 18 when I signed. I was right out of high school. Scared? No. If it hadn't worked out, I would have gone to college. I would have gone back and tried to play basketball, probably at Indiana State. Had it been later, I could have gone back to school and started a regular life.

The first time I could do this for a living was 1993, in A-ball [at Fort Wayne]. I had a real shitty first month of the season. But as soon as the weather warmed, everything just clicked. I just started having success [he led the league in wins, ERA, shutouts, and strikeouts that year]. I said, "OK, I can do this."

In the minors, it's tough. In rookie ball and extended spring, it's tough, because you don't have too many older guys around you.

In Minnesota [Hawkins spent seven-plus seasons with the Twins], I played with Kirby Puckett. I played with Paul Molitor and Bob Tewksbury. [Kent] Hrbek was around. [Harmon] Killibrew was around. Tony Oliva was around all the time. And there was [Twins manager] Tom Kelly. Tom Kelly is No. 1 on that list.

T. K. always stressed respecting the game. Win or lose, respect the game. You need to be able to look yourself in the mirror and know you gave 110 percent. Don't cheat yourself and don't cheat the game.

Actually, talking to Moli was good for me. He'd always say, "You guys can talk to me, because I'm a hitter. I know what goes through our minds. I don't know what goes through a pitcher's mind, but I know what's going through our minds." We talked to Moli a lot about hitting. We talked a lot about a lot of things. He's the greatest. Moli is a good, good dude. He showed how you carry yourself on and off the field. Definitely a professional.

Kirby too. He got in some trouble off the field. But when he was playing, when he was between the lines, a model citizen. They can say what they want to about Puck, but when he played, he played hard.

Moli and Puck. I played with two Hall of Famers.

Sergio Mitre . . . I took him under my wing. I just tried to explain the game to him: how a rookie is supposed to carry himself, that you represent your team, your family, yourself—when you're at the ballpark and even if you're not at the ballpark.

You don't think about these things when you first get here. You get so caught up in finally just getting here—your dreams come true—that you forget about the little things that go along with it.

That's what I would always tell Sergio. I said, "Sergio, you're so quiet. Sergio, nobody in our clubhouse knows you as a person." But that's how rookies are. I know him because I met him at the Cubs Convention, talked to him in spring training, went to dinner with him. The first two months of the season, I hung out with him a lot. I knew Sergio.

I think a lot of guys in the clubhouse—I don't think they know Sergio. He didn't go out of his way to let people get to know him. I'd tell him, "Man, let your teammates know what you're thinking. I hate using the term—but it's just a term, OK?—but if I have to go to war, I want him, him, and him with me. But we don't know you, Sergio, because we don't know what you're thinking."

The thing is, where did he come up from, Double-A? That's a big jump. That's a big jump. I was always telling him that when I came up to the big leagues, we were terrible. I had a chance to suck. He came to a team where we're expected to win, so he had no room for error. No room for error.

I talked to him this past Saturday. I said, "See you soon."

A lot of young guys, they don't respect the game. They don't respect the veteran players. I don't know why. It's the era, I guess. When I came up, when I was learning, it was total respect.

When you're a rookie, you have to carry other guys' bags. Other than that, it's pretty easy. When I was a rookie, we had to carry bags and stuff.

Chuck Knoblauch made us wear red Reeboks for two weeks. On the road, when we were away from the stadium, we had to wear red Reeboks for two weeks.

Last year in Minnesota, we made all the rookies dress up in Hooters outfits. I've had some instances where I've had some cut pants, but the thing is, don't get too mad. [Baseball tradition: Rookies get their shirt-sleeves and pant legs cut on at least one getaway day.] You can't get too mad, because if you do, they're going to pick on you. They're *going* to pick on you. Just roll with the punches. It's all fun and games. If you can't take a joke, you're in the wrong sport.

[Laughing] **You're talking to *me* about dealing with the media?** I played with guys—Moli, Puck—who were great with the media. Those are every-day players, too. Just being a pitcher—I'm not saying we're not that impor-tant—I'm just saying why do you need to talk to the setup man?

Don't judge me until you've walked a mile in my shoes. Like I told the media here, I can do what you do, you can't do what I do. I can go to school to be a journalist, writer, write a column, right? I can go to school to learn that, right? But you can't go to school to learn how to throw a 95-mph fast-ball.

[I remind him that I can blow a save just as easily as he can.] You sure can. You sure can. But you got to get to this point first. You can't get to this point without getting out of the Gulf Coast League, rookie ball. I started at the bottom.

I don't want to be the center of attention. I don't. Let me do my job and go home. We got guys working their asses off every game, getting four, five at-bats a night. Talk to those guys. I understand sometimes that I need to talk, but let me talk when I'm ready to talk. When I'm sitting at my locker icing my arm and I turn around and there's 50 people standing around me, where they got me surrounded and I can't move—I don't like that. I'll let you know when I'm ready to talk. But don't be standing around me.

It was totally different [in Minnesota]. But I had a different relation-ship. I didn't like the media in Minnesota. I had one person I talked to and that was [*Minneapolis Star-Tribune* reporter] Jim Souhan. One person, be-cause I couldn't trust nobody else.

Souhan was consistent. That's all I ask. Just don't be writing about me when something goes wrong. If you're going to blast me in the paper, that's fine. You're entitled to write what you want. At least say, "How you doing today?" But don't, when you see me, go tucking your tail and run like a bitch.

I'm different. I'm different from everybody else. I'm a unique fella.

They should know we're fucking crazy, so leave us alone. If I was sane, I'd still be starting.

GAME 67

Friday, June 18, 2004 . . . Oakland Athletics 2, Cubs 1 . . . Wrigley Field . . . Cubs NL Central pennant flies: Tie-Second (37-30) . . . Stuff: ESPN's Tim Kurkjian, one of the best baseball writers who ever tapped a keyboard, offers his early NL All-Star choices. There isn't a single Cub on his list of starters (fair enough) or short list of candidates (no Aramis Ramirez?). . . . The Curse in Reverse: Florida Marlin starter Josh Beckett is hurt again. . . . Tribune baseball writer Phil Rogers determines, through assorted statistical analyses, that Sosa is worth about two victories per season. . . . The Cubs unveil architectural drawings for a proposed multipurpose building/parking garage next to Wrigley.

Sammy Sosa returns to the lineup for the first time since May 15. Baker has dropped him from his pre-sneeze place in the order (third) to cleanup.

11:04 His Samminess emerges from the dugout carrying two bats and walks slowly across the field to the batting cage under the right-field bleachers. Sosa is going casual during the pregame batting session, wearing a Cubs T-shirt, shorts, blue socks, cross-trainers, and the usual Sammy assortment of wristbands.

11:46 Sosa meets the press.

Was the rehab at the Cubs' Double-A team in Jackson, Tennessee, necessary?

"I've always been a great hitter, but I decided to go to the minor leagues because I wanted to be ready from the first day. . . . But I went down there to make sure everything is OK. I'm happy to be back. I'm ready to go."

The last time you hit cleanup?

"I don't really remember. I'll probably hit fourth not for long, until I get back in a groove."

Is your customary beeline to right on the agenda, what with the just-healed back and all?

"I don't think the sprint to right field will do nothing to me."

Thoughts on sub Todd Hollandsworth?

"I've got to give him credit. He did a great job and represented very well. I'm very happy about it. I'm back."

Thoughts on the recent Cubs road trip?

"They played very well, no question about it. I want to come back and do my job. Everybody got to . . . continue and do good. Now that I'm in the lineup, we have to feel more happy. We're back together."

Do you enjoy the country life of Jackson?

"I'm a city boy."

12-ish Salsa music plays again on the Sosa end of the clubhouse.

1:21 Sosa sprints to right field. The bleacher crowd responds with the usual "Sam-my! Sam-my!"

2:39 The PA announcer introduces Sosa as he makes his way to the batter's box in the bottom of the first with two outs and Michael Barrett on second. Sosa taps home plate umpire Mark Wegner with the knob of the bat and then does his usual maintenance work—digging a hole the size of an irrigation ditch near the back of the box with his cleats.

The at-bat:

Foul ball . . . swing and a miss . . . ball high . . . ball inside . . . ball inside, wild pitch, Barrett to third . . . swing and a miss. Strikeout.

2:48 Bobby Kielty lines a ball deep to Sosa, who makes a nice catch.

3:04 Sosa watches Mark Kotsay's home run clear the right-field fence. Moments later, the ball sails back over his head and toward the infield.

3:26 Sosa again, this time in the fourth inning with two outs, nobody on: strike called . . . soft liner to right for the final out.

4:04 Two outs, none on in the sixth for Sosa.

Called strike . . . called strike . . . foul to right . . . strikeout swinging.

5:00 The A's lead, 2-1, in the bottom of the ninth. There are two outs, none on. Sosa is up. The sellout crowd rises as one. This is a perfect confluence of player and situation.

Right-handed reliever Chad Bradford, a sidearmer, is on the mound. The crowd chants, "Sam-my! Sam-my!" Sosa pokes at the ground with his cleats, takes three practice swings, and moves his fingers on the handle of the bat as if he were playing the clarinet.

Strike one swinging . . . ball one inside . . . ball two high . . . strike two swinging. Then . . . a grounder to shortstop Bobby Crosby. Crosby throws to first baseman Eric Karros, the former Cub. Game over.

As Sosa walks slowly back to the dugout, someone literally turns off the stadium lights. Karros taps Sosa on the rear with his glove. Sosa doesn't acknowledge the gesture and soon disappears down the tunnel leading to the clubhouse.

GAME 68

Saturday, June 19, 2004 . . . Cubs 4, Athletics 3 . . . Wrigley Field . . . Stat of the game: Mark Prior goes just five innings and 85 pitches before leaving with the Cubs trailing, 3-1. . . . Stuff: Unlike the day before, when CSI's William Petersen bounced his ceremonial pitch, actor Vince Vaughn actually reaches home plate with his throw. Vaughn is so money, he doesn't even know he's money.

> *"That was huge today. That might be the biggest win of the year—'til that next one."*

—Dusty Baker on the Cubs' two-run, game-winning rally in the bottom of the ninth

Today's comeback victory proves an essential baseball truth: If you go up there clueless, you'll walk back hitless.

Michael Barrett arrived at the plate in the bottom of the ninth inning with one out, the Cubs trailing by one, and Lemons Todd Hollandsworth on second and Todd Walker on first. What happened next is why Barrett is in the big leagues and you and I are playing 16-inch softball with guys named Maury.

An afternoon earlier, in the Cubs' 2-1 loss to the A's, Barrett led off the ninth inning against temporary closer Chad Bradford. Barrett grounded out to second for the out. Big whoop, right?

Turns out it was.

"I tried to take as many pitches as I could yesterday," Barrett says now. "Sometimes you try to take a little bit to get something later. I knew he'd be the closer for the next few days."

He knew it because the sidearmer Bradford retired the Cubs' side in order Friday and earned his first save. So sure enough, A's manager Ken Macha called on Bradford in Saturday's game.

This time Barrett had a clue. No longer was Bradford's funky sidearm delivery a surprise. Barrett's first thought: "Obviously, stay out of the double play," he says.

The more you watch baseball, the more you realize it is a game of successive decisions, some obvious, some almost imperceptible. Barrett wanted to stay out of the double play, so he decides to . . . bunt?

"All day I'd been flirting with the idea of bunting," he says.

To the rest of the Cubs Nation sitting in its Barcalounger, this means Barrett was trying to move Hollandsworth to third and Walker to second with one out. That way a long fly ball scores Hollandsworth and we've got a tie game.

Except that Barrett saw more than you and me. He saw third baseman Esteban German playing way back, back enough to hail a cab on Waveland. He saw a sidearm reliever. Sidearm relievers—and Barrett says he has some experience catching these kind of guys—have a tendency to fall toward the first-base side of the mound. In other words, they have trouble fielding bunts toward the third-base side. Plus, says Barrett, "we had Mo [Alou] and Sammy [Sosa] coming up."

So on Bradford's first pitch, Barrett half-squared to bunt. At the last moment, he pulled his bat back, but it was too late. Strike one. Barrett shook his head, but he was really more mad at himself.

"It wasn't a good pitch to bunt," he says.

"Hey, I'm glad he didn't bunt," says Baker.

That's because Barrett then lined a 1-1 pitch down the right-field line that squirted off the grass and toward the corner. A's right-fielder Jermaine Dye got to the ball fast enough, hit the cutoff man, and then watched as

Walker slid belly first, arms extended sideways like wings, over the plate for the winning run.

Walker was enveloped by teammates. Hollandsworth hugged Barrett. The Cubs had their biggest win of the season—until the next one—and all because a day earlier Barrett had decided to take as many pitches as possible from Bradford.

Afterward, Barrett is escorted to the interview room. He's still wearing his Cubs cap and looks as if he wants to spray someone with champagne.

"I've never really been a part of something like this," says a beaming Barrett, whose team has won seven of its last eight. "It's awesome. It's great."

You get the feeling his Cubs teammates don't know exactly what to make of Barrett. It's as if his joy has taken them by surprise, like the way Magic Johnson once stunned the usually stoic Kareem Abdul-Jabbar with a five-alarm postgame embrace.

But the Cubs had better get used to it. Barrett's smile isn't going anywhere.

"Without question, this has been a dream," he says. "That hit right there was comparable to my first Major League hit. That was incredible. It's just awesome."

I can't help myself. I smile too.

GAME 69

Sunday, June 20, 2004 . . . Cubs 5, Athletics 3 . . . Wrigley Field . . . Cubs NL Central pennant flies: Second (39-30) . . . Stat of the game: Carlos Zambrano, looking more like a no-brainer for the All-Star team, grinds out his eighth win. An added bonus: no silly tantrums . . . Stuff: Moises Alou steps to the plate in the first. WGN's Steve Stone tells viewers Alou is a fastball hitter and that A's starter Barry Zito might try to sneak his average fastball past him on the inside part of the plate. Moments later, Alou lines Zito's average inside fastball over the left-field wall.

Eric Karros's career with the Cubs lasted exactly one season, or, more precisely, 114 games and 336 at-bats. He hit .286 with 12 home runs, 40 RBI, and 37 runs. Respectable numbers, but nobody at Cooperstown was rushing to clear wall space.

Karros was a platoon player, and at 2003's end the Cubs chose not to pick up his option. His departure and subsequent signing as a free agent with the Oakland Athletics were generally noted by nothing more than a single line on the agate page of your daily newspaper. His appearance today as a pinch hitter (0-for-1) will get the same treatment.

But Cubs followers should remember Karros the same way he remembers them. With fondness.

The October 26, 2003, Sunday edition of the *Chicago Tribune* featured a full-page thank-you note from Karros to the city of Chicago. It featured a black-and-white photo of a smiling Karros high-fiving Cubs teammates, presumably after a homer that helped beat the New York Yankees (and Roger Clemens) that season. Below the fold is this message:

> *Thank you to the Chicago Cubs fans and the entire Cubs organization for your support. You have all provided my family and me with an unbeatable experience and memories to last a lifetime.*
>
> *Warmest regards,*
> *Eric Karros*

The full-page ad cost about $25,000—and that's with the company discount he got as a quasi-*Tribune* employee. Otherwise, it would have run him about $75,000.

"The money wasn't the issue," he says. "I wanted to say thanks."

Pause for incredulous facial expression by author. Since when does a ballplayer, especially one who spent less than seven months with a Chicago address, spend $25K for a group hug with strangers? But that's Karros's point: In a season's time, he and Cubs fans went from blind dates to having a crush on each other. When the '03 season ended so abruptly with the NLCS loss to the Florida Marlins, Karros and his wife, Trish, decided to offer a proper farewell. He wanted . . . *needed* closure.

"After that game I stayed around the city for about four more days, just tying up loose ends, and sure, I felt bad personally, but I felt like . . . we just let everybody in the city down," he says. "But then I'd go into a restaurant, or I'd be out publicly somewhere, and people would just come up and say, 'Hey, you know what, thanks for a great summer. This is the most memorable summer I've ever had in my life here with the Cubs.' Or 'Hey, you brought our family together. We started watching games together. We hadn't spoken.'

"At first you're thinking, 'Ah, that's bullshit. It's people just coming up saying this sort of stuff and whatever.' But if it was just one or two people, I'd say whatever. But it wasn't. The impact we had on everybody, the sincerity that these people showed me . . . you know, it was literally depressing walking around the city and going places those last few days. I had to keep telling myself, 'Hey, it's gonna go on, there's next year.' But this was really the only time that I was devastated for the *fans*."

Of course, Karros knew he was wheat toast the minute the deal involving the Baltimore Orioles and then-Marlins first baseman Lee fell through. The Cubs responded with their own offer to Lee and that was that. Lee was a Cub. Karros wasn't.

But here's what makes Karros's gesture so pure: He purchased his full-page ad even before the Cubs made their run at Lee. Stay or go, he wanted to say thanks.

"It was easily my most enjoyable experience playing baseball in the big leagues," he says. "It was my most enjoyable year, and I wasn't even an everyday player—and I'd been an everyday player for 12 seasons in LA."

Now he plays for the A's, his third team in as many years. It's fine, but it's not the Cubs.

Win or lose, Karros says Cubs fans would leave notes of encouragement on his car. A chef at a nearby restaurant cooked him whatever he desired. When the Cubs beat the Atlanta Braves to advance to the NLCS, Karros returned to his Wrigleyville rental to find a little something on his doorstep: a balloon tied to a can of Old Style. Read the note: "Wish you could have cracked this one open with us. Congratulations. We're all proud of you."

"Those sort of things happened throughout the season," he says. "I'd like to explain it, but I wouldn't do it justice. The experience itself is the only way to do it justice."

Winning helped. A lot. So did a roster where everyone got along. This was no 25-players, 25-taxis type of team.

"That was as close of a team as I've ever been on," says Karros. "Usually, there will be a guy or two you don't care for—it's like that on every team. On some teams, you may be that guy. But on that team anybody would hang out with anybody. It wasn't like the Latin guys are going here, the black guys are going here, the white guys going there. Everybody got along very well. That's very rare in any team sport."

Remember the Yankees' visit to Wrigley in '03, their first trip to the

North Side since sweeping the Cubs in the 1938 World Series? Karros does. "Those three days against the Yankees were easily the most electric atmosphere I've ever been exposed to, including playoff games, Dodgers-Giants games, anything. After I hit the home run [a seventh-inning number to left off reliever Juan Acevedo], I got a curtain call, and that's kind of when I felt like, 'All right, I am now a Cub.'"

Karros saved things other than memories. He has the ball from the final out when the Cubs clinched the Central Division against the Pittsburgh Pirates. Got everybody on the entire roster to sign it, too. He has his Cubs uni. He has a pair of Mark Prior game-used cleats. He has a cap that Kerry Wood gave him.

His most cherished possession is on tape. Karros kept a palm-cam nearby during the last month of the '03 season. So far he's received at least 20 offers to turn those tapes into a commemorative video to be sold to Cubs followers everywhere. Even former Cubs teammates have asked for copies. But Karros won't do it.

Don't get the wrong idea. There's nothing on the tapes Karros wouldn't show Trish and his three kids. Karros has Pearl Jam's Eddie Vedder talking about his love affair with the franchise. He has clubhouse visitor Michael Jordan spraying champagne when the Cubs clinched the division. He has Sammy Sosa chatting to the camera after getting thrown out of a game. To Karros, selling these moments would cheapen his memories.

And while Karros is on the subject of memories . . .

For the record, he absolves Steve Bartman of any wrongdoing.

"Put it this way: [shortstop Alex] Gonzalez should be happy as heck that [Bartman] gets all the publicity," he says. "Bartman did what everybody else would have done. There were a million things that happened that night that had nothing to do with Bartman."

That was then. Now Karros is an Athletic. But he still roots for the Cubs to win the NL pennant. He still reads their box scores. And he still talks to some of the Cubs on a regular basis. A new uniform doesn't change that.

Can the Cubs make another run at October? Sure, says Karros. But this time they do so with expectations.

"I think this year, anything short of winning the World Series is going to be looked upon as a step backwards," he says.

Whatever happens, Karros will never forget his one lone season as a Cub. So sweet are the memories that he actually considered retirement.

"What went on that season, it was almost grounds for saying, 'I'm shutting it down because I don't know how it's going to get any better,'" he says.

"I could win a World Series somewhere else and I honestly don't know how it could be better. I really don't."

GAME 70

Tuesday, June 22, 2004 . . . Cubs 5, Cardinals 4 . . . Busch Stadium . . . Stat of the game: The Cards blow their first save this month. Geez, that's too bad. . . . Stuff: Wavin' Wendell Kim catches his share of grief at times, but tonight he sends Sammy Sosa home on the potential go-ahead run late in the game. Why? Because Kim knows cutoff man Tony Womack, a gamer with a tender elbow, has mush for a throwing arm. Sosa scores on the play. . . . Some smart guy in the PA booth plays Steve Goodman's "A Dying Cub Fan's Last Request." Yeah, that was a good idea. . . . The Cubs move to within one game of the first-place Cards.

St. Louis Post-Dispatch columnist Bernie Miklasz, who understands the psyche of his baseball-rich town as well as anybody, decides it's time for a Come-to-Jesus speech to Cardinals Nation. After watching the Cards blow leads of 3-0 and 4-3, Miklasz can take it no more.

The opening paragraphs of his column:

It's time for Cardinals fans to drop the arrogant pose and face up to the truth: You don't have the Cubs to kick around anymore. This is not your father's patsy. You'll need to find another chew toy. You'll need a fresh punch line to finish your Cub jokes. You need to come up with some fresh material instead of constantly referencing 1908.

I am not saying that the Cubs will win the NL Central. I am not saying that the Cubs' recent success over the Cardinals comes with a lifetime warranty. I'm not saying that Cardinals fans should like, or even admire, their rivals. I'm not channeling Harry Caray here.

But if nothing else, respect the Cubs.

Miklasz loves his town, but he's no homer. Of course, the column goes over like a sack of tire irons. E-mail response is 70/30 against. The nice rip jobs merely suggest he move to Chicago. The ugly ones tell him where to stick the Gateway Arch.

Miklasz's response:

It's a little difficult to explain. As much as I admire Cardinal fans—and you can make the argument they're the best fans in baseball—when it comes to the Cubs I'm a little put off by this arrogant attitude, by the way they look down on the Cubs. You hear what they say: They're chokers . . . we don't have to worry about the Cubs . . . they've never won anything.

But go back to last September. If anybody choked, it's the Cardinals. In the biggest games of the year (a five-game series in St. Louis in early September), the Cardinals lose four of five.

Anyway, I don't buy into this Curse stuff. You want to tell Cardinals fans, "Why are you people talking about 1908, talking about Bartman? They're kicking your ass!"

I know that stuff is great material. I know people like to talk about that, about 1908, 1945, 1984, Bartman. But live in the moment a little bit. The Cubs have a hell of a team.

When Cards fans sit around and say the Cubs are doomed, they're cursed, that you don't have to worry about Chicago, what they're really doing is discrediting the really hard-earned victories won by the Cardinals.

People e-mail me and say, "Why do you love the Cubs? Why don't you understand the rivalry? You don't know your history." But what does that have to do with Mark Prior and Kerry Wood? Or Aramis Ramirez? Or Derrek Lee? Or Michael Barrett?

Look at the Cardinals. Cardinal fans want to call the Cubs chokers, but what about the Cardinals in '85, in '87, in '89? What about [Tony] LaRussa, who's a hell of a manager, but they've been in the NLCS three times and haven't won it. With all due respect to the great Cardinal fans, look at your own house.

I'm not saying the Cubs are chokers. I don't think the Cubs losing to Florida was choking. They just ran into a hot team. That happens in the playoffs. It's the roll of the dice. When Mariano Rivera gave up the winning hit against the Diamondbacks in the World Series, does that make him a choker? No, he had a bad night.

I don't think the Cubs lost that game [Game 6 of the 2003 NLCS] because of Bartman, just like I don't think the Cardinals lost that game [Game 6 of the 1985 World Series against the Kansas City Royals] because of [umpire] Don Denkinger.

I still believe it's the Cubs' division to win. I think they're the team to beat. They've got the starting pitching. Their bullpen makes me nervous and I don't think their defense is the best, but their lineup is very good.

The Cardinals have been underproductive at the corner spots in the outfield. They have no shutdown pitchers in that rotation. They just don't have the firepower of five starting pitchers that the Cubs do. They hope they can get six gritty innings out of their starters and then hand it over to the bullpen, which has been very good.

I also don't think the Cardinals took total advantage of the Cubs' predicament when they had all those injuries. But there's a long way to go, isn't there?

GAME 71

Wednesday, June 23, 2004 . . . Cardinals 10, Cubs 9 . . . Busch Stadium . . . Cubs NL Central pennant flies: Second (40-31) . . . Stuff: Weirdest game of the season so far. The Cubs gag away a four-run lead, get their reliever (Mercker) and starting catcher (Michael Barrett) thrown out of the game, and pinch hitter Jose Macias bats twice in the sixth inning. Meanwhile, Cards reliever Steve Kline shoots a bird at St. Louis manager Tony LaRussa from the bullpen. This comes after reliever Julian Tavarez, thinking Kline is coming into the game, tries to hand LaRussa the ball at the mound. LaRussa refuses to take it and keeps Tavarez in the game. . . . Curse in Reverse: Marlins starter Josh Beckett goes on the DL.

Today is the 20-year anniversary of "The Sandberg Game," so named after Ryne Sandberg hit two game-tying homers off one of the greatest relievers of all time, Cardinals closer Bruce Sutter. One homer came in the bottom of the ninth, the other in the bottom of the 10th. The Cubs won the game an inning later and Sandberg finished with five hits and seven RBI.

June 23. Figures. Sandberg's jersey number was 23.

Rick Sutcliffe, now 48, was in the Cubs' dugout that day. Acquired earlier in the month from the Cleveland Indians, Sutcliffe had already beaten Pittsburgh in his first Cubs start and would finish the regular season with a remarkable 16-1 record. Without him, the Cubs never reach the NLCS.

But June 23, 1984, belonged to Sandberg. That's the way Sutcliffe, now an ESPN broadcaster, San Diego Padres roving pitching instructor, and manager-in-waiting, will always remember it—and everything else about being a Cub.

On the Sandberg Game:
I'll never ever forget it. It was unbelievable. It was actually my wife's first game ever at Wrigley. We had gotten traded, and my first start at Wrigley was going to be the following day. As I walked out after the game, my wife, who's almost in tears, says, "Are all the games here like that?"

On realizing he wasn't in Cleveland anymore:
I was being entertained by the fans up until he hit that homer in the ninth.

I had been with the Dodgers, and I remember getting off the bus in San Francisco as a 19-year-old kid and there was like a six-year-old kid with a sign and it said, "Fuck the Dodgers." I thought, "Wow, they really don't like us." So I knew about rivalries.

I was there [with the Cubs] for a couple of games against the Phillies before we went on the road. And then I started against Pittsburgh and then we came back to play St. Louis.

I remember that whole game. It was up and down, but it was more the Cardinal fans were up. I watched the games. I always did. I wasn't a clubhouse guy. I paid attention. I loved baseball. But at Wrigley, a lot of times you don't even know what the score is until all of a sudden in the seventh inning this big guy with the big glasses gets up and starts singing. I'm looking out at everybody and I'm thinking, "They really like this, man. It's kind of fun."

Then, at that time, you look at the scoreboard and go, "What the hell's the score, anyway?" That's kind of the whole experience at Wrigley. It's so much more than a baseball game. And that's what I was caught up in that day.

So I know what the score is, and here comes Bruce Sutter, and, OK, the game's over. It's my job to go out there and win tomorrow. That's what I had already started thinking about.

Bobby Dernier had an 0-2 count and battled back. I don't even know how he did it. It was like a miracle that he got on. When Sandberg hit the homer, it was like, "Golly, this is going our way." But if Dernier doesn't get on, none of that would have ever happened.

On one of his favorite 1984 moments:
No, there's no Sutcliffe Game. But I think the one game that fans remember me by is the clincher in Pittsburgh.

We had had a tough road trip. We got beat up a little bit in St. Louis. I remember walking to the bullpen—there were only about 10,000 people there, and all of them were there to see the Cubs—and I saw a huge sign by this family. It said, "39 Years of Suffering Are Enough."

So I actually called the guy down as I was walking to the bullpen and asked him, "What does that mean?" And he told me: "We haven't been to the playoffs since then."

Not being cocky or whatever, I just said, "We're gonna end it tonight for you." He had driven a long way and brought his family.

Anyway, I drove in a run that night. And earlier, Jody Davis had told me, "I want to catch the last out." I knew what he meant. He wanted a strike-out. He didn't want a fly ball or ground ball to end it. So I had that in my mind after I got the first two outs: "OK, I have to strike this guy out." And that's what happened.

So we celebrate, we go in the clubhouse, and then it's over. We're in Pittsburgh. What the hell are we gonna do? There's nothing to do.

I'll never forget, though: Somebody from WGN said, "C'mon outside. [WGN producer] Arne Harris has something for you."

We all grabbed a beer and sat on the Astroturf. And there on the big screen in Pittsburgh, Arne Harris had programmed in to what was going on back at Wrigley Field. It was absolute craziness. It wasn't until right then that I realized what we had done that night.

On being a Cub:
Cub fans, they take you into their home with WGN and whatever else it is now. Also, the Cub fan takes the Cub player—the ones they like—into their heart. Generally, everywhere else, the fans know you, you're in their mind. But there they take you into their hearts.

My whole plan when I became a free agent in '84 was to play in '85 for my hometown team. My dream growing up was to play in Kansas City.

Just sitting there once the season ended, working on a contract basically with the Royals—that's when the letters started coming in from Cubs fans. And in the letters, the Cubs fans were apologizing for the ink being so smeared . . . because they were crying as they wrote it. It was, "Please come back." It was stuff from the heart.

That's what brought me back. It's just the passion that they have. It's so sincere.

On the rigors of broadcasting:
I think broadcasting is the Lord's way of getting even with me for not doing my homework when I was a kid. I was an athlete, I coasted. But when you're doing these games, I'm studying a minimum of four hours a day.

I know what you're thinking: "I listen to the jerk, and it sure doesn't sound like it."

On the 2003 season:
Nobody pulled more for the Cubs than I did. I'm a Padres fan, a Cubs fan, and a Coors Light man. That's probably the only difference between me and Harry. He drank Bud and I drink Coors.

On Cub reunions:
We had the 20th-anniversary party at the Cubs Convention back in January. I was told there were like 19 of the 25 guys who made it back. It was sold out. You couldn't get another person in there.

I said a few things to the crowd, and then I said, "C'mon, Ryno, you're gonna say something." And he did. For the first time ever, Ryno spoke.

GAME 72

Thursday, June 24, 2004 . . . Cardinals 4, Cubs 0 . . . Busch Stadium . . . Cubs NL Central pennant flies: Tie-Second (40-32) . . . Stuff: Sammy Sosa, who's only been in the big leagues for 15 seasons, gets completely fooled on a deke by center fielder Jim Edmonds. Sosa gets thrown out at home (no blaming Wavin' Wendell on this one) by about 600 feet. . . . Uh-oh: The Astros trade for Kansas City Royals star center fielder Carlos Beltran.

Rey Ordonez weeps in the players' lounge after this one. Nine years in the big leagues and you cry after your team of exactly 27 days loses a game in June? Not only that, but he also apologizes to Dusty Baker for his part in the shutout defeat. Isn't that against players' union rules?

"First time that's happened in a long time," says Baker later.

The fourth inning is what eventually reduces Ordonez to tears. With bases loaded and one out in a scoreless game, he dinks a ball back to Cards pitcher Chris Carpenter. Carpenter throws to catcher Mike Matheny for the force, who throws to Albert Pujols at first for the double play. It turns out to be the Cubs' best scoring chance of the evening.

Ordonez owns three Gold Gloves and holds the National League record for fewest errors (four) in a season by a shortstop. But that was five long years ago. Tonight he also bungles a potential double-play throw in the bottom of the fourth inning—a play, he says, he's made a million times in his career. Again, there is one out with the bases loaded.

What could have been an inning-ending double play becomes a four-run Cardinals inning. Ordonez, who has as many errors as hits this season (three), is pulled for a pinch hitter in the seventh, but that only gives him more time to think about his two crucial mistakes. By game's end, he's a mess.

"The last thing I want with bases loaded and one out is to do that," he says. "And that other [play] with bases loaded . . . I'm feeling badly, I feel sorry," he says. "It's tough to say that, but I have to. It's like I have to get it out of my body."

The Cubs aren't buying it. Clement tells reporters he isn't sure they could have turned the double play even if Ordonez hadn't dropped the ball while trying to make the throw to second. Other teammates stop by and try to console Ordonez.

"The man has a love for the game," says fellow Lemon Tom Goodwin, who knows how lineup-card-thin the margin of error is for a reserve player. "We all know Rey. We all know what he's done in the past. He's a great player. In no way, shape, or form was what he did the reason we lost that game."

They might not have been *the* reasons why the Cubs lost this game, but they were close. Ordonez has been around long enough to know that. The proof is in the tears.

GAME 73

Friday, June 25, 2004 . . . Cubs 7, White Sox 4 . . . U.S. Cellular Field . . . Cubs NL Central pennant flies: Tie-Second (41-32) . . . Stuff: Mayor Richard M. Daley chats with Dusty Baker before the game. Daley, who proudly professes his allegiance for the South Siders, arrives wearing a White Sox cap. . . . Blair Kamin, the noted architecture critic for the Tribune, weighs in on the proposed Wrigley expansion plan. Kamin describes Wrigley's features as "soft, continuous curves as sensuous as the voluptuous hills in Grant Wood's paintings of Iowa." Hey, Blair, if you're going to write like that, get a hotel room, will you? Anyway, Kamin says the HOK architects responsible for the proposed Clark Street multipurpose facility and parking garage need to "raise the level of their game." Agreed.

You don't interview White Sox manager Ozzie Guillen as much as you and your tape recorder hang on for dear life. Between the Venezuelan accent, the staccato chatter, and the interesting combinations of nouns and verbs, Guillen is a tough transcribe. But good gosh, can he talk. And talk. And talk. Better yet, he usually has something to say.

Guillen was born in the San Diego Padres organization but was raised by the White Sox. He played 1,743 games for the Sox, made brief stays in Atlanta and Tampa Bay, and retired in 2000. Cubs followers last saw him as the Florida Marlins' third-base coach in the 2003 NLCS. Guillen has a World Series ring to show for that season.

We chat in the White Sox's dugout after his pregame filibuster with beat reporters. The highlights:

On the Cubs-White Sox series:
To me, facing the Cubs is like facing any team. Is it a big series because of the Cubs? No, it's a big series because we're in a pennant race, and so are they.

A lot of people think I want to bluff myself about facing the Cubs. I'm not. I got a lot of friends who are big-time White Sox fans. But nobody in this town—nobody . . . nobody, maybe one—is a bigger White Sox fan as Ozzie Guillen. Only guy is a bigger fan than me: Jerry Reinsdorf.

But I hate crosstown games, because that take away my day off.

On Wrigley Field:
Two years I played at Wrigley Field. With Atlanta. I liked going there. It was nice. You come to Chicago and you no go to Wrigley . . . it's like you go to New York and you not see the Statue of Liberty. That's why the ballpark is packed. That's the only difference.

On the size of Wrigley crowds:
When I was playing, there were only 5,000 people in Wrigley Field, sir. Why? Because they was horseshit. I'm telling you the truth.

On why the Cubs have so many sellouts now:
Sammy Sosa. That's the reason.

[I tell him, "You're probably right." Says Guillen: "No, I'm not *probably* right. I know I'm right. I don't say things to be wrong. Sammy Sosa."]

Wrigley Field or Old Comiskey Park?
Old Comiskey Park. It's easy to park. You have better seats. Wrigley Field had a real bad game field. Comiskey Park had the best infield in baseball. The best infield in baseball. I played there for a real long time, so that's why I say it.

On the differences between Cubs fans and White Sox fans:
Yes, there is a difference. Maybe 10 percent of the Cubs fans are not real Cubs fans. They're there for the game, the city, and Wrigley Field. White Sox are pretty tough. They can boo anybody in a heartbeat. [For Cubs fans] to boo at Wrigley Field, that's hard for them to do.

Me, I never got booed [at home]. Never. Because I played my ass off here. I might be booed as a manager.

On the Marlins being down to the Cubs, 3-1, in the 2003 NLCS:
No panic. We weren't supposed to be there. They were. They were supposed to be there. Obviously, their pitching staff was a lot better. When you've got Kerry [Wood] and Prior in your staff, you have a real good pitching staff. Now you add [Matt] Clement, you add [Carlos] Zambrano, that's loaded.

On Game 6 of the NLCS—The Bartman Game:
You know, when the Bartman situation happened, we didn't even realize that. They make it up, that thing, after they lose. If they win, that thing the next day, they don't even know that kid catches the goddamn ball. They didn't win, so now they're making a good excuse, that that's why they lose. I'm not saying it was their players [who said this], I'm saying their fans. That's part of baseball.

On alleged Fox TV network bias in the NLCS:
Fox, they didn't want us. They gave out red and blue jackets. Our players threw them in the garbage can. Red and blue. Cubs and Red Sox [colors].

I kept two.

On if the 2004 Cubs were better than the 2003 Cubs:
On paper, yes. They got a better pitching staff.

But you know what? That team was not better than the Marlins.

We [the Marlins] got better catcher, better first base, better second base, better shortstop, better third baseman, and better center field. And we got [Miguel] Cabrera in right field now. The only thing that was better than us was Sammy and Moises [Alou]. Everywhere else, we were better on the field.

On what would happen if the Cubs played the White Sox in the World Series:
That'd be dangerous. Both good and bad way.

It's so funny. I say this for my kids and my fans, not me, because I was never in the stands. If you go to Wrigley Field with a White Sox jersey, maybe a couple of people will say, "Hey, get outta here." But if you come to White Sox with a Cubs jersey on a regular day, you better be careful. A different type of fans.

GAME 74

Saturday, June 26, 2004 . . . White Sox 6, Cubs 3 . . . U.S. Cellular Field . . . Stuff: Two more hits for Corey Patterson, who doubles, homers, and raises his average to .280. Not so hot is Sammy Sosa, who goes 0-for-3 with a sac fly. Sosa is 6-for-27 (.222) with two RBI and no homers since his return. . . . Available for purchase outside The Cell: White Sox jerseys with BARTMAN on the back. . . . The White Sox don't come right out and say it, but it's obvious they love beating the demonstrative Zambrano. . . . After the Sox win, Jumbotron operators flash a Cubs logo with a slash across it. . . . Who said interleague play is fair? The Cubs get the White Sox, the Cardinals get the baseball-impaired Kansas City Royals. The Cards also get a victory, dropping the Cubs four games out of first.

There it is again, that White Sox ad that throws a high hard one at Cubs futility. It plays to cheers on the U.S. Cellular big screen.

> *The White Sox present . . . a comparison.*
> *Them vs. US.*
> *They: Are lovable even when they lose.*

We: Hate losing.
They: Champions in 1908.
We: Champions as recently as 1917. (And who can forget 1906?)
They: Believe they're cursed.
We: Agree.
They: Got Wood.
We: Got lumber.
They: Have a fan who says, "Woo."
We: Don't.
They: Need tickets? See a broker.
We: Call 866-SOX-Game.
Oh . . . and the mayor likes us better.

Brooks Boyer, the 32-year-old marketing director for the White Sox, is the brains behind the ad campaign. Boyer played hoops at Notre Dame, majored in both finance and computer applications, and later earned an MBA at DePaul. He isn't afraid, as he likes to say, to "get down and dirty."

This campaign isn't dirty, but it isn't Zest-soap-clean either.

"We wanted to be a little more aggressive marketing our team," says Boyer, who was an early-season replacement for 15-year Sox marketing VP Rob Gallas. "We wanted to have a little fun. Our campaign has nothing to do with the Cubs. Our campaign is about the White Sox. It's about us. And Sox pride."

No it isn't. It's about giving a wedgie to the Cubs, which is fine, even welcome. Who says crosstown rivals have to like each other? Boyer can talk about "celebrating our uniqueness" all he wants, but the Us vs. Them ad also celebrates Cubs failings. That's why Boyer needed approval from Sox managing partner Jerry Reinsdorf (Reinsdorf actually rewrote one of the lines) and why the phone calls to the Sox front office are coming in at a 40-1 pace in favor of the ad.

A Milwaukee-based advertising agency conceived the idea, but it was Sox front-office employees who helped shape the copy.

"Now it got mean and nasty," Boyer says. "We had a whole list, and we picked the four ones that were best. We wanted to be tongue-in-cheek, and it worked."

A few suggestions from the brainstorming session didn't make it. Actual nominees:

They: Own a newspaper and a TV station.
We: Don't.

They: Have offices in a tower.
We: Have ours in a ballpark.
They: Got Dusty.
We: Got Ozzie.

"And Ozzie's sandwich is kicking Dusty's sandwich's ass," says Boyer, referring to a Subway contest featuring sandwich creations of Sox manager Ozzie Guillen and Dusty Baker.

The Us vs. Them ad first ran on June 8. You can find it online, on Sox broadcasts, and on the Jumbotron. It's been a huge hit.

Of course, the Cubs aren't thrilled. Cubs Senior Marketing VP John Mc-Donough noted somewhat sarcastically that it's always nice to be the center of a Sox ad campaign.

Boyer didn't expect a thank-you note or much more than McDonough's polite, but terse, response.

"We knew they weren't going to spend any money to respond to us," Boyer says. "Their tickets are all sold. I've told people over and over again that I'm excited the Cubs are sold out, because that means I own the market, unless you want to go see a scalper."

The technical term for this is spin. Boyer would give anything to be sold out for the season.

"Damn right," Boyer says. "I'd be foolish not to. I'm very envious of their position in the market. But they've earned it. They have good marketing people over there. They know they play in a shrine, and they use that to their advantage—and they should.

"They're lucky because they really don't have to [market the Cubs]. The team and the ballpark market themselves. They put a couple of ads in the paper saying tickets are on sale and they're all sold. God bless them. They haven't had to get down and dirty and attract people and come up with plans and market their players. They're in a great position."

This isn't finished. Boyer, the former ballplayer, is treating the Cubs like they're DePaul during the Meyer Era. And you know how Irish hoopsters felt about *that* rivalry. In his own ballpark, a visiting Cubs fan held up a sign mocking the ad campaign:

We: Sell out games.
They: Only sell out when we come.

So make no mistake, Boyer wants what the Cubs already have, which is why you should ignore the following:

"I haven't paid attention to them at all," he says. "Like I said, I really don't care what they do. My guess is they don't care what we do either. We're just going to compete. We're going to get out there and we're going to become a very strong marketing and sales force in this market."

Spoken like a politician. No wonder the mayor likes the Sox better.

GAME 75

Sunday, June 27, 2004 . . . White Sox 9, Cubs 4 . . . U.S. Cellular Field . . . Cubs NL Central pennant flies: Tie-Second (41-34) . . . Stuff: Six games ago, the Cubs were a victory away from a first-place tie with the Cardinals. Now they're five out . . . A pregame team meeting fails to make a difference. The Cubs commit three errors (nine in the last five games) and make another baserunning mistake (Corey Patterson gets deked into a double play). . . . Sammy Sosa hits two home runs. . . . The Curse lives: Mike Remlinger (shoulder tendinitis) goes back on the DL. Todd Hollandsworth fouls a ball off his shin in the third inning and leaves the game.

There is a famous photograph, taken about 15 years ago, of then-Cubs manager Don Zimmer and the only Chicago baseball writer famous enough or, more correctly, good enough to plop next to him and chew on a stogie the size of a lead pipe.

The baseball writer is Jerome Holtzman, who hasn't done much during his career except be inducted into the Baseball Hall of Fame, author the quintessential baseball book, invent the save, unknowingly mentor about 1,100 beat reporters, become MLB's official historian, and bring new meaning to bushy eyebrows.

Holtzman has taken so many writers under his wing that he barely has any feathers left. He held my hand on the Cubs beat in 1996. He's sprung for dinners at spring training. He's sat in dugouts and imparted wisdom to anyone smart enough to listen.

When I first met him years ago, he was wearing dark pants, pin-striped shirt, and suspenders. Today he appears on the field wearing . . . dark pants, pin-striped shirt, and suspenders. The eyebrows are still thick as Bermuda grass, and the baseball talk is 100 proof.

Holtzman is 78 now, and he walks with the slight help of a Buford Pusser–sized wooden cane. With a dab of pine tar, Sosa could go 2-for-3 with the walking stick.

He is here to be honored by the Chicago chapter of the Baseball Writers Association of America. Twenty-five of his peers, a *Tribune* photographer, and White Sox chairman Jerry Reinsdorf are in a small auditorium located between the two clubhouses.

"It's nice to be eulogized while you're still alive," says Reinsdorf, who first met Holtzman shortly after purchasing the Sox 23 years ago.

Reinsdorf tells a story or two. Then *Daily Herald* Cubs writer Bruce Miles tells a story or two. Then longtime *Sun-Times* baseball writer Toni Ginnetti offers another testimonial, followed by a touching anecdote by *Daily Southtown* columnist Phil Arvia. What was supposed to be a brief acknowledgment of Holtzman's contributions has turned into a full-fledged but well-deserved lovefest.

Holtzman leans back in his chair, smiles, and offers a couple stories of his own. If the game weren't about to begin, no one would budge.

I'm lucky. A few hours earlier, I sat in the dugout as Holtzman imparted more wisdom. I took notes.

Advice to Writers
Get there early and you won't get scooped.

Covering Baseball in 2004
I was 29 years as a beat guy. It was me and two other [beat] guys. It wasn't the masses like it is now. I would talk to [manager] Al Lopez, then somebody else would talk to him. There wasn't a pregame press conference. There wasn't a postgame press conference.

[Cubs hitting coach Sarge Matthews stops by. They chat about Gary Matthews Jr.]

Pete Rose in the Hall of Fame
I'm against him all the way.

Cubs Assessment
I think they're a pretty good ballclub. They had a lot of injuries, lost their key players: Kerry Wood, [Mark] Prior, Sosa. But I think the potential is outstanding. They have a lot of good hitters.

The bullpen isn't as good. The bullpen has been a little erratic. A lot of bullpens are leaking these days. That's because the starters are going fewer innings and the pressure is getting greater.

If a relief pitcher has an 80 percent success rate, that's pretty good. [Goose] Gossage had 90. [Dennis] Eckersley had 95. [Mariano] Rivera and [Eric] Gagne have very good success rates. But still, a lot of bullpens are struggling.

Inventing the Save Category

Nineteen-sixty is when I did it. I had no idea it would become so important.

I helped relievers make a lot of money. Oh, sure, I heard from some of them. Jeff Riordan was always thanking me. Gossage was appreciative. Eckersley, Jose Mesa always made it a point to say something. And I'll tell you another one: David Cone. But Mesa, he hugged me and hugged me.

[Cubs GM Jim Hendry stops by. "How's my favorite Hall of Famer?" Moments later, here comes Baker. "How ya doing, Mr. Holtzman? They honoring you today? They should be."]

Baker Assessment

I like Baker. He knows how to handle players. Baker knows how to handle his men.

Cubs, White Sox Predictions

I think they're both going to make the playoffs. But anybody can win it all. Tampa Bay can win it all.

The Cubs and Streaks

I think they're pretty good, but you don't know. I don't believe in momentum in baseball. Every day is a new day. What happens yesterday has no impact on what happens tomorrow. Every game is separate. Every game has to be won.

GAME 76

Tuesday, June 29, 2004 . . . Cubs 7, Astros 5 . . . Wrigley Field . . . Stat of the game: Battle of the Beltrans. New Astros center fielder Carlos Beltran homers off Cubs reliever Francis Beltran. . . . Stuff: St. Louis loses, Cubs win—move to within 3½ games of first. . . . A Cubs beat reporter, who should know better, tells Baker that his club resembles a Little League team on the base paths. Baker's temper flares. "You don't call my team Little League," he snaps. . . . Corey Patterson, professional hitter (two words you wouldn't have used earlier in the season), raises his average to .284. . . . Cubs ratings on WGN-TV are the highest they've been in 13 years. . . . Super Lemon Todd Hollandsworth is on crutches because of a severe shin bruise.

The latest fan voting figures for the All-Star Game are available. The starting National League eight, as of today: 1B: Albert Pujols, Cardinals; 2B: Jeff Kent, Astros; 3B: Scott Rolen, Cardinals; SS: Edgar Renteria, Cardinals; C: Mike Piazza, Mets; OF: Barry Bonds, Giants; Ken Griffey Jr., Reds; Sammy Sosa, Cubs.

Nothing personal, but Sosa belongs on the 32-man NL roster like I belong on the Chippendales calendar. Sosa missed more than a month, is hitting .278 with 12 homers and 29 RBI, and has one less strikeout than hits. The Astros' Lance Berkman, the Cubs' Alou, the Marlins' Miguel Cabrera and Juan Pierre, the Cardinals' Jim Edmonds, and the Phillies' Bobby Abreu are all more deserving.

But fans are fans, which is why every big league player, coach, and manager also receives ballots. Their choices help determine 16 of the NL All-Star Game reserves.

You should have seen some of the Cubs filling out their ballots. It looked as if they were taking the LSATs.

"The votes should go to the guys having the best year," says Todd Walker, always a voice of baseball reason. "I disagree with a guy getting voted on because he's a great player, even though he's not having a great year. It's not just a courtesy vote. It should go to the guys who are having good years."

So, uh, Todd, who'd you vote for?

"I'm not going to tell you that," he says.

Dusty Baker shares the same philosophy on player selection.

"I try to be fair and go on who's having an outstanding, outstanding year, and not necessarily go on names," he says.

Any Cubs on the list?

Baker says he can't divulge that kind of information, though he is willing to campaign for some of his players. Baker's short list of deserving

Cubs includes Matt Clement, Carlos Zambrano, Moises Alou, Aramis Ramirez, and Michael Barrett. You can make a case for each, though the one no-brainer pick has to be Ramirez, followed by Zambrano and Alou.

Derrek Lee picked Alou. He also picked Ramirez. And Barrett. "I voted for almost everybody on this team," he says.

But he didn't vote for himself, despite a .302 batting average, 10 dingers, and 46 RBI.

"I've had a good first half, but [Cincinnati's Sean] Casey is hitting .350-something, and Thome has 20-plus home runs," he says.

I can respect that. I can respect it more than the fans punching Sosa's name on the ballot.

GAME 77

Wednesday, June 30, 2004 . . . Astros 3, Cubs 2 . . . Wrigley Field . . . Cubs NL Central pennant flies: Tie-Second (42-35) . . . Stuff: With two outs in the ninth, closer LaTroy Hawkins gives up the game-winner against Carlos Beltran. Hawkins, who still isn't chatting with the media, doesn't get much sympathy. "Wow, I really feel sorry for LaTroy," mutters one beat reporter in the postgame interview room. Hawkins, by the way, has been approached by a media outlet to write a column. He declines. The pay stinks, he says. . . . Dusty Baker still can't use Todd Hollandsworth because of a bruised shin. Turns out Hollandsworth lost feeling in his feet when he first fouled the ball off his shin last Sunday.

Ole Lyse, 81, and his wife, Lois, 80, are ushers at Wrigley. Ole works Aisle 15, which includes most of the seats directly behind the Cubs' dugout and over to the on-deck circle—about 160 fans in all. You don't mess with Ole.

Born in Norway, Lyse came to Chicago when he was six, was raised on the city's North Side, and spent 25 years as a sheet-metal man for Wrigley Gum. His hands are as big as waffle irons. After I exchange a handshake with him, my fingers want to report to the stadium first-aid station.

Ole retired in 1985. Six years later, tired of watching television and putzing around the house, Ole and Lois applied for the usher positions after reading about the job openings in their church bulletin. "And we're not sorry we did," says Ole.

The Lyses don't miss a game. Barring illness (knock on ivy), they'll work all 81 home dates.

The gates have just opened when Ole and I start talking. He wears the usher-issued red polo shirt (crowd control wears light blue shirts), khaki pants, and a warm smile. His gold-colored chamois, which he uses to wipe down the seats, is draped nearby on an armrest. Midway through the interview, a fan—a regular at Wrigley—approaches him. She wants to show Ole photographs of her newest grandchild.

Ole gushes about the kid. The woman beams, turns to me, and says, "Isn't Ole great? He's the best usher in the whole park."

I've seated Hillary Clinton, Robert Dole, Governor Jim Thompson, Matt Damon, Jim Belushi, Bill Murray. Governor Blagojevich comes here and sits with his daughter. There's been a lot of variety.

Bribe offers? It has happened, yes. That is a complete no-no. We try to keep the integrity of the ballpark. I've been offered a fair amount. Our response: "We don't do this at the ballpark."

We are offered tips. We don't accept tips.

I had one the other day who tried to sneak by. He said he wanted to give a player a candy bar. That's a new one. Fella came along, he wanted to go down there and give him a candy bar.

We get paid by the hour. We have a five-hour mininum. Yes, we're paid above mininum wage.

During the first four innings, it's quite busy. We're busy seating people. But then we do get a chance to watch the game, or some of the game. My favorites were the 1998 playoffs, the Sammy-McGwire home-run-record chase, the Kerry Wood strikeout game. But the most fun were the playoffs in 2003. It was something we Cubs fans had been hoping for.

That 2003 season, that was the first year since we've been working here that we saw the ivy change color in the fall. We had never been here that late in October.

The best part about the job is the fans and the ballpark. A lot of the fans come here because of the ballpark, because it's an old-fashioned ballpark. You see people come up the stairwell and get their first look at the place. That never gets old. They're amazed how close they are to the field.

I'm the same way. There's always excitement coming here. I don't think that will ever leave me.

JULY

••

GAME 78

July 1, 2004 . . . Cubs 5, Astros 4 . . . Wrigley Field . . . Stuff: Before the game, Kent Mercker starts walking up the stairs on the far right of the dugout and then stops. "Haven't gone that way all season," says the superstitious Mercker, who uses the middle stairs instead. What happens? He gives up a game-tying three-run homer to Carlos Beltran in the eighth. . . . Sammy Sosa, who is booed earlier in the game, hits the game-winning walk-off home run in the bottom of the 10th. Sosa was 1-for-12 with six strikeouts in the series before sending Brad Lidge's first pitch onto Waveland. That's career dinger No. 552. . . . Something you don't see, well, ever: Catcher Michael Barrett registers an unassisted tag out on an attempted steal of second by Morgan Ensberg.

Michael Wilbon sits at an outdoor café table at Navy Pier, his recently de-livered strawberry daiquiri (strawberry daiquiri?) all but ignored as he punches the keypad of his Nokia. The Chicago skyline looks drop-dead gorgeous in the late-afternoon sun. And speaking of gorgeous, a conga line of summer-attired women saunters up and down the famous pier. It is the kind of perfect July day that makes Chicago winters worth enduring.

Wilbon, who is here on vacation visiting family, notices none of it. In-stead, he has the cell pressed to his right ear and wears the look of someone who's worried their 401(k) just went belly up.

"Hey, this is Wilbon," he tells whoever just answered the phone in the *Washington Post* sports department. "Can you do me a favor? Can you tell me who won the Cubs game? They were tied in the ninth."

A long pause. Then relief.

"They won, 5-4," he says to me. "Sosa hit a home run."

The daiquiri glass gets raised. "Cheers," he says.

Wilbon, 45, is a Chicago native, St. Ignatius and Northwestern graduate, star of print (longtime *Post* sports columnist, bestselling author) and airwaves (cohost with Tony Kornheiser on ESPN's *Pardon the Interruption*). You might find a nicer guy, but you'll have to do some serious looking.

Wilbon cares deeply about five things: family, friends, writing, equality, and sports, specifically the Cubs. He calls me near midnight an evening earlier to ask about a rumor he'd heard: Matt Clement for Nomar Garciaparra—any truth to it? He wants to know how Prior has looked, how Dusty Baker is holding up, how Wood's rehab is coming along.

It would be wrong to merely describe Wilbon as a Cubs fan. He is an addict. The Cubs hooked him on the hard stuff decades ago and no stay at the Betty Ford is going to make him go clean. He is like so many Cubs followers, the equivalent of baseball chain smokers. It is a love/despise relationship.

Wilbon still mourns the 2003 NLCS loss. In fact, when he pronounces Steve Bartman's name—and I don't think he even realizes he does this—Wilbon says, "Bart Man," as if the guy were some sort of evil cartoon character who battles SuperMoisesMan.

Anyway, here's five-plus minutes with Wilbon, a Cubs lifer.

I've got a Michael Jordan story to tell you. It's the Division Series against Atlanta in 2003. They win Game 3 but lose Game 4. I wind up going to dinner with Jordan and John Cusack—they had been at Game 4. This is Saturday night at Gibson's, and Jordan says, "Whattya doing tomorrow?" I say, "You're going to laugh at me, but I've got to fly back and do the Redskins-Eagles game."

He can't believe it. He says, "Let me get this straight: You've lived in Chicago all your life. You've been a Cub fan your whole life. Game 5, Kerry Wood's pitching in Atlanta, and you're going to *Redskins-Eagles*?"

"I've gotta go. I've gotta work. I gotta go to the game."

He goes, "No you don't. Get on the plane with me."

See, he's flying down to Atlanta. He's going down to Game 5. He's going.

I say, "What are you, crazy? You're flying around to see the Cubs?"

He goes, "I've gotta lend them *something*. I've gotta give them whatever I got."

Whatever support he had in him he was going to give. The great irony, of course, is he's the greatest winner in the history of the world, certainly in the history of Chicago. And now he's affixed himself to this sinking ship. He knows he's a winner, but now he's doing what he can for the other franchise. This is a guy who played for the enemy White Sox.

He kept telling me I was crazy. He was laughing at me for going to an NFL game the next day. He kept saying, "I've gotta give them what I got." He was going to support this team. The greatest winner in the history of this losing-ass city was loaning himself to the Cubs. That's how much he cared about them.

I grew up on the South Side. Clark Street turns into Shields. If I stood on a real tall pair of stilts at my house, I could look straight down the line to Comiskey Park. It was 82nd to 35th, 47 blocks south.

But when you grow up as a black in the city of Chicago, at least then, the rich, famous black people lived in our neighborhoods, even though we didn't have anything. This was a time when Ali was at a place called the Tiger Lounge, on 79th Street. If you went by the Tiger Lounge, Ali would be there a lot of nights. This is when Ali lived on the South Side of Chicago.

Famous black people lived in the same neighborhoods as ordinary, middle-class, poor, working-class black people, all in a two-, three-mile radius. We all lived together—South Side or the West Side. Walt "No Neck" Williams lived in my neighborhood. He was a White Sox utility man, an outfielder. Bill Melton, former home run champ, a white guy, roomed with Walt Williams. These guys would stop by our Little League games. They were the grand marshals of our Little League parade in 1970. My team was the Sox. We wore those red and white uniforms that the Sox wore. I have a picture of me and Bill Melton, home run champ, wearing that uniform. I was 11.

Billy Williams lived in the same neighborhoods. Ernie Banks lived there, and so did his twins, Joel and Jerry. They played for the Cubs. Ernie Banks Ford sponsored the Cubs Little League team. Fergie Jenkins would drive us back to the South Side. You'd see him and say, "Mr. Jenkins, can you teach me how to throw a sinker?" There were no groupies, and if there were, we didn't know it. The groupies were kids. They were us.

These players, they lived where you lived, so I never rooted against either one, Sox or Cubs. I never hated the Cubs, even though they were on the North Side.

The interesting part comes in 1969 when the Cubs are having That Season. This is the only place in America where 69 doesn't mean [sexual] position, it means collapse.

The Cubs were rolling and my brother and I—I was 10, he was 8—wanted to go to Wrigley and see a game there. We watched the games on TV, but now we wanted to go see the Cubs.

We had never been to Wrigley. We had never been to the North Side. If you were black growing up on the South Side, the North Side might as well have been separated from the South Side by the Berlin Wall. You were not going to the North Side. And I'm sure kids on the North Side were not coming to the South Side.

But we wanted to go see the Cubs. I wanted to see my idol, Ernie Banks. My first two idols in life were Ali and Ernie Banks. But my father said no. He wasn't going to take us to Wrigley Field, and the reason was this: In 1947, my father went to see Jackie Robinson play at Wrigley Field and he got turned away. He vowed he would never set foot in Wrigley Field again, and he didn't.

Now fast-forward to 1969, 22 years later. My mother said to him, "You know, that's a long time ago. You've got to let it go. They want to go to the game. Take them to the game." So all four of us got on the train to Wrigley Field. It seemed so far that I thought we needed a hotel room. I didn't know where the North Side was. I didn't know how to get there. Blacks were associated with the South Side of Chicago. The North meant, like, Minnesota—The Great White North Side. Anybody my age who grew up here would understand that.

So I went to Wrigley to see Hank Aaron and the Braves. The Cubs won and Hank Aaron hit a home run. It couldn't have been any better for me.

By the way, my father never went there again. He went that one time. He died in '86. He died after the Super Bowl.

Now, if my memory is correct, the White Sox were taken off 'GN in 1970 or '69. They put them on the first pay-per-view ever, I think. So every day I'd come home and watch the Cubs. I couldn't watch the White Sox.

In the early '70s, if you were 12 years old, you went wherever you wanted to go. And even though my high school [St. Ignatius] was closer to Comiskey, my parents wouldn't let me go there. Comiskey was in the middle of the projects. But you could go to Wrigley and not even tell your parents. You'd get out of school at 1:25, which is when the Cubs games started. So you'd play hooky the last period, be on the train by 12:40, and be in your seat by the first pitch.

There is a difference between Cubs and Sox fans. It's like the difference between New York and Chicago. Cubs fans don't acknowledge that White Sox fans exist. More appropriately, it's like the difference between Chicago and Milwaukee, or Chicago and Indianapolis. Chicago doesn't even know where Milwaukee is. It's the same thing with Cubs fans. They're not even sure where Comiskey Park is.

But White Sox fans hate, *hate* Cubs fans. And maybe the New York–Chicago analogy is better. I went to Comiskey [author's note: Again, true Chicagoans simply can't call it U.S. Cellular] last weekend for the series, and White Sox fans hate Cubs fans. Cubs fans are like, "Who are you again? What's your team?"

There's a certain arrogance about Cubs fans, about Wrigley. They've always had a superior ballpark. But here's the thing: Comiskey has a better view than Wrigley, but only if they had turned the stadium around to face downtown. That's the best skyline view in America.

If I could invite three people to Murph's for a beer and burger, it'd be Banks, Santo, and Fergie Jenkins. Those were my baseball idols.

It's hard for me to watch Santo. It's hard to know he's had to deal with the diabetes, deal with the amputations. It's hard to deal with him not being in the Hall of Fame. I think he was the most underrated baseball player of his time, and not just at third base. Him and [Boston Red Sox] Jim Rice are the two most underrated players of the last 45 years. And I'm not totally biased, because I have no ties to Boston.

I wore No. 10 in Little League because I loved Santo.

I'd like to talk to those three because I'd like to know what they thought happened in '69. I'm obsessed with '69. I can't get over it. I can't get past it.

I don't tell Tony [Kornheiser] anything about the Cubs. New Yorkers don't understand the Cubs. They have no idea what it is. New York is so big.

He doesn't get it. He didn't get it that there was going to be a Bartman on the show, didn't know what it was going to be. No New Yorker gets it. There's a pathology involved with the Cubs.

If the Cubs won it all, I wouldn't do anything. I would just sit there and say, "I saw them do it."

My mother is 86. She cried when they lost last year. My mother's been here in Chicago 61 years. They have not won. She's been here *61* years and she's never seen a World Series game.

You know what, I don't think she's going to see it. I don't think *I'm* going to see it. I'm 45. No, last year was the year. I hope I'm wrong.

America can't be told about the Cubs. People have to come and sit in Wrigley Field. They have to come for a day game, for a series against the

Cards, or maybe the Astros. They have to watch them lose. They need to understand how, even after an 18-16 loss to the Phillies, how upbeat people are here. They need to know how this team touches this town, how seriously people take this stuff. They take it to heart. It hurts.

I didn't talk to my wife for almost a good day after the Game 6 [NLCS loss]. I talked to her after Game 7 because I knew they were going to lose, so I was fine with that. I talked to her during Game 7, but I did not talk to her at all during Game 6. I couldn't. And I didn't talk to her the next morning, part of the next afternoon. And I *know* I'm typical. I know I'm no different than X number of Cubs fans.

Harry Caray. During my senior year in college, me and another guy did a senior project for the Chicago Historical Society on Harry, an oral history. We go meet Harry at his apartment on North State and we're sitting there with Ike Cole playing the piano in the background and we're talking with Harry.

I don't remember much about the conversation, but we were talking with Harry.

You know, New Yorkers think they have all these great announcers, but they're such idiots. They don't have anybody like Harry Caray. They've never had anybody like Harry Caray.

There's not another Harry. He was at his best with the White Sox. Him and Jimmy Piersall. The greatest pairing of play-by-play man and color analyst that I'll ever see in my lifetime.

Bill Murray screaming out of the broadcast booth "Your mother wears combat boots" could be the greatest line ever uttered on the air. That was the greatest performance ever in a broadcast booth. I watched every second of it. I loved it. I wish I had a tape of it.

If Bartman came up to this table, I'd tell him, "Get away from me." I'm embarrassed I feel that way. Intellectually, I know it wasn't his fault. But yet I feel it was. I'd rather play golf with O. J. than with Bartman. I bashed Bartman on television, and I regretted it that night. But the next day, I said it again.

I would hope the Cubs win just to save his life here. He can't have a life here until they win.

So sad. So sad. I wish I wasn't like this, but there's nothing I can do about it. I have to accept it.

GAME 79

Friday, July 2, 2004 . . . Cubs 6, White Sox 2 . . . Wrigley Field . . . Stat of the game: "Big Z," as Dusty Baker likes to call Carlos Zambrano, earns his ninth win and all but locks up an All-Star Game invite. . . . . Stuff: Kent Mercker plays soft toss with his daughter. Matt Clement watches her throw for a few moments and says, "She's got a better arm than you." Says Mercker: "Yeah, why didn't she face Beltran yesterday?" Pitchers never forget dingers. . . . The Curse lives: Aramis Ramirez leaves the game in the sixth with a strained groin. Todd Hollandsworth and his bad shin are destined for the DL. Zambrano leaves the mound with his cramped fingers curled like the Wicked Witch of the West's. . . . White Sox GM Ken Williams rags hard on the Tribune's Paul Sullivan for suggesting in print that Sox star (and soon-to-be free agent) Magglio Ordonez could become a Cub.

The Baker managerial philosophy:

"Just hustle. Go hard. Have fun. We're here to have fun, and hopefully make lots of money. That's the focus."

And strategy?

"No strategy. I just want them to hustle and stick with the plays. I'm fine, as long as they give their best. And they've got to have fun out there."

Does GM Jim Hendry know about this? No strategy? Make lots of money?

Oh, wait, this is *Melissa* Baker, Dusty's wife. She's managing the Cubs wives/significant others vs. the White Sox wives/significant others in a pregame softball charity event at Wrigley. It isn't her first time running a team. Melissa also managed the Giants wives, etc. vs. the Oakland A's counterparts when Dusty worked for San Francisco.

"When I left, we were 7-2," she says of her Bay Area record.

So, like her husband, she left because of contract problems with the other Giants wives?

"Yeah, it was contract problems," she says, laughing. "Yeah, among other things. And we like Chicago."

Melissa played basketball and softball in college. She has a jock mentality, as evidenced by a pregame fall by Darren off the wooden dugout seats.

"Is he bleeding?" she says, standing about 10 feet away.

"No," says MLB.com reporter Carrie Muskat, who dabs the tears from Darren's eyes with a towel.

"Then tell him to shake it off."

There are certain unspoken rules when you're the wife of a big league manager or player. Shortly after their marriage, Melissa asked Dusty's father for a couple of tips on understanding her new husband.

Mr. Baker's tips: "After he loses, leave him alone for an hour and he'll be all right. If you hassle him during that hour after a tough loss, then he'll probably snap at you or say something he don't really want to say. The second thing: On a full moon, don't let him out of the house because he don't know when to come home."

So after, say, the Game 7 NLCS defeat, Melissa didn't bother asking Dusty if he wanted to play Twister?

"No, we don't really say a whole lot," she says. "I just kind of give him some time. What helps is that sometimes if Darren wants to play or just goof around, then it makes things a little easier. But for him to come home and stew on it—no, that doesn't happen very often."

Melissa is the one who organized the Cubs-Sox charity game. The proceeds are split between Cubs Care and White Sox Charities. If all goes well she'd like to make it an annual event, with the 2005 game at U.S. Cellular. In other words, she has a few items on her plate.

"I just kind of have my own things going and he has his," she says. "It's his job. It has its perks and stuff, but we're just regular people."

Sure, just regular people. Just like the time Melissa beat Dusty in a game of Ping-Pong at the house of Giants player Chili Davis.

"She don't want to hear it, but I was drinking that night and my equilibrium was off and I got upset and accidentally broke the paddle and threw it out the window," says Dusty. "She's beating me and laughing, and I don't like that."

Dusty recovered. If anything, he has a greater respect for Melissa. She can beat him at Ping-Pong and remember those two rules from her father-in-law.

"You definitely got to be a special person," says Dusty of baseball wives. "You got to have tolerance. You have to understand your husband's work."

By the way, the Bakers finish the day 2-0. Melissa wins. Dusty wins. No quiet time tonight.

GAME 80

Saturday, July 3, 2004 . . . Cubs 4, White Sox 2 . . . Wrigley Field . . . Stat of the game: The game goes only five and a half innings, thanks to persistent rains that turn Wrigley into South Carolina marshland. . . . Stuff: The Curse lives: Todd Hollandsworth (shin) goes on the disabled list, Aramis Ramirez (groin) is lost for at least three to five days. . . . WGN Radio play-by-play master Pat Hughes passes the 3,400-game broadcast mark for his career. . . . Rey Ordonez, who hasn't hit a home run since dinosaurs roamed the earth, sends a Felix Diaz pitch into the left-field bleachers. . . . Sammy Sosa hits a fifth-inning homer to right that somehow slices through the monsoon conditions. Then he makes what might have been a game-saving sliding catch in the top of the sixth.

Fifteen hours ago, Brendan Harris was in the visitors' dugout at Omaha's Rosenblatt Stadium sipping on a cup of coffee, trying to stay dry as the Iowa Cubs waited out a rain delay. Then he was summoned to manager Mike Quade's office.

Quade didn't say a word at first. Instead, he smiled and shook Harris's hand.

Harris was going to the big leagues.

"Those next five minutes, I don't really remember anything," he says.

This is how it works. One minute you're in Triple-A getting $20 a day in meal money. Then Ramirez strains his groin, Hollandsworth goes on the DL, and the big league club suddenly needs a player, preferably an infielder.

Harris can do that. He was drafted in 2001 as a third baseman and later moved to second base. He left the Iowa Cubs with a .311 average, eight homers, and 26 RBI in 56 games. In June, he hit a Teddy Ballgame-like .400.

"He's been hot lately," says GM Jim Hendry.

Harris is insurance, a body to help get the Cubs to the All-Star break. He doesn't mind a bit.

The remainder of Friday night was spent making travel arrangements from Omaha to Chicago, as well as accepting congratulations from teammates. Harris called his parents, too; they're making the trip from upstate New York to Wrigley. Then he tried to relax and get some sleep. Fat chance.

"My roommate Bill Selby [431 Major League at-bats] told me about the first time he was called up," says Harris. "He said we might as well stay up and order a movie or something, because it was going to be tough to get some sleep."

Selby was right. Harris couldn't sleep, so they watched *Terminator 3* on the hotel cable.

This morning, he took a 6:30 flight to Chicago and was in the Cubs' clubhouse before 9. Now he sits by himself in the dugout wearing his new uni and watches the White Sox take BP. He wore No. 23 in the minors, but no way is he getting Ryne Sandberg's number. So hello No. 19.

Later, Harris is told to grab a mitt and play catcher. As the lowest-ranking rookie, he has to catch the ceremonial first pitches of some yahoos from a local bank. You think Harris minds? He'd trim the ivy if Dusty Baker asked him.

Before he left Omaha, some of the Iowa Cubs such as Trenidad Hubbard and Calvin Murray, guys with big league experience, offered some advice to Harris. "Make sure you enjoy it," they told him.

No problem there. Harris is already enjoying the difference.

Big league meal money is $77.50 a day.

GAME 81

Sunday, July 4, 2004 . . . Cubs 2, White Sox 1 . . . Wrigley Field . . . Cubs NL Central pennant flies: Second (46-35) . . . Stat of the game: Glendon Rusch pitches eight shutout innings. How'd this guy lose 12 games in 2003? . . . Stuff: The William Hung of Seventh-Inning Stretch singers—Mike Ditka—makes his seventh appearance as the guest conductor. . . . Carlos Zambrano, Moises Alou, and Sammy Sosa are named to the NL All-Star Game roster. . . . LaTroy Hawkins blows his fourth save in 15 save situations. . . . Just 81 more regular-season games to go.

A Wrigley Field ground rules quiz:

Sosa hits the top or face of the screen in front of the bleacher wall and the ball bounces back on the field. Home run or still in play?

Corey Patterson drives a ball over Carlos Lee's head. The ball settles into the vines. Lee doesn't bother to look. Double or still in play?

It is physically impossible for a ball to land in foul territory between the left-field or right-field grass and the walls along the farthest points of the left- or right-field foul lines. True or false?

Alou pulls a ball down the left-field line. It hits the foul pole above the painted mark. Home run, double, or foul ball?

This is why you talk to Charlie Reliford, the crew chief of the umpiring crew working this weekend's Cubs-White Sox series. This is Reliford's 15th season in the big leagues. He knows each and every one of the 13 Wrigley Field ground rules by heart. In fact, there isn't much Reliford doesn't know about the place.

On Wrigley:

It is absolutely one of my favorite trips. I love coming to Wrigley. I think there's something special about it. The fans, the day games, the atmosphere, the history. Even The Babe played here.

I had the Yankees-Mets Subway Series. This year I have the Cubs-White Sox. Those are special games.

On Wrigley and its 13 ground rules:

We discuss them with both managers at home plate of the first game of every series, so both teams should know them. It's not the easiest park, but it's not the hardest. I always tell people this is one of the things that make baseball unique. If you go to a basketball game, the actual playing dimensions are the same. In baseball the infield is the same, but the rest of the stadium dimensions are unique.

On balls sticking in the vines:

That is not a significantly hard call for us, though we might have to make a delayed call on it. But if it sticks, then it's a ground-rule double. Sometimes the players panic; the players get anxious because possibly they're thinking we're not going to make a call. But we will. Sometimes it seems a little delayed.

What happens is a player raises his arms to signify the ball is stuck. When you see them throw up their hands, that's when you go out there and look. But if that player starts searching for it, well, if he plays it, he better find it.

On the outfield baskets:

In the early '90s—I'm going to say in 1990—I actually had fan interference over the basket. That's because the fans are so close everywhere. Obviously, the baskets cut down on most of that, but there's still the possibility of fan interference.

On the foul poles:
It is a good park to umpire in, but some of the more difficult aspects of it are the foul poles. In the new parks, there's usually a three-foot screen all the way up the poles. In Wrigley, those screens only go about halfway up the pole.

On Wrigley's winds:
At all times in the rotation, each umpire is assigned a coverage area. When the winds are significant, the ball will start in one area and drift to another umpire's coverage area. The way we deal with that is once the umpire goes out, he's going to take it even if it drifts into another umpire's area.

On adding a new ground rule at Wrigley:
The only area of concern I have deals with the new renovations, where they created a recessed space between the dugout and the wall because of the new seating. That's an area where the batboy or the ballperson are sitting. Right now if your catcher or fielder runs over there and trips over people, or a chair, that's too bad. What might have to be considered is putting a line where the corner of that recessed area juts out. Make the space inside that recessed area a dead area.

On hitting the left-field and right-field foul lines:
When I first came to the big leagues—when I came to Wrigley—I was told it was impossible to hit a ball foul without first hitting the wall. So I got a ball and laid it between the foul line and the wall. It can be done, but it would take a miraculous shot to land and not hit that wall.

GAME 82

Monday, July 5, 2004 . . . Milwaukee Brewers 1, Cubs 0 . . . Miller Park . . . Stat of the game: The Cubs have scored three runs during Matt Clement's last 31⅔ innings. . . . Stuff: A bouquet of birthday balloons (as well as a gag gift of the inflatable variety) is waiting for Cubs hitting coach Gary Matthews, now 54, when he arrives at the clubhouse. . . . Tough day for Dusty Baker. Not only do the Cubs lose a game in the standings to St. Louis, but Baker takes a foul ball flush on the ribs during Jose Macias's ninth-inning at-bat.

Miller Park has all the charm of a really nice airplane hangar. But say this for the place: It's clean, it's relatively new, and the bratwurst with special sauce is to die for.

Problem is, the Brewers haven't come within a foul pole of success since Robin Yount and Paul Molitor were teammates. They haven't had a winning record since 1992, and haven't played in the postseason since the 1982 World Series. And once the Green Bay Packers crank up their training camp in July, the Brewers suddenly become a statewide afterthought.

This year is a little different. The Brewers are now four games over .500 and still within viewing distance of the first-place Cardinals. But on most nights here you can hear crickets chirp.

Except when the Cubs are in town.

There's a reason why I-94 is a major revenue source this week for the Wisconsin State Police. You'd camp out with a radar gun, too, if you saw all the Illinois tags.

The Brewers now have two sellouts this season: One on Opening Day, one today against the Cubs. They'll have another one on Wednesday, and another one on Thursday.

The Cubs are the baseball box office equivalent of *Spider-Man 2*, especially in Milwaukee. In 2003, the Cubs accounted for three of the four Brewers sellouts, and 228,004 of the team's 1,700,354 home attendance. In just seven games, the Cubs accounted for 13.4 percent of Milwaukee's total gate. Nobody else comes close.

Jim Bathey is the Brewers' assistant vice president for ticket sales. He meets me just outside the glass doors of the team's administrative offices on the loge level of Miller Park. If he were any happier, he'd break into spontaneous song and dance.

"We've already sold all of our tickets for the game," he says. "The capacity is 41,900. We are prepared to sell as many as 4,000 standing-room-only tickets."

Cha-ching. The Brewers get 45,016 for today's game, the second-largest crowd in Miller Park history. Sellouts are expected Tuesday and Wednesday, too.

Bathey knows who butters the Brewers' bread. According to the team's research, about 40 percent of all trackable tickets for the Cubs-Brewers game were purchased by people with Illinois addresses. No wonder Chicago is Bathey's kind of town.

"The White Sox were always a big draw for us in Milwaukee," says Bathey, whose office features a *Mr. 3000* movie poster (he makes a brief appearance in the Bernie Mac baseball flick, filmed, by the way, at Miller Park). "Then, when we moved to the National League, the Cubs became even a bigger draw. From a business perspective, based on the fact that we've had 11 consecutive losing seasons, the first thing I look at when we receive our schedule each August is when do we play the Cubs."

There isn't enough black ink to handle the take of a Cubs visit. The three-game series during the 2003 Labor Day weekend drew 131,254, a Miller Park record. "Well over 50 percent [of those crowds] last September were Cubs fans."

Bathey nearly had a litter of kittens when he saw the 2004 schedule last August: 10 games at Miller Park, but all of them were weekday games, and bunched in a seven-week time frame. Weekday games are usually box-office death. "We know if we have the Cubs on the weekend, we'll sell out," he says.

But the Cubs' success of 2003 has translated into boffo Brewers sales, no matter the day. It's as simple as supply and demand.

"Once [the Cubs reached the NLCS], we felt a lot better about the schedule," Bathey says. "From a business standpoint, we knew that it would be that much more difficult for Cubs fans to get a ticket at Wrigley Field. And those fans, being 90 minutes away, we felt confident that a lot of them would have no alternative but to come on up."

Cubs fans have actually purchased the $640 20-game season-ticket packages from the Brewers. The reason? The deal allows them to pick what games they want to attend. So they choose the 10 Cubs games at Miller Park and usually fill in the rest with Cardinals and Houston Astros dates.

"If you were to look at all sports, Cubs fans and Packers fans are among the most loyal, regardless of the team's performance," Bathey says.

I ask him if he's jealous.

"At times," says Bathey. "My job is to put as many fans in the ballpark as possible, and when I see the Cubs do that even when they're not winning, sometimes you wonder why. You wonder if there's anything we could be doing differently."

I kiddingly suggest growing ivy on the outfield walls.

Bathey breaks into a sheepish grin.

"We are," he says.

GAME 83

Tuesday, July 6, 2004 . . . Brewers 4, Cubs 2 . . . Miller Park . . . Stuff: Brendan Harris gets his first start. Ron Santo approaches the rookie before the game and gives him the same advice Ernie Banks gave Santo in 1960: Pretend you're facing Triple-A pitching. Harris gets his first big league hit and RBI on a double to right center. . . . The Cubs drop five games behind the evil Cardinals.

Jack Lopez got sent down to the minors today.

He knew it was inevitable, but it's still hard to pack up your Nike glove, your cleats, your bats (the ones with the just-shaved handles), and say good-bye to everyone. Some of the other players stopped by to wish him well, but let's face it, it's always an awkward time in the Cubs clubhouse when a kid—a good one, too—gets shipped out.

Lopez didn't say much. He never does. That's what everyone liked about him. He listened, learned, did whatever was asked. And now he's gone. About the only thing he said before hopping on his flight to Orlando was "I'll be back later this summer."

I only talked to him once during his cup of coffee with the Cubs. It was just before he left. He wore his Cubs uni (good ol' No. 59) and mostly stared straight ahead as he sat on the padded dugout seat at Miller Park. When you asked him a question, he didn't blurt out the first cliché that came to mind. Lopez took his time. He was thoughtful.

Just the other day, he was out there warming up with Cubs first-base coach Gene Clines. What an arm. Everyone could see his talent.

Michael Barrett used to pull him aside and work with him on his footwork, show him how to cut a sliver of time on the catch and release. And Aramis Ramirez would always tell him, "Don't try to pull everything." Even in faraway Seattle, veteran Mariners DH Edgar Martinez sent his regards. Martinez and Lopez go back a long ways.

Lopez never got an official at-bat, but he did get some occasional TV time. He was the one always wearing a batting helmet, as if to show Dusty Baker he was ready, prepared. I liked that about him. His best friend back home would always tell everyone, "I saw Jack on the Cubs game again," but nobody believed him.

Lopez says he'll be back. But if he isn't, he'll always have a handful of incredible mementos and memories. There's a photo of him, Sammy Sosa, and Barry Bonds. He even got to try on a 2002 San Francisco Giants NL championship ring. Lopez wants one of those rings. All the great ones do.

I'm going to miss Lopez. He was always one of the first guys in the clubhouse, and nobody worked harder on his daily conditioning program than Lopez. He didn't swear. He didn't dip. He always had a shy smile for anyone who said hello.

And now he's in the minors. Actually, he is a minor. But that's how it goes for Cubs batboys. Here today, home in Orlando tomorrow.

Lopez, the 11-year-old son of Cubs bullpen coach Juan Lopez, is back with his traveling Little League team. Former big leaguer Dante Bichette is the team's coach, and Lopez's godfather is none other than the Mariners' Martinez. So it's no surprise what Lopez wants to do when he grows up.

"Play in the Major Leagues," he said that day in the dugout.

That's when Juan interrupted. "What's before baseball? What did I tell you?"

"Oh, yeah," said Jack, after a long pause. "School is first."

You've never seen a father more proud of a son.

GAME 84

Wednesday, July 7, 2004 . . . Brewers 4, Cubs 0 . . . Miller Park . . . Stuff: Brewers fans wave the brooms. . . . No Aramis Ramirez, no runs. The Cubs are averaging less than two runs since Ramirez (groin strain) became a spectator July 3.

Three days ago, only a few hours before the Cubs played the White Sox, Media Relations Director Sharon Pannozzo delivered Carlos Zambrano the news.

"Hey, Carlos, by the way, Jim [Hendry] is running late and he told me to tell you that you made the team."

This is how Zambrano, 23, learned he was a National League All-Star. The Brewers congratulated him tonight by milking 108 pitches out of him before he left after 5⅔ innings. He also broke a bat over his knee and once again threw a hissy fit that almost got him booted out of the game by home plate umpire Phil Cuzzi.

Kids.

Zambrano drops to 9-4, and afterward he was his usual apologetic self. You've heard it before.

The likable Zambrano is a pin-striped drama club on the mound. Fist pumps. Pointing. Dirt kicking. Yelling. The thing is, it's hard to stay mad at Zambrano. You see him walking around the clubhouse, all 6-5, 255 pounds of him, and you're struck by his innocence, almost his naïveté. Is playful the right word? But then he gets on the mound and he becomes more emotional than a soap opera diva.

But here's why you give Zambrano the benefit of the doubt: When Pannozzo told him he had made his first All-Star Game roster, Zambrano immediately called his agent, his buddies, and his pastor. Then he called his family in Puerto Cabello, Venezuela.

"They don't understand," he says. "My dad, he knows just a little bit. But my mom doesn't know anything about baseball. She only know that I'm in the big leagues."

If it were up to Zambrano's old man, Carlos wouldn't be playing baseball. That's how it was with Zambrano's five older brothers.

"He don't let my oldest brother play baseball, because he's a tough type of religious guy who don't believe in baseball," says Zambrano.

Alberto Rondon is the guy who scouted Zambrano. They signed him in 1997 as a nondrafted free agent. Zambrano's father reluctantly approved his son's new profession.

"I was lucky," says Carlos. "My dad was getting old. He recognized that somebody had to do something for the family. So he let me and my younger brother play baseball."

Zambrano, who helps provide financial support for the family, bought his parents one of those satellite dishes big enough to track flocks of geese migrating south. His folks see him on TV but have no real appreciation of their son's growing reputation as a star and occasional flake. That's OK; his peers do.

Zambrano might be a bit of a goof on the field, but his heart is in the right place. He remembers watching All-Star Games as a kid, and later made it a goal to play in one if he reached the big leagues. Surprise.

Zambrano leaves for Houston after Sunday's game. He'll share a clubhouse with his favorite player, Roger Clemens. And he plans on asking for lots of autographs.

"You want to have something to show your parents, your grandparents, your kids," he says. "They see that and they can say, 'He was an All-Star.'"

Pride. That's something even Zambrano's old man should understand.

GAME 85

Friday, July 9, 2004 . . . Cardinals 6, Cubs 1 . . . Busch Stadium . . . Stat of the game: The Cubs' offense, which has taken a leave of absence to pursue other interests, scores exactly one run. . . . Stuff: The Cubs now trail the Cards by seven games, which is why nervous followers are tracking the wild-card standings. But last year at this time, the Cubs were only two games over .500, and as late as July 26 they trailed the first-place Houston Astros by 5½ games. . . . The Curse in Reverse: Josh Beckett is on the DL and the Marlins drop to .500 and fourth place in the NL East.

The last time Mike Remlinger pitched was June 23, at this very same Busch Stadium. That was the night the Cubs could have moved into a first-place tie with the Cardinals. Instead, they blew a 9-5 sixth-inning lead and have slowly fallen behind the more efficient and better-balanced Cards. With tonight's loss, the Cubs have dropped eight of the 14 games they've played since the devastating June 23 defeat.

Remlinger threw eight pitches that June evening. He also got the loss. The next day, he went on the 15-day disabled list with left-shoulder tendinitis.

Remlinger is a Dartmouth man, so he's known ivy long before he saw Wrigley. He has a degree in economics, as well as a refreshing and thoughtful perspective on all things baseball. But no amount of education, Ivy League or otherwise, can change a simple, indisputable truth: It sucks being on the DL.

"In baseball, when you're not in this clubhouse, you cease to exist," says Remlinger. "When you go on a rehab [assignment] or get sent to the minor leagues, you cease to exist. As much as your friends and teammates feel for where you are, No. 1, you can't help them. And No. 2, they're certainly not going to trade positions with you."

This isn't Remlinger's first time on the DL. He missed almost the entire

1988 season (strained left elbow), and made subsequent visits to the DL in 1992 (strained left elbow), 1999 (strained muscle, left side), 2000 (left elbow stiffness, allergic reaction), 2002 (strained left groin). After the 2003 season, he underwent arthroscopic surgery for left rotator cuff debridement, which is a fancy way of saying they snipped off some tissue. That partly explains the two DL stays in 2004 (one beginning in March, and again in June).

Now he stands in front of his locker, a mummylike ice wrap hiding his left shoulder and much of the University of Tennessee T-shirt he's wearing. Remlinger can read the standings as well as anyone. The Cubs need hitting, but they also need left-handed relievers, the more the better.

But there's the rub. He wants to come back, but his tender shoulder isn't so sure. So he remains on the DL, travels with the team, undergoes treatment, tests his shoulder, and waits. He is of the Cubs world, but he isn't entirely in it. Such is life in injury limbo.

"I think that's one of the things that makes us unique—not just baseball players, but all athletes—is you have that mentality," he says, walking away in midsentence every so often to spit some dip into a garbage can. "You can spend eight months with somebody, even years with somebody, depending on how long you've been teammates, and see them go down, and the next day you walk out there like they're not even a part of your life anymore. That's the way it has to be."

Remlinger is at the fringe of the Cubs' lives. They see him return from the field after a throwing session . . . they care, but compassion goes only so far.

"When it's game time, you have to go with what you have," he says. "If you worry about what you don't have, it takes away from your ability."

Remlinger will earn the oddly configured $3,983,333 this season, so he isn't asking for sympathy. His 44-year-old brother hangs drywall for a living, so Remlinger knows there are plenty of working stiffs dealing with their own aches and pains.

But there were times during the 2003 season, more than anyone will ever know, when Remlinger would wake up and not be able to lift his left arm. It was only after a long, hot shower that his shoulder would begin to loosen and the range of motion would slowly return.

"Everyone deals with something," he says. "It's part of the deal."

For Remlinger, it takes anywhere from three to six weeks for his arm to recover after a season's worth of use. This year, who knows? His arm and shoulder felt relatively wonderful before he made a rehab stay with the Iowa Cubs earlier in the season. Then the dull ache arrived.

"That's one of the hardest things as a younger player to figure out, the difference between 'Am I hurt? Or do I hurt? Is there something physically wrong and I'm going to make it worse? Or do I just hurt and this is what I'm going to have to deal with?'" says Remlinger. "When you talk about the difference between older and younger players, that's the difference."

Remlinger wants to play. You don't go through all this rehab for any other reason.

I ask Remlinger if it's worth it. Is it worth the pain?

He pauses in midstep toward the garbage can.

"Depends if we win."

GAME 86

Saturday, July 10, 2004 . . . Cardinals 5, Cubs 2 . . . Busch Stadium . . . Stuff: Matt Clement gets no run support and loses. What else is new? . . . The Cards have won eight consecutive games. They lead the Cubs by eight in the standings. Maybe a wild-card spot is a more realistic goal, after all.

There's always one guy on every team a writer can go to when all else fails. Reliever Kent Mercker is that guy on the Cubs.

Mercker has spent 13-plus seasons in the big leagues and owns a World Series ring (1995), a complete-game no-hitter (1994), the first combined no-hitter in National League history (1991), and a sense of humor that ought to be cloned. Considering how things are going on this road trip, you need a sense of humor.

Then again, Mercker is the same guy who spent four days in intensive care after suffering a cerebral brain hemorrhage in 2000. You tend not to sweat the small stuff after one of those.

Anyway, the baseball world according to Kent Franklin Mercker:

Best Stadium
Wrigley Field. Just because of the history.

Best Bullpen
I'm going to say San Diego—not the new one [PETCO Park], but the old

one. It was the best not because you could see it from the stands, but because no one could see you. You could throw bad and no one would know. Fans couldn't see you, and your teammates couldn't see you.

Best Visitors' Clubhouse
Colorado. Coors Field.

Best Home Clubhouse
I'm going to go with Cincinnati. But it's almost too big.

Best Fans
It's a tie between the Cubs and the Red Sox. What makes them different is the passion. It's handed down, it's generational. You don't find any yuppie Red Sox fans. They've got their hats that their grandfathers gave them. It's the same hat. And they leave their season tickets in their wills. They just hand them down. That's passion.

Best Mound
Dodger Stadium.

Best Place to Get Ripped by Fans
It used to be San Francisco. When I'd come into Chicago with the Braves, yeah, you're sitting right in front of them along that right-field foul wall, but they're not violent. They're on you, but they're not violent. Now? Philly. I guess it would have to be Philly.

Best Food Spread in Visiting Clubhouse
Houston. St. Louis is a close second.

Best Pampering in Visiting Clubhouse
It's not the National League, but the guy in Tampa Bay is the best. He has a guy who comes in and gives you a haircut. He's got a guy who cleans and shines your shoes during the game. After him, it'd be Houston, then St. Louis.

Best City
Chicago. That's because of the city and the day games. You get to see the city more because of the day games. I like Atlanta a lot, too. But Chicago's the best.

[An MLB.com poll of a cross section of players confirms Mercker's choice. Chicago finishes first, New York second as a travel favorite.]

Worst Stadium

It's not in this league. It's U.S. Cellular. For as new as it is, they built it like a cookie cutter. What everyone was trying to get away from, they did. And they don't have enough shower pressure. Their showers are terrible. Remember, you can make up for a bad stadium with nice showers.

Best Shower Pressure

Dodger Stadium.

In fact, if I was telling someone how to build one of these new stadiums, I'd tell them start with the shower pressure and build up from there.

Worst Fans

Montreal. Very apathetic.

Worst Mound

Cincinnati.

Worst Road Trip

Puerto Rico. But we might have had bad timing. We went on Good Friday. We were there Friday, Saturday, and Sunday. The whole country was closed. Got rained out the first night. Got a split doubleheader the next day. It was 100 degrees. Had an hour-and-a-half rain delay on Sunday. Then a six-and-a-half-hour flight back.

Best Restaurant

It's in Chicago—Ron of Japan. It's on East Ontario.

Best Hotel

Grand Hyatt in New York. And you know why? You can close your curtains and in the morning you don't know it's daylight. Good curtains.

GAME 87

Sunday, July 11, 2004 . . . Cubs 8, Cardinals 4 . . . Busch Stadium . . . Stat of the game: Who cares? The Cubs finally win. . . . Stuff: It's a toss-up on story lines. Kerry Wood rejoins the rotation, goes five strong innings, and picks up his first win since April 24. It also marks the first time this season Wood and Prior have been in the same rotation. Or you have Sammy Sosa, who drives in five runs in an absolute must-win game. . . . Mike Remlinger comes off the disabled list. Rookies Michael Wuertz and Jon Leicester are sent to Iowa.

Numbers at the All-Star break:

The Cubs are seven games behind the Cardinals in the NL Central, one game behind the San Francisco Giants in the wild-card race.

The Cubs rank third in NL batting, seventh in runs scored, second in total bases, second in home runs, sixth in RBI, 14th in walks, seventh in strikeouts, and have the third-fewest errors.

The Cubs' pitching staff ranks second in NL ERA, eighth in home runs, second in strikeouts, tied for sixth in walks, and third in hit batsmen.

The Cubs currently have five players (Ryan Dempster, Todd Hollandsworth, Alex Gonzalez, Todd Wellemeyer, Joe Borowski) on the DL.

The Cubs are sixth in NL home attendance (1,611,019), though it should be noted they've had eight fewer home dates than the league-leading Giants (1,935,965).

The Cubs have outdrawn the White Sox by about 600,000, an average of about 16,000 per home game. (Of course, the Sox have a slightly better record than the Cubs at the break, and lead the AL Central by a half-game.)

Eric Karabell couldn't give a squat about most of these numbers. With the exception of several team offensive, defensive, and pitching categories, ESPN.com's fantasy baseball guru is interested only in individual production.

A first-half analysis:

Derrek Lee (.304, 12 HR, 49 RBI, 42 R, 6 SB)

Karabell then (April 11): "I've already done about 10 drafts, and I think he's overrated because people think he's going to steal a lot of bases."

Karabell now: "I was right on the money. He's not running. He does hit for average and he hits a ton of doubles. He's not going to hit 30 homers."

Lee is what he is. He's not a 40-home-run guy, not a 20-steal guy. He'll finish with 25 home runs, 100 RBI, 10 steals, a .300 average—all things that were easy to predict."

Mark Grudzielanek (.286 [only 70 at-bats], 1 HR, 5 RBI, 8 R, 0 SB), Todd Walker (.283, 11 HR, 29 RBI, 47 R, 0 SB)

Karabell then: "I would rather have Walker than Grudzielanek, but I probably wouldn't be too high on either one of them."

Karabell now: "I would think Grudzielanek would play more in the second half because, one, he gets to more balls than Walker. He's a legitimate .280 hitter. Really, the Cubs do it all wrong. If only they would put guys in the top of their order who would take a walk, get on base. I can't believe their leading walk guy [Lee, 33 BB] is on pace for 60 walks. Typical Dusty Baker."

Alex Gonzalez (.244 [only 90 at-bats], 3 HR, 7 RBI, 11 R, 1 SB), Ramon Martinez (.261, 2 HR, 23 RBI, 16 R, 0 SB), Rey Ordonez (.172 [58 at-bats], 1 HR, 5 RBI, 2 R, 0 SB)

Karabell then: "At a position where fantasy has seen 10 solid guys go in the first five rounds of the draft, Alex Gonzalez will get forgotten."

Karabell now: "Shortstop is a total wasteland. Gonzalez has missed most of the year. Ramon Martinez can't hit at all. He has 15 extra-base hits—yecch. But whatever I said about Gonzalez still stands."

Aramis Ramirez (.326, 15 HR, 56 RBI, 60 R, 0 SB)

Karabell then: "The potential is there for him to hit 30 homers and knock in 100 runs, assuming the defense doesn't take him out of the lineup, and I don't think it will. He doesn't get hurt. . . ."

Karabell now: "Right on the money. He's missed a couple of games [try eight, and counting]. The only thing out of the ordinary is that .326 average, because he doesn't walk. He's still not a top-five third baseman, but he's close."

Moises Alou (.276, 19 HR, 49 RBI, 51 R, 2 SB)

Karabell then: "Moises Alou is old. He's older than I am. He's older than you. . . . If he knocks in another 91 runs and hits .280, then I guess I'll just be wrong."

Karabell now: "I was wrong about Alou, who is actually not older than you, is he? He's older than me. All I can say about Alou is that he started out fast. Part of that is because Sosa was out of the lineup and he got to move up in the order. He did hit under .200 in June, though. He's dropped below Sosa in the order, and he should be below Ramirez. His 19 home runs at the break are shocking, but those other numbers are on pace. Good for him."

Corey Patterson (.274, 10 HR, 35 RBI, 45 R, 9 SB)

Karabell then: "A huge upside . . . He still has the potential to hit 30 homers and knock in 100."

Karabell now: "I would agree on the upside part, but I think we're getting to the point where he's not going to realize that upside. He's not even on pace for 20 home runs and 20 steals. And his walk-to-strikeout rate remains horrific [25/77]. Really, it's one of the worst in baseball for a guy with potential like this. I don't blame the ACL injury anymore. I blame Patterson's makeup. He refuses to learn the strike zone. I no longer think he's going to be a 30-home-run hitter. Right now, he's a pretty big disappointment in fantasy."

Sosa (.279, 16 HR, 39 RBI, 33 R, 0 SB)

Karabell then: "He shouldn't miss any time this year, assuming he doesn't cork his bat or doesn't get hurt. He could hit 45 to 50 home runs, and I think he's a safer bet to do that than Bonds in '04."

Karabell now: "Well, we couldn't have predicted another injury for him, especially the injury he had. When he went on the DL for sneezing, which I couldn't make up, that obviously affected his numbers. In terms of pure numbers, when Sosa's been in the lineup he's done what I expected him to do. He should still hit 30 home runs, which isn't bad considering he missed a month of the season."

Michael Barrett (.291, 10 HR, 43 RBI, 29 R, 1 SB)

Karabell then: "I don't like their catcher, I can tell you that. He's not in the top 20 of catchers, which, frankly, is hard to do, considering this guy is a veteran. I'm not a big fan of Barrett. He's probably a real nice guy, but he's not a really good player."

Karabell now: "Michael, I owe you dinner. He's hitting .291 and is on pace to hit 19 home runs, but he still hasn't cracked the top 10 of fantasy catchers. But did I, or anyone else, think he would be one of the better catchers in fantasy baseball? No. Is there a guarantee he'll do this in the second half? No. He's still prone to hot and cold streaks. Please, trade this guy now."

Mark Prior (2-2, 4.00 ERA, 40 Ks, 16 BB)

Karabell then: "He's got to stay healthy. If he does—and he's had problems with that Achilles—I think he could be a monster this year."

Karabell now: "Prior has made only seven starts, so we still don't have the complete story on him. We've seen periods of dominance, and we've also seen a guy who's been wild. That happens when you return from injury. Could he be one of the best pitchers in the second half? Absolutely. It wouldn't shock me if he won 10 games in the second half. Long term, I worry that he's going to break down still."

Kerry Wood (4-3, 2.72 ERA, 57 Ks, 16 BB)

Karabell then: "He's had five seasons and he still hasn't won more than 14 games."

Karabell now: "Wood won't win 14 games this year, mainly because he missed two months because of that triceps injury. There were big red warning signs because of overuse. Could he again be a top pitcher in the second half? He could be. But think about this: Wood and Prior missed a combined 15 starts in the first half. It's amazing the Cubs are still in the race. But from a fantasy standpoint, I would have to see 200-inning seasons in the next year or two to make them top picks in the next three, four years."

Greg Maddux (7-7, 4.51 ERA, 77 Ks, 18 BB)

Karabell then: "Maddux will win his 300th game in 2004. He shouldn't be forgotten in fantasy baseball. However, there has been a disturbing trend in Maddux's pitching the last couple of years. I think he'll win 15 games."

Karabell now: "Maddux hasn't been as good as I expected, mainly because he's been way too hittable. He's on pace to give up 37 home runs, which isn't like him. He'll win his 300th game and he might get to 15 wins this season. I wouldn't even put him in my top 20 right now. He's pitching more like a Brewer than a Cub. Of course, it would help if he had an infield."

Matt Clement (7-8, 2.91 ERA, 123 Ks, 45 BB)

Karabell then: "He could win 15 and strike out 200 guys if it goes well."

Karabell now: "At this point, I'll take Clement over Wood because I know he's healthy. He should win 15. Clement is a very underrated pitcher. It's hard to get a hit off him, hard to get a walk off him. Clement has really been a solid fantasy find, and you got him five rounds after you got Wood, so good for you."

Carlos Zambrano (9-4, 2.61 ERA, 104 Ks, 47 BB)

Karabell then: "If I had my choice of Zambrano or Clement, I would take Clement."

Karabell now: "Based on their current ERAs, you'd have to say Zambrano has had a better first half than Clement. What Zambrano has done—and I'm talking about throwing something like 110 pitches per start—it's still hard to believe he hasn't developed arm injuries. Arms just aren't meant to do this. I'd still take Clement over Zambrano in the second half, because of those pitch counts. And it would be hard to project an ERA like [Zambrano's 2.61] in the second half."

Joe Borowski (2-4, 9 saves, 8.02 ERA, 17 Ks, 15 BB), LaTroy Hawkins (2-1, 11 saves, 2.47 ERA, 34 Ks, 7 BB)

Karabell then: "Right now Borowski can't be considered a top 10 closer, mainly because his setup man is just as good as he is."

Karabell now: "Well, there was no foretelling that Borowski's shoulder would give out like this, turning him from an unhittable closer to a soft-tossing right-handed pitcher. Hawkins is having a great season, and he should keep the closer role for the rest of the season. I bet they don't let [Borowski] back."

GAME 88

Thursday, July 15, 2004 . . . Cubs 4, Brewers 1 . . . Wrigley Field . . . Stat of the game: Thirty-six pitches. That's how long Mark Prior lasts until he grimaces ever so slightly, shakes his head twice, and departs shortly thereafter with tenderness in his troublesome right elbow. Group depression ensues. . . . Stuff: The Cubs' starting rotation of Kerry Wood, Mark Prior, Greg Maddux, Matt Clement, and Carlos Zambrano remains intact for exactly 1⅔ innings. . . . Those Nomar Garciaparra-to-the-Cubs rumors continue to linger. . . . Oh, yeah, the Cubs win the game, thanks mostly to Glendon Rusch's 5⅓ innings of no-run relief work. . . . Pregame scene: Wendell Kim rolls a couple of baseballs down the third-base line. He wants to see if the grounds crew has tinkered with the tilt of the base paths. Nope. The balls roll foul. . . . Home plate gets a fresh coat of Krylon white spray paint for the second half of the season.

The Wrigley first-aid room, located off the street-level concourse area near the main entrance, is hopping today. It isn't like the day an elderly lady was brought here with a gunshot wound to her leg (a police officer sitting behind her stood to cheer, causing his gun to fall to the ground and discharge upon impact), but it has potential.

Someone has tried to break into the supply closet again, this time breaking off a piece of a screwdriver in a failed attempt to crack the door lock. If only they knew there's no drugs in the supply closet.

As a stadium worker tries to remove the closet doorknob, an elderly Wrigley usher is wheeled into the room. He has a gash on the top of his head. Turns out he got hit by a foul ball during batting practice.

"I won't sue," says the 80-year-old usher, named Val. "I just want two World Series tickets, home and away."

An attendant holds a slightly blood-soaked Gatorade towel to Val's head. No stitches will be required, but Val's work night is finished. Cubs officials contact his son and arrange for Val to receive a ride home.

A few minutes later, Phyllis "Peach" Donnan walks in. Donnan, 49, works as an RN at Northwestern Memorial's cardiovascular intensive care unit. She's been moonlighting at Wrigley's first-aid room since 1980. This is like Kerry Wood shutting out the Cardinals during the day and then playing in a softball beer league that night.

Wrigley's medical facility looks like Brezhnev decorated the place. Very Soviet, and about as modern, too. There's a *Physician's Desk Reference*, the 1998 edition. There are two aging blue sofas and a love seat in the "waiting room." There's at least one working TV, four examination tables, a bathroom, a play area of sorts, a defibrillator, a wheelchair, and a stretcher. The medicine cabinet includes antacid tablets, sunblock, aspirin, Tampax, and throat lozenges. Johns Hopkins, it isn't.

Donnan doesn't mind. After all, this is nothing compared to her real job or her real life. Her husband passed away three years ago, leaving Donnan to raise a son and daughter. She works in ICU, which tends to keep things in perspective. And so far this week she's had to endure a root canal, Internet service problems, houseguests, and a broken sink pipe that flooded part of a room.

"That's why I was late," she says, describing her search for a plumber.

Donnan checks on Val, on the stadium carpenter, on a worker who has been nicked by a stadium delivery cart. Then she sits on one of the Lee Elia-era sofas and talks about her second job.

I used to come out and watch the ballgames all the time. Then [one of the former team physicians] asked me to help him out one day. I didn't have anything else to do, so I said, "Yeah, I guess so." Next thing you know, I'm here every day for the last 20-some years.

I work in the cardiovascular intensive care unit, and have for 25 years. I call this my recreational job. I love it. I've been a lifelong Cub fan. My father was a very devoted Cub fan. His greatest moment was when I was asked to come out here one day, and it's ballooned into this.

Back in the mid-1970s, when the team doctor would admit ballplayers to the hospital, or the Wrigley family to the hospital, he'd put them on this little unit that I happened to be assigned to. So I took care of the elder Wrigleys and some of the ballplayers when they had their surgeries. So that's how I came to know the whole Wrigley thing.

We always have the TV on in here. Even if you're busy, you can hear the crowd outside before you see what happened on TV because of the TV time delay. So you can stop and look up and see what's going to happen. But there are days I never see a pitch because it's so busy.

I get paid for watching ballgames. And I think it keeps a professional balance. I do life-and-death stuff downtown all the time. It's a lot more intense there. Here, it's mostly Band-Aids and aspirin. We'll get a cardiac arrest here maybe one, two times a year. It happens. But we have a pretty good survival rate, actually. We have defibrillators throughout the ballpark. We have physicians in the ballpark, and I page them if I need them. We've had a number of [cardiac-related deaths], but we've had a number of saves, too.

But the bulk of what we do is treating people who are overheated, who get blisters from walking too far to the ballpark, skinned-up knees. Usually pretty simple stuff.

Every day someone gets hit by a baseball. They don't always get hurt, but some do. The seams on the baseball are raised like a zipper. If the skin is taut, those seams will cut. There was one guy who actually lost an eye because of a baseball. Men tend to try to catch those balls, so they dislocate their fingers. Women tend to be turned sideways talking to someone. I know that sounds sexist and I probably shouldn't say that, should I?

To keep my sanity, I learned years ago that when I walk out that hospital door, to leave the job there. That's how I've been able to stay in the intensive care business for 30 years. When I walk out, I forget. I couldn't tell you who I took care of yesterday.

GAME 89

Friday, July 16, 2004 . . . Brewers 3, Cubs 2 . . . Wrigley Field . . . Stat of the game: Matt Clement drops to 7-9, despite a 2.98 ERA. . . . Stuff: Reliever Todd Wellemeyer comes up, infielder Brendan Harris is sent down. . . . Hendry continues to recite the requisite GM-speak concerning possible trades, but it's obvious the Cubs are trying to work a deal. They're averaging only 3.3 runs during the last 18 games, so that means a Nomar Garciaparra trade, right? If so, we're talking about a three-way deal with the Arizona Diamondbacks and Boston Red Sox. . . . True story: After the Cubs lost the three-game series in Milwaukee July 5-7, Ron Santo came home wanting nothing more than a lick or two from the family pooch. Instead, the dog ignored him. So Santo asked his wife, Vicki, to lick his face. And she did.

Gary Pressy hands me his business card. White front, black lettering.

CHICAGO CUBS ORGANIST

Sports Events

Parties

"I also play at the ice arena in Crestwood, and I work for Lowry Organ Company," he says. "That's L-O-W-R-Y."

Whatever. When Pressy spins in, his obit won't say anything about selling organs or working the Saperstein wedding. Pressy's legacy will forever be linked to that 122-key (61 on top, 61 on bottom) organ in the end booth of the Wrigley press box.

As gigs go, nobody in Chicago has had a better run than Pressy, who was born and raised in the same South Side neighborhood as Cubs ticket manager Frank Maloney. Think about it. Pressy is booked for at least 81 dates a year. He plays to a full house of 40,000-plus—or close to it—every gig. And not once has he had a costume malfunction.

This is his 18th season at Wrigley. It's also the 64th season organ music has been played at the place. In fact, says Pressy, the Cubs were the first Major League team to play organ music.

Organs aren't my favorite musical instrument. I hear an organ and I immediately look around for the Mormon Tabernacle Choir. But for some reason, organs and baseball hit it off. Must be the acoustics.

I find Pressy in the press box cubicle that houses him, his Lowry, and the stadium PA announcer. Batting practice hasn't started yet, so he has time to talk.

When I was five years old I'd be in the backyard playing baseball and saying, "All right, and now our National Anthem," like I was Jack Brickhouse. And then I would hum the National Anthem.

Or I would get home from school, turn the game on—Cubs or Sox—hear the organist playing, and think, "Hey, I like it." I thought it was cool.

I started playing when I was six. I played piano for six months, and then I switched to the organ. I just like the sound of the organ. To me, the organ is easier to play.

I would take lessons religiously every Saturday. Kids would be lining up to play baseball, but I'm going to my music lesson. I was never pushed into it.

I filled in at the Bulls games in the early '80s, before Jordan. The crowds weren't much. You'd entertain 2,000 people, play everybody's favorite song. I was also doing games for Loyola basketball, the Chicago Sting, DePaul basketball. But I wrote letters to John McDonough [Cubs Senior VP of Marketing and Broadcasting] and said if the Cub job ever opened up I'd be really interested in it.

In 1986, I filled in for three games at Wrigley. Then I got a call in mid-March of 1987 from John McDonough. I got an interview and audition. It was a snowy day there. I played the Canadian anthem, the American anthem. John said wing it for 20 minutes, so I did a bunch of songs and some little charges that I do.

I got the job on April Fool's Day.

They're going to put a new organ in here before the next homestand. We've had the Heritage model in here for 10 years. We're going to switch to the Legacy, which goes for about $20,000 to $25,000.

To do this job, first of all, you have to be a baseball fan. You have to know when to play, when not to play. When the other team is up, I hardly play. You don't want to interfere with the game. Once he's in the batter's box, you don't play. That's standard. We get a policy on that every year, and we follow that.

Also, mix your music up. I try to play a variety of music, from Big Band sound to the current stuff. The people want to hear everything, on the organ and on the CDs. You've got to be flexible.

I play little theme songs for each batter.
Todd Walker—"Walk Right In," "I'm Walking," "These Boots Are Made for Walking" . . . Corey Patterson—"Centerfield" . . . Sammy Sosa—I do a salsa-like rhythm. Or "Let's Do the Hop" . . . Moises Alou—"Louie, Louie" . . . Aramis Ramirez—"You're Sixteen" . . . Alex Gonzalez—"Alexander's Ragtime Band" or "Eight Days a Week" . . . Derrek Lee—"Dare Me" . . . Kerry Wood—"Classical Gas" or "The Heat Is On" . . . Greg Maddux— "Welcome Back," "Reunited," "The Gambler," "Seems Like Old Times" . . . Mark Prior—The USC fight song or "Let's Hear It for the Boy" . . . Matt Clement—"Pennsylvania Polka" or "My Darling Clementine." That's stuff you just don't hear on the CDs.

The players usually like what I choose. The one guy who did ask me to change his song—and he was really nice about it—was Todd Haney. I'd play the *Green Acres* theme song. He said, "I appreciate it, but my whole life I've been Mr. Haney. So could you play something else?"

In 1990, the Cubs were playing the Atlanta Braves here and we had a long rain delay. I was playing during the rain delay. They ended up calling the game, and afterward Don Sutton, who's a broadcaster with the Braves, comes by and says, "You're our player of the game. We'll send you a watch."

Well, I got this Longines gold watch. It's a $700 watch. And it's engraved with the date and *Gary Pressy, Atlanta Braves Star of the Game.*

I was just doing my job.

When Jack Brickhouse passed away, his wife, Pat, asked if I'd play at his funeral. I played "To Dream the Impossible Dream." And when they were wheeling the casket out, I played "Hey, Hey, Holy Mackerel."

Mark Grace, he was pretty good to me. I'd play "Taking Care of Business." He was in a movie with the same name. It was filmed in Wrigley. When I'd play it, he'd be down there warming up and he'd tip his cap to me.

The last song I played in the 2003 season was "Auld Lang Syne." I would have played longer, but TV wanted to do interviews and they didn't want music on the field.

For a 1:20 game, they'll want music on the field beginning at 10:30, in time for batting practice. We play CDs then.

[Pressy thumbs through a box of CDs featuring mixes, *American Bandstand*, and "Old Style Polka" by The Polkaholics. Just then an usher taps on his door.

"Dusty Baker wants you to play these," she says.

It's a "Now 13" mix and a Temptations CD. Pressy doesn't hesitate. Out goes his selection, in goes Baker's choices. The Polkaholics will have to wait.]

GAME 90

Saturday, July 17, 2004 . . . Cubs 5, Brewers 0 . . . Wrigley Field . . . Cubs NL Central pennant flies: Second (49-41) . . . Stat of the game: Greg Maddux wins career No. 297. . . . Stuff: WGN's nationally syndicated show Pet Central *gets a call tonight from a dog owner whose pooch continues to ignore him. The caller? Ron Santo.*

Pressure? Tony Cooney snacks on pressure like it's a handful of cocktail peanuts.

You think it's hard trying to scratch out a hit against Eric Gagne in the bottom of the ninth? Try doing what Cooney does, which is somehow cram about $2 million worth of luxury vehicles into a Cubs players' parking lot that is slightly smaller than Darren Baker. That's 20 spaces divided by more than 25 Cubs rides. Do the math.

Cooney, all of 21, oversees some of the most precious property at Wrigley. The Cubs players' lot is located right across the street from the fire station on Waveland. It is protected by a chain-link fence, a couple of gates, and Cooney.

Cooney was 17 when he started parking cars at Wrigley. He's a North Sider and grew up near Lane Tech. And if he were any more serious about his job, you'd think he was parking missiles for NORAD.

"I'm so careful with them, like a baby," he says, standing in the middle of the packed lot, his Motorola HT600 walkie-talkie crackling with chatter. "I protect them so much. I've never got in an accident in the players' lot. I've never put one scratch on any of the players' cars. It's almost like a Cal Ripken streak. His streak was broken, but hopefully mine won't be."

The lot has enough high-priced merchandise to make a State Farm agent hyperventilate. All the biggies are represented: BMW, Mercedes, Lexus, Range Rover, Hummer, Cadillac. I could buy a beach house in Wisconsin on the tinted window concession alone.

Cooney's job is to squeeze this auto showroom into the unfriendly confines of the dinky lot. Seasoned valet parkers would weep.

"It's a big bear," says Cooney. "I don't know how Boston is, but I know Fenway's lot is real small. This lot is real small, but the cars and SUVs are getting bigger. So all these cars are like a puzzle and I have to fit them in."

Cooney maneuvers a $90,000-plus Mercedes into spaces as thin as Paris Hilton. Plus, he has to worry about scraping the fence, backing up into cement walls, or dinging a car door while extricating himself from these Trumpmobiles.

"They have ultimate total trust in me," says Cooney of the players.

Only one player has a permanent special parking spot: Sammy Sosa. His SL 500 or Range Rover is parked just outside the stadium hallway leading to the lot. "For safety reasons," says Cooney. "There are so many fans who want his autograph."

The other players are parked on a first-come, first-served basis. The Hummers, pickups, and larger SUVs are lined alongside the outer fence. The sedans and smaller SUVs (say, the Beemer X-3s) are crammed into the remaining spaces. Overflow parking runs down the middle of the lot.

These aren't short days for Cooney. He's here at least five hours before game time, just in case a player gets to Wrigley early for treatment. Plus, he can keep an eye on the autograph seekers who gather around the entry gate on Waveland.

Most of the players start pulling into the lot about four hours or so before the first pitch. There's a 15-minute period where Cooney looks like he's working the parking garage at the Bellagio. Sprint here. Sprint there. The only thing missing are the claim checks.

There are no tips—at least, not very often. Cooney gets paid by the hour (he won't divulge salary, only a tight-lipped "Not much") and is expected to park and unpark the cars. Dusty Baker parks his Chevy in an adjacent lot, as do the Cubs execs. Cooney will occasionally help out there, but the players' lot is his No. 1 priority.

When he first started, Cooney had a serious case of star/car-gazing. After all, how often do you get to meet Sosa *and* his new-car smell? But the thrill factor lasted less than a week. Now Cooney is unfazed by the players or the window stickers.

"It's just a job, but it's a very cool job," he says. "It's something to look back on 15, 20 years from now and say, 'I parked that Hall of Famer's car.'"

About 30 minutes after today's game, I walk down to Cooney's parking lot. He already has about half the cars prepared to go. The engines are running, the AC units are cranked up, the driver's-side doors are cracked open for quicker access. Cooney takes pride in the little touches.

By the time the final player leaves the clubhouse, makes his way down the concourse and through the hallway leading to the lot, Cooney will have put in another 10½-hour day. Then he'll go find his own car, a 2000 Nissan Altima.

"I have to park it on the street," he says. "Wherever I can find a spot."

GAME 91

Sunday, July 18, 2004 . . . Brewers 4, Cubs 2 . . . Wrigley Field . . . Cubs NL Central pennant flies: Second (49-42) . . . Stuff: Aramis Ramirez is back in the lineup for the first time since July 2. He takes the collar. . . . The Cubs drop eight games behind the Cardinals, making the upcoming two-game series against St. Louis the most important of the season.

It's Sunday, which means it's time to ask a question that has haunted and perplexed theologians from the Evangelical Reinhold Niebuhr, to the Jew Martin Buber, to the Catholic Pierre Teilhard de Chardin.

Is God a Cubs fan?

Actually, none of these famed intellects probably knew who the Cubs were, except maybe the midwesterner Niebuhr, who authored what is known as the "Serenity Prayer," which could double as the Cubbie fan anthem: "God, give us grace to accept with serenity the things that cannot be changed . . ."

Niebuhr must have been a Cubs follower during the 1950s and most of the '60s.

I contacted an expert on this Cubs/God thing—Father David F. Ryan, executive director of Maryville Academy. Father Ryan isn't a world-renowned theologian, but he does have certain qualifications that separate him from all other religious eggheads.

First of all, he was a longtime friend of Harry Caray, which gives him some Cubs cred. One of his most prized nonsecular mementos is a photograph of him and Caray taken years ago at the now long-gone Barclay Club in Chicago, where Caray originally sponsored an annual Thanksgiving/Christmas dinner for the children of Maryville Academy (the tradition continues these days at Harry Caray's restaurant, courtesy of Dutchie Caray). His other favorite keepsake is an actual music/lyrics sheet of "Take Me Out to the Ballgame" used in the WGN booth by Caray.

Father Ryan flew to Palm Springs to be with the family when Caray had his stroke. He was one of two priests who administered last rites to Caray (Caray always liked 2-for-1 nights). He was a celebrant at Caray's funeral at Holy Name Cathedral (Caray died February 18, 1998). And Caray's grave site at All Saints Cemetery in Des Plaines (Section 42 West, Block 22—you'll know Harry's marker by the baseball and glasses frames) is only an "it could be . . . it might be" fly ball or two from Maryville Academy property.

Fittingly enough, it was Father Ryan who "blessed" the Cubs' 2004 season minutes after the Bartman Ball was zapped and reduced to angel pasta. Remember?

"We ask for the good blessing to gather some evening in the cold of Wrigley Field in October to once again celebrate a World Series in the great city of Chicago with the Chicago Cubs!" Father Ryan told the congregation that night in a street tent just outside Caray's restaurant.

In addition, Ryan is a lifelong Cubs fan, attends games at Wrigley, and isn't against mentioning the Cubs during homilies, during the petitions of the mass, or even during funerals.

"Whenever I have a funeral for someone who lived to be 98, 97, 96 years old . . . if I know they were born before 1907, I always bring up during the course of the mass that this is a very unique person," says Ryan. "This person was actually alive the last time the Cubs won a World Series. There have been millions of people who have lived and died and not experienced that reality."

Which brings us back to God and His apparent grudge against the Cubs. There are four possible reasons for this: There is no God . . . there is a God, but he has a few other things on his agenda . . . God owes George Steinbrenner money . . . God never forgave Orval Overall for losing Game 1 of the 1910 World Series against the Philadelphia Athletics.

"I think part of being a Catholic—and it's the same to be a Cubs fan—is that you have to have a sense of long suffering," says Ryan. "We've been waiting a long time for a World Series championship, and some part of faith's dimension is to be able to suffer, and to be able to suffer gladly. So it helps to be a Cubs fan and be a Catholic. There's that idea of suffering that goes along with it in an appropriate sense. Also, the Catholic belief is eternal hope, too. I have eternal hope the Cubs will turn it around."

I ask the good Father if he ever saw the movie *Patton*, where the famed general summons his chaplain and demands he write a prayer asking the Almighty for fair weather—the better to attack in. The chaplain reluctantly does as ordered. Good weather ensues. The U.S. Army is victorious.

"Yes, *Patton*, I know it," says Ryan. "Patton says, 'Get me that chaplain. He stands in good with the Lord and I want to decorate him.'"

Well?

After a slight pause, Father Ryan finally gets it.

"Maybe," he says, "it is time to write a Cubs prayer."

Bless you.

GAME 92

Monday, July 19, 2004 . . . Cardinals 5, Cubs 4 . . . Wrigley Field . . . Cubs NL Central pennant flies: Second (49-43) . . . Stat of the game: Cards starter Chris Carpenter wins his 10th game, which is four more than the combined season totals of Kerry Wood and Mark Prior. Incredible . . . Stuff: Sun-Times *columnist Rick Telander has seen enough. "The Cubs are finished," he writes in today's edition. . . . Alex Gonzalez called up, Rey Ordonez sent down. This is the first time since April 9 that the Cubs have had their Opening Day lineup. . . . Wavin' Wendell Kim sends Aramis Ramirez (one day removed from coming off the DL with a strained groin) with no outs in the sixth. Instead of Cubs on first and third, Ramirez gets thrown out at home. Kim later apologizes.*

The author wishes to acknowledge his shallow and frantic breathing patterns as the Cubs begin their slow descent into hell. Said author also would like to mention that he'd rather have his armpits waxed by an angry Bulgarian woman than endure another 2 hours and 22 minutes of whatever it was he witnessed earlier this evening.

Not only do the Cubs drop nine games behind the Cardinals, but they do so in spectacular Cubs fashion, which is to say they explode like a water balloon dropped from the Wrigley Field roof.

Let's begin with Cubs starter Carlos Zambrano, whose on-field antics are as appealing as braided chest hair. Zambrano is an innocent of sorts, only 23, with just 67 career big league starts. He is a work in progress, which is why the Cubs tend to dismiss his indiscretions as misguided youthful exuberance. Fine. The mid-June temper tantrum directed in the general direction of Todd Walker? The on-field gestures? Knucklehead moments, to be sure, but nothing fatal.

Tonight's performance was different. This wasn't innocence, or even ignorance. It was arrogance. It was a first-time All-Star who seems to have forgotten you can't have it both ways.

Example:

With two outs in the first inning, Zambrano plunks Jim Edmonds in the right hip to load the bases. Zambrano squirms out of the jam. But three innings later . . .

With no outs and Scott Rolen standing on first, Edmonds launches a Zambrano pitch so far that air traffic control at O'Hare picks it up on radar. Ballhawk extraordinaire Dave Davison, who grabs the home run ball after it clears Sheffield, tells me later that Edmonds's blast would have hit Murphy's on the fly if not for a tree guarding the front of the bar. In other words, a dinger worth admiring.

And that's what Edmonds does. He stands at home plate and stares at the thing as if it were Chagall's *America Windows* at the Art Institute. Then he glances at Zambrano and takes a leisurely stroll around the bases. Cards lead, 2-0.

Zambrano can't believe it. He stares at Edmonds for most of the home run trot and then, as the Cardinals' center fielder nears the plate, Zambrano cups his hand and starts yelling at him. He tells him to run the bases, to quit with the cocky attitude, to conduct himself like Rolen. Zambrano is giving a 13-year veteran a lesson in baseball etiquette, which is a ballsy move, all things considered. Moments later, the benches clear when Michael Barrett begins gesturing at a Cardinals player in the dugout. It's wonderful theater, but totally unnecessary.

Yeah, Edmonds isn't going to win any league-wide popularity contests. He's a bit of a jerk, but would the Cubs want him on their team? Damn right, they would. And anyway, what did Zambrano expect? As the teams head back to their respective dugouts after the skirmish, old-school Moises Alou tells Zambrano: You hit him, he bombed you . . . such is baseball.

Now move forward to the sixth inning. The score is tied, 3-3. Edmonds comes up with one out, bases empty. Zambrano strikes him out swinging. Instead of turning his back and concentrating next on Ray Lankford, Zambrano wags his forefinger at Edmonds. See? Double standard.

Now on to the eighth inning. With two outs and Tony Womack on third, Rolen sends a Zambrano slider over the left-field wall. Edmonds is up next . . . and gets hit in nearly the exact same spot as the first time. Zambrano, as well as Baker, gets tossed.

In the sweatbox that passes for a postgame interview room, Baker all but absolves Zambrano of any wrongdoing.

The author wishes to mention that Baker is (a) protecting his player, and (b) wrong.

Zambrano follows Baker and says, with an absolute straight face, that he didn't mean to hit Edmonds either time. This is called Method acting.

Meanwhile, Tony LaRussa is in the visitors' clubhouse seething about Zambrano's act. And while LaRussa can slop on the piousness like gravy on mashed potatoes, he has a point this time. Zambrano's schtick is getting old to opponents and, if you had to bet a nickel, to teammates alike.

On the way out of Wrigley, tormented author sees tormented Cub honk Ron Santo. Santo takes a deep sigh and says, "I don't know how much more I can take."

Author still doesn't know if Santo was talking about the game or Zambrano.

GAME 93

Tuesday, July 20, 2004 . . . Cardinals 11, Cubs 8 . . . Wrigley Field . . . Stat of the game: The Cubs blow an 8-2 lead and fall 10 games out of first. Break out the black crepe. . . . Stuff: LaTroy Hawkins gives up the game-winning runs in the ninth and then goes nuts at inning's end. After getting tossed by home plate ump Tim Tschida, Hawkins has to be restrained by Dusty Baker, four Cubs coaches, and one umpire. . . . Longtime Cardinals announcer Mike Shannon isn't so sure the Cubs are toast. "We'll be back here," says Shannon as he leaves the press box. In other words, Cubs vs. Cards in the NLCS? . . . Et tu, Bernie? St. Louis columnist Bernie Miklasz pulls the rip cord on his Cubs parachute and lands safely in Cardinals territory. Writes Miklasz: "On Monday night at Wrigley Field, we saw why the Chicago Cubs are destined to go down as a beaten favorite and one of the biggest flops of the 2004 season." . . . Sun-Times columnist Jay Mariotti after the loss: "It's over. At this point, the Cubs will be fortunate to win a wild-card berth."

So I'm walking down the Waveland side of Wrigley before the game when I see some Cardinals yahoo standing in line alongside the stadium wall to the bleachers entrance. He's wearing a pricey Cardinals replica jersey, complete with stitched name and number on the back:

Bartman. 96.

And under that . . .

Years and counting

Then I notice the handmade signs. He has dozens of them. The yahoo has guts.

I introduce myself and tell him I'm writing a book on the 2004 Cubs season.

"That'll be a pretty short book," he says.

The yahoo is also a bit smug.

His name is Marty Prather and, quite frankly, he's the kind of guy you'd want as a Cubs Nation resident. After all, he has impeccable credentials. He's a working-stiff-made-good (he started as a pizza deliveryman and now owns 12 Domino's franchises), adores baseball (he owns Cardinals season tickets, despite the seven-hour round-trip drive from Springfield, Missouri, to Busch Stadium), and has crisscrossed the Midwest to support the Cards for nearly 20 years. No wonder Prather, 46, is the first fan ever to be inducted into the Missouri Sports Hall of Fame.

Prather was in Cincinnati Monday night, so he missed the Zambrano-Edmonds drama. But no way was he missing the last regular-season meeting between the Cubs and his Cards.

"The Bartman jersey, though, may not be a good idea," he says. "That may push it over the limit."

The bleachers are his preferred seating choice. He has room for his signs and the reception is surprisingly civil.

"It's 99 percent positive," Prather says. "I don't block the view. I keep the signs down. I follow the rules. There will always be one or two guys out there who will take it a little bit too personal, but I've never had a beer poured on me, and I've been coming to the bleachers for 15 years. Security in the bleachers is much better than it is in the grandstands."

In all, Prather has more than 800 hand-painted signs in his collection. Today, he has brought 20 of the corrugated plastic boards to Wrigley. Eight of the 30 × 40 boards are devoted exclusively to the Cubs.

"The only team I do that for," says Prather.

Nobody is going to offer Prather a job on Comedy Central, but his stuff does have its moments.

Moises (crossed out, replaced by *Moist*) *Alou Is a Spray Hitter.*

"Dusty Baker laughed at that one," says Prather. "Alou was laughing. It brought chuckles."

Sammy Sosa wasn't so thrilled when he first saw *Keep the Cork, We'll Take the Champagne.*

"Sosa made a little gesture to me," Prather says.

Prather thumbs through the rest of his collection. His favorites: *Cub-O-Meter: 96 Years and Counting. Anyone Can Have an Off Millennium. Cubs Magic Number: 911.*

In a few hours, these signs will make their Wrigley debut. Prather can't wait.

"This is really a fun rivalry, nothing like New York-Boston," he says. "This is more friendly, though I like the Cubs as Lovable Losers. This year they're kind of competent, borderline cocky. In fact, I think the Cubs will make the playoffs. That scares me. They're built for the short series. We're built for the long run. I really see a Cardinals-Cubs matchup to go to the World Series, which would be brutal."

Some advice to Prather: Don't wear the Bartman jersey at Wrigley in October. If you do, Cubs fans will want to accessorize it.

With beer.

GAME 94

Wednesday, July 21, 2004 . . . Cubs 5, Reds 4 . . . Wrigley Field . . . Cubs NL Central pennant flies: Second (50-44) . . . Stat of the game: Sammy Sosa, hip-deep in a 4-for-26 slump, hits the game-winning homer in yet another rain-storm. Two of his last five homers have come in downpours. Sammy is a mudder. . . . Stuff: LaTroy Hawkins picks up the save. Enjoy it while you can. Hawkins and Carlos Zambrano are getting ready to serve time in MLB's big house. . . . GM Jim Hendry says Ryan Dempster, who is rehabbing in Triple-A Iowa, could be the closer by September. Translation: The Cubs aren't thrilled with Hawkins in the ninth inning, and nobody is holding their breath for a Joe Borowski return in 2004. . . . Wild-card status: two games back.

Covering baseball is the toughest newspaper beat in sports. The deadlines keep Pepto-Bismol in business. The workload is insane. And generally speaking, at least a third of the roster would love to dunk you and your laptop in a vat of Copenhagen spittle.

That's why other sportswriters approach Hal McCoy and all but genu-flect in his presence. McCoy has covered the Reds for the *Dayton Daily News* since 1973—or in Cubs terms, since the Opening Day lineup last featured Ron Santo, Glenn Beckert, Don Kessinger, Randy Hundley, Billy Williams, and Fergie Jenkins. A long time.

McCoy was inducted into the Baseball Hall of Fame in July 2003, which is why fellow writers, broadcasters, and even ballplayers still go out of their way to pay their respects.

No baseball writer has a longer continuous tenure covering a team than McCoy. He's been there for The Big Red Machine, Schottzie, Pete Rose, and Junior Griffey. But six months before the induction ceremony in Coopers-town, McCoy suffered strokes in the optic nerves of both eyes that ren-dered him nearly blind.

He's better now. And he's back in Chicago, where he's spent more time at Wrigley than some of the ivy.

I've been coming here for 32 years. The playing field, the walls, the bleach-ers, they haven't changed a bit. The press box has changed. It used to be down there [he gestures to the seats behind home plate on the mezzanine level]. Once you were in your seat, you were in your seat. If you were in the middle of the row, everybody else had to get up to let you out. In fact, there used to be a hamburger/hot dog grill at the end of press row. You'd just yell what you want.

I remember when Joey Hamilton was with the club. It was cramped in there and I was trying to stay out of everyone's way. Hamilton says, "Don't the writers have anything better to do than clog the clubhouse?" He was being a jerk.

Gabe White [another veteran pitcher on the Reds' roster] says, "Hal McCoy can stand anywhere he wants in this clubhouse. He can sit in my chair and wear my uniform."

That was a great thing to say.

I love the bleachers, the ivy-covered walls. I still think it's a fabulous place to play. The amenities aren't much. But if you throw out the amenities, this is my favorite place to come watch a game.

Last July, I was inducted into the Hall of Fame. The vote was the previous December. That January, this happened to my eyes.

I'm glad it happened then. I didn't want to get the sympathy vote.

An hour after the vote, the phone rings. I answer it.

"Hal, do you know who this is?"

"I know who it is—it's Junior."

"This isn't for quotes, or publicity, or a story. I just wanted to congratulate you."

When I had my eye problems, he had never said anything. Some of the other players always asked about it every day. Not Junior. But I found out later he was asking the other players how I was doing. Classy.

The thing that I remember best about this place is [Reds pitcher] Tom Browning sitting out on a brownstone on Sheffield.

Davey Johnson was the manager then. [Reds teammate] Tim Belcher bet Browning $200 that he wouldn't sit out there in uniform. So during the game Browning sneaks out there and gets on the brownstone.

Somebody in the press box says, "There's somebody dressed like Browning out there. Hell, it *is* Browning."

He sat out there for two innings.

Johnson thought it was funny as hell, but he still fined him.

GAME 95

Thursday, July 22, 2004 . . . Cubs 13, Reds 2 . . . Wrigley Field . . . Stuff: Moises Alou says Cubs announcers Chip Caray and Steve Stone are "negative." Please. Credibility comes with a price, and if that means occasionally annoying the likes of Alou, then tough. Caray and Stone are paid to call and analyze the game, not wave red and blue pom-poms. . . . The Washington Post's *Michael Wilbon officially gives up on the Cubs. He writes: "I've loved them all of my life and I'll happily root for them even though I'm certain to go to my grave without them ever winning a World Series. And while wallowing in Cubbiness last fall, I somehow became a closet Red Sox fan, which is the quintessential loser's doubleheader. Even so, they're both dead."*

Dale Wheeler, 49, grew up about a mile from Wrigley Field. He joined the grounds crew in 1979 and became responsible for the pitcher's mound in 1989. To Wheeler this is sacred ground of sorts. It is baseball's C-cup, the only part of the playing field that is round (18 feet in diameter, if you're scoring at home) and pleasingly plump. Anyway, you should see Wheeler tend to the mound hours before the game. If he were any more loving, he'd have dirt on his lips.

The mound is my baby, so to speak. You start off with a flat first 6 inches off the rubber. Then for every foot down there's a 1-inch drop, so you end up with a 6-inch drop at the 6-foot marker. The mound extends to 10 feet at the bottom, so your height should be 10 inches from home plate to the top of the rubber.

Before the season starts, I'll take a lot of the old clay off and then repack it. The mound is all clay. It's a red type of clay. After a game, I'll sweep out the holes next to the rubber, and where the landing is. I'll water it, put red clay in, tamp it down. Then we'll put in Turface, which is a moisturizer/drying agent. Then I retamp that to make it firm on top. It takes about 15 minutes.

See that roller? That roller is probably the heaviest in the league. It weighs about 250 pounds. I'll roll the mound once at night and once in the morning.

The biggest problem I've always had is that we play the most day baseball in the majors. And no matter what, if it's hot out . . . if it's windy and the sun's just beating on it, the mound is going to dry out. So what we've done the last few years is to put the canvas on it with a mat during batting practice.

I just try to make it consistent every day. Day baseball makes it tough. If we played night baseball, our whole field would be better.

Greg Maddux always said he loved it, too. When he was with the Braves, he told our foreman, "I'd love to fly Dale down to Atlanta and blow up that mound." I told Maddux the next day, "Nice compliment, I really appreciate it."

Sometimes after games he'd say, "Dale, the mound was really nice today."

I don't talk to the players much. I'll say, "Nice game." Sometimes they'll say they liked the mound. But usually if they don't say nothing, it's better that way.

GAME 96

Friday, July 23, 2004 . . . Cubs 5, Philadelphia Phillies 1 . . . Citizens Bank Park . . . Cubs NL Central pennant flies: Second (52-44) . . . Stuff: A city-ordered inspection of Wrigley begins today as workers and engineers try to determine the cause and extent of three separate incidents involving concrete chunks falling off the stadium underside. Earlier in the week, Tribune *columnist Rick Morrissey calls Wrigley "a dump." Morrissey is confusing creature comforts for character. The last time that happened, we ended up with New Comiskey. . . . Wild-card status: one game back.*

About two hours outside of Philadelphia, in the *Deer Hunter*-dinky town of Bangor, Pennsylvania, is the Majestic Athletic headquarters and factory. This is where Cubs uniforms are made. Think Santa's workshop for baseball and you'll understand why I had to be treated for drool marks at day's end.

It isn't exactly the easiest place to find. You take I-95 south out of Philly, then 476 North, then the Pennsylvania Turnpike, then get off at the Allentown exit, then take Route 22 East, to Route 33 North, to Route 191 North. Then you look for the Bangor Car Wash, take a right at Messinger, cross a bridge, take a right at Main Street, then take a left at Majestic Way. Bobby DeNiro and Christopher Walken will point you to the visitors' parking on the left.

The main brick building would send architect I. M. Pei screaming into the night, but who cares, right? Inside the reception lobby is a near-perfect model of Notre Dame Stadium enclosed in a Plexiglas case.

Yeah, the Capobiancos are Domers. Faust Capobianco, Notre Dame class of 1964, took over the family business three years after leaving South Bend. His son, Faust IV (ND Class of '94), is now Majestic's president. Daughter Nicole, who is VP of team services, got her degree across the street from the ND campus at St. Mary's—Class of '95. When I met Faust IV and Nicole, I didn't know whether to shake their hands or belt out the first verse of "Shake Down the Thunder."

Anyway, this used to be a big textile area. Grandma Capobianco started with a blouse-making shop decades ago. Then the family opened its own sewing mill, and eventually Majestic Athletic was born. Today Majestic makes game uniforms for 15 Major League Baseball teams, including the Cubs. Beginning in 2005, Majestic becomes the exclusive provider of all MLB wear.

Bangor's population wouldn't fill the outfield bleachers at Wrigley. Faust IV's graduating class at Pius X High School (what is it with this guy and Roman numerals?) numbered 28. Nicole's was 36. But this is where they were born and raised. And this is where Majestic is staying.

This being chummy Bangor, the Capobianco Lexus SUV parked out front is unlocked and the keys are located right below the dashboard. Do that in Chicago and you'd spend the afternoon down at the precinct filling out a missing-vehicle report.

Our first stop is the cutting facility, located about five minutes away. On the way there, Faust IV mentions that the Cubs will be getting newly designed warm-up jackets next season. Majestic does that about every three years. In fact, it was longtime Cubs equipment and clubhouse man Yosh Kawano who first suggested Majestic try an Olympic collar (zips up and then folds over like a turtleneck) on the warm-up jacket.

Nicole meets with the MLB equipment managers every year. What she ought to do is bring them to Bangor. Geez, you should see the 50,000-square-foot cutting facility. There are rolls and rolls and rolls of fabric, with each roll containing anywhere from 50 to 75 yards of fabric. Faust IV used to play hide-and-seek in these rolls as a kid.

Right now there are nine shades of gray for the road unis they make. The Cubs gray has a blue cast to it. The St. Louis Cardinals gray has a green cast to it. There are even different shades of white. Optic white. Diamond white. Standard white. And there are different widths of pinstripes. We find a roll of Cubs Royal Pride Stripe. According to Nicole, the Cubs pinstripes are about an average width. The Chicago White Sox have very thin pinstripes; the New York Yankees have very thick.

Majestic makes just about everything here except the embroidered emblems, such as the Cubs logo on the home unis. "We call it the Cubs Bull's-eye Patch, which is kind of appropriate since everybody kind of got shot again through the heart [in 2003]," says Faust IV. Funny.

This place really hops around the trading deadline. Think about it: A cluster of last-minute player deals means all sorts of new uniforms.

"It's crazy," says Nicole. "We'll sometimes ship hundreds of jerseys and pants, most of them being custom, in a week."

In 2003, the Cubs completed five separate in-season deals that brought six different players to Chicago: Jose Hernandez, Kenny Lofton, Aramis Ramirez, Doug Glanville, Randall Simon, and Tony Womack. Majestic had to deliver the new unis, and fast. Sometimes it can make and ship a uniform the same day.

"They're really wearing tailored suits," Nicole says.

I had no idea it was this complicated. Or quirky. Did you know that no other team but the Cubs wears a hip patch, which is part of their road uniform? Did you know the Cubs are the only team to wear a National League patch on their batting practice jerseys? Did you know the Cubs are the only team to wear their team logo patch on the right sleeve of their warm-up jackets? "And we couldn't tell you why," says Faust IV.

Nicole introduces me to Majestic's head pattern maker, Michael Panuccio. At last count, he had about 700 different pants patterns and about 100 jersey patterns downloaded on his computer. Each spring, Nicole and Panuccio will travel to the training sites of their 15 MLB team clients, have every player, coach, and manager try on stock sizes, record the alteration requests, and then make the polyester unis. Easy, right? Uh, no.

Take a pair of baseball pants. There are three cuts: regular, athletic, and double athletic (otherwise known as "The David Wells Cut"). You've got a right and left front and a right and left back. From there you can adjust the rise (too baggy or tight in the front or back). You can adjust the calves' width. You can adjust the length. You can adjust the waist, hip, and inseam.

There are also nine different jersey sizes, from size 40 to 56. Majestic will customize a jersey's chest width, sleeve length, sleeve circumference, and jersey length.

Nicole sizes the Cubs. It usually takes about two hours to size everybody on the team's spring training roster. For instance, Sammy Sosa likes his pants legs tapered. He also likes button holes to be cut at the bottom of each pant leg. That way he can slip his cleat laces through the button holes to hold the pants legs down.

Pitchers tend to prefer more room in their jerseys. They like to wear bigger sizes. When, say, Mark Prior tries on a Cubs (royal blue) jersey, the first thing he does is tug at the shoulder. By the way, the Cubs jerseys are considered the stretchiest made by Majestic. They call it a warp knit. It refers to the type of machine used to make the fabric.

We drive to the sewing facility, which is part of the original building Grandma used. Nicole and Faust IV introduce me to Sicilian-born Anna Maria Verniero, 52, a shop operator who has worked at Majestic since she was 17. Anna has done everything at this facility: sewing, printing, frocking, embroidery, quality-control checks.

Someone hands us a Sosa jersey. Majestic puts player ID labels on each jersey and pair of pants it makes. The Cubs label begins with the player's jersey number (21), jersey size (48), the year, and set number (i.e., this is, say, the fourth jersey pattern Majestic has shipped to Sosa this year—so it would read, "S4"). By the way, Sosa wears elastic in his sleeves.

The Cubs have three sets of jerseys—home pinstripe, road gray, and alternate royal blue. And the Majestic staff knows Cubs retail product is among the top 10 in sales. When the Cubs blew that 3-1 NLCS lead against the Florida Marlins in 2003, "it was a several-million-dollar swing in sales, just on the basis of LCS sales, not even World Series merchandise," says Faust IV.

Faust IV, Nicole, and I climb back into the Lexus and head back to the headquarters building. Behind the corporate offices is another warehouse and printing work area where about 2 million jerseys are stored. Well, make that 1,999,999.

Earlier in the day, I mentioned that I was going to buy a No. 10 Ron

Santo jersey when I got back to Chicago. So shortly before my tour is complete, Faust IV and Nicole present me with a newly made road-gray Santo model.

I wear it all the way back to Philly. With pride.

GAME 97

Saturday, July 24, 2004 . . . Phillies 4, Cubs 3 . . . Citizens Bank Park . . . Stat of the game: Carlos Zambrano gets the loss. He's 0-2 since the All-Star break. . . . Wild-card status: two games back.

Ryne Sandberg was in Lakeland, Florida, when I called. He was appearing in an All-Star softball game with Pete Rose, Steve Carlton, and Dave Parker, among others. This is what happens when you get money-whipped by the likes of Kraft Foods. Anyway, Former Major League All-Stars vs. A Team of Grocery-Chain Employees. Whooeee!

"Yeah, I better rest up," said Sandberg.

He was joking . . . I think. You never know with Sandberg. He has a sense of humor as dry as a rusted radiator, and enjoys losing only slightly less than bobbing for apples in a barrel of Atomic Balm.

The 10-time All-Star and member of the Cubs All-Century Team began his pro career as a shortstop in the Philadelphia Phillies organization. He was signed out of high school in the 20th round of the June draft, reached the big leagues late in 1981, and was traded to the Cubs (Sandberg and Larry Bowa for Ivan DeJesus) in time for the 1982 season. He played third base and switched permanently to second base in 1983.

Since retiring after the 1997 season, Sandberg serves as a Cubs spring training instructor and makes assorted personal appearances for the team. I last saw him at Games 6 and 7 of the NLCS against the Marlins. He was sitting in Row 11 of the field-box section of Wrigley with his wife, Margaret. Every so often, he'd lean over and tell her to look for the hit-and-run, or a sac bunt, or a pitchout, or a stolen base, or some other nuance. Sandberg couldn't help himself. You don't play 15 seasons in the bigs and then pretend you don't notice things.

The 2004 season is the 20-year anniversary of the Cubs' NL East division title. Sandberg still has a glass cube that contains a piece of green ivy from the Wrigley outfield wall. Every Cubs player got one that year. Reads the inscription: "1984: The year the ivy smiled."

Sandberg on 1984 . . . and 10 other things:

I say there's no curse. I think besides this 2004 season, I don't know if the Cubs have had the best talent, or the right talent at one time, to go all the way to a World Series or win a World Series. Seems like there's always been one little thing short. I think it's been the players lacking the ability to get the job done rather than some curse.

But that's for the goat's sake. I don't want anybody blowing up a goat. I'm an animal lover.

I didn't see the scouting report on me coming out of high school [North Central, in Spokane, Washington], but I think I could guess what it said. The scout from the Phillies [Bill Harper] had been watching me for a couple of weeks. After a high school practice, he had me stay afterward and run the 60-yard dash. It was raining, the track was wet, but he still walked off the 60 yards. I ran the 60, came back to him, and he looked at his watch and said, "Uh, sorry about that, Ryne, but there must be some mistake. Can you run that again?"

I walked down there again, somewhat reluctantly. All my buddies were already gone, and I wanted to be with them. But I go down there, run the 60 again, come back, and it's the same exact time: a handheld 6.6, which is fast. That was something that really stood out to them, my speed. And also I was a two-sport all-state player in football and baseball, and all-city in basketball. I think back then they were really looking for the all-around athlete.

All the way through the minors, I played shortstop. I didn't change positions until I came over to the Cubs and then won the job in spring training as the starting third baseman. I believe I made 10 errors [actually 12] the whole season at third base, but that September, [general manager] Dallas Green came to me and said, "We've watched you play all year and you've done great. But with your offense, your range, your quickness, we'd like to try you at second base for next year." So I finished my rookie season that September playing at second base. I'd played a little second base in winter ball in Venezuela.

I could have played third base my whole career, definitely. And I thought

I was going to be a shortstop. I was a good shortstop coming through the minor leagues. I thought I was going to be a Major League shortstop.

Playing at Wrigley Field, every day can be a little bit different. The first thing I did was always check the wind. I checked the flags, the ones out in center field. I'd check the flags every time I'd run out to my position. The wind can change during a game two or three times at Wrigley Field.

I checked the infield grass every day. Because of the weather, sometimes they didn't mow the grass until the second day of the series. Sometimes the tarp would be on and they wouldn't mow the grass. For the most part, they like to keep it a little bit on the longer side because of all the day games. Their chance to work on it is very early in the morning or late after the game. With all the day games, they can't afford to cut it too short and risk losing a whole batch of infield grass. They tended to keep it on the long side for that reason.

For day games, the sun is straight up for at least three-fourths of the game. I never took the field at Wrigley without a pair of sunglasses on, whether it was sunny or cloudy. I wore them no matter what.

My first Major League at-bat was in a Phillies uniform. I was a September call-up in the '81 season. They had won the World Series in 1980 and were on the verge of going to the postseason again.

My first at-bat was against Kent Tekulve, an ace reliever for the Pittsburgh Pirates. A submarine guy. He was in his prime. I walk up to the plate, and he comes submarine with a fastball that had more movement . . . it looked like a wiffleball coming in there. I took it for strike one. I say, "OK, that's what it looks like." Then, boom, he does it again. Same pitch, different location. I took that—strike two. I say, "OK, now I got to battle." Here he comes with same pitch, different location. Strike three. Three pitches. All looking. Strikeout.

That was my first feeling of "Wow, this is a different league." I had six at-bats that September and actually got my first hit as a Philly at Wrigley Field off of Mike Krukow. Then I ended up getting traded that winter to the Cubs.

In '82, when I moved over to second base for a couple of games in September, we were playing the Phillies. Pete Rose was standing on second base and there was a break in the action. I think we were changing pitchers or something.

So Larry Bowa, who was playing for the Cubs now and was an ex-teammate of Rose's, walks over and starts talking to him at second. I'm a rookie, but I kind of wander over there, act like I know what I'm doing. You know, I'm gonna go talk to Pete . . . yeah, right. I mosey over to the bag and stand there. And Bowa goes, "Hey, Pete, whattaya think of Ryno switching over to second?" And Pete looks at me and he says, "I think he'll be an All-Star second baseman."

And you know, two years later I went to the All-Star Game, and I went for 10 straight years.

My last at-bat at Wrigley Field was a Sunday game against the Phillies and Curt Schilling. It was my third at-bat of the game. I'd already doubled off the wall against Schilling. [Cubs manager] Jim Riggleman came down about the sixth inning and said, "Ryno, this can be your last at-bat if you want it to be." I said, "OK, that's fine."

So I went up there, got a split-fingered pitch, and got a base hit to left field. I'm talking to the first baseman and here comes a pinch runner, Miguel Cairo. I gave him a high five running by and ran by the mound, and Curt Schilling tipped his hat to me, which caught me off guard. The whole stadium gave me a standing ovation. That was pretty awesome.

I'd pay to see Alex Rodriguez, Roger Clemens, Ichiro, and, uh . . . I think the reason this is tough is because I get great seats from the Cubs. I don't have to buy a ticket. I've never thought about buying a ticket. And I've seen all these guys play in person.

Let's see . . . wait, Pedro Martinez. And I'd pay to go watch Don Zimmer sit on the bench. I actually went to games because he was coaching.

I signed a contract to make $500 a month at rookie ball. My signing bonus was for about $28,000. I bought my first car. A Dodge Duster. Used, by the way. They were pretty hip at the time.

One of my best friends still works for the Cubs, and I visit him every time I go there: Yosh Kawano, the clubhouse guy. He'll be dressed in his white sailor hat, his white T-shirt, and khaki pants. He's been there for more than 60 years.

That really takes me back to the first time I walked into spring training at Fitch Park, and there's my uniform hanging up, No. 23—which I hated. I tried to talk to Yosh about giving me No. 14. He says, "No, that's retired. That's Ernie Banks's number." I said, "Who's Ernie Banks?"

I was 20 years old. I didn't know anything about the Chicago Cubs. No. 14 is what I wore in high school. To me, 23 was a crazy number. I thought maybe if I established myself I could change the number.

Yosh was the first guy I saw walking in when I reported. Saw him every year for 15 years. He was probably the last guy I saw walking out. He took care of me.

I kept things. I've got the ball from my first hit in the Major Leagues. I didn't have any bats at the time because I was a September call-up. So when they told me I was going to hit, I looked through the bat rack and that's when [shortstop] Larry Bowa came up to me: "Hey, Ryno, take this one up there." So I used one of his bats.

I've got that bat and the baseball, but here's what happened. I made contact with the ball right on the lettering of the baseball. The lettering from the baseball came off right onto the bat.

The MVP trophy is another thing. It signifies the '84 season we had as a team, a city, an organization.

I've got a lot of things that were firsts. I've got a bat signed from my first All-Star Game. That was in '84 at Candlestick Park in San Francisco. I take two steps out of the locker room walking onto the field, and this photographer comes up and says, "Ryno, George Brett is looking for you. He wants his picture with you. You're his favorite player."

I said, "You're kidding." But I look up and here's George Brett running over. We posed for a picture. I've got a copy of that. That was pretty cool.

GAME 98

Sunday, July 25, 2004 . . . Phillies, 3, Cubs 2 . . . Citizens Bank Park . . . Cubs NL Central pennant flies: Second (52-46) . . . Stat of the game: Michael Barrett breaks up Eric Milton's no-no in the ninth. . . . Wild-card status: two games back.

Noted Cubs philosopher Ernie Banks once said, "The riches of the game are in the thrills, not the money." He's right, of course. Memories are what connect us to the past and to the players themselves. We care more about the decimal point in Greg Maddux's ERA than the decimal point in his salary.

The National Baseball Hall of Fame is familiar with Banks and Cubs thrills. It has Ernie's jersey from 1971, which was his final season as a Cubs player. It has the bat used by Johnny Evers in the 1906 World Series, the ball from the final out in the 1906 Series (the heavily favored Cubs lost to the White Sox's "Hitless Wonders"), Harry Caray's glasses/goggles, Kerry Wood's cap and game ball from his 20-strikeout performance against the Houston Astros in 1998 (had tickets . . . didn't go . . . I live in shame), World Series pins from 1945, Ryne Sandberg's cap and spikes from 1988, every copy of the Cubs monthly magazine, *Vineline,* except Volume 1/No. 1, a scientific research report commissioned by the team in the mid-1930s called "The Chicago Cubs Experimental Lab Reports," a Wrigley Field folding seat removed from the stadium in 1986, the bat used by Hack Wilson to hit his 47th homer in 1930, watch fobs presented to Mordecai Brown in the 1907 and 1908 World Series, assorted bats, assorted game-used bats, batting gloves, jersey, cap, spikes, and batting helmet from Sammy Sosa's glorious 1998 season, and, among other items, Cubs 1984 World Series tickets, which were printed but, alas, never used, thanks to the team in the Burger King unis.

Mary Bellew, Hall of Fame assistant registrar and loyal Cubs fan, has been cataloguing donated items since 1995. If it's in the Hall, Bellew has a record of the item either in her computer database or on paper.

Bellew is enough of a Cubs fan that she once took her husband, Joseph, to the final 1989 regular-season game at Wrigley for a birthday present. Bellew sounds like a Ray Kinsella novel just talking about it, all gooey and misty-eyed.

Anyway, Bellew keeps track of, give or take a few, the 1,800 bats, 800 jerseys, 500 gloves, and 6,300 baseballs in the Hall of Fame's collection. That means the ball thrown by Ferguson Jenkins for his 3,000th strikeout in 1982 sits in the same climate-controlled room (65 degrees, 45 percent humidity) as a ball signed by Pope John Paul II. Sosa's bats share cabinet and shelving space with the Bambino's lumber. Rogers Hornsby's wool flannel jersey is wrapped carefully in acid-free tissues and stored in an acid-free box, just as a wedding gown is preserved.

"There's tobacco juice stains on some of the older ones," she says.

You want to hold that ball used by Fergie? Then you've got to wear white cotton gloves. That way no skin oils touch the item. The Hall of Fame is so particular about its collectibles that it sends them to a special conservation lab for cleaning.

The jersey Sosa wore after hitting home runs No. 61 (to tie Roger Maris's record) and 62 (to surpass it) almost never made it to Cooperstown and the cleaning lab. In the bedlam of the Cubs' clubhouse that September 13, 1998, day at Wrigley, equipment manager Yosh Kawano took Sosa's No. 21 jersey and threw it in the dirty clothes pile for washing.

"We had to send Billy Williams back there to get it from Yosh," says Jeff Idelson, VP of Communications and Education for the Hall.

Idelson, along with then-assistant John Ralph, were at Wrigley to try to coax a few mementos out of Sosa. The jersey was high on the wish list, as were any of the bats Sosa used during that Summer of Sammy and Mark McGwire.

Ralph, who now works for MLB.com, followed Sosa during the last three weeks of that season. Idelson was assigned to McGwire. In fact, it was Idelson who brought Maris's bat to St. Louis for a Cubs-Cardinals series. Sosa swung it a few times in the visiting clubhouse and asked about the specs. Thirty-three inches, 32 ounces, he was told.

"This is the same kind of bat I use," Sosa said.

"Well, if you were fortunate enough to reach Maris's number, we were hoping you'd donate a bat," said Idelson.

"I'll be right back," Sosa said.

A few minutes later, he returned with a donation. "I used this bat to break Hack Wilson's record [Wilson hit 56 homers in 1930]," said Sosa, handing the black Rawlings to Idelson. "Don't worry. I understand the importance."

Sosa has been a sweetheart to the Hall. In 1998 alone, he donated the black Rawlings used for his 18th homer in the month of June, the Rawlings used for home run No. 57, the natural-stain Rawlings bat used for Nos. 59 to 62, the black Hoosier bat used for his last three homers of the season (Nos. 64, 65, and 66), his batting helmet, batting gloves, Nike spikes (size 12, if you're interested). He also gave the Hall the jersey he wore when he hit his career 400th home in May 2001, and the black Easton bat he used to hit career No. 500 in April 2003. (X-rays were done; no cork in any of them.)

There's more. The Milwaukee Brewers sent the home plate used at County Stadium when Sosa hit Nos. 64 and 65 in '98. Idelson and Ralph also returned to Cooperstown that season with a treasured No. 3 placard from the Wrigley Field scoreboard (Sosa hit a three-run dinger for his

60th), as well as a No. 1 placard (a solo shot for his 62nd). They also have the ball from No. 62, and their very own box of Slammin' Sammy cereal.

There are a few other Cubs items the Hall would love to get its white cotton gloves on. Those phantom 2003 Cubs World Series tickets would be a nice addition. And Tim Wiles, the Hall's director of research, continues to search for the only issue—Volume 1, No. 1—missing from the library's collection of *Vineline*.

Oddly enough, the Hall isn't interested in remnants of the Bartman ball.

"It's a vital moment in Chicago history," Idelson says. "In terms of baseball history, it's not a very poignant moment. It was a foul ball. That, to us, wasn't a defining moment."

But what about the $113,824 paid for the ball by the owners of Harry Caray's? What about ending the Bartman Ball Curse? What about a ball whose destruction is carried live on national television?

"I grew up in Boston," says Idelson. "I understand all about jinxes, curses, and voodoo. From our standpoint, it's not a significant moment."

Tell it to Moises Alou.

My personal favorite Cubs artifact can be found in a Cooperstown greenhouse. Samantha Newby, the team's manager of media information, sent it to Idelson in an egg carton.

It is ivy from the Wrigley outfield wall. When it grows up, it will climb and creep up the side of the Hall of Fame. No catalog card necessary.

GAME 99

July 26, 2004 . . . Cubs 3, Brewers 1 . . . Miller Park . . . Cubs NL Central pennant flies: Second (53-46) . . . Stat of the game: Matt Clement wins his first game since June 8. . . . Wrigley North is packed again: 41,585.

The phone rings. Figures. I'm two bites into a carefully constructed ham-and-Swiss on sourdough. I make a beeline from the dining room table, maneuver around the kitchen island, hydroplane on the hardwood floor near my office door, grab my cheapo Time-Life operator-like headphone, poke a forefinger at the Talk button on the cordless, and offer nothing more than a gruff, dismissive "Wojciechowski." After all, this screws up my whole lunch break.

"You wanted me to call," says the voice—commanding, older, as authoritative as a police precinct sergeant. "This is Studs Terkel."

Yikes! Already? I had sent the fawning Eddie Haskell–quality interview request ("Gee, Mr. Terkel, you're the best . . .") only three days earlier. Since when do Pulitzer Prize winners fall for desperation? And so promptly?

But the great Terkel, long the de facto conscience of Chicago, has a spot for baseball as soft as a broken-in mitt. The preeminent oral historian played sportswriter Hugh Fullerton—and played him well—in John Sayle's *Eight Men Out*. Terkel knows the game. Better yet, he knows the Chicago game played on the North and South Sides. In fact, you could steal several of his book titles and apply them to the Cubs. What better way to describe the futility of following this tortured franchise than *Hope Dies Last*? Or *Hard Times: An Oral History of the Great Depression*. (Pre-Bartman, of course.) And remember, Terkel is familiar with sinking ships—he was born the same year the *Titanic* met an iceberg.

Terkel is 91, a bit hard of hearing, but remains as sharp as a No. 2 pencil. He was a longtime friend of the late Mike Royko, the Pulitzer Prize-winning Chicago newspaper columnist, 16-inch softball enthusiast, and lifelong Cubs follower.

Our conversation was more monologue than Q&A:

"I've got to speak truthful. Once upon a time there were baseball fans. There were North Side and South Side fans. Cubs fans were honest-to-God fans, as were Sox fans. Then came TV and exposure. Wrigley Field became a place to *go*. Most fans would go there like they would go to the Auto Show, the Air Show, the Taste of Chicago, Buckingham Fountain.

"A great many Cubs fans—and I live on the North Side, so I see them . . . I see the SUVs and the others—they know about as much about baseball as I know about Einstein's Theory of Relativity.

"With the Cubs, it has little to do with baseball. It has more to do with a certain institution of baseball. They're lovable. They lose. Then there are the dinosaurs—the Sox.

"Cubs fans, basically with few exceptions, are old people, or young people with IQs—and I'm going to appropriate Gore Vidal's famous quote—of room temperature: 75. Do they know about Hack Wilson, Gabby Hartnett, the teams of the past? Have they heard the humorous 'Miksis-to-Smalley-to-Addison Street'? To be a fan, you have to be a fan of baseball history.

"Where does the idea of throwing back a baseball begin? It's called being a 'homer.' That began with the Cubs. That's not a baseball fan. A baseball fan keeps a homer hit to him. But that's just me. I'm giving you my view of baseball.

[A confession: I was casually taking notes, thinking Terkel and I would begin the actual interview after a few minutes of baseball pleasantries. Then I realized that this was Terkel's version of a Cubs oral history. This was the damn interview. I turned on my computer, fired up Microsoft Word, and then asked if, well, he wouldn't mind starting over. The world's most accommodating political activist—or "lifetime hellraiser," as *Mother Jones* magazine once described him—paused for a moment and then got after it, baseball-wise.]

"I was saying the Cubs fan is a unique species. Not a baseball fan in the unique sense of the word. Now I'm not saying just rubes go there, that it's just people from Indiana or wherever, who want to be there. Those who attend—and I watch them closely—they haven't an idea about baseball. They aren't there for baseball. They sing that horrendous, ridiculous song ['Take Me Out to the Ballgame']. Those are cosmetics to cover a team that is there. A team that has a history of losing.

"Mike [Royko] and I were talking about this. He was a Cubs fan, though I couldn't understand that about him. But in his last column he said the Cubs lost because their owner, P. K. Wrigley, waited so long to sign any black ballplayers. It was the last club in the National League to bring up a black ballplayer—[Ernie] Banks and [Gene] Baker [in September 1953]. Boston was the last in the American League.

"This was the time when Branch Rickey had hired Robinson. That might have been the reason they've been so far behind.

"But Wrigley Field, it's a place to go. It's been so exposed on TV. It's like a place to be. You've seen their faces in the crowd. You know.

"But do they have any sense of baseball history? Do they know about Rogers Hornsby, Riggs Stephenson, Gabby Hartnett, how Connie Mack outfoxed Joe McCarthy putting in a slow pitcher instead of Lefty Grove? Do they know about Miksis-to-Smalley-to-Addison Street, 30 years after Tinker to Evers to Chance? Knowing that makes you a fan.

"They need to question. Question the judgment of the manager. Question. Why did he bunt? Now they wait for Sammy and the home run.

"I haven't been to Wrigley for a couple of years. I used to sit in the center-field bleachers with Bill Veeck. I see better on TV than I see at the ballfield.

"I would be, if anything, a Sox fan. The Sox are raggedy. At the same time, Sox fans aren't that bright.

"I saw the 1945 World Series. The Cubs and Detroit Tigers. Warren Brown was the dean of sports correspondents in Chicago. A friend of his asked, 'Who's going to win the World Series, the Tigers or the Cubs?' He said, 'I don't think either can.'

"I could have seen that World Series game of 1929. I was going to McKinley High School. Jimmy O'Hare, my friend in school, said, 'Let's go to Cubs Park. The Athletics are going to open up in Cubs Park. There's standing room only.'

"Instead, I stayed for Psychology 1 class. I missed the game. He went to it. That was the game where Connie Mack started Howard Ehmke. A slow-throwing pitcher. He completely fooled the Cubs. [Ehmke's Opening Game victory—he struck out 13 Cubs—would be his last in the big leagues.] And I stayed to listen to a lecture on gorillas, on Gestalt psychology. I could have seen that game. That's a big regret. I could have seen that game, except for that damn Gestalt psychology.

"Back then Madison and State, that was the busiest street there was. You had the Boston Store, which was more reasonable, more affordable. There was Carson and Marshall Field, which was more expensive.

"On the eighth floor of the Boston Store they had an electric score-board. You watched that scoreboard. This was 1929, the year the Cubs blew an eight-run lead in Game 4. Hack Wilson lost a Mule Haas fly ball in the sun [actually two]. The A's won in five games.

"Back then kids knew the players. There were 16 teams, eight in one league, eight in the other. St. Louis had two teams, the Browns and the Cards. Boston had two teams. Philly had two teams. The furthermost west-ward was St. Louis. Kids knew the managers. They knew the lineups.

"There's a history to baseball. I think a fan to me, an old-time baseball fan, has a sense of some past. Cubs fans are an example of exposure on TV. It's the thing to do.

"And then, of course, The Curse. The Curse has been visited on us. What have we done to sin, oh, dear? What can we do to atone? Maybe wait for the Second Coming?

"Does that make any sense to you?

"OK, so long."

GAME 100

Tuesday, July 27, 2004 . . . Cubs 7, Brewers 1 . . . Miller Park . . . Stat of the game: Greg Maddux wins his third consecutive game and career No. 299. . . . Stuff: GM Jim Hendry gets a win on his birthday. . . . Wild-card status: one game down.

I interviewed Bartman today!

He was driving to some godforsaken farm town in Indiana when he returned my call. My call! It's the first and only interview Bartman has done since that fateful October 14, 2003, evening at Wrigley.

I had sent him a letter weeks earlier explaining the *Cubs Nation* book project, but never heard a peep back. I figured that was that. But then, this morning at about 8:45, he calls on his cell phone and says he has plenty of time to kill during the drive.

One question: Does it make a difference that I was talking to *a* Bartman and not *the* Bartman?

The Bartman, at last check with his attorney/brother-in-law/spokesperson, still is lying lower than a grubworm. But *my* Bartman, the one on the phone, is none other than actor/improvisational comedian Brian Boland of world-renowned The Second City.

Boland plays Steve Bartman in The Second City's production of *Doors Open on the Right.* The premise of the show is simple enough: Bartman is to blame for everything. The NLCS loss. The economy. Racial division. Political corruption. Weapons of mass destruction. You name it, it's Bartman's fault.

The cleverness of the show, which runs eight times a week, isn't confined to the use of Bartman. The lyrics are a Jamie Lee Curtis scream, and the skits are seamlessly woven. But Boland gets the biggest laughs when he makes his first appearance as Bartman, groping haplessly for the infamous foul ball. His parents disown him. His grandfather threatens him. His girlfriend dumps him. But wait, there's more.

A bride throws a bouquet of flowers to the wedding party. At the last moment, Boland's Bartman appears out of nowhere to make a leaping but bungled grab.

Firemen rush to the scene of a house fire. A frantic mother, holding her newborn in her hands, is told to toss the infant down to the pleading crew. As the baby falls toward their outstretched arms, Bartman bursts onto the scene . . . and drops the kid.

Boland, who moved from California to Chicago when he was five, watched bits and pieces of the 2003 playoffs. Before and after shows, even during intermissions, Boland and the rest of the cast kept track of the Cubs. Then came the Bartman moment. Remember the call by WGN's Pat Hughes? Bartman does. He was listening to the 'GN broadcast on headphones.

"Three-two pitch . . . Fly ball to left . . . Toward the line . . . Alou's over . . . Does he have room? . . . And leaping up, Alou cannot make the play!"

A show was born.

"There's no getting around that that was the moment that turned everything," says Boland. "Whether it should have had that impact or not is open to debate. It really shouldn't have, but it did. It goes back to the end of the show where we say, 'Should we blame this man for all our woes?' Pretty regularly, someone, or several people in the audience, will shout, 'Yes!'"

Cast member Antoine McKay was the first to suggest incorporating a Bartman component into the 2004 Second City revue. Jean Villepique, a Second City veteran, began writing assorted lyrics. Costume designer and stylist Tracy Thorpe assembled the Bartman collection: blue Cubs cap, black headphones, glasses. Boland provides the look of bewilderment.

"People recognize who he is, so I think the whole assemblage of headphone, hat, and glasses is such an instant icon," says Boland. "If there was a logo for Bartman, it could easily be done with a line drawing, just like the Harry Caray one with the glasses, or the Mike Ditka scribble. I don't think anyone will forget Bartman's image.

"The opening song of the show, there's a line, 'No one will remember your name,' which obviously isn't true about Bartman. He is permanently etched in Cubs fans' minds. Just like no Boston fan will forget the name Buckner. That's why I never underestimate the degree to which the Cubs Nation will take anything, step on it, expand it. Knowing the history of the Cubs, it's similar to the Red Sox's lore of disappointment."

Out of the indelible memory comes comedy.

"I play him like an innocent at first, which I think he is," says Boland. "The poor guy. I remember him writing that initial statement, something like 'from the bottom of this broken Cubs fan's heart,' or whatever the exact quote was. I feel sorry for the poor guy. He has really eschewed any sort of media coverage. He just wants to disappear and hide under a rock.

"The funny thing is, I think if Bartman made a cameo at our show, I think he would actually be cheered and applauded. I don't think his life would be in danger if he came to our show. It was open to question there for the first couple of days after [Game 6]. Now people would laugh and cheer. Certainly, he would be heckled as well. But at this point, I think enough time has passed where it's like, people realize it wasn't really his fault."

The White Sox will move to Wrigley before Bartman appears on The Second City mainstage. Someone claiming to be Bartman's cousin attended the show and afterward told cast members that he didn't like the portrayal of his relative, nor did he think it was the least bit funny.

But the cousin misses the point. By blindly blaming Bartman for the world's ills, they are, in fact, absolving him. That's the genius of the show.

"The idea was we were going to go all the way back to the beginning of that moment where Bartman screwed up and see if maybe something would be different," says Boland. "What happens if he'd backed everybody away and he didn't touch the ball? And, of course, true to the Cubs' track record, why don't we just let Moises drop the ball anyway, like he probably would have done since, you know, he's a Cub. So that's where we go. We're actually on [Bartman's] side. It just doesn't seem that way at first.

"Hopefully, the audience, if it's paying attention, there's an understanding. They're like, 'Yes, classic. Of course, that's what would have happened. It's *not* this guy's fault. Sometimes things just happen and it's *nobody's* fault.'"

I ask why Boland is driving to a godforsaken farm town in Indiana. He says he has a lead role in an independent movie. He plays a Mennonite farmer who accidentally maims his daughter in a baler accident.

Now, *that's* funny.

GAME 101

Wednesday, July 28, 2004 . . . Brewers 6, Cubs 3 . . . Miller Park . . . Stuff: Now it's 11 games behind the Cardinals. . . . Wild-card status: two games back.

I don't know much about baseball bats, but Mark Grudzielanek does. All hitters do. If it were a category on *Jeopardy!*, they'd wear out the clicker button.

I thought a bat was a bat. Some are longer than others, some heavier than others, but you slap some pine tar on it and you're ready to go, right?

Not even close. Big league hitters are as particular about their bats as the PGA Tour boys are about their clubs. A bat has a *feel* to it. A pro ballplayer can pick up a bat, swing it a few times, and tell you within a few ounces the weight and within a few quarter inches the length. They can tell you if the weight is balanced or end heavy, if the handle is thin, moderate, or thick. Most of all, they can tell you if it's game-worthy.

"Sometimes you can't figure it out, but it just doesn't feel right," Grudzielanek says. "So you'll use it for BP or something."

Grudzielanek broke into the big leagues using a Rawlings ash bat. Maple is the tool of choice, says team clubhouse manager Tom Hellmann, of about 65 percent of the Cubs. Grudzielanek made the switch about four seasons ago. This is a little odd, considering Grudzielanek had his best season as a pro (.326 for the Los Angeles Dodgers in 1999) using the more traditional ash bats.

But loyalty to a certain kind of wood goes only so far. Ask Grudzielanek for a bat inventory and he pushes aside the T-shirts and warm-ups hanging in his locker and starts counting. The maple bats lean against the locker stall wall like rakes in a toolshed. There are six of them, all black (Grudzielanek uses only black bats), and in two different makes and models: the Old Hickory J 143 and the Tuff Bats Pro 64 X Bat.

This is the easy-to-reach supply. There are more stacked nearby in boxes. And Grudzielanek also keeps a few Rawlings pro-grade maples in reserve. The Cubs buy the bats, and the bat reps make sure each player always has at least a dozen or two available.

Old Hickory uses maple from Appalachian region forests. This is the same maple, says the company, used in the furniture industry. Meanwhile, Tuff Bats gets its maple from the hardwood forests of Pennsylvania, New England, and Quebec. Only a few dozen of the X Bats are made each day. For you or me, a Pro Maple will run $80 apiece, less for the big league teams, which buy in bulk. An ash bat? About half that.

But maple is denser than ash and the grain more "closed," which usually means it lasts longer, *feels* harder, and, says Grudzielanek, makes a ball go farther.

"You try to keep a bat around as long as you can," he says. "With maple you can do that. With ash, one bad pitch, or one hit off the end, and you tend to change bats a little more frequently. If you're swinging well, you tend to want to keep that bat around."

Grudzielanek uses a 34-inch, 31.5-ounce bat. The X Bat prototype is 33½ inches, 31 ounces.

"Some guys tend to use different [length and weight] bats depending on how they feel, who's throwing, that sort of thing," he says. "I don't change a whole lot. I pretty much use the same bat throughout the season. If there's a situation with two strikes, I just choke up a little bit, that's all."

Grudzielanek pulls a J 143 and a Pro 64 from his locker. The Old Hickory model gets the call for the game. Together, they go 0-for-4.

GAME 102

Thursday, July 29, 2004 . . . Cubs 4, Brewers 0 . . . Miller Park . . . Stat of the game: Here's why Brewers management loves the Cubs: This four-game series set a team record for attendance (167,136). . . . Stuff: With the trade deadline only two days away, rumors continue to swirl. Maybe that's why Matt Clement asks MLB.com writer Carrie Muskat, "Where am I going today?" . . . Commissioner Bud Selig stops by the press box and says the new netting at Wrigley Field will "solve" the falling-concrete problem. Selig also says he'll be there Sunday to watch Greg Maddux go for career victory No. 300. . . . Todd Hollandsworth still can't run because of nerve damage in his right shin, but he can smoke cigars. He had a son this morning—Tugg. . . . The Oakland A's designate Eric Karros for assignment. . . . Wild-card status: two games back.

Sammy Sosa finishes dressing and then nods to the media herd waiting a respectful distance away. Minicam lights overpower his features. Tape recorders and microphones nearly tickle his chin.

Sosa hit a two-run homer in the decisive four-run sixth inning today. Along with the single he hit in the first, Sosa's average inched up to .274. He now has 10 home runs and 20 RBI for the month. This will be a friendly, carefree exchange with the Cubs star.

Uh, no.

Sosa isn't impolite, just careful. Careful with his words, with his smile, with revealing his emotions.

"People always worry about me," he says. "I know how to make adjustments at the plate. When I'm healthy, I can produce. Maybe you can put that in the paper and those people can leave me alone now."

Sosa isn't done.

"It's not getting to me," he says. "I really wanted to say that I'm OK. I really appreciate it, everybody trying to help me. The only guy who has to make adjustments at the plate is me. I've been doing it all my life."

Fair enough. But facts are facts. The ninth-greatest (and climbing) home run hitter in the history of the game has heard boos this season. Lots of them. This happens when you have as many strikeouts as hits (73) and you whiff every 3.6 at-bats. Sosa has 561 more home runs than me, but you don't need to be Hank Aaron to see that the guy has scuffled, 10/20 July or not.

Five of those 20 RBI came in one game. I'm not knocking the big game, but you get the point. Sosa is hitting an inexplicable .167 with zero homers against lefties (he isn't alone; Alou is hitting .219 with one homer against left-handers). Last season, Sosa hit .333 against lefties and entered the year with a career .297 average against them. So something is wrong.

The Cubs have tried to drop hints to Sosa. This is a proud player, so you have to be delicate with such suggestions. That's them. If it were me, I'd say, "Sammy, have you noticed you're so far away from the plate that you're nearly in Madison?"

Pitchers aren't dummies. They see Sosa can't possibly cover the outer quarter of the plate, so they throw there, or just outside of it. Most of the time, they get Sosa to whiff, tap out to the right side, or pull a grounder to the left side.

Nothing against Sosa, but he isn't the best position player on this team anymore. Aramis Ramirez is, and if all things were equal (no egos involved), I think Baker would seriously consider dropping Sosa to the five hole and let Ramirez hit third or fourth. But he can't. Ramirez is still nursing a strained groin. And Sosa is Sosa.

But at some point it will happen. Sosa is 35, and as his skills decline, Baker's power currency increases. Sosa is still a dangerous offensive weapon, but his games played, batting average, home runs, RBI, runs scored, walks, and hits have declined in each of the last two seasons. Those same numbers are tracking lower across the board in 2004, too.

Sosa isn't very good at aging gracefully. In a way, I respect his stubbornness. But just because he does Pepsi ads and puts up a 10/20 for July doesn't mean problem solved.

This isn't the magical 2001 Season of Sammy. This is 2004, the Season of

Grinding. If Sosa really wants to make adjustments that matter, try these: Stand closer to the plate, and offer to move down in the order. It beats Baker doing it for you.

GAME 103

Friday, July 30, 2004 . . . Cubs 10, Phillies 7 . . . Wrigley Field . . . Cubs NL Central pennant flies: Second (56-47) . . . Stat of the game: Aramis Ramirez hits home runs No. 19, 20, 21—all no-doubters. Stuff: On an overcast, 70-degree day, Phillies catcher Todd Pratt inexplicably pulls an industrial-sized water hose from the maintenance facility under the left-field bleachers and begins spraying down the crowd. Bleacher-savvy Cubs fans thank him by tossing beer cups and serenading Pratt with chants of "Assssssss-hole." . . . Sammy Sosa rarely budges from his spot in right field, which is why the grounds crew had to reseed the worn, brown patch while the Cubs were on the road. One problem: Pigeons kept eating the seeds, which forced the crew to put netting over the area, which caused the grass to turn lime green. Sosa looks like he's standing on a Popsicle. . . . The Cubs' marketing department gets Maddux's reluctant OK to put his name and career win total on the scoreboard until No. 300. . . . The Curse in Reverse: Josh Beckett drops to 4-6 after losing to the Expos. . . . Wild-card status: one game back.

The Cubs return to Wrigley to find it wearing a black hair net. Three separate incidents of falling concrete chunks have resulted in a city-mandated series of inspections and installation of safety netting.

Team president Andy MacPhail makes an appearance in The Cave, where he addresses a media mix of sportswriters and skeptical city reporters. Both sets of reporters pretend they know something about structural engineering.

"The good news," says MacPhail, is that "Wrigley Field is structurally safe and sound and, to use [the engineers'] words, [safer] than buildings half its age."

The bad news: MacPhail says the Cubs used "incorrect judgment" and "were slow" to react to the incidents themselves.

It also doesn't help that the Cubs failed to secure city building permits for previous repairs (Mayor White Sox is going to love that), and questions persist about several of the concrete ramps. Otherwise, it looks as if the Cubs are going to survive this PR disaster, though the aesthetics of Wrigley are taking it in the shorts these days.

Earlier that morning, I notice Paul Rathje, the Cubs' longtime director of stadium operations, having his daily pregame chat with the Wrigley ushers and security personnel. A few minutes later, I hear applause from the Wrigley workers. Weird.

Then word leaks out: Rathje has resigned.

"Everyone loves him," says one of the blue shirts (security). "There were tears. But he had always said if it stopped being fun, he was going to call it quits."

I see Rathje on the field after the game and shake his hand. He says his departure has nothing to do with the concrete controversy; he was just tired of it all. Tired of the hours, of missing his family.

Conspiracy experts will say he was forced out by the Cubs. But had you seen him that day, a sense of relief on his face, you would have known differently.

GAME 104

Saturday, July 31, 2004 . . . Phillies 4, Cubs 3 . . . Wrigley Field . . . Cubs NL Central pennant flies: Second (56-48). . . . Stuff: Workers continue to inspect the concrete underside of Wrigley. On the ramp leading up to the press box is a half-filled bucket of concrete chunks. . . . In one of the all-time great puff pieces, a Tribune *arts reporter writes in today's edition that the new protective netting "does not spoil the beloved traditional ambiance at Wrigley. The netting . . . adds a fun new accessory to Wrigley's crumbly underbelly." Hey, kids, falling concrete: fun! . . . Sammy Sosa enters the game with 10 homers and 21 RBI in July but is only hitting .173 against lefties (0 HRs, 5 RBI, 52 at-bats). This, well, sucks. Does Sammy listen to suggestions? "Sometimes," says Dusty Baker. "Next subject." . . . Country singer Toby Keith sneaks into the WGN booth to see Ron Santo. . . . A crowd of 39,086 pushes the Cubs' home attendance to 2,007,402. It's the earliest the Cubs have ever reached the 2 million mark.*

It is 3:06 P.M. The 3 o'clock trading deadline has come and gone and the Cubs haven't done a thing. No Nomar Garciaparra. No Orlando Cabrera. No nothing. Instead, there is the dull ache of another Matt Clement loss and the end of another very modest two-game Cubs win streak.

I pack my computer bag and debate whether to rush down to the postgame interview room/sweatbox or simply watch Clement and Dusty Baker on the closed-circuit TV in the air-conditioned media dining room. I wuss out and choose comfort.

Baker enters the room. Someone asks him about the Cubs not making any deals. Baker says he just came from the field to the interview room, so he hasn't had a chance to talk with GM Jim Hendry yet.

Uh-oh.

I have a flashback to Baker's daily pregame interview in the dugout. That's when he said, "What you see today could be a prerequisite of another trade. Look at Michael Barrett. Look how we got Michael. Michael spent one day with Oakland, never put the uniform on, and ends up with us. It was already orchestrated to be a three-way trade. That's the thing you see more now. You see more three-ways. There's money involved."

Just for grins, I call the baseball editor at ESPN.com and ask if the Cubs somehow squeezed in a deal.

"They got Nomar," says ESPN's Scott Ridge. "Alex Gonzalez is in the deal. They're filing the papers right now."

What? The Cubs haven't said a peep about a trade.

I hang up the phone. Ron Santo walks by.

"Ron, have you heard about Nomar coming to the Cubs?"

He smiles. "I knew about it a couple hours ago," he says. Then his face grows serious. "Who were the other players in the deal? Did you hear if Clement was part of it?"

Clement? I didn't know Nomar was part of it until a minute ago. In fact, I didn't even know there was an It.

"All I've heard is Gonzalez," I say.

Santo explains there have been rumors of a proposed deal involving Clement and Gonzalez for Nomar and pitcher Derek Lowe. I grab my bag and do a Maurice Greene to the Cubs' clubhouse door on the concourse level. Ryan Dempster walks out, followed by clubbies carrying two massive suitcases. (Maybe Dempster got dealt. The Red Sox need pitching.) Then Clement, looking as if he needs a hug, follows a few minutes later. He gets that hug from wife Heather and then holds son Mattix.

Dempster, Clement, and Gonzalez for Nomar and Lowe?

That's when I see Hendry and Scott Nelson, the Cubs' director of base-ball operations, make their way from the administrative offices to the club-house. Here we go.

I reach the interview room moments before Hendry walks in. The place is packed. And hot. Now I know what it's like to be a chicken breast in a George Foreman Grill.

"Well, we had kind of a long and complicated affair here, but we ended up being involved in a four-way trade," begins Hendry.

The Cubs trade Class-A pitcher Justin Jones to Minnesota for first base-man Doug Mientkiewicz. Then the Cubs trade Gonzalez, Francis Beltran, and Brendan Harris to the Red Sox for Garciaparra, Class-A outfielder Matt Murton, and cash considerations. Then Boston trades Gonzo, Bel-tran, and Harris to the Montreal Expos for Cabrera.

Turns out Baker had laid out a trail of bread crumbs earlier in the day, but no one picked up on his hints. Mientkiewicz was a Cub for an hour or so. It was a multifranchise deal. It involved cash.

In essence, the Cubs give up one starter (the slick-fielding but career-.243-hitting Gonzalez) and two prospects for a five-time All-Star who will be a free agent at season's end, and Murton, a former first-round pick in 2003 who, like Nomar, also played at Georgia Tech.

"I think it's the kind of thing that everybody's happy," says Hendry.

Happy? Hendry looks as if he wants to pop a bottle of Dom, take a chug, and then spray the rest on the sweat-soaked reporters. This isn't a trade, it's a surgical strike. At day's start, you would have given the Cubs a 10 percent chance of getting Garciaparra and maybe a 50 percent chance of getting Cabrera.

"When I got out of the car this morning at about 7, I was prepared for this being a real big day for the Cubs, or I'd be hanging my head a little bit," says Hendry.

The deal itself didn't begin to reach critical mass until about noon. That's when the possibility of a two-team trade grew to three teams, and later four teams. And though Hendry won't discuss specifics, it's obvious prized prospects Angel Guzman and Felix Pie were never going to be part of the package. Not so clear was the fate of Clement.

"I've told the media, told Dusty, told Matt Clement . . . Matt Clement wasn't going for Nomar straight up," Hendry says.

True. Hendry did tell Clement a day earlier that he wasn't going to deal the pitcher for a position player. But offers change. So do business decisions, which is why the rumor of a Clement/Gonzalez-for-Nomar/Lowe proposal refused to die.

Clement didn't have a clue about today's deal until Greg Maddux approached him in the clubhouse minutes after the game ended.

"Does Gonzo know he got traded?" Maddux said.

"I don't know," said Clement. "Who'd he get traded to?"

"Boston."

"For who?"

"Nomar."

Clement, fresh from the shower, quickly toweled off and got dressed. As he was putting on his shoes, it hit him.

"I better check and see if I got traded," he thought.

Clement walked up the clubhouse stairs to Baker's office, but the manager wasn't there. Then he asked the Cubs coaches about the trade. They didn't have the details. That's when Baker walked in.

"Hey, man, did I get traded?" Clement said.

"No, man," said Baker.

Who knows how close Clement came to being an ex-Cub, but I could have sworn I saw Dempster in the bullpen before today's game. At the risk of sounding like Oliver Stone, there might have been an emergency plan in place had Clement been dealt with Gonzalez for Nomar and Lowe. Dempster could have been activated to the roster and started the game. Instead, Gonzo, Beltran, and Harris are gone, and Clement is on his way to a Toby Keith concert.

Gonzalez's departure isn't much of a surprise. The combination of Gonzalez, Ramon Martinez, and Rey Ordonez at shortstop has been an offensive disaster. It didn't help that Gonzalez missed 70-plus games because of injury, or that he's hitting .217 (0-for-3 today) with just eight RBI. Nobody in the Cubs organization will come right out and say it, but if Hendry didn't get Garciaparra, he would have figured out a way to get Montreal's Cabrera.

In a pure baseball sense, the Cubs kicked some serious butt in this trade. Garciaparra, 31, is a career .323 hitter with playoff experience and two AL batting titles. He isn't the defensive player Gonzalez is, but the Cubs need runs more than they need ESPN Web Gems.

Boston GM Theo Epstein is going to catch heat for this one, but it's not like he was going to re-sign Garciaparra anyway. Not after owner John Henry tried moving him in the off-season for Alex Rodriguez. So Epstein gets Cabrera and hopes he puts up numbers. If he doesn't, Ben Affleck is going to be pissed.

Montreal GM Omar Minaya is thrilled. No way was Cabrera, a free agent at season's end, going to return to the Expos.

Minnesota GM Terry Ryan is doing OK, too. Mientkiewicz is hitting .250 with five homers and 25 RBI, which isn't exactly what the penny-pinching Twins had in mind for $3.5 million this year.

Deals like these are either prearranged and announced early in the day, or they get thrown into the microwave an hour or so before the trade deadline. This one was a microwave job.

According to league sources, the deal is more complicated than Hendry ever lets on:

At about 1 P.M., the Red Sox tell the Cubs that if they can engineer a trade that eventually brings Mientkiewicz and Cabrera to Boston, then they'll move Garciaparra to Chicago. Hendry, say league sources familiar with the deal, then works out the Jones-for-Mientkiewicz swap, but with a condition: If Hendry can't swing the Nomar deal before the 3 o'clock local deadline, then the Twins have to take back Mientkiewicz. For this, Cubs fans should forever thank Ryan. Had Ryan not given Hendry such flexibility (after all, there's no way the Cubs need another first baseman), Garciaparra might still be in a Red Sox uni.

The deal lurches forward. But here's the rub. The Cubs, Red Sox, Twins, and Expos are running out of minutes.

Minaya likes the Gonzo-Beltran combination from the Cubs, but he has reservations about taking Murton from the Red Sox. Now it's five minutes until the deadline. The deal is thisclose to falling through.

As the clock ticks, Hendry makes a decision. The Cubs will include the well-regarded Harris in the deal, but only if they get Murton in return. Minaya thinks about it and finally says yes. The trade is submitted to MLB offices with exactly two minutes to spare.

Because of the complexity of the deal, MLB doesn't approve the trade until nearly 3:30. By that time, the Cubs-Phillies game is long over and ESPN is reporting Nomar is history. Gonzalez thinks he's been traded to Boston. Baker calls him into his office and tells Gonzalez the really bad news: He's going to the salt flats of baseball, Montreal.

Meanwhile, Cubs reliever LaTroy Hawkins calls former Minnesota Twins teammate Jacque Jones. The Twins are playing the Red Sox tonight.

"You don't have to worry about facing Nomar," Hawkins says. "We just got him."

I walk into the clubhouse at 4:43. Hendry, finally through with a series of live TV interviews on the field, arrives moments later. Hendry has spoken with Garciaparra's agent, Arn Tellem, but not with Nomar himself. He gives Nomar's cell number to Cubs traveling secretary Jimmy Bank. Transportation and lodging arrangements need to be made for Garciaparra, who is in Minneapolis with the Red Sox.

Just then, Gonzalez walks around the corner and makes his way to his locker. His size-46 Cubs home jersey hangs from a hook, and five Rawlings Big Stick bats, two Wilson gloves, and a pair of blue Adidas cleats clutter the locker floor.

Bank approaches him. Bank shakes Gonzalez's hand and wishes him well. Clubhouse assistant Gary Stark is next.

"You want to keep a jersey?" he says.

A long pause. "Yeah, I'll take one," says Gonzalez.

"One of each color?"

"Yeah."

Stark wants to know how many bats Gonzo wants shipped, but Gonzalez isn't paying attention. Instead, he's watching the latest ESPN News update of the trade.

"Nomar Garciaparra is on his way to the Chicago Cubs," begins the anchor. "The Cubs have been awful at shortstop this year. The Cubs' shortstop problems? Bad."

Gonzalez says nothing. There are two small Cubs jerseys placed on his locker stool. His children, Tyler and Analise, were going to wear them on Cubs Family Day. A few moments later, Gonzalez grabs the kids' jerseys and walks out the door.

Barrett, still in gym shorts and a Cubs T-shirt, sits in a nearby leather recliner and stares at an ESPN graphic on the trade. I ask him about his jersey number, the same No. 5 that Nomar wears.

"Hey, I was here first," he says, sort of laughing.

Barrett has always worn No. 5 or a multiple of five. His brother, who played against Nomar in college, wore No. 5. His wife wore No. 5. But Barrett, who grew up in Atlanta and used to watch Nomar at Georgia Tech, will do the right thing. He always does.

Boston's Epstein appears on the plasma.

"I liked the club before," Epstein is telling the Boston media. "I like the club more."

You lose Nomar and you like the club *more*? Yikes.

Bank is on his cell phone. He's already spoken with the traveling secretaries for the Red Sox and Expos, and he's booked a flight for Gonzalez to join his new team in Florida. Garciaparra will arrive tonight at O'Hare at

11:08. A limo has been arranged. But Bank still needs to find out if Nomar uses an alias on the road, and if he knows where the Cubs' clubhouse is. After all, Garciaparra has never set foot in Wrigley.

It has been a long, bizarre day. Unlikely deals have been brokered. Seven players' lives have been turned upside down. Ridiculous questions have been asked. (A reporter repeatedly pesters Hendry about the possibility of future waiver trades. Hendry, who is fresh from acquiring NOMAR FRICKIN' GARCIAPARRA, is polite at first. But after the third waiver deal inquiry, Hendry has had enough. As the press conference breaks up, he tells the reporter that the Cubs are going to trade for Sandy Koufax.)

As the clubbies begin to vacuum the carpeted floor, I hear Boston's Epstein speak the day's essential truth.

"It's not something we woke up thinking we were going to do," he says of the Nomar trade.

Nobody did. But with all due respect, I'm guessing the Cubs will be more excited about seeing Garciaparra walk through this clubhouse door tomorrow than the Red Sox will be when Mientkiewicz and Cabrera arrive.

AUGUST

· ·

GAME 105

Sunday, August 1, 2004 ... Cubs 6, Phillies 3 ... Wrigley Field ... Cubs NL Central pennant flies: Second (57-48) ... Stat of the game: Nomar Garcia-parra singles in the seventh for his first Cubs hit and RBI. ... Stuff: The Sports World store across the street from Wrigley is selling authentic Cubs jerseys with Nomar's name and No. 8 (for now) number. Price: $199, which is $40 more than the usual Cubs authentics there. The jerseys are flying off the rack. Nomar, whose entire career was played at Fenway Park, on the charm of fellow golden oldie Wrigley: "I'm sure Wrigley doesn't become Wrigley until all the fans are there." ... Wild-card status: one game back.

Minutes before Greg Maddux takes the mound, Jimmy Farrell carefully places the game ball directly behind the middle of the pitching rubber. The 83-year-old umpires' room attendant has left a hand-printed message in the inch-wide space between the two red seams of the ball:

W

For Win.

Farrell does this only for special occasions, and what could be more special than Maddux trying to win career game No. 300, at Wrigley, in front of family, friends, and dignitaries, with newly acquired Garciaparra making his first Cubs start at shortstop? No wonder the lines to the ticket windows stretched around the sides of Wrigley. This is double dating at its finest: Maddux and history, Nomar and drama.

A day earlier, at 5:15 mass at Holy Name Cathedral in downtown Chicago, Farrell noticed Ed Montague standing near the back of the church. Montague is the crew chief of the four umpires working the Cubs-Phillies series. Farrell alerted the priest, who promptly approached Montague and ushered the surprised umpire to one of the pews near the front of the stately cathedral. Then the priest blessed Montague and said, "This is for tomorrow."

It is just a number, 300. But in baseball it takes on a richer meaning. A .300 average for a hitter is the accepted starting point to determine greatness at the plate. It is the most basic of equations, baseball's indisputable version of four quarts equal a gallon. But 300 victories is exalted numerology, not so much a measurement of greatness as it is a definition.

Jim "Pud" Galvin of the Pittsburgh Alleghenies won his 300th game, the first player to do so, in 1901. Maddux attempts today to become only the 22nd pitcher to reach that mark. In between, says the Elias Sports Bureau (with an assist from *Sun-Times* baseball writer Chris DeLuca), more than 7,500 pitchers have made big league appearances.

Of the last seven pitchers to reach 300 victories, six of them had easy-to-read business cards. Roger Clemens, Nolan Ryan, and Tom Seaver: power pitchers. Phil Niekro: knuckleball artist. Steve Carlton: master of the hook. Gaylord Perry: Vaseline spokesman. They were craftsmen, but in easy-to-recognize ways.

Not so with Maddux. Maddux's 299 wins are the product of baseball judo, where Maddux takes a hitter's strength and transforms that force into a weakness. He convinces you to swing at pitches that come tantalizingly close to the plate but never quite over it. You think a pitch ahead. He thinks through the entire at-bat.

Maddux has never pitched a no-hitter. He has thrown five one-hitters, but the only stat that truly matters to him is what Farrell has written on the ball today: *W*. He has won Cy Youngs and Gold Gloves, but his most prized baseball possession is the World Series ring he received as a member of the 1995 Atlanta Braves. That is the essence of Maddux.

It has been a strangely charged day, even by Wrigley standards. There is Maddux's quest for 300 wins. There is Nomar in Cubby pinstripes. There is the wild-card race. Nobody is immune to the day's events. Dusty Baker details a conversation he had a night earlier with his new shortstop.

"Hey, man," he told Garciaparra, "you got here in time to witness [this] and help him win his 300th."

There are no guarantees, of course. The Phillies have scored the fourth-most runs and RBI in the National League. And the wind is blowing out.

Maddux emerges from the dugout at 12:56 with pitching coach Larry Rothschild and catcher Paul Bako. They walk down the left-field line to the bullpen area, where Maddux begins his warm-up session. The crowd of 39,032 showers him with such spontaneous, heartfelt applause that the normally unflappable Maddux is momentarily overwhelmed, especially when he sees his two children sitting near the on-deck circle.

At 1:02, Nomar receives his first standing O of the day. Maddux gets his at 1:04. At 1:20, Maddux reaches the mound, picks up the ball, sees the *W*, and glances into the Cubs' dugout at Farrell. At 1:22, he delivers the first pitch of the game to Jimmy Rollins. Montague calls it a strike. Bless you, Father.

Rollins parks the next pitch in the right-field bleacher basket. Abreu jacks a homer to right center. Maddux faces seven hitters in all and trails, 2-0, at half-inning's end.

The Cubs tie the game in the second, and it stays that way until the fifth, when Maddux hits Marlon Byrd and later watches him score as Sosa misplays a Rollins single. By the middle of the inning, Maddux is on fumes. When he returns to the dugout, he tells Baker, "You've got to watch me. I'm running out of gas."

This is true. Ryan Dempster, who has the misfortune of making his remarkable comeback from Tommy John surgery on the same day as Maddux's start and Nomar's debut, takes the mound to start the seventh inning. Figures. The Cubs score four runs in the bottom of the inning, worm out of a bases-loaded jam in the eighth (thank you, Mike Remlinger), and then watch LaTroy Hawkins get the save. Maddux will have to wait until next Saturday's start in San Francisco.

Maddux is 38. He had thrown only 87 pitches, but had done so on a day that felt much hotter than the game-time temperature of 83 degrees. Baker would have let him try to finesse his way through the seventh, but Maddux has too much respect for the game.

"I would have loved to go out there, and maybe try not to walk somebody, and hope they hit it at somebody," he says. "But that's not right. It's not fair to the rest of the guys, or the team, or the city. It's not the way you're supposed to play the game."

Maddux didn't get his 300th, but the Cubs got their 57th. It was a *W*, but not the way Baker, Farrell, and the crowd of 39,032 had hoped for.

"All he's got to do is keep breathing," says Baker. "He's going to get to 300."

If only it were that easy. But that's the secret of Maddux. He makes it look that way.

GAME 106

Tuesday, August 3, 2004 ... Cubs 5, Rockies 3 ... Coors Field ... Stuff: Michael Barrett trades his beloved No. 5 to Nomar Garciaparra for little more than a promise that the new shortstop will seriously consider signing an extension with the Cubs. .... The latest leak out of Boston is that Garciaparra, who is from California, wants to play for a West Coast team in 2005. (Chicago is on the west coast of Lake Michigan.) Red Sox officials also have intimated that Garciaparra orchestrated the Cubs trade by lying about his Achilles injury, that he was aloof and moody, that he had to be talked out of a trade demand by his agent, that he's greedy. Next Red Sox allegation: Nomar Garciaparra— Al Qaeda leader ... LaTroy Hawkins converts his fourth consecutive save.

The happiest Cub isn't Garciaparra, who escaped from Boston management, or Barrett, the Montreal Expos refugee. The happiest Cub has one victory since June 8, is 8-10 overall, and always seems to pitch on the day his teammates score bupkus. The happiest Cub is Matt Clement, mostly because he's still a Cub.

It was dicey for a while. Remember the rumor Michael Wilbon heard weeks ago? Clement for Nomar, straight up. Then came a more plausible scenario: Nomar and Derek Lowe for Clement and Alex Gonzalez.

"I heard that too," says Clement.

Clement heard everything. You can't help but hear the rumors as the trading deadline draws near. In 2001, Clement nearly had to be treated for shock when the San Diego Padres traded him to the Florida Marlins. The following year, when he and Antonio Alfonseca were traded to the Cubs for four players (including Dontrelle Willis), Clement wasn't so surprised. He was 27 and the Marlins wanted to go young and cheap.

This time, who knew?

"A couple weeks ago, [GM] Jim [Hendry] had said to me, 'I'm not trading you. There's no way I'm trading you,'" says Clement. "Maybe I was naive, but I just said to myself, 'I'm going to believe him. I'm not going to sit here and worry about it or anything else.'"

That's nice. But the bearded Clement, who looks like he's late for an Amish barn raising, couldn't entirely shake the thought of a trade.

"There were so many rumors flying around about pitchers, and everybody needing pitchers," he says. "But yet my name was only mentioned for one team? I just didn't think [Hendry] was making me available, or else you would have heard my name with other teams."

Then came news of a deal. That's when the other side of his brain kicked in.

"I have to admit for an instant, when I first heard Gonzo got traded to Boston and we got Nomar, I thought, 'Oh, maybe. Maybe [Hendry] found something he just couldn't pass up.' But you know what? I love Chicago and I'd love to play here the rest of my career, but if I was going to go somewhere, it wasn't like I was going to a team in last place. I was going to a team that was basically in the same place in the standings as the Cubs are right now. So at least I was mentioned to go to a good team with a good offense, with a good history and a fun place to play."

Hendry and Baker are Clement guys. Baker stuck with Clement in 2003 when the right-hander was 2-6 entering June. Clement has never forgotten Baker's loyalty, nor will he forget Hendry keeping his word.

"It's a good feeling to know the Cubs thought that much of me, especially since I'm a free agent at the end of the year," Clement says. "It's not like I'm a guy they have signed for six years. Hopefully, that bodes well for getting something done in the future. That's what I wish for."

Clement is worth keeping for all sorts of reasons. He gives you innings, strikeouts, and lots of quality starts. The only thing he hasn't been able to do this season is give the Cubs more wins.

"This has been such a strange year for me," he says. "This is finally how I've wanted to pitch my whole career. I've been working my butt off, busting my tail to get to this level, as far as throwing the ball. It's showing everywhere except the won-lost record. There's been a lot of tough losses, a lot of tough no-decisions. But I'm keeping the team in the game every game. I've told myself, 'When I walk out of the clubhouse, it's done.' Stuff like this can eat you up and ruin your season when you're losing a lot of close games like I have."

As always, Clement leans on three reliables to get him through the tough times: religion, family, and Greg Maddux.

"You know, you learn a lot from Greg Maddux on how to act," he says. "I read an article about him yesterday where he said one of the best things he learned when he was young was to leave the game at the park."

So that's what Clement does. He leaves it all at the clubhouse door—the perplexing 8-10 record (despite a 3.03 ERA), the frustrating dry spell, and the trade rumors. Especially the trade rumors.

GAME 107

Wednesday, August 4, 2004 . . . Cubs 11, Rockies 8 . . . Coors Field . . . Stuff: The Curse in Reverse: The Marlins' Josh Beckett loses to the worst team in the majors, the Arizona Diamondbacks, and drops to 4-7. . . . The Tribune *reports that some Cubs players want Steve Stone and Chip Caray booted from the team charter plane. Knowing some of the Cubs, they probably want them booted while the plane is in the air.*

Sammy Sosa hits career home run No. 563, tying him for eighth with Reggie Jackson on the all-time list. Twenty years ago, before Sosa ever did his first post-homer bunny hop, Omar Minaya was a scout and coach with the Texas Rangers. Minaya is now the general manager of the Montreal Expos, but he still remembers the summer of '85, when he first saw Sosa in Puerto Plata, Dominican Republic.

He was a small kid, but he was very much like the way he is right now: very energetic, very confident. A big smile on his face. But when he took the field, he was all business. You had to like his energy. You had to like his smile.

He had a good arm, but a long swing. He hit the ball with some authority, but he was not strong. He was only 16, 5-10 at the time. He didn't run that well, but he didn't *know* how to run that well. But you could see he was a prospect. What separated him from the other guys was the desire to achieve. He almost had an independence, a confidence about himself. He was open to learning the [English] language, open to interacting with different people.

There was no doubt he was going to be strong. Sammy's father was rock solid. I knew he was going to have that same body as his father. They're solid.

There was a tryout. I think there were about five kids there that day. I thought he was going to be a prospect. I thought we had to sign him. Sammy was also in the Toronto Blue Jays camp [in the Dominican Republic]. They had a baseball school. They were looking at him to sign him. We gave him a $3,500 signing bonus. That's what it was. That's what most guys got down there [as nondrafted free agents]. That was the average.

I use the word *fortunate*. I was very fortunate to be part of Sammy in his early years. I never thought he'd be the player he is. But my instinct told me he was going to be a good player. When he was traded to the White Sox [in 1989] I remember telling him, "Somebody wanted to trade for you. Somebody wanted you." Sammy was like, "Hey, look, I understand."

No way did I think this would happen. You'd be lying if you said that. I was just hoping I was signing a guy who would get to the Major Leagues. Some scouts say, "Oh, I knew it." I wasn't that smart. The moment he got faster is when he became a different player. But I never thought he was going to hit like that. My original thought was he was going to be a 15-to-25-home-run guy. In those days, that was average power. I thought he was going to be a five-tool player. He did that.

GAME 108

Thursday, August 5, 2004 . . . Cubs 5, Rockies 1 . . . Coors Field . . . Cubs NL Central pennant flies: Second (60-48) . . . Stat of the game: Mark Prior throws a season-high, pain-free 108 pitches. Better yet, he gives up zero runs in six innings at Coors Field, the stadium where ERAs go to die. . . . Stuff: The Cubs are 4-0 with Nomar, as well as a season-high 12 games above .500. . . . Carlos Zambrano bags his appeal of a five-game suspension. Zambrano could have hired Johnnie Cochran to argue his case to Major League Baseball and it wouldn't have mattered. . . . Wild-card status: two games up.

Earl Shaevitz opened his Wrigleyville-based Sports World store in 1977. Those were lonely times.

"We used to count the people coming into Wrigley," he says. "You could do that in April when the weather was drabby, or in September when the Cubs were 25 games out."

And now?

"It's the greatest show on earth. It's like the Barnum & Bailey circus."

Business is good, very good, at Shaevitz's store directly across from Wrigley. He says "99%₁₀" of the merchandise is Cubs or Wrigley Field related, which is why the gruff, Chicago-born Shaevitz has a soft spot for this team. If you want something with a Bears or White Sox logo, good luck. "It'd be like a treasure hunt to find Bears and Sox stuff here," he says.

Shaevitz won't divulge his age or his sales figures, but he does say business has tripled since Sports World opened its doors 28 years ago. Now he crams 200 different items into just 3,000 square feet of sales space. When he first started selling baseball merchandise out of a cardboard box 40 years ago, the inventory was limited to pennants and buttons. Now he has a staff of 15 working the counters during home games.

"I've been through the highs and lows here," Shaevitz says. "But you figure they can't lose forever. This is giant now. This is a cult now, this team."

You think he's kidding? Shaevitz used to close his store in February and vacation in Florida. But that was before he opened a website and noticed the sales orders climb each week. "You stay in Florida," he told his wife. "I'm going back." Now he's closed for business only twice a year: Thanksgiving and Christmas.

During the 2003 NLCS, Shaevitz kept Sports World open from 6 A.M. to 11 P.M. He received orders from as far away as England. He even had several customers purchase Cubs items and have them shipped to their sons stationed at military outposts in Baghdad. (This isn't unprecedented. In the Cubs' clubhouse at Wrigley is a photograph of a fortified bunker in Iraq. A Cubs flag flies over it.)

"The playoffs were unbelievable," he says. "There was a fever."

Everybody, including Shaevitz, ran a temperature. When the Cubs were a single victory away from reaching the 2003 World Series, Shaevitz contacted his local New Era baseball cap rep and ordered 12,000 Cubs hats with World Series logos. The New Era people nearly fainted.

"They got scared," says Shaevitz. "They were worried because I ordered more caps than the Cubs did. They're thinking, 'What if this guy doesn't pay us?'"

So Shaevitz sent a down payment of $100,000. The next day, the Cubs were eliminated from the playoffs. Shaevitz got his check back, but he has little doubt he would have sold every one of those caps.

Shaevitz has a list of old reliables in the store. The 1908 World Champion T-shirts have been big sellers for years. The same goes for the 1969 Cubs logo T-shirts. The 1914 road and home throwback caps do very well, as do the traditional Cubs blue caps. "And anything with Prior on it sells," he says. "[Kerry] Wood too. It's like bread and butter."

Sosa merchandises sells, "but Prior surpasses him, and Aramis Ramirez is going past him too," says Shaevitz. Ron Santo, Ryne Sandberg, and even Mark Grace authentic jerseys do brisk business, as do the newly delivered Garciaparra jerseys. Earlier in the week, Shaevitz was sweating out this whole Nomar jersey number situation. Would Michael Barrett give up his No. 5 for Nomar? Shaevitz needed to know, and fast, because he wanted to order Nomar T-shirts. Plus, he'd just had a handful of No. 5 Nomar authentic jerseys delivered by his seamstress (it took all night to do the stitching).

"But our biggest impulse-buy items are the baby outfits," says Shaevitz. "That's an automatic. People can't help themselves."

Shaevitz has his share of clunkers, but always figures out a way to move product. Maybe that's why he was on the phone recently giving advice to a good friend in Boston who was stuck with Nomar merchandise. His tip: Stick the stuff on a sales rack in the back of the store, price it to go, watch the bargain shoppers go nuts.

The law of averages and the perfect location have treated Shaevitz well. Shopping mall developers always talk about the need for an "anchor" store. Wrigley Field is Lakeview's anchor store. Nobody knows that better than Shaevitz, who says about 90 percent of business is generated because of the magnetism of the historic stadium.

And if Wrigley, his personal gravy train, crumbled to the ground one day?

"Retire," he says. "Why go on?"

GAME 109

Friday, August 6, 2004 . . . Giants 6, Cubs 2 . . . SBC Park . . . Stuff: Bartman impersonators in the crowd: eight. . . . The Cardinals, who already have the best offense in the NL, acquire Larry Walker from the Colorado Rockies. . . . Joe Borowski rejoins the Cubs. . . . Wild-card status: one game up.

Baseball America, sort of the Bible of seamheads, once wrote that Cubs special assistant Gary Hughes is one of the top 10 scouts of the twentieth century and one of the best player-development executives of the 1990s. If it were up to his boss Hendry, Hughes would already have a bronze bust in Cooperstown.

"If you gave him the choice of taking a couple days off or getting on a plane and watching the Lansing Lugnuts, he'd pick watching the Lugnuts," says Hendry.

Hughes started scouting for the San Francisco Giants in 1967, moved to the New York Yankees in 1978, oversaw the Montreal Expos' scouting system beginning in 1985, joined the Florida Marlins in the same capacity in 1992, had brief stays with the Colorado Rockies and Cincinnati Reds, then accepted Hendry's job offer in 2003.

Hughes discovered 146-game winner Bob Knepper in the wine country of northern California. He signed a college infielder with a decent arm—some kid named John Elway. More than 60 of the players his staff signed and developed played in the majors. And any thank-you notes for the Marlins' 1997 World Series championship should also be CC'd to Hughes.

Wearing one of his signature Tommy Bahama silk Hawaiian shirts (he has 40 in his wardrobe collection), Hughes, 62, waxes poetic about his 37-year career.

I played the game, though not very successfully, into college. If I was rating me: below-average running, slightly below-average arm, pretty good hitter but no power, adequate fielder, real good instincts. Your basic one-tool player.

Scouts in the Hall of Fame? Definitely. Me? No. That top-10 thing, that's very flattering, but without thinking I can probably come up with 25 others who are better.

I think the writers should be honored. I think the broadcasters should be honored. I think umpires are in it. The fact that scouts aren't in it is ridiculous.

My dad was a salesman. In business, nothing happens until somebody sells something. In this business, nothing happens until somebody discovers someone. We're like the salesmen of this business. After sales, it's development.

The scout whose name comes up most times is a guy named Howie Haak, who was with Pittsburgh for years. He's passed on now. He did a lot of work in Latin America. Was a character. A very hardworking guy. And had great judgment. [Haak discovered Roberto Clemente, Manny Sanguillen, and Tony Pena, among others.]

Here's what you do: Hire good people and let them do the job. It's so simple, yet how many businesses don't do that? They hire good people and try to put their thumb on them and say, "This is the way we're going to do this." Well, there's a lot of ways to do things. There's a lot of ways to scout. I always tell scouts, "Don't worry about what I'm doing. Let me figure out what you're doing. Let me know what you think a player is. Don't give me what you think I want, because it's probably going to be wrong."

The type of player that I like is an athlete. It goes back to high school. Jim Fregosi was a high school player of mine. He could do anything. He could run. He could throw. He could catch. He had power. Great fielder. He could really run. And he played every sport there was, including track. Once he stopped doing all those things and concentrated on baseball, he just took off. I always felt if you got a guy with great athletic ability and have him concentrate on one thing, i.e., baseball, you got a chance to get a special player. Not a good player, but a special player.

Best picks? Marquis Grissom in the third round was probably the best guy we took [in Montreal], as far as not a No. 1. Charles Johnson [drafted No. 28 overall and signed by the Marlins in 1992] was a three-time All-Star and three-, four-time Gold Glove winner. But getting Marquis Grissom in the third round and having him become the player he's become is really special.

I'll tell [any scouting director] to listen to your people and go with your gut. In the end, if you're going to be any good at it, you got to have a pretty good gut feel.

I got out of being the scouting director at the right time. It's a shame what's happened now. And I was partly responsible. I was giving out these ridiculous bonuses to unproven high school kids. And it hasn't stopped. The whole financial thing of the game has changed. It's a runaway train.

If you asked me if I could do one thing over, well, the biggest mistake I made was not signing Charles Johnson out of high school. [Johnson was the 10th overall pick in 1989.] It was a $25,000 difference and I went on principle. It was a deal where his agent, Scott Boras, was holding him out. Twenty-five thousand dollars apart now is nothing. And I refused to change, to go up on the offer, because it was a matter of principle. I thought I was doing it for the good of the game. It was stupid. I hurt the Montreal Expos. But we ended up getting him three years later [in Florida].

I did [the scouting director gig] 10 years—6 years with Montreal, 4 with Florida. That was enough. I wasn't worn out or anything. It was just time for somebody else to do it. Had I stayed a couple more years I probably would have burned out.

My job now: I'm responsible for the American League and National League West. I watch those teams and our minor league teams. I think that's the most valuable thing I do. The key to our business—and I got this quote 20 years ago—"is knowing what you have." I got the quote from Andy MacPhail. I read it somewhere and saved it.

Best team I've seen is Anaheim. I told these guys, "The guys you played [in mid-June] are the guys we're going to play in October."

Of course, I also liked Smarty Jones to win the Triple Crown.

GAME 110

Saturday, August 7, 2004 . . . Cubs 8, Giants 4 . . . SBC Park . . . Stat of the game: Greg Maddux wins career game No. 300. Does anything else matter? . . . Stuff: 15 of the 25 players on the Cubs roster, including five of the six relievers, contribute to Maddux's 300th. . . . Maddux is now 11-7 this season, 4-0 since the All-Star break, and leads the Cubs in victories. Hard to believe he only had two wins on May 13. . . . Memo to Sammy Sosa: According to St. Louis Post-Dispatch's Bernie Miklasz, NL MVP favorite Scott Rolen stopped by manager Tony LaRussa's office after the Larry Walker trade and offered to move down from fourth to fifth in the batting order.

Excerpts from accounts of Maddux's big day, all suitable for pasting in the family scrapbook:

With Saturday's 8-4 decision over the San Francisco Giants, Maddux becomes the 22nd pitcher in baseball history to attain the 300-win milestone. Fourteen of the other 21 are dead, and yet it's a safe bet they had a more animated reaction to the 38-year-old Cubs right-hander joining their club than he did.

—Dan McGrath, *Chicago Tribune*

Asked how he'd celebrate, Maddux said: "I don't know. I'll do something."

He was relieved, more than anything, to get the big number out of the way. He just wanted to move on.

Back in the visitors' clubhouse, where his teammates waited, two message boards saluted Maddux's milestone and captured his sentiment:

300!

First bus 4:55.

—Gwen Knapp, *San Francisco Chronicle*

The Braves were playing in Arizona on Saturday while Greg Maddux was pitching in San Francisco, but they kept close tabs on his pursuit of his 300th victory.

When Maddux got it, they reacted as if he were still a Brave and not a Chicago Cub.

"He was as much a part of our success when he was here as anybody," said third baseman Chipper Jones, who reached the Major Leagues with Atlanta in September 1993, the first of Maddux's 11 seasons with the Braves.

"We all feel like we had a little part in [his success], but I don't think there's any doubt who the main contributor was. It's him," Jones said. "He's the best pitcher I ever played behind."

—David O'Brien, *Atlanta Journal-Constitution*

There's a reason he's the best control pitcher we'll ever see. Even on the day when his place among baseball's pitching giants was validated, he had to follow a personal protocol, the hard and true ground rules of the professional's professional. What was the advice handed down years ago by Ralph Medar, the former scout who taught him the intricacies of pitching? "Movement is more important than velocity," he told a short, skinny, Las Vegas teenager. Well, that applies to celebrations, too.

—Jay Mariotti, *Chicago Sun-Times*

Maddux began the bottom of the sixth by giving up singles to Alfonzo and Pierzynski. Pitching coach Larry Rothschild went to the mound and removed Maddux in favor of Jon Leicester.

"He said, 'You better watch me,'" Baker said. "I sent Larry out. Larry said, 'You might have to take him out.' I said, 'Hey, man, if you have to take him out, you do it.'"

—Bruce Miles, *Daily Herald*

Greg Maddux received a champagne and beer shower in the visiting clubhouse at SBC Park after winning his 300th career game Saturday.

The beer—six cans' worth—came courtesy of the Cubs' bullpen.

"We have a low-paid bullpen, so we couldn't splurge," reliever Kent Mercker joked.

—Jeff Vorva, *Daily Southtown*

If he's the last to win 300 games, Maddux did so efficiently and intelligently and primarily with ground-ball outs, not with 98-mph fastballs. The milestone win took 594 starts and 4,115⅓ innings to achieve, beginning with his first Major League start and win on Sept. 7, 1986. He was wearing a Cubs uniform then, too.

—Carrie Muskat, *MLB.com*

GAME 111

Sunday, August 8, 2004 . . . Giants 6, Cubs 3 . . . SBC Park . . . Stat of the game: The Gladiator goes 0-for-Bay Area. He's hitless in his last 17 at-bats. . . . Stuff: Even ESPN's Joe Morgan, a longtime Sosa honk, mentions during the broadcast that Sammy needs to move closer to the plate. . . . Greg Maddux will donate his shoes and cap from win No. 300 to the Hall of Fame. The HOF will get his glove at season's end.

The last time I had spoken to Andy Pafko was at the Cubs Convention in January. His smile was warm and gentle, but his handshake could have cracked a walnut. He was 82 and still leaving bruise marks.

I noticed the small but distinctive ring on his left hand.

"This?" he said. "This is my '45 World Series ring. Every time I see Ernie [Banks], I say, 'Hey, Ernie, how many of these do you have?'"

Pafko played center field on the last Cubs World Series team, so he's earned the right to woof a bit. Those 1945 Cubs were beaten in seven games by the Detroit Tigers, the same franchise against which the Cubs recorded their first (1907) and last (1908) World Series championships.

Sixty-eight Cubs, past and present, attended the Convention that day. I don't know how many fans were crammed into the hotel ballroom for the player introductions, but I do know the fire marshal must have taken the day off. Wayne Messmer sang "The Star-Spangled Banner." "If you're interested in joining in," he said, "we're singing it in the key of B-flat—just like it will sound like in October." New Cub and former Florida Marlin Derrek Lee got booed. Mark Prior, Jody Davis, Dusty Baker, and Ron Santo received thunderous ovations, though nobody got more applause than Ryne Sandberg.

But here's what stuck with me: All these Cubs legends, but the only one with a Cubs World Series ring was Pafko, who played from 1943 to 1951 in Chicago, and later returned to the Series with the 1952 Brooklyn Dodgers and won one with the 1957 Milwaukee Braves.

I give Pafko a call today. He still lives in Mt. Prospect. He still watches the hometown team. And he still hopes he's not the last Cub to wear World Series jewelry on his finger.

Of all the players, a great player like Ernie Banks never got a shot at a World Series. All those great players—Randy Hundley, Billy Williams, Ernie, Ron Santo—never got their shot. I feel sorry for those guys.

Ron is such a die-hard Cub fan. I feel sorry for that poor guy up in the booth. He gets so involved, you'd think he was playing. What a thrill it would be for him if they made it. After all he's been through physically. That would be a great tonic for Ron.

How lucky can a guy get? All the clubs I played on went to the World Series. Three of them. I got three rings, but I cherish that Cub one. That's my favorite.

I joined the club at the end of the season in '43. I had played in the Coast League. I was batting champion. Then I played 13 games for the Cubs. My first game, I got two hits, drove in four runs. I thought, "Oh, my God, this is a piece of cake."

I was wrong about that.

The first time I saw Wrigley Field, I thought I died and went to heaven. There were four of us who came to Wrigley Field. We took the train for three days. The first guy I ran into was [Cubs third baseman] Stan Hack. He says, "Welcome to Chicago. Welcome to the big leagues, Andy." He made me feel at home.

Playing in a World Series . . . you can't describe it, honestly. I'll never forget that first game in Detroit. They play the National Anthem, and there you are. That's the biggest thrill a ballplayer can have. I get goose bumps just talking about it right now.

We faced Hal Newhouser in that first game. I think he won about 28 ballgames that year, was the MVP. But I had three hits in my first World Series game, and I also threw out a runner at third. I often think about that World Series. The older you get, the more you think about it.

I'll never forget that seventh game. We played in Chicago. Us against the Detroit Tigers. They got five runs in the first inning. We lost that seventh. [Long pause.] That was a heartbreaker.

My last year as a player was 1959, with the Braves in Milwaukee. I stayed on as a coach with the Braves. Then I scouted for a couple of years. Then I managed for a couple years in the minors. And you know who played for me in West Palm? None other than Dusty Baker.

I'm 83. I was born in 1921, in a little town outside Eau Claire, Wisconsin, called Boyceville. They had an Andy Pafko Day, and on the plaque it says, "Andy Pafko loved the game. He would have played the game for free."

My late wife saw it and said to me, "You did, honey, you did."

With the Cubs, I think I made $500 a month. My World Series share with the Braves was about $9,000. What are the winners' shares now? About $250,000?

I don't begrudge the ballplayers of today. But I think we had more fun. It's not a game anymore. It's money. Money talks.

They're having Andy Pafko Day at Wrigley Field August 25. I'm so thrilled about that. I get to sing at the Seventh-Inning Stretch and throw out the first pitch. No curves. I'll be lucky if I can reach home plate. Maybe I'll cheat up on the grass.

On occasion, I watch them when the opportunity is there. Looks like they got a pretty good ballclub. But it's one thing to pick them in a magazine to get to the World Series. You got to do it on the field. Hopefully, this is the year. At least, I think so. If anybody deserves it, it's these Chicago fans. They're so loyal, so faithful.

I'd like to see a World Series in Chicago. I'm not getting any younger. I'd like to see one before I leave this earth.

GAME 112

Tuesday, August 10, 2004 . . . Padres 8, Cubs 6 . . . Wrigley Field . . . Cubs NL Central pennant flies: Second (61-51) . . . Stuff: Nomar Garciaparra, who has hit second in the lineup since coming from the Red Sox, is moved to his more familiar No. 3 spot. For 60 games this season (and in seasons past), the spot belonged to Sammy Sosa. But the self-proclaimed "gladiator" enters the game hitting only .238 since returning from the DL and is mired in a 2-for-24 slump. So what does he do? Goes yard in his first at-bat for career No. 564 and passes Reggie Jackson on the all-time dinger list. . . . Baker on why he doesn't drop Sosa lower in the order: "I considered that. We just can't lose him psychologically and spiritually." . . . It's '70s Night, which means lava lamps in the TV-radio booths, disco music by Gary Pressy, and guest conductor Erik Estrada singing "Take Me Out to the Ballgame." Estrada is so off-key that structural engineers worry about more concrete cracks at Wrigley. . . . Wild-card status: one game up.

Sure, the Seventh-Inning Guest Conductor series has had its comb-over moments over the years. Ty Somebody of a home-improvement show?

Another high school state champion? Gary Sandy? Nothing personal, but those are seventh-inning bald spots.

Still, the conductor schtick gets my endorsement because it means well. And where else can you get Ozzy Osbourne mumbling and slurring his way through Albert Von Tilzer's classic?

I have a wish list of guest conductors: a duet by Ozzy and Mike Ditka . . . the two remaining Beatles . . . Barbra Streisand and William Hung . . . a once-a-season recording of Harry Caray doing the song.

The Cubs have a slightly less ambitious list. According to Joe Rios, manager of Special Events, Player Relations and Entertainment, the Cubs would love to hand a microphone to . . . White Sox honk and Chicago mayor Richard M. Daley, Michael Jordan, Elton John, Bruce Springsteen, John Mellencamp, Dan Aykroyd, Kevin Garnett, Billy Crystal, Tom Hanks, Billy Bob Thornton, Phil Cavarretta, Hank Aaron, Willie McCovey, Willie Mays, Pete Rose (if he's ever reinstated by Major League Baseball), Matt Damon, and the crown jewel of Chicago crooners, Oprah.

Daley—and you have to respect this about the man—has a jones against the Cubs, as well as a loyalty to the Sox. He didn't even make a booth appearance during the 2003 NLCS. The rest of Rios's A-list has been done in by schedules or lack of interest.

In the meantime, we get our share of conductor memories. Pressy, who provides the musical accompaniment on that Lowry, provides the highlights.

On Harry: "With Harry, it better be done right. We had a glitch with the sound system one day and he could not hear the organ. So it didn't go great. He comes shuffling down the hall after the game and yells, 'Gary!'

"So I tell him, 'I guess we had a little problem with the sound system.'

"He says, 'Fix it, dammit!'"

On the Big Moment: "About 95 percent of the time, they'll come up and rehearse. If it's a professional singer, I'll ask what key they want it in. If it's not a professional singer, I'll say, 'Here's what we do: You'll make a little intro and then I'll [he hits the C note] . . . and you'll start singing.'"

On the post-Harry era: "Dutchie [Caray] was the first to sing. She was nervous. But there wasn't a dry eye in the house."

On Ditka's 4.2-second rendition: "Ditka, he was golfing, and I guess he was a little late. It was the top of the seventh, there was a double play, and, bang-bang, the inning's almost over. And here comes Ditka running up—and you know how many steps there are coming up here—and he has the artificial hip, and, well, it was crazy.

"He comes dashing in the 'GN booth and Steve Stone says, 'Here comes Mike Ditka.' Ditka just goes into it. I'm hanging on the C, but he just starts with 'Aoneatwoathree,' and off we go. He was singing in a polka tempo as opposed to a waltz.

"The thing is, we scored seven runs in the bottom of the seventh. We ended up winning the game. So I call that the Knute Rockne of 'Take Me Out to the Ballgame.'

"And I'll tell you what, Mike Ditka put that sucker on the map."

On legendary Los Angeles Dodgers broadcaster Vin Scully: "He's been the best nonprofessional singer. He's like an Irish tenor. He sang it, and I was like, 'Oh, my.' "

On ESPN's Dick Vitale: "You could hear him on Lake Shore Drive."

On ice skater Nancy Kerrigan: "She was, uh, a little off. Yeah, a little off. She was—just put it that way."

On comedian Jackie Mason: "I have no idea what he was singing. And neither does he."

On Cuba Gooding Jr.: "He sat out on the ledge."

On Shania Twain: (Pressy almost begins to hyperventilate.) "Whooo. Shania Twain."

On keys: "Kenny Rogers sang it in C. Harry sang it in D. Ozzy . . . it didn't matter."

On Ozzy: "You know when clouds are gathering and there could be a storm? That was Ozzy. His wife kind of guided him along. They came in and I explained everything to them. He tried it—but I think he was singing it backwards. But his wife was so nice.

"Then it was time for the real thing. He walked down the hall, grabbed the mic, and basically hummed it. But he did say, 'Let's get some runs.' He did all right."

On his personal wish list: "As far as singers, I'd love to get Barry Manilow, Billy Joel, and Elton John. Nonsingers: John Havlicek and Bobby Orr."

GAME 113

Wednesday, August 11, 2004 . . . Cubs 5, Padres 1 . . . Wrigley Field . . . Stuff: Game-time temperature: 59 frickin' degrees . . . A TV guy approaches Joe Borowski for an interview. "Ryan?" says the TV guy, who thinks Borowski is Ryan Dempster. . . . Dusty Baker and Sammy Sosa have a private meeting about Baker's recent comments concerning The Gladiator's fragile ego. "Everything's cool," Baker says. Sosa, standing much closer to the plate these days, doubles and later scores on a sac fly.

My rental apartment is five blocks straight down Waveland to Wrigley. Every day I walk past the Bleacher Bums lined up against the outer walls, sometimes as early as five hours before the first pitch (the gates open two hours before game time). I stop and introduce myself to Gary Stromquist and his buddy Dave Rossi—Nos. 1 and 2 in line.

Stromquist, 46, drives a forklift for a local manufacturing company. He wears a Cubs cap, Cubs shirt, Cubs warm-up jacket, a pair of batting gloves, and a Louisville Slugger outfielder's glove.

Stromquist: "I've been coming out here since I was a kid, with four years interrupted by the Navy. I always sit in left field. Even if I get here late, I always try to find a seat there.

"I wouldn't trade a bleacher seat for a box seat. I wouldn't trade it for a skybox. And I'd have to think before I said no to trading it for a seat in the dugout."

Rossi: "No to the dugout?"

Stromquist: "Look, the bleachers, they're a rip-off, man. They went to a premier-tiered pricing system in 2003 and they're doing it again this year. It used to cost $2 a game in the '80s. Now they let the season-ticket holders in first, then us. It's every man for himself. But I love it in those seats. You're out in the sun. And I've known these people for, like, 25 years. They're like family. We've been through weddings, divorces, their kids getting married. There's no other park where you know people like that. Maybe Fenway, but not Comiskey. It's not like that minor league team on the South Side.

"In fact, I remember I came here the first time when I was eight or nine with my dad. The thing I remember most is that he only had two beers that game.

"But I tell people, especially if it's a cold day, that the bleachers are going to be in the sunshine. If you sit far enough down in the bleachers, then it's going to block the wind. It might be 45 degrees, but in the bleachers it will feel like it's 50 or 60. No wind."

Rossi: "I live in St. Louis."

Stromquist: "Yeah, but don't hold that against him."

Rossi: "I've got a Cubs tattoo on my left arm. It's the Cubs symbol—the old frowning Cub bear. And there's one coming on the right arm later this summer. I've got to even it out. That tattoo, that's the best thing my ex-girlfriend ever got me."

Stromquist: "Except for your freedom, right?"

Rossi: "Yeah, she was good for one thing."

GAME 114

Thursday, August 12, 2004 . . . Padres 5, Cubs 4 . . . Wrigley Field . . . Stuff: Bruce Froemming, and the umpiring crew that cornea transplants forgot, botches yet another call in this series. Froemming somehow doesn't see Nomar Garciaparra tag the bag on a force-out at second in the sixth inning. The Padres score two runs. Later, during a rain delay interview on WGN-TV, the Tribune's Paul Sullivan says, "And before I go, I want to thank Bruce Froemming for 30 years of screwing the Cubs." Sullivan is referring to Froemming's ball-four call in the ninth to ruin Milt Pappas's perfect game in 1972. (After this game, Froemming says he blew the Nomar call.) . . . The Cubs Internet chat rooms are buzzing after Sammy Sosa's strikeout in the sixth inning. Viewers of the game say they swear they saw Sosa drop an F-bomb on the crowd as he returned to the dugout. Sosa finishes 0-for-5 with four strikeouts and is now 4-for-36 during the last nine games. He waves away reporters after the game.

A sampling of the faxes received by Ron Santo and Pat Hughes in the 'GN booth during today's broadcast (some didn't quite make it on the air):

From Heather and Todd Faga, Washington, Illinois

Dear Pat and Ron,

My husband and I would like to someday save a puppy from a shelter. We would like to name it Santo. If you could be any dog, what would you be? I was thinking a big, beautiful white Labrador. What do you think?

From Barbie DDDDDoll, Rolling Melons

Dear Mr. Santo!

I'd like to get you REAL, REAL warm like HOT HOT HOT!!! HOW-EVER YOU LIKE IT!!!!!!! I accommodate ALL requests (as long as it's cash up front)!!! But I'd give you a BIG BIG BIG BIG BIG DDDDDiscount!

I LOVE YOU!!!!!!

From Ethel Huberty, McHenry

Dear Ron & Pat—

Do you think this weather is God's way of telling the Cubs to get ready for October? I can find no other explanation for fall weather in the middle of August . . .

From Matthew, Des Moines, Iowa

Dear Ron + Pat,

I love listening to you both. You make work fly by. Ron, hope to see that old No. 10 Cubs jersey in Cooperstown someday.

I have been a Cubs fans for my whole life and a Sosa fan since he came over from the Sox. But don't you think it is time for him to move down in the order to give Ramirez and Lee a chance to deliver?

Thanks for the entertainment.

From Ed Blazina, Ottumwa, Iowa

Ron + Pat:

I listen to you every day with the sound off on the TV. You are the best. I am a die-hard Cub fan who, as a 12-year-old, attended the '45 World Series. I still have a scrapbook full from the Herald-American. *My question—I assume when a player is called up from AAA, he receives minimum Major League salary. If he is sent back down, does he get cut back to AAA salary?*

P.S.—Loved your comment last night about your hairpiece not being a "rug."

From Randy H., Glencoe, Illinois

Hi Pat & Ron!

I'm a catcher too. I'm wondering why Barrett doesn't try to catch every ball pitched at him. He seems to let them go when no one's on base. I'm thinking if he tried to catch them all, he would have less get past him. At least, that's what my Coach (my dad) says I should do. So I thought I'd ask an EXPERT such as yourself!

Thanks a lot.

From Bob Pap, Greektown

Hey Nor & Tap,

Did you guys know that your names are not palindromic, but form words backwards and forwards?

From EP Fanatics

Good day Mr. Ron Santo and Mr. Pat Hughes:

So, can you be honest with us and admit that Prior DID NOT have an "Achilles" problem that caused him to miss spring training. But he did/does have a psychological problem with his MIND and pitching?

From Robin W, Oak Park

Hello Mr. Ron Santo

I noticed that Nomar has some mannerisms similar to my little brother's. He's 8. He has Tourette's Syndrome, but he doesn't swear like the other kids. Do you know anything about this? Robbie is interested.

Thank you, great allstar.

From Jimmy Kaddafer (10), Barrington

Hi Mr. Santo & Mr. Hues

Are you staying warm? Which ballpark (excluding Wrigley) is most visually appealing? Which feeds you the best?

From Jeremy Bos, Iowa City, Iowa

Ronnie and Pat,

I love the Cubs and love listening to you guys at work and at home. In reference to last night's discussion as to what a Padre is, who cares? Leave the piece on Ronnie, and stay a Cubbie.

From Tom McLaughlin

Ron,

I've been involved in religious education in the Archdiocese of Chicago and even was a monk for a while. So let me fill you in on Friars.

Friar is what men in the Franciscan order are called. . . . They are pictured with that bald spot because they all were tonsured. They had their hair cut in that special way to show they were members of the clergy. But back then being a member of the clergy meant not being a lay person. It didn't mean you were an ordained priest as it does today. . . . Most were priests. The priests were called "Padre."

From Tim Eisenhut

Why do the Cubs have their home dugout on the 3rd base line? Most teams have their dugout on the 1st base line.

To: Ron Santo & Pat Hughes

Please wish my daughter, Katie Cavarretta, a Happy 25th today. She's sitting in the upper deck, enjoying the game (rain delay). This is the one place that she wanted to be on her birthday. Also, please say a big hello to Katie's Great Uncle, Phil Cavarretta.

Thanks,

Mick Cavarretta (Phil's nephew)

GAME 115

Friday, August 13, 2004 . . . Dodgers 8, Cubs 1 . . . Wrigley Field . . . Stat of the game: Three Cubs relievers (Glendon Rusch, Kyle Farnsworth, and Jon Leiceister) pitch a combined one inning (the ninth) and give up six runs. In Farnsworth's last three outings (a combined one inning), he's given up six hits and six runs. . . . Stuff: Grant Johnson, the Cubs' first pick in the June draft, agrees to a deal. . . . Geez, what a surprise: St. Louis wins again. . . . Wild-card status: tied for first.

I sit in the stands for this one. First-base side. Section 224, Row 8, Seat 7. I want to see what my Cubs peeps think about this team. After watching them watch these guys waste a wonderful 6⅓-inning effort by Greg Maddux, I can now report exactly what they think of their beloved Cubbies: not much.

It isn't the losing so much, but the *way* the Cubs lose. Check that—it *is* the losing, *and* the mind-numbing, sometimes unfathomable ways they lose. Plus, a lot of these people seem to be very close friends with the Bud and Old Style vendors.

Most of their frustration and anger is directed at The Gladiator, Sammy Sosa. Sosa is still greeted warmly by the Bums during his customary sprint to right field at the beginning of the game, but the reception is decidedly more mixed when Sosa steps to the plate for his first at-bat. I'm guessing two-thirds of the crowd cheer, the rest boo. Sosa's skin is as thin as papiermâché, so I'm also guessing The Gladiator is seething as he reaches the box.

Sosa singles. The 60-something-year-old lady sitting next to me records the hit on her scorecard. "About time," she says.

This is the general mood among the paying spectators. They've just about had it with being understanding. They're restless, nervous, cranky. The season is 114 games old and they want to see something—anything— good happen. Gary Pressy playing "Won't You Come Home Bill Bailey," on the ol' Lowry organ between innings isn't enough anymore. This is what happens when you've got a team built for late October that's playing like a team built for October 3, the final day of the regular season.

The Dodgers score a run in the first, matched by a Cubs run in the bottom of the inning. It stays that way until the sixth, when the Dodgers move ahead, 2-1. In between, Sosa ends the third inning with a man on second, and ends the fifth inning with men on first and third. The fly-out in the fifth is the one that turns the crowd of 39,105 against him.

Someone in Section 222 stands and holds up a sign.

Red Line—$3.50
Cubs Tickets—$36
Hard Hat for Concrete—$50
Sosa At-bats—Useless

Sosa isn't the reason they lose this game, but he helps. Moises Alou goes 2-for-4 with an RBI, but he also grounds into a double play in the eighth when Dodgers reliever Darren Dreifort can't find the plate with a pack of hound dogs. And unless you're a sadist, there's no real reason to review the ninth-inning exploits of Farnsworth & Associates. They stunk. Why say more and scare the kids?

It would be nice to report that the crowd stayed until the end. And they did stay—until Farnsworth was replaced by Leicester. Then they dowsed Farnsy with enough boos to make Sosa feel good about himself. That done, most of the audience bolted for the exits like a herd of stampeding bison.

The afternoon wasn't a complete washout. There was a touching moment in the bottom of the second when Maddux stepped to the plate and received a well-deserved standing O. Maddux acknowledged the fans with a quick wave of the hand, which in Maddux's Old School world is about as good as it gets for public displays of emotion.

And Patterson, who endured the wrath of Wrigley earlier in the season, continued to earn admirers. Sosa ought to learn from the 25-year-old Patterson (it's his birthday today). Patterson has hit in seven different lineup spots, has incorporated the bunt into his game, and has never said a peep when benched on occasion. In other words, he's adapted.

Sammy? Not so much.

Mia Francesca restaurant on Clark calls my name at game's end. Outside the stadium, I see a shapely woman wearing a red halter top with iron-on lettering. I stare at her chest, which doesn't go over real well with the ball-and-chain wife.

"Gonzo's Gone . . . I'm 30 . . . What Now."

What now? Well, I'm going to order the roasted chicken, but that's probably not what the woman wants to know. The Cubs are 6-5 in the post-Alex Gonzalez Era and now tied with the Padres for the wild-card spot. And the Cardinals are so far ahead (13½ games) in the NL Central that you need Mapquest to find them. This is why the unrest is Guinness thick.

I'm going to take the Maddux approach, which is to shrug it off. There's still 47 games left, so there's time. But I've got to tell you something.

I'm in the minority.

GAME 116

Saturday, August 14, 2004 . . . Cubs 2, Dodgers 0 . . . Wrigley Field . . . Cubs NL Central pennant flies: Second (63-53) . . . Stuff: Go figure this team. On Fri-

day, the Cubs play like they couldn't make it to Williamsport. Today, they're flashing leather and holding a lead. . . . Ron Santo broadcast moments of note: In the last week or so, Santo has discussed the environmental threat of global warming, and has accidentally called Garciaparra Omar, Mark Prior McGwire, and Mark Grudzielanek Grunzielanek. Strangely enough, we know exactly what and who he means. Also, if Santo can't remember your name, he calls you "Big Boy." And finally, this story courtesy of WGN Radio's Andy Masur: Santo once asked Masur to help him find his lost hairpiece. Masur returned to Santo's hotel room and eventually found the clump of hair stuck to the adhesive end of a FedEx box. Rather than tear the hairpiece from the tape, Masur delivered the entire box to Santo. . . . Wild-card status: one game up.

Joe Borowski, soaked in sweat, sits in the near-deserted Cubs' clubhouse. He's 10 minutes removed from his second simulated-game throwing session. This one lasted 35 wonderful, pain-free pitches.

Borowski has been on the DL since June 5 with a strained right shoulder. Sure, it's strained; there's a torn supraspinatus muscle in his throwing shoulder. The supraspinatus, according to medical opinion, is the muscle in the rotator cuff most likely to take it in the shorts. It wasn't designed to throw a baseball.

Then again, Borowski isn't exactly the prototype for a closer. As recently as the 2000 season, he was playing for an independent minor league team in Newark, and later for a Mexican League team in Monterrey. He was drafted in the 32nd round by the White Sox in 1989, traded to the Baltimore Orioles for Pete Rose Jr. in 1991, and traded to the Atlanta Braves with another pitcher for Kent Mercker. He later had a few sips of coffee with the New York Yankees in 1997 and 1998, and banged around the minors until 2002, when the Cubs brought him up for good. In 2003, he converted 33 of 37 save chances.

Not bad for a guy who used to make ends meet by working in a Maidenform bra factory in New Jersey. His grandmother helped him get the job.

"It was all right," he says. "I used to load up the carts with the raw fabric, put it on the ladies' tables, and they'd go to work. Shoot, I made better money doing that than I was making during the baseball season. But more than anything, I loved playing baseball. That's why I didn't think of anything else but playing baseball."

So Single-A meant something a little different to Borowski than the rest of us.

Borowski is a meaty 6-2, 225 pounds. He has that *Goodfellas* "dis" and "duh" and "ain't" Jersey accent. He came up the hard way, which is why he savors every minute in the bigs and takes nothing for granted.

"Shoot, I was making $1,000 a month up until I finally made the big leagues in '95 with the Orioles," says Borowski, 33. "My first year was, like, $850 in rookie ball and $1,000 a month the next couple of years. I lived at home in the off-season, and I pretty much lived check to check."

Borowski made $410,000 in 2003, then signed a two-year deal that pays him $2 million this season and $2.3 million in 2005. Now he'd like to earn it.

His last appearance was a June 4 blown save and subsequent loss against the Pittsburgh Pirates at Wrigley. His ERA was 8.02, opponents were hitting .303 against him, he had 17 strikeouts and 15 walks. Something was terribly wrong.

"Coming into spring training, I felt fine," he says. "It just seemed like as spring went along my arm started getting tired instead of getting stronger and stronger, you know? It was never sharp pain. There was never a day where I couldn't lift my arm or anything. It was just a feeling that you were carrying around a five-pound weight in your arm. Halfway through spring that's how it felt, but then it'd feel better and I'm thinking, 'OK, now we're going to bounce back. I'm over the dead-arm period.'"

Borowski's arm would feel better, but the radar gun still fell asleep when he threw. His velocity was down, his anxiety up.

"There were some mind games being played," he says.

His right biceps hurt, so Borowski figured he had tendinitis. But this tendinitis didn't go away. Neither did the hitters. When he gave up two hits and two runs in the loss to the Pirates, that was it. Borowski underwent a series of tests that revealed the muscle tear in his shoulder. The biceps pain was the result of what doctors call "referred" pain.

"The last thing on my mind is that I'm going to have something wrong with my shoulder," Borowski says. "I never ever felt anything there. But when they get done testing and they say, 'shoulder,' it's like getting hit by a truck."

Borowski has had his share of hit-and-runs. Try keeping the faith when you've got a 5.50 ERA for Newark, or you give up six earned runs in 1⅓ innings for the Cubs in your first-ever big league start.

So Borowski went on the DL and did what he does best. He grinded. He rented an apartment in the Phoenix area, brought his family there, and spent five hours a day at a physical rehab clinic. "If I was down there by myself, I would have definitely went nuts," he says.

Equally worse was that Borowski was disconnected from the Cubs. He still talked to coaches and trainers on the phone, but watching the games on TV was agony.

"That was the worst part," he says. "At least if you're [at Wrigley] doing rehab, you can feel you're part of it. But when you're that far away you just feel helpless, like you can't do anything. But I had to do it. I needed five hours a day, and there's no way I'd get that done here. Everybody else is trying to get ready for a game, and I needed personal attention."

When he first started the rehab, Borowski couldn't lift a five-pound weight above his head without wincing. "Now I do 50 pounds without a second thought," he says.

Everything is about strengthening the muscles around the supraspinatus, but also about reacquainting your mind to the game. Borowski didn't start playing catch until the middle of July. His shoulder muscles are pumped, but his arm still is learning what to do again. He threw a mini simulated game a few days ago and basically had to introduce himself to the mound again.

"But the difference between that day and today is huge," Borowski says, all but beaming.

A minor league rehab stint is a given. After that, who knows?

"I've tried to look at my career from the perspective of, I've been through so much already, this is just another thing thrown into the mix," he says, wiping the beads of sweat from his forehead. "I didn't get down on myself. I didn't say, 'Why me?' I just went and said, 'I'm going to prove, mostly to myself, that I can come back from this and pitch effectively in the big leagues again.'"

The comeback countdown continues.

GAME 117

Sunday, August 15, 2004 . . . Dodgers 8, Cubs 5 . . . Wrigley Field . . . Stat of the game: The Cubs' bullpen takes it in the shorts again. Mark Prior leaves in the seventh with a 5-2 lead, but then Kent Mercker, Kyle Farnsworth, Jon Leicester, and Glendon Rusch go to work. Farnsworth is beyond brutal. . . . Stuff: In a pregame ceremony, Maddux is summoned to the field by a brass quartet and then presented with a framed photograph from his 300th victory, a plaque, and a framed "3-0-0" using placards from the Wrigley scoreboard. A blue flag bearing his name now flies atop the stadium roof. Maddux's "speech" lasted less than a minute. . . . Wild-card status: a three-way tie with San Diego and San Francisco.

Jim Riggleman spent five seasons as manager of the Cubs. His .472 winning percentage (374-419) is better than that of 28 other former Cubs managers, which is all you need to know about the franchise's history of success.

Riggleman is now the bench coach of the NL West-leading Los Angeles Dodgers. At some point, someone is going to give him another chance, right?

Q: *Do you realize that no manager since Leo Durocher (1966-1972) has managed more Cubs games than you?*
Riggleman: Actually, I did know that. That happened when I passed Don Zimmer in length of service. But the Cubs have changed managers so many times. There's been three since me. But it looks like they're stable now.

Q: *Your first season was 1995. What was the state of the organization when you arrived?*
Riggleman: To be honest with you, I thought there were a lot of great possibilities. It was a major market. There was some talent there with [Mark] Grace and [Shawon] Dunston. I knew that the farm system was not strong. The reason I knew that was because when I was with the Padres and we were having the fire sale, I remember [Padres general manager] Randy Smith—he was mandating the fire sale—deciding who we were going to get for trading [Fred] McGriff, [Gary] Sheffield . . . what prospects we could get. I remember him getting to the Cubs [and their list of prospects] and him saying, "They don't have anybody, flip to the next team."

I knew we probably would go through the free-agent market rather than developing young players to help us immediately at the big league level. And we immediately made trades. We got [Jamie] Navarro and [Brian] McRae. They did a good job for us. But we really didn't have many players come through the system and help us. You've got to have prospects down there for two reasons: to come up and help you, or to have them to acquire other players. That's the way the Yankees have done it, how Boston has done it.

Q: *How exactly did you get the job?*

Riggleman: I'm going to be perfectly honest with you. Here's the way it happened: When I was the manager of the Padres, Joe McIlvane was the GM. Ownership told him, "You've got to get rid of all these players." Joe resigns. He says the heck with that. Randy takes over. Joe was my security blanket. So in a perfect world, Randy would want Bruce Bochy as his manager.

We had the fire sale, we're losing ballgames [47-70 in 1994]. I didn't hear from anybody [in management] from August to October. Randy and I talk. He says, "The new owners have given me permission to offer you a one-year contract, but the Cubs have called and they want to talk to you." He intimated that I really should talk to the Cubs.

But I did not want to leave the Padres. I felt like I was building something there. But it turned out to be a smooth transition. Randy gets his guy. I get two years instead of one year. And I get to go to Chicago and manage. But I would have preferred to stay in San Diego. On a one-year contract with new owners coming in, I thought if we lost a few ballgames they'd get rid of me. If I'd been offered a two-year contract, I would have stayed.

Q: *You finish 73-71 in 1995, 76-86 in 1996, and then along comes an 0-14 start to the 1997 season. That had to be a living, breathing nightmare.*

Riggleman: In the off-season I saw the schedule, and I'm saying to myself, "Geezus, we're opening up with Florida, Atlanta, Florida again, then Atlanta again. That year Florida had gotten [Kevin] Brown and they had [Al] Leiter and [Alex] Fernandez. Then it was [Greg] Maddux, [John] Smoltz, and [Tom] Glavine in Atlanta. Our first 10 games that's who we played. So there was a chance it was going to be very tough to win ballgames with who we were playing.

My concerns came to fruition. The season opens up and Sammy [Sosa] is struggling. Everybody was struggling to hit. Grace was the only guy swinging the bat well. Then he pulled a hamstring and had to go on the disabled list. It just accumulated.

At one point, after 10 games [and losses], [GM] Ed [Lynch] says to me, "Jimmy, we got to win a ballgame. What are we doing?"

I said, "Ed, it's as simple as this: They can hit our pitching, we can't hit theirs."

We just couldn't compete with those better teams. Those teams played in the division championship. Atlanta ended up playing Florida.

Q: *Is it possible to have a low point during a 14-game losing streak?*
Riggleman: In the 12th loss—we played just an absolutely horrible game against the Rockies [a five-hit shutout with three errors]—there were some amateurish mistakes. So after that game, I said to the players, "You'll be glad to know you can tell your grandchildren that you participated in the ugliest game played in Major League history today."

Q: *In 1998, two wonderful things take place: Kerry Wood arrives, and the Cubs reach the playoffs for the first time since 1989. What are your memories of that season?*
Riggleman: I felt like going into 1998 we were putting our best ballclub out there since I'd been associated with the Cubs. I felt good about [Kevin] Tapani, [Mark] Clark, and [Steve] Trachsel. They weren't classic No. 1s, but more like No. 3s. The other thing is we went out and acquired Rod Beck. We really put together a team. It was a little bit like the Cubs have now. It was built around power and good starting pitching and a good ninth-inning guy. We didn't steal bases and we weren't a great team at sustaining a rally.

But I don't feel like anybody could have won any more games with that club than we did.

Q: *And you were there May 6, when Wood struck out 20 against the Houston Astros, and eventually became the first Cubs pitcher to win Rookie of the Year.*
Riggleman: We were hearing about this kid Kerry Wood in the minor leagues who might not be too far away. But the reason he came up was Bob Patterson twisted an ankle. I needed a left-handed reliever in the bullpen, so I put [Terry] Mulholland there and he was madder than hell. Then we brought Kerry up. But it wasn't like I was saying we *had* to have Kerry Wood up here. Circumstances brought him up there.

I remember the first time he came on the field. He had this [protective] sleeve on his elbow, and I'm thinking, "Oh, my God, here's this great young pitcher and he comes here with *that* on." We had heard stories that he had a thin ligament in his elbow and that it might be a problem.

But on [May 6], oh, my God, it was just unbelievable. It was not a great day to pitch. It was a sloppy, miserable day. But on that day he just completely overmatched them. You could argue he pitched probably the greatest game in the history of Wrigley Field. Billy Williams and Ron Santo were involved in a perfect game pitched by [Sandy] Koufax, but they said this was more impressive.

Q: *You go from a 90-73 season to a 67-95 season in 1999. Then you get fired. What happened?*
Riggleman: I thought we were going out there with what I felt was even a better ballclub than what we finished up with in 1998. We started out good, but we got old real quick. All of a sudden, [Mickey] Morandini, [Jeff] Blauser, and [Gary] Gaetti, around May or June, they weren't playing as well as they had in the past. [Benito] Santiago and Kerry Wood blew it out in spring training. Kerry, in his first appearance . . . he's done for the year. Everything that could go wrong went wrong. I felt like the club got away from me a little bit. It became the longest, most miserable year I've ever experienced as a manager.

Q: *Did you know you were going to get canned?*
Riggleman: It was kind of hanging over my head quite a bit throughout the second half of the year. It was just kind of a feeling everybody had. And I probably caved in to the feeling instead of fighting it.

The way I rationalize it is I know I can manage. But sometimes another voice needs to be heard. Sometimes it just starts falling on deaf ears. The death knell for me was my one really good year there was sandwiched between two terrible years. Plus, if you're a manager for five years someplace and you have not won anything, there just becomes a feeling with the media, talk radio, the fans of "Let's try something else."

Q: *Anything you would have done differently that season?*
Riggleman: I'm not going to name names, but there were some personalities that weren't mixing well there. I think I lost some respect from some ballplayers on that club because they thought that, "Hey, Jim doesn't have much juice here." I knew I was being disrespected by some players on the club, but they were still on the team.

Q: *Do you think you'll get another chance to manage?*
Riggleman: Well, I'd like to manage again. It's been five years now.

GAME 118

Tuesday, August 17, 2004 . . . Brewers 3, Cubs 1 . . . Miller Park . . . Stat of the game: Another Cubs loss (7 of their last 10), another game lost in the wild-card standings, another game lost in the Central standings to the Cardinals (an astounding 15 back) . . . Stuff: The Brewers are going to start sending a limo for the Cubs. They get the win (they're 4-1 vs. the Cubs at Miller Park this season), and they get another sellout (41,174). . . . Ron Santo approaches the beleaguered Kyle Farnsworth in the clubhouse before tonight's game. He half-jokingly tells Farnsworth to grow his hair, forget about shaving—"get ugly," he says. Santo wants Farnsworth, who pitches as if he has self-esteem issues, to start projecting an intimidating image.

I'm officially ready to ralph.

How can a Cubs team with the best starting-pitching ERA in the entire big leagues, a lineup that includes a gladiator/future Hall of Famer (Sammy Sosa), five guys with 15 or more home runs this season (Sosa, Aramis Ramirez, Derrek Lee, Moises Alou, Corey Patterson), a five-time All-Star (Nomar Garciaparra), a three-time manager of the year (Dusty Baker), one of the best pitching coaches in the business (Larry Rothschild), a home crowd *on the road,* an off day to rest . . . lose to a last-place Brewers team whose starter had lost his last five consecutive starts?

I thought we were going to have to break out the defibrillator for Santo when second-base umpire Wally Bell reenacts *The Hellen Keller Story* and botches a call in the fourth inning. Then again, the Brewers already had all the runs they would need for the night.

Still, Santo had to leave the visitors' radio booth for a few moments to cool down. He walked down the press box hallway and later could be heard railing against the umpires. You could have used his forehead as a Benihana grill.

Everyone is a bit cranky these days. Before the game, Garciaparra agrees to a brief interview with the Milwaukee and Chicago writers. He answers the questions as if he's been deemed a hostile witness by Judge Wapner.

I notice a gold pin on his left wristband. So I ask him about it.

"It's a guardian angel," he says, making it fairly clear there won't be an explanation of the pin's origin.

Sooooo . . . pause for awkward silence. Someone begins another question, only to be interrupted by Garciaparra, who says he has to go stretch.

There's something funky going on here. Losing can do that. It can crank up Santo's blood pressure. It can affect a shortstop's disposition. It can create scapegoats, such as Mr. Bell.

But Bell's gaffe isn't the reason the Cubs are doing an August belly flop. There is something more ominous at work here than a second-base umpire who needs night-vision glasses. Maybe it's as easy as this: These Cubs are doomed.

Tonight's loss was ground zero of the season. It is the first time Baker's frustration level boils over in the postgame interview session. Sitting at his desk in the clubhouse, a scowl owning his face, Baker mutters an occasional "damn," followed by a "God, it's frustrating. It's very frustrating."

Baker is in the mood to vent.

"It's frustrating to make mistakes," he says. "It's frustrating to see that sometimes we can't get that two-out hit. We're not getting enough base hits. It's frustrating totally. Maybe we need this to shake us up some. Just shake it up, period. Everybody just break something and get it out of you."

Bruce Levine of WMVP asks him to clarify. Sure enough, Baker meant what we thought he meant: time to beat the hell out of, say, a dugout Gatorade cooler.

I don't spend much time in the clubhouse. What's the point? The place is so quiet you can hear the Cubs chewing on their postgame meals.

There is time to recover—not much, but enough. The Cubs have 44 regular-season games to figure out how to become a team again. Forget the Cardinals. They can't catch St. Louis even if Scott Rolen and Albert Pujols retire tomorrow. But somehow, despite this wretched stretch, the wild-card spot remains within easy reach of the Cubs.

Maybe Baker is right. Maybe someone needs to go postal here. This calm, collected, even-keel thing isn't working. Why not stir it up? Throw a few clubhouse chairs, win a few games, then have a toga party. Simple.

Something needs to change. The Gladiator, who stiffs the reporters for a fifth consecutive game, has just eight hits in his last 51 at-bats. Alou, who didn't play tonight, isn't doing much better (14 for his last 66). Ramirez is playing on one leg and spends his postgame in a familiar spot: on the trainer's table, an ice-pack wrap on his thigh. Even the guardian angel took the night off—Nomar takes an oh-fer and commits an error.

Baker keeps saying there's a difference between a sense of urgency and panic. Urgency is OK. Panic is a sign of weakness.

I have no idea how he feels about barf bags.

GAME 119

Wednesday, August 18, 2004 . . . Cubs 7, Brewers 5 . . . Miller Park . . . Stuff: Matt Clement ties a career high with 13 strikeouts, gives up three runs, but gets no decision. . . . The Cubs use four relievers, none of them named Kyle Farnsworth. Farnsworth is in the Cubs' version of mental rehab.

Ninety minutes before game time. I glance at the lineup card taped to the clubhouse wall leading to the Cubs' dugout.

Patterson, Lee, Garciaparra, Alou, Sosa, Ramirez, Walker, Barrett, Clement.

Wait a second—Sammy Sosa batting *fifth?* The Gladiator hasn't been out of the No. 3 or cleanup spot in nine-plus years. So either this is Ashton Kutcher's idea of a joke, or Dusty Baker pulled the trigger on a move, however symbolic, that had to be made.

Turns out I'm half right. Baker pulled the trigger, but Sosa handed him the gun.

"I was a little upset last night after the game," says Baker, sitting on the padded dugout bench. "I went upstairs [to the Pfister Hotel bar] and I had a couple of Scotches—I know you're not supposed to say that—but that's what I did. Then I got back to my room and my wife said Sammy had called three times. So I called him, and he answered the phone immediately. He just told me he thinks it's better for the team—with the way he's been going and stuff—that he should drop himself down in the order. I told him I'd been thinking about it for a while. He just said he wanted to do what was best for the team to help us get to the playoffs and get to the World Series."

Baker was more than a little peeved after Tuesday evening's loss. His son could sense it.

"Daddy, why are you so upset?" said little Darren.

Here's why: The Cubs had lost 7 of their last 10 and were a mess.

"I was glad [Darren] was there, because I was about to get real mad," says Baker. "I'll tell you, I don't like that real-mad guy. That's a bad guy."

The real-mad guy breaks things. The real-mad guy punches things. "That's why I've got scars all over my hands," says Baker.

The sort-of-mad guy drinks Scotch and counts slowly to 10. Then he heads back to his room at 1 A.M. and returns a call from the proud Sosa.

I've bashed Sosa more than a few times, but I'll give him credit for making what must have been an extraordinary admission: that for the moment he is no longer the straw that stirs the Cubs' drink. Too many strikeouts, too few hits.

Remember what Baker said way back when on Opening Day in Cincinnati, when Sosa was in the three spot: "Your third hitter is generally your best hitter." Sosa isn't the Cubs' best hitter these days. Not even close. Sosa recognized that, even on the same night he accounted for the Cubs' only run with his 26th dinger.

"It was a good move, a good, noble move," says Baker, who has never had a player make such a request. "It was a good team move."

Sosa, who hasn't spoken to reporters in days, is approached by the *Sun-Times*'s Mike Kiley. Kiley is Sosa's guy. It happens on beats. A certain player trusts a certain writer more than anyone else. Sosa trusts Kiley.

Kiley asks Sosa if he's willing to chat about the move. This is right before Sosa's group is supposed to take BP. Sosa says he'll talk, so we encircle him near the bat rack. We're crammed so close, I swear I can smell the wintergreen chaw Sosa has stuck between his cheek and gum.

First things first: Sosa says he and Baker are fine. "He's always been behind me," says Sosa, who's been thinking about the switch for about a week. "I appreciate that. I'll hit fifth for the rest of the year, or whatever he wants, whatever he needs."

Someone asks if Sosa has been hurt by the criticism.

"This is part of the game," he says. "At the beginning of the year, they were booing Derek Jeter and Alex Rodriguez. Those guys knew what they have to do. The situation, it's the first time it happened to me. It can happen to anybody. I need some support, and some people support me. Booing is not going to help."

I don't know if Sosa batting fifth is going to help, but it can't hurt. If nothing else, he shows Baker and his teammates that he cares. He also spares Baker of having to do the deed himself. It's a win-win.

"Nothing has been easy for myself," Sosa says. "Now everything will go back to normal. We just have to go out and win some games."

Geez, what a day. First a closed-door meeting with Baker doing most of the talking. Now Sosa coming clean. The only thing missing was a group hug.

"I just know down in my heart that sooner or later water seeks its own level," says Baker. "I know there's going to be a time where he's going to get hot and carry us."

It isn't tonight. Sosa goes 0-for-5 with two strikeouts, but it's the gesture that counts. The Cubs win in extra innings, and Garciaparra and Moises Alou combine for five hits (Nomar has three doubles), three RBI, and a run scored. So guess who is among the first to congratulate them?

Sosa.

GAME 120

Thursday, August 19, 2004 . . . Cubs 9, Brewers 6 . . . Miller Park . . . Stuff: Uh-oh—Chicago Buildings Commissioner Stan Kaderbek, on what turns out to be a disputed tip from a Chicago-based L.A. Times reporter named P. J. Huffs-tutter (who?), orders another round of independent reviews of Wrigley. If the reports aren't satisfactory, Kaderbek says he'll shut the place down. . . . Wild-card status: a half-game back.

Tom House calls from the Detroit airport, where he's waiting for a connection back to San Diego. Actually, it's *Dr.* Tom House (thanks to a Ph.D. in psychology), and he's the closest thing to a guaranteed beer on a bar bet: What former big league pitcher with 29 victories and 33 saves is in the Baseball Hall of Fame not once, but twice?

That would be House, who doesn't have a plaque at Cooperstown but does have a starring role in two prominent photos in the HOF. Only House has the distinction of being pictured catching Hank Aaron's record-breaking 715th home run while standing in the Atlanta Braves' bullpen and, in another exhibit, throwing a football with the great Nolan Ryan.

The Aaron story has been told countless times.

"I caught Aaron's ball," he says. "I ran it in and gave it right to him.

There was a crowd around him and he was hugging his mom. When I gave it to him, he said, 'Thanks, kid.' "

The Ryan moment came much later, when House was a pitching coach with the Texas Rangers. I remember those footballs because I was there as a reporter for the *Dallas Morning News.* I remember thinking, "What kind of kook has his pitchers throw footballs?"

But House has always been a baseball nontraditionalist. He's gone against the grain so often that he has grass burns.

"Baseball is a game of failure coached by negative people in a misinformation environment," says House, who has authored or coauthored 19 books on pitching.

House, who has always been a decade or so ahead of the learning curve, is cofounder of the National Pitching Association, whose most notable disciples include Ryan, Randy Johnson, and Mark Prior. In fact, Prior and House, part of the USC baseball mafia, are tighter than cowhide and stitching. They're friends first, mentor/student second.

The NPA is sort of the Botox of baseball. Through biomechanics analysis, performance psychology, physical training, and metabolic management, the NPA staff tries to "minimize the breaking-down process" of a throwing arm. In short, House and his experts have created an anti-aging template.

House first met Prior when Mark was a high school freshman. It was obvious Prior had a terrific arm, but House was more impressed with the family: Prior's mother was an educator, his father a former Vanderbilt football player—both valued work ethic and integrity. If you could combine that athletic potential with the family core values . . .

"He was like a big doofus 14-year-old who wasn't hooked up," says House.

The NPA features motion-analysis cameras that can shoot anywhere from 600 to 1,000 frames per second. A pitcher's motion is reduced to a stick figure, and that figure's windup and delivery is graded on an efficiency model House and his experts have created. Nearly 400 big league players are in the NPA video library.

"Nobody has a perfect delivery," says House. "Greg Maddux probably comes the closest to our theoretical model of perfection. The most perfect of the hard throwers is Nolan Ryan. And Charlie Hough, the knuckleballer, is the most perfect of what we call the 'freak' pitchers."

And Prior?

"He's the poster child for the complete package," House says. "His mental profile is right up there with the best we have in the system [the NPA has more than 10,000 profiles]. It's not like he's a robo pitcher. But he's probably the most predictably consistent pitcher of all the people we have. He's in the upper echelon in all the things we think contribute to a long, healthy career."

This season has been anything but healthy for Prior. He missed the first two months of the season because of tendinitis in his right Achilles. Then came the elbow problems in mid-July. He has one win since June 25, only three for the season, and his ERA is an unattractive 4.97 (nearly two runs higher than his career average).

"Believe it or not, we actually try to talk about various scenarios," says House. "For example, what it's like to pitch when you're not 100 percent, or what happens when the media turns on you. This is the first time he's experienced something where he's not quite right. It's the first time he's had to experience criticism."

House and Prior are in regular contact with each other. They do so with the blessings of the Cubs. House's roommate with the Braves was Dusty Baker.

House has traveled to Wrigley several times this summer to see Prior. He was there the day Prior pulled himself out of the July 15 game. He was there to see the frustration as Prior dealt with injuries and the media.

"He's very guarded right now," says House. "He's actually been hurt a little bit by the venom aimed in his direction. He's really got a heart of gold. He could have done better [with the situation], but remember he's only 23. He'll get it. He was just a little surprised how people went after him."

There is a perception that Prior's father, Jerry, and House were responsible for the ultraconservative approach taken when the right-hander wasn't activated from the disabled list until early June. But House says the Cubs, influenced by past injury problems with Kerry Wood, shared that approach, if not encouraged it.

This latest injury—"discomfort" in the posterior area of the throwing elbow—added to the frustration and tension. Prior was examined not only by Cubs' doctors but also by the renowned Dr. Lewis Yocum and Dr. James Andrews. About a month ago, after an understandable amount of hand-wringing, a consensus was reached among the Cubs' medical staff and outside specialists: Let Prior pitch. So the Cubs let him pitch, but with the knowledge that he wasn't 100 percent healthy.

"He's not right," says House. "He tells me, 'Tom, it doesn't feel right. But as long as they tell me there's nothing else I can do to make it worse, I'm going out there.' He's pitching on Saturday. Know what he said? 'Tom, I'm going to go Mach 3 with my hair on fire.'

"He's not right physically, but he's not scared. Watch him."

House has a plane to catch. I've got a yard to mow. But we'll both be doing the same thing Saturday: watching Mr. Near Perfect with his hair on fire.

GAME 121

Friday, August 20, 2004 . . . Cubs 9, Astros 2 . . . Minute Maid Park . . . Cubs NL Central pennant flies: Second (66-55) . . . Stat of the game: The Cubs hit six home runs. . . . Stuff: Don't laugh, but Glendon Rusch might be the Cubs' MVP. . . . Ah-ha, now I see: Garciaparra touches that gold guardian angel pin between every pitch. . . . Joe Borowski gives up two walks, no hits, and one un-earned run in his first rehab appearance at Iowa. . . . Wild-card status: a half-game back.

I corner a National League scout who has seen the Cubs more than a few times this season. He remains a believer.

"I'll tell anybody I talk to that this is the club that everybody wants to keep out of the playoffs. This is the [World Series champion Arizona] Dia-mondbacks of 2001. It's like [Curt] Schilling and [Randy] Johnson, then off days, then bring back Schilling and Johnson.

"That rested power pitching is a hell of a weapon to have in the playoffs. Kerry Wood missed a couple of months. Mark Prior missed a couple of months. If they get in the playoffs, you're going to see a strong contingent of power pitchers that you're going to have to face, and you're going to face them constantly because of the postseason schedule with all the off days.

"I hope our club gets in the playoffs and I hope they don't, because I'd rather face any other pitching staff than theirs.

"What you have here is a predominantly right-handed lineup that can hit right-handed pitching. And they can mash left-handed pitching. It's a very good ballclub—and I think Dusty said it right—they haven't hit their stride yet. When they do, they're going to be a tough team.

"Now, Sammy . . . I've been telling guys, 'He's getting close.' Have you seen how hard he's hitting the ball? The games I saw recently [at Wrigley] . . . the wind was blowing in. Any other August, he would have had three home runs in two days. Just watching him, he looked like his old self. He has 28 homers, and he missed a month.

"As far as weaknesses, they're still not a great defensive ballclub, but I don't think they've ever professed that they are. But they're a very good power-pitching ballclub. They can kill your rally with strikeouts, so the ball isn't always going to be in play. If you're striking people out a lot and you have fly-ball pitchers, then your defensive weaknesses are less likely to show up. But you know who I think is a good defensive player? Ramirez. And Lee and Patterson are the others.

"I don't think Garciaparra changes this team, but I think he makes it that much better. Their depth in the lineup goes that much farther. Now you've got [Michael] Barrett hitting seventh or eighth, and he can hit the ball out of the ballpark.

"The bullpen is good. They don't have that classic dominating closer, but they've got guys who aren't afraid to have the ball in the eighth or ninth inning. I think they'll be fine there.

"You've got a veteran ballclub here that knows how to play. They're not going to be intimidated by any situation that comes up. They've been there before.

"I'm not going to let you use the word *fear*, but I do not want to see this team in the playoffs."

GAME 122

Saturday, August 21, 2004 . . . Astros 4, Cubs 3 . . . Minute Maid Park . . . Stuff: So much for going Mach 3. Mark Prior pitches well enough to win, but he also gives up a two-out, two-run single to rookie pitcher Brandon Backe. . . . A win would have put the Cubs atop the NL wild-card standings. Instead, Jose Macias commits a ninth-inning throwing error and LaTroy Hawkins blows the save chance. Oh, the humanity. . . . Aramis Ramirez is 3-for-20 on the road trip, Sammy Sosa is 4-for-22.

Tim Isaacson is a New Era sales rep for the North Side of Chicago and parts of Indiana. He sells Cubs caps, including the ones the players wear—the handmade-in-the-USA (there's a 22-step process in making a single cap), MLB-approved 59Fifty model.

Isaacson resides in La Grange Park, is married, has two kids, and lives and dies with the Cubs. When you make your living off straight commission, you do that.

Last year during the playoffs was brutal. It was the craziest three weeks of my life. We have to go out and write what-if orders: what if they win the NLCS . . . what if they win the World Series. I was working the concession trailers outside the ballpark, getting home at two in the morning. Then I was getting cell calls at 7 A.M. from guys looking for product. Our New York guy—he sells Yankees stuff—goes through it every year.

We had all these manufacturers ready to go. We lined up embroidery houses in Chicago. Air freight companies . . . ready to go. When they're up 3-1, people get permission to make these things. If they get in the World Series, the sky's the limit.

I had people coming out of the woodwork looking for product. Hey, get in line. They'd say, "I thought you were my friend." I'd tell them, "I don't have any friends this week."

For the playoffs in '03 we geared up and made 100,000 Cubs 59Fifties. All we had to do was put the World Series heat seals on them. But you know what happened. If the Cubs had won, we were oversold on product. Who knows how many hats we would have sold? Millions. With the Marlins, we couldn't sell out what we had.

Game 6, The Bartman Game . . .

After that game, I just called my wife and said I'm going to be home late. I had a buddy down there with me. He was my designated driver. There was a bar, the New Orleans bar or something, about three blocks away from Wrigley. Just stayed there. That's when I got home at 4:30 in the morning after drowning my sorrows.

And I didn't have a good feeling about Game 7. When Florida scored those runs, I'm thinking, "What am I going to do with all these orders when [the Cubs] lose this game?"

When it was over, I shredded the smaller orders and saved the bigger orders in a file. I was dying.

Here's what you need to understand: There are 81 home games, right? That's 81 Christmas days to me. If I miss a homestand, I miss six days of Christmas. If I don't get product there, I'm missing Christmas.

Dark Royal is the official cap color for the Cubs. The Dodgers use a Dark Royal. So does Texas. With the Cubs, it's just a classic-looking cap. Very plain, very classic.

In the urban community, that Cubs logo doesn't do a lot for them. People in the urban communities like the Yankees cap, or Boston. After that, you almost have to throw L.A. in there, maybe even the White Sox. But to the baseball fan, the Cubs cap is probably No. 3, right up there with the Yankees and Boston.

How many do we sell? Someone just asked me that this week, and it's a tough number to figure out. For the Cubs, we'll probably sell between 75,000 and 100,000. With the White Sox, probably 30,000.

The numbers [on Cubs caps sales] were way up this year. We did more business in the first half of this year than we did in all of last year. That's how nuts it was. And once you get in the playoffs you can make up your numbers in two weeks for the entire year.

It's August 21 and I'm worried. We're a half-game out in the wild card. I either want them losing right away or winning right away. Win me 10 in a row, man, or lose me 10 in a row. Just put me out of my misery. It's all about inning by inning, pitch by pitch. Isn't that brutal?

GAME 123

Sunday, August 22, 2004 . . . Cubs 11, Astros 6 . . . Minute Maid Park . . . Stat of the game: Corey Patterson goes 3-for-5 with two runs and an RBI. He's raised his average to .288 and is batting .375 since moving to the leadoff spot August 1. . . . Stuff: Bizarro game. Kerry Wood, ahead 10-2 and two outs away from qualifying for one of the easiest wins of his career, gets tossed by home plate umpire Bill Hohn after hitting his third Astros batter of the day. Wood is the victim of crummy control and the earlier ejection of Astros starter Roy Oswalt (he nailed Michael Barrett on purpose).

I thought Ed Hartig, the Cubs' de facto historian, was some old codger who grew up watching Gabby Hartnett and used to take the trolley to Wrigley. I figured he lived in a Loop studio apartment with a cat, wore Old Spice, and washed his socks in the sink.

Instead, I get a 39-year-old father of two who resides in Bolingbrook. His full-time gig is as a statistician for a chemical company. His act-of-love gig is as a baseball info guy who provides historical research to sportswriters and the Cubs' media relations, publications, and marketing departments. He knows stuff.

In 1970, he made his first visit to Wrigley, and life has never been the same since. Twenty-five years later, Hartig was giving tours of Wrigley for Cubs Care charities. A year later, he was writing a history column for the team magazine, *Vineline*. Now he's the team's personal Baseball Encylopedia. For this he gets paid the grand total of zilch.

I ask Hartig to do the near-impossible: pick an all-time Cubs team. This is like asking Upton Sinclair to pick a favorite beef product . . . it can't be done. Or can it?

"I tried to limit players to their years with the Cubs," he says, "so Rogers Hornsby, while one of the great second basemen of all-time, doesn't make the cut. Sorry—Greg Maddux and Grover Alexander don't, either."

It's his team, so I'm not going to throw a fit. Hornsby played for the Cubs from 1929 to 1932. Maddux did most of his heavy lifting with the Atlanta Braves, and Alexander had a hell of a 1920 but isn't among the team's all-time leaders in any of the major pitching categories.

Hartig picks two players at each position, five starters, one reliever, one manager.

First Base: Cap Anson (Cubs 1876-1897)
Hartig: Cap led the NL in batting four times, hit over .300 in 19 of his 22 seasons as a Cub [White Stocking], and was the first Major Leaguer to reach 3,000 career hits. Named captain [equivalent to today's manager] in 1879, he helped guide the Cubs to five pennants. Anson is the Cubs' all-time leader in runs, hits, doubles, and RBIs.

Sub: Mark Grace (1988-2000).

Second Base: Ryne Sandberg (1982-1994, 1996-1997)
Hartig: A winner of nine consecutive Gold Gloves and a 10-time All Star, he had 20 errorless streaks of at least 30 games. Add to that he scored at least 100 runs seven times, is the all-time leader in home runs for a second baseman,

and that he stole over 300 bases. Ryno drove in 100 runs twice and in 1990 won the home run title, the first second baseman to lead the NL since 1925.

Sub: Billy Herman (1931-1941).

Shortstop: Ernie Banks (1953-1971)

Hartig: Mr. Cub played more games at first base than at shortstop, but it was as a middle infielder where he earned back-to-back MVP honors in 1958 and 1959. Ernie hit 40 home runs five times between 1955 and 1960. At the outset his fielding was erratic, but he improved to win a Gold Glove and led NL shortstops in fielding three times. Ernie is the Cubs' all-time leader in games, at-bats, total bases, and extra-base hits.

Sub: Joe Tinker (1902-1912, 1916).

Third Base: Ron Santo (1960-1973)

Hartig: After his departure, the team struggled for the next 30 years finding a suitable replacement. A nine-time All-Star and five-time Gold Glove winner, Ron consistently led NL third basemen in putouts, assists, and double plays. He also hit at least 25 home runs and drove in 90 runs every year from 1963 to 1970. Named team captain at age 25, Santo played in at least 154 games in 11 consecutive seasons.

Sub: Stan Hack (1932-1947).

Left Field: Billy Williams (1959-1974)

Hartig: Williams had 2,711 hits and 426 home runs—392 of them as a Cub. The 1961 Rookie of the Year, Billy was the Cubs' iron man, playing 1,117 consecutive games—then an NL record. He hit 20 home runs and drove in at least 84 runs in 13 consecutive years.

Sub: Riggs Stephenson (1926-1934).

Center Field: Hack Wilson (1926-1931)

Hartig: Wilson led the NL in home runs in four of his first five seasons as a Cub, batting .313 or higher each season. In 1929, he topped the NL with 159 RBI while hitting 39 homers. A year later, he dwarfed those numbers, driving in a Major League-record 191 runs and hitting 56 home runs—and doing it in only a 154-game schedule.

Sub: Andy Pafko (1943-1951).

Right Field: Sammy Sosa (1992-   )

Hartig: Sammy was the team's first 30-30 player. Sammy has hit at least 36 home runs and driven in 100 RBI each of the last nine seasons, and he's the only player to hit 60 home runs in a season three times. In 2004, he overtook Ernie Banks as the Cubs' all-time home run leader and should challenge the 600 mark by the end of the 2005 season.

Sub: Frank "Wildfire" Schulte (1904-1916).

Catcher: Gabby Hartnett (1922-1940)

Hartig: Hartnett was behind the plate for three pennant winners (he missed most of the 1929 season), including his 1935 MVP season. Named player-manager during the 1938 season, his "Homer in the Gloamin'" helped lead the Cubs to another World Series.

Sub: Johnny Kling (1900-1908, 1910-1911).

Starting Pitcher: Mordecai Brown (1904-1912, 1916)

Hartig: A farming accident left his right hand permanently disfigured. It also gave tremendous spin on his pitches. Nicknamed "Three Finger," he won 20 games six consecutive times, and from 1904 to 1910 his highest ERA was 2.17! When he wasn't starting, Mordecai was one of the most dependable relief pitchers in his era.

Rotation: Fergie Jenkins (1966-1973, 1982-1983), Charlie Root (1926-1941), Ed Reulbach (1905-1913), Hippo Vaughn (1913-1921).

Relief Pitcher: Bruce Sutter (1976-1980)

Hartig: Bruce saved 31 games in 1977 but missed much of the season with an injury. With him, the Cubs were a first-place team, building an 8½-game lead. Without him, they slumped to a .500 finish. Two years later, he saved 37 games and won the Cy Young. In 88 of his 133 saves as a Cub, he tossed more than one inning, and 31 times he went more than two innings.

Setup: Lee Smith (1980-1987).

Manager: Frank Chance (Manager 1905-1912)

Hartig: The first baseman in the Tinker-to-Evers-to-Chance double-play combination, Chance led the Cubs to four pennants and two World Series titles in his first five full seasons as player-manager. In 1907, he convinced team owner Charlie Murphy to officially adopt the name Cubs for the team.

Bench Coach: Charlie Grimm (Manager 1932-1938, 1944-1949, 1960; Coach 1941, 1961-1963).

GAME 124

Monday, August 23, 2004 . . . Cubs 8, Brewers 3 . . . Wrigley Field . . . Stuff:
Chicago Building Commissioner Stan Kaderbek deems Wrigley safe for
tonight's game. Make no mistake: This is about public safety, but also about a
public feud between Mayor Richard Daley and the Tribune, which is owned
by the same company that owns the Cubs. The city's latest thumbs-up
prompts this deliciously pithy response from Cubs president Andy MacPhail:
"The city has conducted enough inspections of Wrigley Field by now, that
they should be satisfied we are not printing a newspaper here." . . . The Curse
of the Bambino meets the Curse of the Billy Goat. Nomar Garciaparra misses
his third consecutive game with a just-divulged strain of the left wrist. . . .
Hank Borowy spins in. Borowy, 88, was the last Cubs pitcher to start a World
Series game. . . . The Joe Borowski Rehab Tour: 0-2, 21.60 ERA . . . Wild-card
status: tied for first.

I walk into Wrigley at 2:45 today and there it is: another group of corporate
wonks fielding grounders and fly balls, and taking batting practice. It's pathetic, really. Overweight, overaged, and underathletic goobers making
fools of themselves in their shorts, sneakers, and replica Cubs jerseys.

And I'd give anything to be one of them.

Greg Huff, one of the lucky corporate-wonk few, took his cuts today.
Huff, 42, lives in Plainfield and is a CFO of a suburban company. He's here
as a guest of Bank of America, which paid a fee to use Wrigley and a handful of its coaches for the pregame outing.

"They're trying to get my business," says Huff of his Bank of America
hosts.

So this is a glorified bribe. If so, where do I sign up for a BOA checking
account?

"This is a childhood dream," says Huff. "I've been a Cub fan my whole
life. As a kid, you want to be Ernie Banks, Ron Santo . . . those guys."

Third-base coach Wendell Kim hits soft ground balls to some of the
BOA-sponsored "players." Pitching coach Larry Rothschild hits fly balls to
another group in center field. The remainder of the party takes their hacks
in the batting cage.

Some of the swings are straight from Spasms-R-Us. The fielding is of the Frank Thomas quality. And you don't even want to know about the fly balls.

Huff drills a couple of liners to the outfield during his eight or nine swings. "I didn't hit it like [Banks or Santo] did, but I got it out of the infield. Not bad, considering I haven't swung a bat in 20 years."

Nobody comes close to clearing the ivy wall, but that figures. The wind is blowing in, and the bats are leftovers from Rey Ordonez's brief stay with the Cubs.

Huff uses an old glove he dug out of a basket in the garage. "At least it didn't have dry rot," he says. He cleanly fields Kim's grounders, but he somehow lets one of Rothschild's fly balls drop behind him.

You think Huff cares? While waiting his turn in center, Huff unclips his cell phone from his belt and calls his father, a lifelong Cubs follower, in Minnesota.

"Dad, I'm in center field at Wrigley," he says.

A pause, and then . . . "Cool," says his old man.

An hour later, and Huff still can't believe the reaction.

"He's 68, and I don't think I've ever heard him use the word *cool.*"

GAME 125

Tuesday, August 24, 2004 . . . Cubs 13, Brewers 4 . . . Wrigley Field . . . Stat of the game: Derrek Lee hits a grand slam, Moises Alou drives in a career-high six runs. . . . Stuff: Matt Clement wins for the first time since July 26.

Still no word from Major League Baseball on Kerry Wood's latest incident involving the umpiring crew of Gary Darling, Brian Runge, Mark Carlson, and the esteemed Bill Hohn. Hohn is the guy who tossed Wood from Sunday's start for plunking, accidentally or otherwise, one too many Houston Astros. Wood didn't go ballistic on the field, but afterward he did pop off a bit in the papers.

Under normal circumstances, that would be that. But the Cubs, and Wood especially, are on some sort of MLB double-secret probation. That's one of the reasons why there's an MLB umpiring official at Wrigley on what seems to be a fairly regular basis.

I ask Wood if we can talk about the art of coexisting with umpires. After all, it is such a strange dynamic: pitcher, home plate umpire . . . separated only by 60 feet, 6 inches and subjectivity.

This amuses Wood.

"Me?" he says. "I don't know if I've really learned how to yet."

Wood was born and raised in Irving, Texas, which is just outside Dallas. He watched former Longhorn Roger Clemens. He was there at old Arlington Stadium the night Nolan Ryan pitched his seventh no-hitter.

"Left-field bleachers, halfway up," he says. "Got free tickets at the grocery store. Minyard. We were collecting tickets in the bleachers after the game was over."

These were Wood's pitching role models. Ryan was a stoic, hardball pitcher, and a hardass too. Clemens is the same way. Give no quarter, take no crap.

"They never got really excited when they got a big out," says Wood. "It's like they expected to get a big out and then it was time to get back to business to the next inning, or the next hitter, or the next pitch. I kind of liked the way they walked around the mound, how they handled the game."

So Wood behaved in a similar way. His unspoken deal with hitters: You don't embarrass me, I won't embarrass you.

But no one taught Wood how to deal with big league umpires. Wood was 20 when he was called up from Triple-A Iowa in 1998.

"When you first come up," says Wood, "a couple guys will say, 'Hey, don't do anything with this ump because he might think you're showing him up.' A veteran might say, 'Good luck tomorrow. You've got so-and-so. Don't piss him off.' But there's no dos and don'ts. I mean, it's pretty much clear-cut what a pitcher can do on the mound."

It is, but it isn't. Even in Wood's six-plus seasons there has been a gradual change in player-umpire etiquette.

"When I first came up, you could ask a guy where a pitch was," says Wood. "If he called it a ball, you could ask where it was—I've seen Randy Johnson do that a bunch of times. A pitcher could have thought it was a strike where it crossed the plate, but the umpire thought it was maybe too high, too low. So you kind of ask, with a hand gesture, 'Where did you have that? Is it down? Up?'

"But this year I've seen where a guy will ask that, and it ends up in a shouting match, the mask comes flying off. I think they're taking a lot less questioning from players."

Wood isn't exactly Mr. Social when it comes to the men in black. He pitches. They call balls and strikes. That's it for niceties.

"The day I'm pitching, all I see is a mask," says Wood, who would be hard-pressed to tell you the first names of most of the big league umpires. "But I think it would be beneficial to learn the umpires. I think that's what makes Greg Maddux and Barry Bonds so successful at what they do. I don't do that. We see so many different umpires. It's a mask back there to me. I'm out there to do my job, and they're out there to do their job."

This makes no sense to me. If building bridges of understanding works with a 300-game winner and the best hitter of our generation, shouldn't it work for Wood?

Wood shrugs his shoulders. "Yeah, I guess," he says. But his body language says something else: WWND (What Would Nolan Do). Nolan wouldn't cultivate or nurture a damn thing with an umpire.

I ask him what he'd tell a rookie pitcher about umpires.

"When a rookie's up—and especially if they've had some hype with them along the way, like [Mark] Prior—he got tested," says Wood. "They test you a little bit to see what's going to happen. If you've got a rookie going against a guy who's been in the league eight years, and the guy in the league is getting a few calls, it seems like sometimes the rookie doesn't get the same benefit if it's close. But that's how it is. You just go out and pitch. When I was a rookie, I never felt like I deserved to get the borderline calls because I wasn't around the zone."

The umpire hazing, if you can call it that, usually ends after the first season, says Wood. "But this is from a player's standpoint," he says. "[Hazing] could not even be happening. We could just be thinking it's going on. But when you first come up, you don't really question anything. You definitely don't want to get a reputation."

Does Wood have a rep with the umpires?

"I hope not," he says. "Obviously, the [April 17 incident] was probably my worst. And there was a time in San Diego a couple years ago where I thought a pitch was a strike, so I kind of yelled down. After I yelled, I turned around, got on the mound, looked up, and the umpire's got his mask off looking at me. He doesn't know if I was yelling at myself, yelling at him. I told him to put his mask back on, and here we go. But I stayed in there."

Carlos Zambrano shows his emotions on the mound. Wood shows his intensity. Sometimes he shows it a little too much, which is why he's always doing the compare-and-contrast thing when he sees other pitchers throwing a small fit.

"If I see somebody standing out there yelling, I'll turn around to somebody in the dugout and say, 'Do I look like that when I'm doing that?' If they tell me, 'Yeah,' then I don't feel so good."

Has anybody told you that? I ask.

"No. They tell me it's not that bad."

So they lie? I say.

"Yeah," says Wood, "they lie."

GAME 126

Wednesday, August 25, 2004 . . . Cubs 4, Brewers 2 . . . Wrigley Field . . . Cubs NL Central pennant flies: Second (70-56) . . . Stat of the game: Paul Bako hits his first dinger in two years. Brewers starter Doug Davis reacts as if the batboy just hit the thing into the bleachers. . . . Stuff: LaTroy Hawkins blows his second consecutive save opportunity, as well as Greg Maddux's 13th victory of the season. . . . The Cubs move a season-high 14 games above .500. . . . Chicago Mayor (and lifelong White Sox fan) Richard Daley, talking as if a piece of Wrigley concrete knocked him silly, is asked by reporters about the Cubs. His response, duly noted in today's edition of the Sun-Times: *"They should get a team." This is interesting, since there's a better chance of Daley becoming a Republican than there is of his beloved Sox making the playoffs. The Sox are 61-63 and so far out of the postseason chase they need an AWACS radar plane to see the AL Central leaders. . . . My* Sports Illustrated *arrives in the mail. An unnamed big league general manager says of the Cubs: "You think they should win the wild card, but for a team with veteran players and a veteran manager, they make way too many mistakes on the bases and in the field." This is true. Moises Alou gets doubled up at second today after wandering off the bag on a fly ball. . . . Wild-card status: one game up.*

With the score 2-2, Mark Grudzielanek leads off the bottom of the ninth with a slicing fly ball that appears to land just outside the right-field foul line. But wait—first-base umpire Mark Wegner signals it fair, and

Grudzielanek reaches third on the questionable double and a throwing error by stunned right fielder Brady Clark.

Bako pops up to second. Pinch hitter Todd Walker pops up to third. Corey Patterson steps to the plate. And so does Steve Stone, who is a viewer's best friend. His call:

Stone: That was a good job of pitching by [Luis] Vizcaino, as he gets everything upstairs, and he's two-thirds of the way there, but Corey Patterson stands in the way of Vizcaino getting out of this inning. Corey is 1-for-9 against Vizcaino, but you've got the right-hander [Derrek Lee] due up next.

Chip Caray: It may sound unconventional, but how about a bunt? You've got a third baseman playing first base on a wet infield. I know there are two outs, but you might have a better shot that way.

(Patterson swings away.)

Caray: No sign of it. Strike one, out of play. Branyan even with the bag at first, Bill Hall on the outfield grass at second, Durrington even with the bag and base runner over at third . . . At the belt, strike two.

Stone: They're going to go upstairs and try to throw a high fastball by him. I wouldn't think that Vizcaino would try any kind of slider, because that's a pitch that winds up in the dirt. Let's hope Corey can lay off [the high fastball].

(The crowd yells, "Cor-ey! . . . Cor-ey!")

Caray: One ball, two strikes. The Cubs got a leadoff three-base gift. Can they unwrap the present and win it, 3-2?

(Vizcaino throws a fastball high and inside. The count is 2-2.)

Caray: Well, that will make the outer portion of the plate a little more inviting to Vizcaino, you would think. Corey's gone the other way a lot of late.

Stone: You're only thinking about a high fastball as hard as [Vizcaino] can throw it. [Vizcaino gets the sign from catcher Chad Moeller.] No, now he's gone to a slider, it appears.

(Patterson pulls the pitch foul.)

Caray: It slides over the roof of the ballpark.

Stone: I'm real surprised he went to a slider in that situation, but he got it inside enough.

(The Fox Sports Net camera crew shows two nuns in their seats, rosary beads in plain sight.)

Caray: Pull some strings, ladies, will you?

Stone: Another slider from Vizcaino and this one probably ends.

(More chants from the crowd. Vizcaino gets his sign from Moeller.)

Stone (in disbelief): He is going with the slider.

Caray: Two-two . . . Swing and a high fly ball hit to right field. Back goes Clark . . . on the warning track . . . at the wall . . . it's a homer! A game-winning home run!

[There are a half-dozen replays of Patterson's homer. Stone was right. It was a slider.]

GAME 127

Thursday, August 26, 2004 . . . Cubs 8, Astros 3 . . . Wrigley Field . . . Cubs NL Central pennant flies: Second (71-56) . . . Stat of the game: Mark Prior wins for the first time at Wrigley since Game 2 of the 2003 NLCS. . . . Stuff: Steve Stone takes one look at the center-field flags and winces. He once gave up five homers in 2⅓ innings at Wrigley, one shy of tying the record for most dingers allowed by a pitcher. "[Cubs manager Jim] Marshall comes out and says, 'You've had enough.' I said, 'Why? The record's six.'" . . . Wild-card status: one game up.

Catching the ceremonial first pitch isn't the worst job in baseball (that distinction goes to whoever has to clean the spittle- and nuclear-waste-drenched dugout floors after a game), but it's on the short list.

It's one thing to catch the first pitch on Opening Day, when it means something. It's quite another to drag your butt out there in late August and squat for an endless procession of FOTCs (Friends of the Cubs), or the occasional celeb who can't hit the side of Wrigley from a foot away, much less 60 feet, 6 inches.

Jon Leicester is the current squattee, assuming the duties July 21, when he was recalled from Iowa and became the new guy again. Earlier in the season, from June 6 to June 27, Leicester also had to trudge out to the plate before home games. Then Michael Wuertz was recalled and Leicester got a reprieve.

That's how it works. Low man on the seniority pole gets stuck trying to catch 40-footers, screamers that sail high or wide, or, if the moons are aligned, an actual strike.

"I've done it so much I can evaluate who's better at it than other [cere-monial pitchers]," says the 25-year-old right-hander. "For the most part, I'd say 6 out of 10 reach the plate, which is actually pretty good. But they all say how nerve-racking it is, how much farther it looks to the plate when they're on the field, compared to seeing it on TV. I think more fans need to do this so they can get an idea of what pitchers go through. It does look easy, but it's a lot tougher than it looks."

The red-haired Leicester, who looks as if he ought to be scooping ice cream at the local Oberweis, recalls his first time on the Wrigley mound. Sort of.

"June 9," he says. "Against St. Louis. I remember being out there, but it was kind of a whirlwind as far as nerves and emotions. It was kind of like an out-of-body experience a little bit. When you play the game for so long, the game slows down for you. But that game, everything was so fast-paced that my mind never got a chance to catch up. There's a big crowd, a lot of emotion, and it's like you've never played the game before, like you're pitching for the first time. I just went into muscle-memory pitching."

Leicester entered the game in the fifth inning, with the Cardinals ahead, 5-3. All he had to do was face National League MVP candidate Scott Rolen, three-time All-Star Jim Edmonds, Reggie Sanders, and So Taguchi.

"I did all right," says Leicester. "I struck out Rolen. With Edmonds I threw it a little high and tight and he got a little upset. So he hit a home run. Then I struck out Sanders and got Taguchi to pop up. Those aren't slouch hitters, by any means."

And how did he begin his day? By trotting out to the plate before the game and catching a few from two guests of Old Style, and then Chicago Bears quarterback Rex Grossman. Now he waits for September to arrive.

"That's when they expand the rosters," he says. "They can't do it soon enough."

GAME 128

Friday, August 27, 2004 . . . Astros 15, Cubs 7 . . . Wrigley Field . . . Stuff: This loss could leave a bruise. Michael Barrett and Roy Oswalt chirp at each other at home plate, both benches clear, Kerry Wood gets scorched for eight runs in 4⅓ innings, Kent Mercker gives up a hit, two walks, a run, and pops Oswalt in the thigh—all in just one-third of an inning—and returns to the clubhouse to call the Cubs' PR staff to complain about Steve Stone and Chip Caray for stating the obvious: that Oswalt was pitching his Astros off. And later, as the Tribune's Dave van Dyck reports, Mercker gets into a heated postgame shouting match with the umpires in the dugout tunnel. Kyle Farnsworth pitches the ninth, gives up six hits and six runs, and then tosses his glove into the stands after finally retiring the side. . . . A new ceremonial first-pitch low: Jon Leicester has to retrieve the throw of Disney character Goofy. . . . Wild-card status: one game up.

Don Patterson sits at one of the many wobbly tables in the media dining room and pretends he's thrilled to be answering my questions. This is a big day for Patterson. His youngest son, Eric, just signed a contract to play for the Cubs, and his oldest son, Corey, is moments away from batting leadoff in the bottom of the first. Don would very much like to be in his seat right now, but he made two rookie mistakes: He stopped in the dining room just long enough to be recognized, and he's too polite to say no.

A few minutes earlier, Eric concluded his own mini news conference in the back of the press box. The now-former Georgia Tech star is four years younger than Corey and four times as talkative. That's no knock on Corey, but it's obvious Eric is the more social of the two brothers.

"The one that just signed?" says Don. "Hey, there's nothing introverted about Eric. Now, Corey, he's been like that ever since he was one year old. He's always been a very intense kid."

Don lives in Atlanta and watches the Cubs games on the tube. He saw Corey's average dip into the .240s, saw him on the bench when the slump was at its worst, saw Dusty Baker move him up and down the batting order (as low as eighth) in hopes of sparking something. And he heard the boos.

"I actually came up and watched a couple of games when [the boos] were taking place," says Don. "One of the things I tried to do with him was take a negative situation and put a positive spin on it. I said, 'Look, let's take you out of it as a professional baseball player. Let's put you in the shoes of the Chicago Cubs fans. Be a fan for a day. Be a fan for a week. Because you need to understand it isn't anything personal.'"

If it's my kid, I'm fuming. But Don, who played defensive back for the Detroit Lions (1979) and New York Giants (1980), knows better.

"I watched their games on TV earlier in the year, and even recently, and guess what—Sammy Sosa gets booed at Wrigley Field," says Don. "So if they can boo an All-Star, they can certainly boo a young player trying to get established in the big leagues. You're not immune from being booed as a superstar, or if you are a kid trying to get established. It's part . . . of . . . the . . . game. And you have to realize that at a very early age.

"And by the way, when there was criticism earlier in the year, he did an excellent job of dealing with it. You know what he told me? He said, 'Dad, I believe in me. It's going to come. It's just a matter of time.' I said, 'I know.'"

Don glances up at the TV in the dining room. The Astros already lead, 4-2, in the second. Corey has walked and scored on a Nomar Garciaparra RBI single. Now Barrett is popping off to Oswalt. The benches clear.

"You're missing a good game," says Don. "You sure you don't want to go watch it?"

Ah, a clever attempt on Don's part. But, no, there is work to be done. I ask about Corey's on-field demeanor, which is mostly impassive.

"When you don't know him, and you don't know his personality, and you just see his outer shell as a baseball player—and then you take a baseball fan who sees that, and sees the struggles . . . then you can certainly understand their reaction," says Don. "But I don't think there's a person in the world who enjoys getting booed—at least not in their home ballpark."

Corey enters the game hitting .293. His average, on-base percentage, and steals have all spiked since moving to the leadoff spot. But his bump in production can also be traced to some behind-the-scenes baseball therapy that would make Dr. Phil proud.

It was Baker who arranged a recent meeting between Hall of Famer Billy Williams and the 25-year-old center fielder. Williams first saw Corey in 1998, shortly after the high school senior had been drafted with the No. 3 pick. A nervous Patterson worked out with the Cubs in Atlanta and couldn't hit a thing that day. Williams told skeptical Cubs players and coaches to watch Patterson the next day.

Sure enough, Patterson had a boffo workout. What did Williams see that the others didn't? It was something simple: Rather than sulk after the unimpressive first workout, Patterson had jogged to the outfield and chatted up other players. Williams figured if the kid was smart enough to initiate conversation—to adapt to an intimidating environment—he'd be more comfortable the next day.

So that's what Williams discussed in their latest conversation: how to adapt. Meanwhile, Cubs coaches worked with Patterson on his bunting, his base stealing, his approach on certain pitch counts. Most of all, they did the positive-reinforcement thing. Forty-five points later . . .

Corey strikes out to start the third inning. As he walks back to the dugout, there's a slight grimace, nothing more. Of course, I've seen the same expression after he doubles off the wall. He shows nothing. Or does he?

"Absolutely," says Don.

"What's the tip-off?" I ask.

"I can't tell you. I won't tell you that."

"Is it something he does on the field?"

"No. But if you watch him close enough, you'll see it. It sticks out like a sore thumb."

If that's true, it's the smallest thumb in America.

Don pulls out his tickets. He wants to join his son.

"Keep in mind, this is Eric's day," he says. "And it's a big event for Corey to have his brother join him in the Cubs organization. I'm up here today not to see Corey play but to celebrate Eric becoming a Cub."

By the way, Corey strikes out in the fifth and flies out in the eighth. But no boos.

GAME 129

Saturday, August 28, 2004 . . . Astros 7, Cubs 6 . . . Wrigley Field . . . Stat of the game: Carlos Zambrano throws 125 pitches, his second-highest total of the season, in just 5⅔ innings. Zambrano later suggests he got squeezed by home plate umpire Eric Cooper. Didn't look that way from my seat, and none of the Cubs rush to support Zambrano's theory . . . The Cubs are 13-23 in the all-important one-run games.

We've all done dumb things in our lives.

I once informed the great Reggie Jackson that the only way he'd ever get a Gold Glove is if he spray-painted it himself. I still have burn marks on my ears from his F-bomb-a-thon the next day near the batting cage. I deserved it.

Then there's Kyle Farnsworth. If Dumb were a nation, Farnsworth would be the capital.

Today we learn that Farnsworth will be out a minimum of three weeks, probably more, because he decided to do a Paul Edinger and attempt a 35-

yarder with a dugout tunnel cooling fan after Friday's ninth-inning melt-down. He suffered a severe contusion and almost hyperextended his right knee. Now the knee is the size of his August ERA (19.29) and the Cubs have no choice but to place him on the 15-day disabled list.

The official reason as reported to league offices: right knee contusion and sprain. The unofficial reason: brain cramp.

Cynical Cubs followers will rejoice. In Farnsworth's last eight appearances, half of them in garbage time, the right-hander has pitched a total of 5⅓ innings and given up 14 earned runs, 14 hits, 3 walks, and hit a batter. Good riddance, right?

But Farnsworth, despite his obvious lack of confidence and frail mental state, is still worth having in your bullpen. He can still hit triple digits on the radar gun, and when he's right, as he was for most of the first half of the season, Farnsworth is a rally killer.

But when he's wrong . . .

"Obviously, the frustration yesterday got the better of him," says GM Jim Hendry.

Obviously. Also obvious is that the Cubs are clinging to a one-game wild-card lead with 33 games remaining. Farnsworth becomes the 14th different Cubs player to spend time on the DL, but more important, his absence puts additional pressure on a bullpen with its share of issues. LaTroy Hawkins has blown his last two save opportunities. Ryan Dempster is still finding his control. Jon Leicester has done an admirable job, but he's still a rookie. Mike Remlinger is pitching well but has to be used carefully. Kent Mercker pitched poorly in his last outing. Todd Wellemeyer gave up four hits, three runs, and a walk in his most recent appearance, which was in Omaha. And who knows when, or if, Joe Borowski will make it back from Triple-A Iowa.

Farnsworth is now on crutches, and so are the Cubs. Before Friday's loss, the Cubs had won eight of their previous nine games. Now they've lost two in a row and enter Sunday's final game against the Astros in desperate need of a win and tranquillity.

"We're going to find a way to piece it together and get it done, despite the injuries," says Hendry.

"I think he'll be strong and fresh when he comes back," says Baker.

What else do you expect them to say? Hendry and Baker have no choice but to try to turn Farnsworth's negative into a Cubs positive. So far the only positive I can think of has to do with Leicester: With Wellemeyer the newest player on the roster, Leicester doesn't have to schlep out to home plate for the first-pitch pregame ceremony any longer. Whooee!

Farnsworth is as enigmatic a player as I've seen. Physically gifted, mentally delicate. As is his custom, he declined all interview requests today. So we're left to judge him by his actions, not his reasons for those actions.

Reading between the carefully chosen words of Baker and Hendry, I think we've seen the last of Farnsworth in a Cubs uni this season and seasons to come. He is a pitching contradiction, the Cubs' version of Nuke LaLoosh. But unlike *Bull Durham*'s LaLoosh, Farnsworth never quite figures it out. At least, not here, or not yet.

We all do dumb things, but Farnsworth did his during a playoff run when, says Hendry, "it affects not just [Farnsworth], but everybody else." There wasn't any sympathy in his voice when he said it, either.

It has been a strange, even bizarre seven-day stretch, complete with threats of stadium closings, victories, beanballs, confrontations with opponents and umpires, bench clearings, a blowout loss, another one-run loss, a Houston surge, and Farnsworth in street clothes. Maybe that's why Baker, his daily pregame media update complete, sits on the dugout bench longer than usual, drops his head, and covers his face.

"I feel like I'm on the Raiders," he says of this week's events.

This makes sense. Cubs followers want what Al Davis wants, no matter the circumstances.

Just win, baby. With or without Farnsworth.

GAME 130

Sunday, August 29, 2004 . . . Astros 10, Cubs 3 . . . Wrigley Field . . . Stat of the game: Ten Astro runs today, 7 on Saturday, 15 on Friday. Geez, can't understand how the Cubs lost three in a row. . . . Stuff: Lance Berkman, Method actor, crumples to the ground in the eighth inning after a pitch by Mike Remlinger apparently strikes the Astros' cleanup hitter on the batting helmet. Remlinger, visibly upset by the accident, gives up three run-scoring singles and also walks in a run. But wait. Replays show Remlinger's high fastball completely missed Berkman's head and, at best, nicked his fingers. In other words, Berkman might have been stunned, but he wasn't hurt. Berkman later admits that Remlinger's pitch didn't hit his helmet. . . . The Cubs hit the road for a three-game series at depressing Olympic Stadium in Montreal, and then

three games at Florida, where meteorologists are bracing for the possible ar-
rival of another hurricane by week's end. Perfect.

The Cubs need to take a deep, calm, cleansing breath. Either that, or some Valium.

Losing streaks happen. But the Cubs continue to act as if the defeats are part of a Da Vinci Code-like conspiracy where greater, evil forces are at work.

This series alone featured the habitually pleasant Kent Mercker calling the press box to bitch about Chip Caray, later yelling at an umpire in the dugout tunnel, and then angrily chastising a reporter for writing about it. Huh? You'd think a veteran such as Mercker would have a few more layers of skin, but the pressures of playoff chases do funny things to people. Just ask Kyle Farnsworth.

Carlos Zambrano adds to the fun by clumsily suggesting that Roger Clemens got all the close calls in Saturday's Cubs loss. If Zambrano thinks he got screwed Saturday, just wait until his next start, when the umps thank him for his public comments.

Today the Cubs direct their anger at Berkman, who violates baseball etiquette by essentially faking an injury. That's fine; Berkman's act, as they say in clubhouses everywhere, was "chickenshit." But take away the five runs the Astros score in the eighth and the Cubs still are staring at an L.

The Cubs have lost three out of four, fall into a three-way tie for the wild-card spot, and do so with Kerry Wood, Zambrano, and Clement taking turns on the mound. So maybe it's time for the Cubs to quit worrying about the picture-in-picture stuff and start concentrating on important items, such as, well, themselves.

"Our team is a close-knit team," says Baker. "Our guys don't like people messing with us. We're a happy team. [To say otherwise], that's as far from the truth as you could be. You can be jumpy and be happy. But you're a lot happier, less jumpier when you win a lot of games."

If the Cubs were any more jumpy, they'd be in a padded room. Moises Alou has to lead the league in disputed strike calls and disgusted looks. Even mild-mannered Michael Barrett has had his recent share of nutty moments.

Of course, not everyone is bouncing off walls. Greg Maddux keeps his pulse at a playoff-prescribed steady pace. Corey Patterson does a nice job of staying on point. The same goes for Lee, who got hit by Dan Wheeler today but simply dropped his bat and jogged to first.

But it's clear the Cubs are feeling the heat. The heat of the dog days. The heat of a wild-card race. The heat of expectations placed on them by management, fans, and themselves. The resulting stress causes Mercker to microcritique WGN's Caray, and Baker to defend his relief pitcher's comments.

"There could be some merit to some of it, you know what I mean?" Baker says. "We don't have no crybabies here. And we're not a team that's going to complain unjustifiably, either. Plus, at times, it appears there's more focus on what we haven't done in general versus what we're doing and what we're accomplishing.

"I mean, if you were an outsider coming in, you would not think that we were in first place in the wild card. It would appear from the outside that you were seeing a team that's failing. We're not."

Exactly. So why do the Cubs insist on inventing phantom foes?

Chicago, as Baker accurately observes, is a blue-collar town. But it is not the country's toughest media town. Sportswriters and broadcasters in New York, Philadelphia, Boston, and perhaps even San Francisco, are appreciably more critical than those in Chicago. They're not homers, mind you, but they don't boo Santa, either.

This isn't the first time the Cubs have chafed at the comments of Caray and broadcast partner Steve Stone. Caray and Stone are approved by the team, but that doesn't mean they have to wave pom-poms in the booth. Sure, Stone can sound a bit superior at times, but here's the thing: He's usually right. And even Mr. Bleeds Cubby Blue, Ron Santo, has rightfully criticized this team, especially during this series. What, you're going to pretend the Astros didn't open up a few cans of whoop-ass on the Cubs?

But ask Baker if the Chicago media have treated his team fairly this season and you get "Uhmmmmmm . . . sometimes. Sometimes yeah, sometimes no."

Fair enough. There have been stories, especially during the Mark Prior injury saga, that were flat wrong. But this is the least adversarial collection of media I've seen, and that's not necessarily a bad thing. It's like the epithet Baker says he wants on his tombstone: "Firm but fair." That's how I'd describe the Chicago sports media, generally firm but fair.

"Our guys are a group of proud guys who really don't start nothing, but we don't take nothing, and that's all right," Baker says. "Would you rather have the Lovable Losers or the perception of the unhappy winners? I'd rather have the winners, all day long."

Everybody would, including this particular author doing a book on the 2004 Cubs. But it isn't going to happen if they don't quit sweating the dinky stuff. Never have so few wasted so much energy on Caray, Stone, sportswriters, umpires, and official scorers.

"This has been, by no means, an easy road," says Baker of the season. "It's never an easy road, but some roads [wind] more and are bumpier than others. This has been a winding, roller-coaster-type road. That why I think if we get to the playoffs, I think this team won't panic and will know how to respond to most any circumstance or situation we have."

But first they have to get there. On the greaseboard in the Cubs' clubhouse somebody has written, *Expect to Win!* It's a nice thought, but first the Cubs have to remember an essential truth.

There's no crying in baseball.

GAME 131

Monday, August 30, 2004 . . . Cubs 5, Montreal Expos 2 . . . Olympic Stadium . . . Cubs NL Central pennant flies: Second (72-59) . . . Stuff: Counting tonight's game, 22 of the Cubs' next 31 games are against teams with sub-.500 records. . . . The incredibly brave Lance Berkman, still in the Houston lineup despite not getting hit by a pitch, delivers a grand slam in the Astros' win against Cincinnati. . . . Ron Santo doesn't make the trip to Montreal. He's fine. He just wants to avoid the Customs hassle (do you think he's carrying?) and the time change. . . . Wild-card status: a half-game ahead.

Bill James is the godfather of sabermetrics because he was the first guy to look under the hood of baseball and tinker with its statistical engine. After he turned those numbers upside down, he found a way to explain them— and his new formulas and theories—so the average baseball lunkhead (me) could understand their importance.

I'm not the only one to notice he makes sense. James's collection of books are required reading for anyone who wants to take the Nestea plunge into the deep end of baseball's numbers. After all, there's a reason why the Boston Red Sox hired him as their senior baseball operations advisor.

I've always wondered why Ron Santo isn't in the Hall of Fame. If there were a category for Most Times Heart Broken, then Santo would lead it. He'll say his jersey number being retired in 2003 is his Hall of Fame, and, in a way, it is. But I've seen his face when fans approach him and ask, "Hey, Ronny, when those voters gonna come to their senses?" Santo shrugs his shoulders and offers a sad smile.

Can you blame him? All he did during his 15-year big league career was hit 342 home runs, knock in 1,331 runs, bat .277, lead the National League in walks four times, win five Gold Gloves, earn nine All-Star Game selections, hit .300 or better four times, bat cleanup for 10 of his 14 seasons with the Cubs, collect 2,254 hits—and do it all while dealing with diabetes. It's not his fault the Cubs never reached the playoffs during his tenure. In 1969, The Year of the Collapse, Santo hit .289, had 29 homers, and drove in 123 runs, a career best.

Teammates Billy Williams and Ernie Banks are in, but Santo still has his nose pressed to the Cooperstown window. I don't get it. I contact the esteemed James for his view. His response, via e-mail:

"I claim to be Santo's number one proponent. [But] I have a rule against getting involved in Hall of Fame campaigns. I get asked 500 times a year to weigh in on whether this guy or that turkey ought to be in the Hall of Fame, and I just have a policy of not expressing an opinion.

"Santo (and sometimes Minnie Minoso) are the only exceptions. To me it is clear and unequivocal that Santo is a Hall of Famer."

I push my luck and ask if James would consider a three- to five-paragraph explanation. Shortly thereafter, I hear the sweet sound of "You've got mail." It's the great James.

He writes:

"Third basemen have a special problem getting into the Hall of Fame. If you look, there are like one-half as many third basemen in the Hall of Fame as there are shortstops or second basemen. The special problem is this: that third basemen have to play offense AND defense. Ozzie Smith and Bill Mazeroski don't have Hall of Fame numbers, but people say, 'Well, of course they don't; they were fielders, not hitters.' And then they will rant at great length about the unfairness of electing people to the Hall of Fame based on hitting numbers and ignoring defensive contributions.

"In fact, there are as many second basemen in the Hall of Fame as players at the other positions, but . . . don't bother me with the facts while I am ranting.

"The position that actually gets screwed in the voting is third base. The reason this happens is that the Hall of Fame debate is by nature simplistic, while a third baseman's job is by nature complex.

"There are two sets of Hall of Fame *de facto* standards for hitters: one for outfielders/first basemen, one for middle infielders and catchers.

"Third basemen, who stand on the field a few feet from the shortstops, have very substantial defensive challenges—yet they still seem to be subject to the Hall of Fame standards of outfielders and first basemen. Yet, Santo MET those standards—he has batting numbers which are essentially the same as a good many Hall of Fame outfielders and first basemen, at least if you remember that he was playing in a period when the league batting average was often under .250. AND he was a five-time Gold Glove third baseman.

"Putting guys like George Kell, Freddie Lindstrom, and Tony Lazzeri in the Hall of Fame while you leave out Ron Santo is like putting Dalmatians, Palominos, and Siamese in the zoo while you let the lions roam the streets."

This makes perfect sense to me, but then again, I don't have a Hall of Fame vote. I know this: It's time for the voting zookeepers to leave a gate open for Santo.

GAME 132

Tuesday, August 31, 2004 . . . Expos 8, Cubs 0 . . . Olympic Stadium . . . Stat of the game: Mark Prior's ERA inches toward the unfathomable 5.00 as he gives up five runs in five innings. . . . Stuff: The Cubs acquire outfielder Ben Grieve from Milwaukee and catcher Mike DiFelice from Detroit for players to be named later. . . . As Hurricane Frances moves steadily toward the Florida coast, Cubs, Marlins, and Major League Baseball officials continue to discuss alternative plans for the three-game series that is scheduled to begin Friday evening. . . . Houston's gutty Lance Berkman, still recovering from a pitch that didn't hit him, homers in another Astros win.

Roger Baird's first year at Wrigley was Herman Franks's last. Baird was a part-time maintenance man in 1979 but eventually moved to the field and worked his way to head groundskeeper in 1995. Wrigley is the groundskeeping equivalent of Pamela Anderson. You've got lots to work with, but you better not screw it up.

Baird, 43, and his crew get it right every day. I know this because I usually get to the ballyard four hours before a game, which is two hours after the grounds crew begins applying its daily coat of makeup to Pamela. And it doesn't matter that the Cubs are in Montreal. The field gets TLC on a daily basis.

You should see these guys. They pamper this field as if it were a newborn. The only thing they don't do is burp it.

No detail is overlooked. No amount of work (and they put in at least 60 hours a week, with Baird putting in 70 to 80) is too much. Baird worked himself to the point of dehydration earlier in the season and missed two games while recovering in the hospital. That makes a grand total of four games Baird has missed because of illness since punching in for the Cubs.

A few weeks ago, Baird's father died. Guess who was back at work not long after the funeral? The old man would have been proud.

The first thing I'll do is put up the flags on the foul poles. That's the first thing I do every morning, put up the Banks, Williams, Santo flags.

My favorite thing is coming in on a Sunday when the team is not home. I'll run the sprinklers, cut the grass, maybe paint the foul line by myself. I'll walk around the field checking things. It's real peaceful, a beautiful place.

Ivy, it can be tricky. There's a lot of trimming involved. A lot of people don't know how many man-hours are put into those vines. They grow quite a bit. They're trimmed every single time the team goes on the road. It takes like two days to hand-trim them with, basically, a pair of scissors. You cut the top, then a straight line all the way around. Then you trim around all the numbers [on the outfield wall], around all the doors, and then weeding at the bottom. A lot of work.

I have two kids, Danielle and Roger. They're 18 and 15. A couple of years ago, I think they realized why, from March to October, I'm not around too much. Before, I think it hurt them a lot when Dad wasn't around. Or when I got home I was tired, or I was falling asleep on them. I think they're at that age now where they appreciate and understand why I wasn't around as much as I should have been.

During the off-season, we work on the field until the latest we possibly can, which, if we get lucky, can mean Thanksgiving or maybe even

Christmas. We try to get the field in the best shape possible before winter really rolls in. Once that first frost or snow comes, we try to keep everybody off the field. But we don't cover it.

We've been using the checkerboard pattern in the grass forever. It was here before me. It's just something that when people come out to a game they expect to see that checkerboard pattern. We'll cut it 1 ⅝ in the outfield, 1 ½ inches in the infield.

Now everybody is going to school, learning all the types of grasses. But there's a lot more than just knowing your grass. You better know the clays, how to do mounds, the home plate areas.

Believe me, I walk in this door every day and I appreciate being here. It's a pretty special job. I know there's a lot of people who would like to be in my position, and I'm thankful every day. But it's something that you've got to love. You've got to love what you do, and you better love the game of baseball.

Wrigley itself, I don't think it ever should be changed too much. I do really believe in its tradition.

SEPTEMBER

· ·

GAME 133

Wednesday, September 1, 2004 . . . Cubs 2, Expos 1 . . . Olympic Stadium . . . Cubs NL Central pennant flies: Second (73-60) . . . Stuff: San Francisco loses (thank you, Colorado), San Diego loses (we love the Cardinals), but Houston, led by the courageous Lance Berkman, wins its sixth consecutive game. So does Florida (The Curse lives), which means the Marlins and Astros remain an annoying three games behind the Cubs in the wild-card race. . . . Corey Patterson goes 0-for-Montreal and strikes out six times in 13 at-bats. . . . Wild-card status: one game ahead.

Jimmy Bank's morning begins at 8:15, when his wife calls and wakes him up in his room at the LeCentre Sheraton in Montreal's downtown district. It isn't a long conversation, mostly because the Cubs' traveling secretary is preoccupied by another woman more than 1,400 miles away.

Frances.

The not-so-little lady is a hurricane the size of Texas and is shuffling directly toward the southeastern coast of Florida, which, as the National League schedule would have it, is exactly where the Cubs are supposed to fly after tonight's game. Frances is a Category 4 hurricane—the second-deadliest rating on accepted meteorological scales—packing winds between 131 and 155 mph, causing storm surges anywhere from 13 to 18 feet, and capable of doing "extreme structural damage." It is expected to reach the Florida coastline perhaps as early as Friday evening—when the Cubs' three-game series against the Marlins is to begin—or as late as Sunday. No one knows for sure, especially Bank.

Bank, who has been a big league traveling secretary for 26 years (the last 12 with the Cubs), is in charge of coordinating all things connected with getting the Cubs from one place to another. Once there, he tends to their ticket, per diem, and hotel needs. He is Mr. Trains, Planes, and Automobiles, as well as the unofficial Cubs concierge.

Today is different. Today, as he looks out onto the Boulevard René-Lévesque West, Bank is faced with arranging as many as four different travel scenarios, all depending on the whim and winds of that other woman. Making matters worse—and Bank is the first to say the Cubs' travel inconveniences pale next to the dangers of those bracing for Frances's arrival—is the fact that the team is in a foreign country, which means Customs and a quirky airport curfew that prohibits no outbound flights past midnight. With the Cubs-Expos game scheduled to begin at 7:05 P.M. local time, this could get dicey.

Bank watches CNN for Hurricane Frances updates and speaks at 10 o'clock with Cubs president Andy MacPhail, who is in Montreal with the team. MacPhail has been in contact with the Major League Baseball offices, as well as Florida Marlins officials. Two issues are being discussed: Can the Cubs safely make the trip to south Florida? Will Frances force the cancellation of Friday's opener, Saturday's game, Sunday's game, or the entire series?

With those questions as the starting points, Bank begins to sort the travel possibilities in his mind.

Plan A. If Frances suddenly veers away from Florida, the Cubs are likely to follow their original itinerary, which is to fly to Fort Lauderdale after tonight's game and set up headquarters at the Marriott Marina Hotel, located about 45 minutes from Pro Player Stadium. Thursday is an off day on the Cubs' schedule.

Plan B. Fly into Fort Lauderdale in the wee hours of Thursday, then fly to Fort Myers on the west coast of Florida.

Plan C. Fly from Montreal to Chicago after the game.

Plan D. Circumstances prevent the Cubs from leaving Montreal after tonight's game, which means rebooking the hotel, et cetera.

Bank begins working the phones. His travel case includes his most prized possessions: a pair of battered, three-inch-thick black leather personal phone books now held together by clear packing tape. There are nearly three decades' worth of numbers for players, coaches, managers, front-office personnel, minor leaguers, scouts, clubhouse personnel, security agents, hotels, limo companies, truck companies, airlines, charter bus companies, customs officials, and anybody else Bank has done business with.

"If I lose these," he says, tapping the taped-up phone books, "I quit. I never throw phone numbers away."

The news is not good in Fort Lauderdale, where Bank's hotel contact tells him guests might be evacuated from the property as early as Thursday.

Bank calls the Ritz-Carlton in Naples, which is just south of Fort Myers, and says the magic words to a corporate contact: *"This is important."* Bank doesn't say it often, but when he does, he expects cooperation. He gets it— the Ritz-Carlton will make 53 rooms available for the Cubs.

Bank fires up his Toshiba laptop and checks Accuweather.com for another Frances update. No change—the hurricane is still plodding toward Florida.

By early afternoon, it is apparent that Friday evening's game against the Marlins has no chance of being played. Bank makes his way to Olympic Stadium, which is about eight miles from the team hotel. Once there, he meets with several players, who make it clear the team wants to return to Chicago rather than attempt a flight into south Florida.

Still, no official decision has been made by MLB, the Marlins, and Cubs management. Canceling the games creates a scheduling nightmare, especially during the last month of the season and in the middle of a wild-card race. But Frances isn't concerned about baseball—or anything else, for that matter.

Bank starts using up serious minutes on his Nokia cell. He calls bus companies, truck companies, and hotels in both Chicago and Florida, just in case. He calls new Wrigley Stadium operations director Mike Hill and tells him the Cubs' first choice is to return home, which means the stadium parking lot gates have to be unlocked and the clubhouse made accessible.

Then he has to do his regular job, which is to coordinate ticket distribution for the players (less than 100 requests in Montreal, compared to more than 200 in, say, Milwaukee) and tend to player needs (Ben Grieve needs a hotel and rental car in Chicago).

At 8 o'clock, Bank receives word from MacPhail: The Cubs are going home after the game. Bank addresses the players and tells them they absolutely, positively must be out of the clubhouse and on the bus 30 minutes after the game. The players usually have an hour to shower and dress on a getaway night, but because of the airport curfew the Cubs can't linger.

A police escort is arranged for the Cubs' charter bus. The rooms at the Ritz-Carlton are canceled. Limo services back in Chicago have been alerted. Everything is set, except . . .

The game goes into extra innings.

The game ends at 10:18 local time. No way will the Cubs make it in time. A takeoff extension is negotiated between the airport and United. The Cubs have until 1 A.M.—otherwise they're not going anywhere.

The team is on the bus by 10:50 and at Dorval by 11:15 or so. The players and staff go through Customs without incident (thank Bank for that one—he called Customs officials two months ago to learn the latest rules), but the loading of equipment on the plane by the ground handlers is taking much too long. Bank looks at his watch for the millionth time. It's going to be close.

At exactly 12:57 (Bank checks), the United Airlines Airbus 8320 takes off. About two and a half hours later, the Cubs arrive in Chicago.

MacPhail compliments Bank, as do several other members of the traveling party. None of the players say a peep. Bank doesn't take it personally.

"They're here to play baseball and I'm here to get them to and from the ballgame," he says.

Bank doesn't bother driving to his home in suburban Milwaukee. Instead, he gets a room at the downtown Chicago Hampton Inn. Sleep comes easily.

GAME 134

Monday, September 6, 2004 ... Cubs 9, Expos 1 ... Wrigley Field ... Stuff: Not much happening with the Cubs these days, other than Hurricane Frances wiping out their series in Florida, Kent Mercker getting suspended for three games (and appealing), Sammy Sosa suffering from bursitis of the hip (and missing today's game), Steve Stone getting hassled by Cubs players, and the wild-card race becoming tighter than Carlos Zambrano in compression shorts. ... One Cubs player begins a dugout discussion of Hurricane Frances with "I'm no geologist, but ..." The Houston Astros have won 10 in a row since the Roy Oswalt-Michael Barrett dustup at Wrigley.

Wade Vergon's speech is slurred and his legs don't work so well, which is why he spends his time in a dinged-up, battery-operated black wheelchair parked on the Addison side of Wrigley. You can't miss him. Hell, you can barely get around him, thanks to the stadium wall directly behind him and a sidewalk that narrows at the exact spot Vergon sits in his wheelchair.

Of course, you can do what I've done in seasons past: stare through him as you power-walk by. I mean, he's a panhandler, right?

Today I stopped. I wanted to meet the guy in the wheelchair.

His handshake made my fingers sing soprano. He had the Todd Walker stubble look working, and full Cubs attire. Propped against his chest was a white cardboard sign and a handwritten plea: *Please Help. Go Cubs.* In his left hand he held a white plastic pitcher. It was empty.

"Ten years," he says, his voice thick.

"Ten years you've been coming here?"

"Ten years," he says. "The L is right there." A long pause as he struggles to say the words. "All the people . . . walk by."

The control knob on his wheelchair is held together by duct tape. One of the wheels looks like it's moments from a blowout. He catches me staring.

"I bought this wheelchair," he says. "I bought clothes. I fixed my teeth." Another long pause. "I don't waste the money I make here. . . . I don't drink. I *don't* drink. I use the money strictly for good stuff."

For a night game, he gets here by 3 P.M. Nobody has ever tried stealing his money. Nobody has tried shooing him away. If they do, they'll have to answer to a certain Chicago Police Department sergeant who wrote his name and badge number on the back of Wade's cardboard sign.

I ask him what's the most someone ever dropped into his plastic pitcher.

"A hundred dollars."

"Geez, a hundred dollars?"

He holds up three fingers. Long pause. "Three times."

Someone walks by and tosses 35 cents into the pitcher as if Wade were a tollbooth basket.

"Thanks," he says.

The man nods.

I don't have a C-note, but I dig into my jeans and give him what I can find: five ones. Wade counts the bills and then nearly crushes the ulnar bone in my right hand.

I've got 15 more regular-season home dates. From now on, no more crossing the street.

GAME 135

Tuesday, September 7, 2004 . . . Expos 7, Cubs 6 . . . Wrigley Field . . . Stuff: As part of the Hurricane Frances MLB makeup plan, the Cubs will play a Friday doubleheader against the Marlins at Wrigley, and another one September 20 at Pro Player Stadium. That means 29 games in 28 days. . . . Houston, led by the inspirational Lance Berkman, wins its 11th in a row. . . . As the Cubs do their pregame stretching, a pair of bikini-clad women try to get their attention by dancing on one of the right-field rooftop houses. Several weeks ago, the same duo was spotted dancing topless on the rooftop. The consensus of those who watched: They're real, and they're spectacular.

Is there a more famous greasy spoon/bar than the Billy Goat Tavern? Presidents (George, and George Dubya), vice presidents (Al Gore), Pulitzer Prize winners (Mike Royko), actors (Wheaton's own John Belushi), and assorted dignitaries and celebrities all have found their way to the Chicago institution at 430 N. Lower Michigan Ave.

It is the bar that time forgot. The cash registers are straight out of *It's a Wonderful Life*. The smell of burgers ("Double, the best.") is as thick as proprietor Sam Sianis's Greek accent.

I love this place. Two of my sisters-in-law worked here. My father-in-law, a former Chicago police commander, used to "borrow" a CPD squad car to pick up turkeys for the annual Billy Goat Thanksgiving dinner for the homeless. And my wife would rather have a double and a frosty here than dine at Charlie Trotter's.

Belushi and *Saturday Night Live* buddies Dan Aykroyd and Bill Murray gave it icon status ("Cheezborger! Cheezborger!"), but original owner William "Billy Goat" Sianis, Sam's uncle, provided the most intriguing sports curse this side of the Bambino.

Cubs legends have scoffed at it. Managers have mocked it. Cubs executives have tried to ignore it. But "The Curse of the Billy Goat" endures because the Cubs' streak of non-World Series appearances and championships endures with it.

I walk in near the end of lunch rush. Sianis, who was eight years old when he came here from Greece in 1955, is standing behind the counter. As usual, business is good.

Sianis isn't a big man, but I would think twice about being on the wrong side of his fists. He wears gray pants and a white shirt with the sleeves rolled up to his Popeye elbows. He points to a table near a side wall covered with Chicago newspaper clippings and headlines from decades past. One headline immediately catches my attention.

"Cubs Hex Clings On," it reads.

Between answering phone calls, writing checks to deliverymen, and greeting a handful of Chicago's finest, Sianis offers an oral history of The Curse.

First of all, this started back in 1945. My uncle tried to take the goat to Wrigley Field for the World Series between Detroit and the Chicago Cubs. He had two tickets and they refused to let him in. My uncle says, "I've got tickets. The goat has tickets. Why not?" And they said they can't have animals in the ballpark. So my uncle says, "Ask Mr. Wrigley."

Somebody went up there, told Mr. Wrigley that my uncle was down there, a billy goat was down there, they have tickets, and they want to get into the game. Mr. Wrigley says, "No goat allowed. The goat smell. We don't want any smelly goat in there."

My uncle went back to his tavern at 1855 W. Madison. That was the old Billy Goat there. He stayed there, and later on the Cubs lost. Then he sent a telegram to Mr. Wrigley after the Cubs lost the World Series (in seven games, marking the seventh consecutive time the Cubs failed to win the Series). It says, "Who smells now?" I've got the telegram right over there, behind the bar.

Then people say that my uncle said, "As long as I live, the Cubs, they're not going to win any World Series here." But my uncle, he never told me that. He always tell me that the Cubs are going to suffer "because of what they did to my goat." That I remember.

In 1969, the Cubs have the best chance to win the pennant and the World Series. I remember, sitting right here was David Condon, Mike Royko, Bill Granger, and the Cubs were seven games ahead with 17 games left. And everybody, they were kidding my uncle: "Billy Goat, that's it. The hex is done. The Cubs are going to win the pennant and head to the World Series."

My uncle says with a smile, "Not yet. Not yet. Not yet. Not yet."

So they play, and Don Young dropped a ball in center field. After that, they lost nine out of 10 and the Mets won the pennant that year.

In 1973, I tried to take the goat. Dave Condon, myself, and the goat go in a limo. We had tickets. We get out at Wrigley Field, we walk around with the goat outside. Then Ferguson Jenkins, a pitcher at that time, came out, pet the goat, and he asked me to bring the goat in. But they say no, it's not allowed. So we walk around. But the Cubs are unfair to the goat. They're unfair to the goat. So we left, came down here.

At that time, they were about three games ahead. It was Fourth of July. Then I left for Greece for three, four weeks. When I came back, the Cubs were about four games out of first place. People call down here and say it's the billy goat, it's the billy goat. They swear at me because the Cubs lost. But the Cubs wouldn't let the goat in.

In 1984, they invited me to go there with the goat. I took the goat over there and we won on Opening Day. We won the division and we play San Diego. I went to the playoff games with the goat. We sat out in right field with the goat. We won both games. Then the Cubs left here for San Diego. People from San Diego call me and say, "If you bring the goat here, we're going to kill the goat."

I didn't go, and the Cubs lost three games. Everybody was disappointed. I was sitting here watching the game—the goat was here watching the game—and the Cubs lost. I left the goat here and went home. I was so upset I couldn't find my house. I drive around and I can't find my house. I was so upset because we had the win right there.

Finally, 1997, the Cubs were losing 14 straight games to start the season. So some guy from the radio, he call me and says, "Sam, let's go to the ball-game tomorrow morning and bring the goat." At 9 o'clock he picked me up at Billy Goat, we went down to Wrigley Field. And seminary kids come in from Milwaukee and come to the gate. And he asked them to bring a goat from their farm. So they bring a goat. I had to dress up the goat. We walked around saying, "We got the goat. We got the goat. We got the goat."

Finally, we walked to right field. There was a lady there by the door. I show her the tickets. For me and the goat. She says, "If you bring in the goat, I'm going to arrest you." I say, "Look, let the goat in and then arrest the goat."

So finally John McDonough, he's a good friend of mine, he come out and says, "OK, bring the goat in." Myself, Ernie Banks, and the goat go in. We walked in, walked around the field. It was against Cincinnati.

Then we came back here and the place was packed. All the [TV] channels were down here. So finally the Cubs lead, 5-2, top of the ninth, two outs, and they strike the guy out. Cubs win. I say, "Buy everybody a drink on the house."

But after that, 19, uh, 98, I try to take the goat in [for the NL Divisional Series]. They open the gate, and as soon as the goat cross the gate at the right-field wall, the guy comes over and says, "You take the goat and get out of here." They kicked me out. I went out, came down here, and the Cubs lost to Atlanta. Three in a row they lose those.

Then last year I went with the goat on Opening Day, then two games in a row—the sixth game, the seventh game [of the NLCS]. I went there, but they wouldn't let me in. And the Cubs lost. That was the best chance they had to win the pennant.

And now, I don't think they were right to blame the guy [Steve Bartman] who tried to catch that ball. It could have been anybody. And what about the ball hit to the shortstop? They score eight runs one inning. It was like nobody was in the field.

And you know another bad thing the Cubs did? Why did they destroy that [Bartman] ball? They should have taken that ball and put it in Harry Caray's hand at his statue at Wrigley Field, or in Jack Brickhouse's hand at his statue. People could say, "Let's go see Bartman's ball." But they blow it up.

Now nobody call me from the Cubs. Nobody invite me. It's too late now. They're 16½ games out.

But you know what? If they ask me, I would go to Wrigley Field. I'd find a goat.

(No call comes today. The Cubs lose.)

GAME 136

Wednesday, September 8, 2004 ... Expos 6, Cubs 0 ... Wrigley Field ... Stat of the game: The loss drops the Cubs a half-game behind Houston in the wild-card race (OK, no more Lance Berkman cracks—the Astros have won 12 in a row). . . . Wonder if Nomar Garciaparra notices the Boston Red Sox have won 14 of their last 15 to move within two games of the New York Yankees.

And then, as Bill Murray says in *Stripes*, depression set in.

This was a game so devoid of Cubs highlights that you wanted to chug a frosted mug of Clorox and send it down with a Lysol chaser. In fact, I'm still trying to choose my favorite Cubs moment.

Was it Moises Alou getting doubled off second (again) on a fly ball to right? Was it Sammy Sosa taking a step in before realizing Maicer Izturis's fly ball was going to sail over his head for a "double"? Was it a poorly executed pitchout play where Paul Bako threw the ball into center field? Was it Mike Remlinger's second consecutive Kyle Farnsworth-like outing, where he gave up a two-run homer? Or was it the hilarious Fox Sports Net graphic asking viewers to choose the best bullpen in the league—and list-ing the Cubs as a finalist?

The scorecards being sold at Wrigley tonight feature a beer ad near the bottom of the front cover. *OPTIMISM. Now that's Old Style.* Problem is, it's hard to draw a smiley face on a team that just lost two out of three to an Expos squad that has the second-worst record in the NL.

Montreal starter Scott Downs, who was traded by the Cubs for Rondell White in 2000, entered the game with a 2-5 record and a 7.22 ERA (9.98 in his last three starts). He left with his first-ever complete game and shutout.

But it wasn't just Downs who messed with the Cubs. It was that woman again—Hurricane Frances.

About 4:20 today, as I'm waiting for Dusty Baker in the interview room, I turn on one of the TVs near the side wall. The Channel 7 meteorologist is explaining why we have whitecaps on Lake Michigan today: strong NNE winds caused by the rotation of what was once Hurricane Frances as it makes its way up and across the Northeast. Here at Wrigley, that means the scoreboard flags are pointing directly toward home plate at a stiff 16 mph. In other words, add at least an imaginary 30 feet to the distance between home plate and the left-field and center-field walls.

This isn't good news for the Cubs. The Cubs are mostly a lineup of right-handed home run hitters with uppercut swings. Maybe this would be a good time to adjust.

"The best thing to try to do is just hit it," says Dusty Baker, scoffing at the notion of a "wind" swing. "We have some guys having trouble enough hitting sometimes, much less trying to change the trajectory of the hit."

The Cubs enter the game leading the NL in home runs (198). They're 62-34 in games in which they hit at least one dinger, 12-27 when they don't. Make it 12-28.

The preliminary forecast for Friday's huge doubleheader against the vis-iting Marlins: The winds will reverse, blowing from the south or southeast.

Hold the Clorox.

GAMES 137, 138

Friday, September 10, 2004 . . . Florida Marlins 7, Cubs 0—Cubs 11, Marlins 2 . . . Wrigley Field . . . Cubs NL Central pennant flies: Tie-Second (75-63) . . .

Stat of the doubleheader: Marlins starter Carl Pavano leaves four tickets for Steve Bartman. Pavano was the starter in Game 6 of the NLCS—The Bartman Game. The tickets go unused. . . . Stuff: Dusty Baker says he spent part of his off day in Lincoln Park watching the squirrels. The tranquillity lasts until someone asks about the perception of the Cubs as complainers. "Let's put it in the grave," he says "We ain't no whiners." . . . Bill Murray is in the stands. . . . Cubs great Andre Dawson, now a special assistant with the Marlins, sings, "Take Me Out to the Ballgame." Afterward, he tosses his Cubs cap to the crowd. It lands on a rafter and stays there. Figures . . . I don't think Steve Stone and Kerry Wood will be sharing a table at Gibson's anytime soon. Wood rips Stone on ESPN Radio-1000 . . . Wild-card status: a three-way tie with San Francisco and Houston.

This one is going to hurt a little bit.

Marlins president David Samson pulls up a chair in the Wrigley media dining room as the Cubs are getting whooped in Game 1 of the doubleheader. He has a George Hamilton tan and his beard stubble is straight out of the Don Johnson Collection, circa *Miami Vice.* On the left breast pocket of his silk shirt is a Marlins logo complete with "2003 World Series Champions" stitching.

It gets worse.

On his right ring finger is the largest, single most obnoxious piece of jewelry ever slipped over a knuckle. Samson's World Series ring looks like a semi-truck lugnut dipped in diamonds. Police could set up roadblocks with these things.

"Can I hold it for a second?" I say.

"Yeah," says Samson, who already has done the same today for inquiring Cubs fans seated near the Marlins' traveling party of executives and elite season-ticket holders here for the four-game series. "Look at the work on it. It's an incredible ring."

Sure it is, in a Liberace, Run DMC way. The 14-karat-gold monstrosity weighs 115 grams and includes 228 diamonds, 13 rubies, and a special teal diamond in the engraved Marlins logo.

I look at the side of the ring.

Samson. 2003. 91 Pres 71.

"91 Pres 71?" I say.

"Our record," Samson says proudly. "That's everything to me, because I predicted the number of wins before the season started."

Wonderful. We're so happy for you.

Last October, Samson sat in the first row behind the Marlins' dugout for each of the NLCS games at Wrigley. In the bottom of the seventh inning of Game 6, with the Cubs six outs away from their first World Series since 1945, Samson walked down the concourse and stood outside the entrance to the Marlins' clubhouse. He called his wife, Cindi, to tell her she wouldn't be coming to Chicago for Game 7 after all.

"I was standing on a ramp just outside the door," he says. "People were going crazy. They were screaming on the streets. Screaming in the upper deck. Crazy. I said, 'Honey, it's been a great year. We should be very proud. I'm trying to think of what I should say to [owner] Jeffrey [Loria] and the players when I speak to them. I'll just congratulate them on a great year.' My wife said, 'David, get your ass down in your seat. This game is not over.'

"So I walked through the clubhouse and [catcher] Mike Redmond is getting a cup of coffee. And I looked at him and I said, 'Mike, how 'bout it?' And he just nodded at me like, 'We'll take care of it.'"

Samson all but giggles when recalling the eighth-inning Marlins comeback. He remembers the first-pitch hits, the Alex Gonzalez error ("That's a play he makes 99 and a half times out of a 100"), the morgue-like quality to Wrigley as Florida took the lead.

"One more thing to note that I will never forget," says Samson. "The bus pulled in before Game 6—I was with the players on the bus—and they were selling Cubs 2003 'National League Champion' T-shirts before Game 6 started. Selling them on the street across from our gate entrance. Our players looked at those and it got them going.

"Those shirts were there before Game 6. They were not there before Game 7."

Samson doesn't mention the Bartman incident or the Curse of the Billy Goat.

"I don't believe in those," he says. "You make your own destiny. I don't even want to say it publicly, but if you have self-fulfilling prophecy, well, self-fulfilling prophecies are a very powerful thing. And they're a very convenient thing as well. And I don't mean that in any other way, except to say that two-out base hits are far more important than a curse."

And if Bartman walked into the media dining room right now?

"I'd say, 'I'm sorry. You had nothing to do with us winning and the Cubs losing. You did what anybody would do. It's a very good lesson that your life can change in the snap of a finger.'"

After the Game 7 victory, the Marlins executives eventually returned to the downtown Westin, where they donned bathrobes and watched themselves on the 1 A.M. *SportsCenter* in a hotel suite. Later, the party moved to the Westin bar, where hotel security tried to boot Samson out of the lounge because of his terry-cloth attire. Samson wouldn't budge.

The team hotel during this weekend's series? The Westin. In fact, the Marlins insisted the charter bus driver take the same exact route from the hotel to Wrigley.

"It all came back in two seconds," Samson says. "It's great. It's a forever memory."

Today was the sweetest kind of déjà vu for the Marlins. As they walked into Wrigley's cramped visitors' clubhouse, several players said they could still smell the champagne. That's nice. I know some Cubs fans who would be more than happy to scrub the Marlins' nostrils with wire brushes if the scent becomes too much.

Samson hugged Derrek Lee before the game. It doesn't matter that Lee now wears a Cubs uni.

"To me," says Samson, "he's frozen as a Marlin."

The same goes for Andre Dawson, whose Cubs roots go only so deep. Dawson was presented with a Marlins World Series ring and, says Samson, wears it every day.

"You realize what sort of pain you've inflicted on this city, on this team, don't you?" I ask.

"I just think we're the latest infliction," Samson says. "I don't think you can say we're solely responsible for the level of despondency that pervades the city."

If he only knew.

GAME 139

Saturday, September 11, 2004 . . . Cubs 5, Marlins 2 . . . Wrigley Field . . . Stuff: The scoreboard flag flies at half-mast in memory of 9/11. . . . The Curse Lives: Nomar Garciaparra leaves midway through the game with a groin strain.

The lineup card posted just outside the Cubs' weight room provides a shocker.

Sammy Sosa is batting sixth.

The Gladiator hasn't batted sixth since Bill Clinton's first term in office. To the political atheists, that's 10 years.

The move makes sense, but it still looks weird on the card—like Matt Clement without his chin beard. Sosa has four hits in his last 20 at-bats. He's missed 34 games this season because of hip and sneezing injuries. He's batting .254.

Watching him these days is like watching time-lapse photography: It's as if Sosa is aging before your eyes. He still has the same game-day mannerisms—the exaggerated arching of the back, the tapping of the bat knob on the catcher and home plate umpire during the first at-bat, the sprint to right field, the ritualistic splashing of coffee on the dugout steps, the hustle—but not the vintage Sosa numbers, except, of course, for the Ks.

A day earlier, he struck out twice in four at-bats, prompting the now-predictable boos from Cubs faithful. He says he feels fine. That's what he told Dusty Baker, who can only assume Sosa's troubles are the result of those boos, of confidence issues.

"Some of it is," says Baker, "and some of it is he's trying too hard. Sometimes he's trying to hit an eight-run home run."

Shortly before today's game, Steve Stone sees Sosa on the field.

"It looks like both of us are taking some shots," says Stone.

"That's OK," says Sosa.

Stone, who has been the frequent target of some Cubs players' ire this season, has a soft spot for Sosa. It was Sosa, says Stone, who helped rescue baseball from a near-terminal case of the dulls in 1998, when he and Mark McGwire engaged in a season-long home-run-hitting contest.

But Stone's respect for Sosa extends beyond the field. About eight years ago, Sosa approached Stone and said he had a problem with some of the broadcaster's on-air comments. So Sosa and Stone walked down the dugout tunnel and ducked around a corner for a private chat. When it was done, they shook hands and that was that.

"Sammy's been great ever since," says Stone. "He dealt with it man to man. He didn't do it in the newspapers. He didn't make it personal. He did it privately."

So maybe it shouldn't come as a surprise that during the recent anti-Stone sniping by several Cubs, Sosa has come to the rescue. On the team charter, it is Sosa who always stops by Stone's seat to shake his hand or put a hand on his shoulder—just to show the others that Stone has at least one friend on this team.

Today Sosa arrives at the plate in the eighth inning with the Cubs trailing, 2-1, and Neifi Perez on second with no outs. Sosa has already struck out twice in the game, already heard the boos ping away at his ear flap.

This time he strokes a single, scoring Perez and tying the score. Sosa eventually ends up at third with two outs and the bases loaded. During a moment's break in the action, you can see Sosa put his hands together in prayer and look upward. Sure enough, Lee lines a double in the gap and Sosa scores what turns out to be the winning run.

No one seems to care about lineup cards.

GAME 140

Sunday, September 12, 2004 . . . Marlins 11, Cubs 1 . . . Wrigley Field . . . Stat of the game: Who knows? I quit keeping score on this stinker after the Marlins take a 7-0 lead in the sixth. . . . Stuff: When a ball slices foul into the stands behind the left-field line, Miguel Cabrera playfully mimics Alou's 2003 NLCS Bartman-related tantrum. Be careful about messing with that voodoo, Miguel.

Tom "Otis" Hellmann, the Cubs' clubhouse manager, had prepared everything for the celebration that October 14 night. He had purchased the champagne, helped prepare the clubhouse stage, taped the protective plastic sheeting to each Cubs locker. Then he waited for five more outs and a celebration for the ages.

And waited . . . and waited . . . and waited.

By the time the eighth inning of Game 6 had come to a merciful end, the 2003 NLCS between the Cubs and Marlins was as good as tied, the plastic sheeting removed, and the chilled bubbly pulled from the ice and repacked for the next evening. You know what happened in Game 7, but do you know what happened to Hellmann's champagne?

As Florida put the finishing touches on a 9-6 victory to advance to the World Series, Hellmann decided there was only one right thing to do with the bubbly: He sold it to the Marlins.

"One of the toughest things I ever did was send that champagne over to the other side," he says. "But that's what happened to it. They bought our champagne."

Now he has a new mantra as the Cubs try to squeeze into the playoffs.

"Let's drink it ourselves," he says.

Hellmann has been the home clubhouse manager and unofficial Cubs cheerleader for the last five seasons. Before that, he spent 17 years in the visitors' clubhouse at Wrigley. He came to Chicago in 1983 after working eight seasons as an assistant home clubbie with the Cincinnati Reds.

"I started doing this when I was 17," he says. "For the Reds I got eight bucks a day, $12 for a doubleheader. The check wasn't very much."

Hellmann actually made his on-field debut as a Reds ballboy. His first job: get a ball signed by Johnny Bench and Pete Rose for then-U.S. vice president Gerald Ford. Once the game against the Atlanta Braves began, Hellmann was assigned to a spot alongside the left-field line.

"First inning of my first game of work . . . Hank Aaron hits the home run to tie Babe Ruth," says Hellmann. "He played left field, so at the bottom of the inning I was the first person to toss a ball with him after he hit the home run to tie Babe Ruth."

His hiring by the Cubs was another right-place, right-time moment.

"I just got lucky," he says. "I sent out a résumé a couple of times and the Cubs needed somebody after the Tribune took over. I was available."

The Cubs paid him $100 a week for six months that first year. That's $2,400. The rest he made on tips working the visitors' clubhouse.

The rules were simple enough: Be there on time. Take care of the ballplayers. The more you do for them, the more they'll do for you.

Nothing has changed. Hellmann and assistant clubbie Gary Stark, who started as a Cubs batboy, tend to every Cubs need. For today's game, they were here at 6:30 to prepare the breakfast spread of eggs, waffles, grits, potatoes, bacon, and sausage. Then they put together a lunch spread. Later, they'll start preparing for the dinner cycle.

"Then we make sure the place is clean for them when they come in," Hellmann says. "Hopefully, it will be a happy clubhouse after a win. We'll high-five them all, tell them, 'Great game.' Or if they lose, you walk around quiet and get your work done."

Today is a You-Can-Hear-the-Cubs-Drop-in-the-Standings day.

Generally speaking, each Cub pays about $40 a day for clubhouse services. The "dues" are paid monthly, though some players pay at the All-Star break or even at the end of the season, which can play hell with a clubby's checking account. "You learn how to budget your money," says Hellman, who is married and has three children.

You also learn how to pamper. Hellmann's staff, which also includes his brother Tim, Rich Rupp, and John Vremis, have been known to arrange for players' cars to be repaired while the Cubs are traveling. Remember, the more you do for them . . .

Hellmann has it easier on the road, where the visiting clubbies provide the meals and wash the unis. Instead, he arranges for Baker's luggage to be delivered immediately to the manager's hotel room. Then he'll go to the stadium and set up Baker's office. He'll also inspect the players' unis for rips. Hellmann keeps an entire kit of extra uniform material and a contact list of seamstresses in every NL city for emergency sewing duties.

"You don't grow up wanting to be an equipment man, just like people don't grow up wanting to be accountants," says Hellmann, who lives three blocks from Wrigley. "It's just something that happens. But I love my job. And I know this: I know my biggest thrill is yet to come. Hopefully, it will be this year."

Better yet, maybe it will involve the popping of cork.

GAME 141

Monday, September 13, 2004 . . . Cubs 7, Pirates 2 . . . Wrigley Field . . . Stat of the game: Sammy Sosa's first-inning homer gives him 30 for the year, and marks his 10th consecutive season of 30 or more dingers. . . Stuff: Greg Maddux wins No. 14.

Meanwhile, on the South Side . . .

I stiff the Cubs today and drive down to Sox Park. (I'm sorry, I just can't say, "The Cell." That would be like calling Cubs Park "The Rig.") That's where the Marlins, who cling to the NL wild-card race like a Yorkshire to a postal worker, play the nomadic Montreal Expos.

Not since 1998 has a home team had to play a game at a neutral site. But with Hurricane Ivan doing a drunken walk toward Florida, Major League Baseball decided to do an Ernie Banks and play two at U.S. Cellular—one today, one tomorrow.

This is history. This is drama. This is cheap: only $15 per ticket, with five bucks going toward a hurricane-relief fund. Better yet, you can sit anywhere you want in the lower deck. So wife Cheryl (the South Sider in the family) and I grab a couple of seats in the shade of Section 128, 26 rows from the field. We stare directly down the third-base line. Perfect.

I notice Sox owner Jerry Reinsdorf walking up the aisle. Fans stick their hands out. One man asks for an autograph. Another says, "Hey, Jerry, don't give up."

Then I see a little guy dressed to the nines and carrying a sign.

Cubs 1908 . . . Sox 1917 . . . Marlins 2003 . . . We have a winner!

The guy's name is Tom McCarthy, and he's a limo driver from Elgin. He hands me his card. *Next to Mom, U Can Trust Driver Tom.*

At this point, I'm wondering if Driver Tom has spent too much time breathing from the manifold exhaust. After all, what's with the sign?

"I'm here just to support baseball," he says. "In this town, you're divided. You have to choose between the Cubs' media blitz or Sox management. So I came out here as a baseball fan. I mean, you've got to feel sorry for the Marlins."

I don't feel sorry for the Marlins. Do you think they were dabbing tears when Gonzo booted the grounder last October?

If you wanted to, you could count total attendance by hand. A dad and his kid get up for a concession run. As the dad is leaving, he says, "Can you save me my row?"

Marlins owner Jeffrey Loria has flown in the team public address announcer, the mascot, and the scoreboard sound staff from Pro Player Stadium. Problem is, he didn't fly in another 20,000 people to fill out the place.

I've never been in a quieter ballpark. You can hear McKeon squint. You can hear players call for fly balls. You can hear 44-year-old Fred Gade cheering for Marlins starter Josh Beckett.

Gade isn't here because he loves the Marlins but because he hates the Cubs. I know this because he's wearing a white T-shirt that features the traditional Cubs *C* logo on the front, followed by the letters *h-o-k-e-r-s*. On the back of the shirt it says, "The Cubs Suck.com."

I walk down two rows and grab a seat directly behind him. Turns out Gade lives in Aurora, is a lifelong Sox fan, and owns an auto body shop. Monday is an off day, so he decided to spend the afternoon at the ballyard.

"A National League game for $15 out here at Comiskey?" he says. "I couldn't pass that up. And anyway, I bet Florida last year in the World Series and won $1,500. They were 15-1, and I put $100 down on them even before they clinched the wild card, before the NLCS. I took them mainly because of the odds. I honestly would have taken the Cubs, but they were only 8-1."

"So you came to thank the Marlins?"

"Not really," he says.

"OK, so you're here to root against the Cubs by rooting for the Marlins?"

"That's exactly why I'm here," he says.

Gade is anti-Cub because he says the team gets too much media attention. But what really gets him steamed is the Wrigley crowd.

"I don't feel they're true baseball fans," he says. "Wrigley Field is the only place you can turn to your left and someone is playing a video game on a cell phone. And three seats to your right, a lady is reading a book during a game against *St. Louis.*"

"And, what, White Sox fans are direct descendants of Judge Landis?"

"There's no question Cubs fans aren't as knowledgeable," he says. "I'll give you an example. Edgar Martinez is here with the Mariners. He gets a standing O on his last at-bat. People here knew he's retiring. You would have never seen that on the North Side."

Beckett gives up a quick run.

"C'mon, Josh!" yells Gade. "Wild pitch. Unbelievable."

I ask him about Wrigley. He can't honestly like this place better than the ivy and bricks, right?

"I love Wrigley Field," he says. "I'm just not a fan of the team. I did have one favorite player—Mark Grace—but he's gone. I used to take the L from Oak Park and sit in the bleachers there for $1.25. Now you can't get a ticket. That's what's nice about this park. You can come out here and always get a seat."

"But can't you just support your team without not supporting the other?" I say.

Gade looks at me as if I've just asked him to gnaw on his own foot.

"That game last year with the famous Bartman incident?" he says. "I was on top of the world when that happened. That night, I was on the phone calling all my friends about it. And then they blow up a ball on national television? You gotta be kidding me."

"But aren't most Sox fans simply jealous of the Cubs?" I say.

"No question," he says. "It's probably the media attention. The Cubs are the only team to make the front page when they lose. As a Sox fan, it's really irritating."

The Expos score another in the first before Beckett gets the third out.

"Gawd," says a disgusted Gade.

It's time to leave. Gade wants to watch the game, plus the lovely Cheryl is back with two frosties. I ask one last question.

"What happens if the Cubs make the playoffs? Then what?"

"I would not root for them unless they got to the World Series," he says. "And even then it would be more for the city than the Cubs."

I guess I can respect that.

The Marlins win, 6-3, with all six Florida runs coming in the bottom of the eighth. The crowd of 4,003 goes wild.

Or at least, Gade does.

GAME 142

Tuesday, September 14, 2004 . . . Cubs 3, Pirates 2 . . . Wrigley Field . . . Stuff: The Gladiator tells reporters, "If they let me play, I'm going to produce. Let me play and I will do the job I always do." . . . Kyle Farnsworth throws a simulated game. No word if he kicked a simulated fan afterward. . . . Glendon Rusch and Kerry Wood discuss wine in the clubhouse. You know, just like Don Drysdale and Sal the Barber used to. . . . The Curse Lives: The Marlins beat the Expos again at U.S. Cellular and do it, sigh, thanks mostly to a muffed ground ball by shortstop Alex Gonzalez.

No player has ever hit the Wrigley Field scoreboard. Not Aaron, not Ruth (I know, American Leaguer, but he played in World Series games here), not Bonds, not Mays, not Robinson, not McGwire, not Schmidt, not Sosa. That's 8 of the top 10 home run hitters of all time and not one of their more than 5,000 combined dingers came within a lavatory line of actually reaching the nearly three-story, 75-foot-wide piece of minimalist baseball architecture.

Live ball, Perfect Storm winds, andro, corked bat, sweet spots, jet streams. . . none of it matters. The great Roberto Clemente came close in 1959, and the pretty good Bill "Swish" Nicholson gave it a run in 1948. Otherwise, nothing worth writing Stats Inc. about.

Just for fun I bring a pair of Bushnell binoculars with a laser ranging system to Wrigley. I stand at home plate and aim at the lowest point of the scoreboard. One click to activate the laser range finder, another long click to get the distance.

According to the Bushnell, it's 507 feet.

Hall of Famer Billy Williams hit 392 career home runs as a Cub—some long ones, too—but nothing that would have caused sweat marks on the scoreboard. Ask him about the possibility of hitting that scoreboard and he all but checks your forehead for fever. After all, a baseball would have to clear the center-field wall (400 feet), clear the juniper bushes, and still figure out a way to defy gravity until it reached the green paint of the scoreboard.

Williams, his hair now peppered with gray, sits in the Cubs' dugout during batting practice and considers the physics of it all.

One of the longest home runs I've seen here—and I mean by that scoreboard—was during a game we were playing against the Giants. Jim Brewer was pitching. The game was delayed a little bit, and Brewer threw a ball and left it over the plate. Orlando Cepeda hit that one and it landed [Williams leans forward to look at the center-field bleachers] one, two, three, four rows just under the scoreboard.

They say Clemente hit it one, two, three rows under it there. I wasn't here for that. But the longest ball I've seen hit here was by Glenallen Hill. That one was to left field. And it was a day you didn't think the ball was going to carry that well. It was kind of cloudy, gloomy, a heavy-air day. There was a lady sitting up there in the rooftop, and I guess that was about the last thing she thought about doing: seeing that ball.

We never tried hitting that scoreboard in BP. Now, you can hit that scoreboard with a golf ball. I remember Ray Floyd hitting a golf ball at that scoreboard. He hit the ball over the scoreboard out there. [Sam Snead did the same thing years earlier.] But I can't imagine a player reaching that scoreboard. I've seen some tremendous balls coming off Sammy Sosa's bat, but I think Sammy hasn't been close to that scoreboard. That's a long way out there. It has to be 600, 700 feet. That's too far to even think about.

We were playing the Giants, and Ron Herbel was one of my favorite pitchers. I hit one right over the top of . . . see that tree [pointing to beyond the right-field bleachers, and across Sheffield]? It hit the sidewalk, broke a window, and went into the house. That's the longest one I've hit. I didn't care how far they went. I just wanted some.

Ernie certainly didn't hit the ball a long way. We used to call Ernie "First and Second Row" Banks. He hit a lot of them, but he didn't hit them far.

He had that long, smooth, fluid swing. Now, Walt Moryn, he used to hit the ball a long way. Big Moose Moryn. And, of course, Dale Long, too.

What would it take to reach that scoreboard? It would take the wind blowing out, maybe about 50 miles per hour. You got to get a ball up in the strike zone, and the pitcher got to throw the ball about 83 miles per hour, and you've got to hit it just right, on the sweet spot of the bat.

Now I got to leave. Got to go stand around the cage and gaze.

GAME 143

Wednesday, September 15, 2004 . . . Cubs 13, Pirates 5 . . . Wrigley Field . . . Cubs NL Central pennant flies: Second (79-64) . . . Stuff: The Gladiator, bumped up to the fifth spot because Aramis Ramirez is out of the lineup, does the Sammy Bunny Hop twice tonight. He takes a rare curtain call but drops the cone of media silence after the game. . . . Derrek Lee homers, giving the Cubs four guys (Lee, Sosa, Ramirez, and Moises Alou) with 30 or more dingers this season. . . . The bullpen hasn't allowed a run in the last 10 innings. . . . Wild-card status: a half-game behind San Francisco.

The red Spartan Gladiator FF with the Luverne pumps pulls into the concrete driveway of the Engine Co. No. 78 firehouse. An American flag flaps on the back of the fire truck, and a worn Cubs flag flies from the driver-side mirror. Pat Reardon, a 16-year veteran of the Chicago Fire Department, is behind the wheel.

Reardon and his three-man crew have been out on drills. Reardon is the lifelong Cubs follower; the other two losers are Sox honks. I introduce myself to Reardon in the firehouse garage, but he looks past me and across the street to Wrigley.

"Excuse me," says the engineer, dipping his hand into a black Nike bag and pulling out a baseball. "I think it's Nomar."

And then he's gone. I watch him jog across Waveland as a taxi sits just outside a steel gate behind the left-field corner of the stadium. Autograph seekers (yes, they're there all the time) make their run at the cab, but with no luck. Even Reardon, wearing his CFD uniform, can't catch a break. The Wrigley security guard hurries the taxi through the gate and the Cub (Garciaparra? Wendell Kim?) slips autograph-free to the clubhouse.

"Couldn't even get near him," says Reardon.

We stand just outside the historic firehouse, which was built in 1915 on the corner of Waveland and Seminary. Sit on the bench just outside the garage door and you get a perfect view of the left-field wall and the grandstands on the third-base side of the field. No wonder this is Reardon's idea of work heaven.

"I originally started on the West Side," says Reardon, 42. "Then I requested to come here in 1999. The location was why, the only reason why. I'm a big Cub fan and I wanted to be closer to the Cubs."

This is pretty close—about 50 feet. Reardon has been coming to Wrigley since he was an eight-year-old Cub Scout. Now he has two young daughters, "and I'm passing that tradition on to them. I took them to the game yesterday."

Out of the corner of my eye I notice something coming toward us. I look . . . and then a wave of water from a fire hydrant washes over me. It's the loser Sox guys.

"That was an accident," one of them says, laughing.

There are about 28 CFD and EMS personnel (Ambulance No. 6 is parked on the curb) working out of this house. "Probably 20 are Cubs fans," says Reardon.

As for perks, the Cubs still let the CFD folks flash a badge for Standing Room Only space on non-sellout days. "But the coolest thing is when you're watching TV in the front here—and it's delayed about one second—and you hear the crowd roar," he says. "Then you know something's going to happen."

A call comes over the firehouse intercom. This one isn't a drill.

"We got to run," says Reardon.

Moments later, the siren sounds. And those two flags wave.

GAME 144

Thursday, September 16, 2004 . . . Cubs 5, Reds 4 . . . Great American Ball Park . . . Stuff: The Cubs are a season-high 16 games above .500. They didn't win

No. 80 until the 150th game last season. . . . Alex Gonzalez, traded to the Montreal Expos in late July, is dealt to the San Diego Padres to replace injured rookie Khalil Greene.

John McDonough speaks so eloquently about the Cubs that you'd never know he grew up a Sox fan. But 21 years of working at Wrigley, the last 12 as the team's vice president in charge of marketing and broadcasting (a Senior VP title was added earlier this season), tend to alter your allegiances.

McDonough is the guy who invented the Cubs Convention (from 2,500 attendees in 1987, to scalpers selling tickets by 1990), now the industry standard for off-season team/fan interaction (41 pro teams now have annual conventions). He introduced Beanie Babies as a baseball promotion. He recognized the gravitational pull of Wrigley on baseball fans, and he marketed it to the point that the 21 highest attendance totals in team history (and I'm including this season, too) came during his watch.

There's more. He nurtured the Harry Caray phenomenom. He hired Ron Santo and later paired him with the perfect partner, Pat Hughes. He reinvented the Seventh-Inning Stretch. He came up with the idea of cutting loaves of bread into slices (OK, I exaggerate).

McDonough, like all skilled marketers, helped change the perception of the Cubs experience. How he did it should be required reading for all business school classes.

His modest Wrigley office is located at the end of a long hallway. There's the usual collection of Cubs mementos on the walls, as well as Bill Walton's autobiography on a nearby bookshelf (he's a huge fan). The phone rings. It's McDonough's assistant reminding him of a scheduled interview with a job applicant. I saw the kid downstairs in the waiting room sweating bullets. He looked like he was only a couple months removed from getting his college diploma and dropping water balloons from the top of the Sigma Chi house.

McDonough glances at his schedule and confirms the time. Then he tells me a story.

"We get lots of applications," he says. "Smart, qualified people. But after we shake hands, exchange pleasantries, I always ask the same question: 'What do you want to do?' If they say, 'I don't know,' the interview is over. I'll spend a few more minutes with them, but in my mind the interview is finished."

See, when it comes to the Cubs, McDonough is a businessman first, a romantic second. It's all about the product.

McDonough on marketing the Cubs:

"What we sell here is hope. We're constantly selling the experience of coming to a Cubs game. Everybody who is affiliated with this organization, and everybody who follows the Cubs, we all hope and pray and think of where we'll be when the Cubs win the World Series."

On the allure of the Cubs:

"Wrigley Field played an enormous role. Harry Caray played an enormous role. The neighborhood played an enormous role. We've gone through significant eras with great players. . . . But I also think there is an unconditional love affair and an unconditional romance that people have for this franchise unlike anything there is in professional sports. It's something very special and very close to indescribable.

"Sometimes when you take the elements and look at this—none of this is based on winning. We haven't won a World Series in 95 years, there's no place to park, all the games are on TV and the radio, and the games are played at a time when it's inconvenient for a lot of people to get there. Yet, on April 17, in the second inning with the bases loaded, there are 40,000 people here, all standing on a 3-2 count. It's amazing. You never, when you work here, become desensitized to it. You respect it. You admire it."

On Harry Caray:

"We certainly made a strategic decision in about 1987, when we heard the murmurs that the White Sox might be moving, to do two things. First and foremost, remember that winning is the greatest marketing idea of all time. That's the greatest idea anyone could ever invent and the only foolproof marketing idea there is. But we made a strategic decision that we were really going to invest in marketing this ballpark, marketing the experience, and really market a 70-something-year-old guy whose credo was 'Live it up, the meter's running.'"

On the working relationship between Caray and broadcast partner Steve Stone:

"Steve was a great supporter of Harry's, very respectful of Harry. A lot of these stories about them having disagreements, that they didn't have a good relationship off the air, that's not true.

"It's like any other partnership. There were issues, but none of them were significant, and I think Harry had great respect for Steve because Steve realized it was Harry's spotlight. It was Harry's booth. I think even the players gave him a pass because he was Harry Caray. I think your modern-day player is very aware as to what the broadcasters are saying, or what they're not saying, in the broadcast booth. If Harry ever became hypercritical at times, I think the players were reverent and understood. I never remember a Cubs player challenging Harry. They realized why there was this sonic boom in '84 and this tidal wave of interest, and I think Harry played a big role in that."

On Jack Brickhouse:
"He certainly deserved a better fate [the Cubs never won a World Series, pennant, division during his broadcasting tenure], but what a great salesman he was. He and Harry Caray were the two greatest salesmen in the history of the franchise."

On Pat Hughes:
"My wife and I and her family were coming back from a vacation in Wisconsin and we turned on a Brewers game. This was at the point where we weren't sure if Thom Brennaman was coming back or not to do our broadcasts. This was probably in June or July of 1995. And for about an hour and a half I happened to hear a day game Pat was doing at Yankee Stadium, and I thought he was just terrific.

"When Thom decided to leave and become the first broadcaster for the Arizona Diamondbacks, we got permission to speak with Pat and set up a meeting at Ron Santo's restaurant in Schaumburg. It became apparent at that meeting that this was one of the great quests in Pat's life—to be the play-by-play broadcaster of the Cubs.

"Ron and Pat . . . they're such polar opposites, so distinct. Pat is meticulous in his preparation. Ronnie is not so much a preparation guy as he is a fan in the heart and soul. You can tell he probably takes these games homes with him. But if you're feeling upset about a loss, or you feel great about a victory, you know Santo is feeling the same thing you do. And I think that's been part of the magic of the two of them."

On the Cubs Convention:
"The idea came to me in 1985, when the team had suffered through a really rough season. I just never really understood why, with one of the greatest brands in the history of business—the Cubs brand—we only market this for six, seven months a year.

"So I made a presentation to Dallas Green. I said, 'Dallas, I want to build a bridge from the end of one season to the next.' It had never been done before where anyone had thought about using the off-season as a marketing vehicle. When I presented it to him, he said, 'Do you think we can make any money?' I said, 'Dallas, I think it will be successful if we can secure the players.' And he was very instrumental in helping us get the players to come to the Convention.

"We've had 16 consecutive sellouts. It has become this mega-event people look forward to, and I think it creates a very collegiate atmosphere. We don't pay the players to come in. We'll pay their expenses, that's it. But they just like getting together with their teammates and friends. I don't care if it's Gary Varsho or Doug Dascenzo, or whoever it is—when we invite them back, I think it revitalizes their life. All of a sudden, they're a star again.

"I remember the first one that Jody Davis came to after he retired. It makes these players feel great about themselves. They realize they're the fabric of this franchise. Jody said, 'You never realize how much you miss this until you come back.' When he came back [to the Convention], he might have had the loudest ovation of any current or former player. I talked to him afterward, and you could just see he was almost overwhelmed emotionally."

On featuring a guest "conductor" during the Seventh-Inning Stretch, despite Caray's death in 1998:
"It was a tough decision because everyone had an opinion. The first part of it is there's no perfect answer. Harry loved celebrities. He was, if there is such a thing, a professional celebrity. He loved being recognized. He loved people yelling, 'Hey, Harry!' He loved to rub elbows with kings and queens. He told me Elvis and Sinatra stories endlessly. He loved having Hillary Clinton up in the booth.

"A lot of people were saying to me, 'John, we should just play the tape of him singing it.' And I went to spring training and actually tried it. We played it once in spring training in '98. You lost the dynamic of the man when you did that. It just fell short.

"I guess the moral of the story is that Harry wasn't as bad as we thought. There are still critics out there who say this isn't the right thing to do, the singers are bad—which we absolutely recognize. But people do ask here: who's pitching and who's singing."

GAME 145

Friday, September 17, 2004 . . . Cubs 12, Reds 4 . . . Great American Ball Park . . . Stuff: Carlos Zambrano wins No. 14, but he also has his traditional knuckle-head moment when, with the Cubs up 6-0, he stands and admires his homer off reliever Mike Matthews. To his credit, Zambrano apologizes (again) for his actions, telling reporters, "After I did that I knew I was garbage and I ran the bases hard. I say, 'Well, if they want to hit me in my next at-bat, I [understand].'" Kids . . . The Cubs win their fifth in a row, but San Francisco wins its sixth consecutive game. . . . For what it's worth, Boston is 33-11 since the Nomar trade, and the Cubs are 25-16. . . . The Curse Lives: Macaulay Culkin, who threw out the first pitch at Wrigley earlier this season, is arrested on drug charges.

Rick Pildes's legal expertise on constitutional law has been cited by the U.S. Supreme Court, which, to reduce it to a baseball simile, is like Ryne Sandberg complimenting your kid on his swing. Having Bill Rehnquist and the gang ackowledge your work is a big deal. In fact, Pildes, a visiting professor of law at Harvard, could be arguing his first-ever case in front of the nine justices as early as December.

Of course, all of it pales next to the landmark case he'll argue tonight on national television in front of a jury in a Yonkers, New York, courtroom. There isn't too much at stake—only the pride of the entire Cubs Nation.

On trial is this notion: Do the Cubs or the Boston Red Sox suffer from the worse curse?

Roe v. Wade it isn't, but as ESPN notes, we're talking about two franchises that have gone a combined 180 years without a World Series championship. During that span, women gained the right to vote, Alan Shepard swung a 6-iron on the moon, 16 U.S. presidents took office, and Janet Jackson's bra sprang a leak.

This is a no-brainer, right? The Cubs haven't been to a World Series since Andy Pafko was leering at Betty Grable pinups in 1945. The Red Sox have made four appearances since then, the latest a scant (for Cubs fans) 18 years ago. I'm no Thurgood Marshall, but that doesn't sound like much of a curse to me. Cubs followers would let Jerry Reinsdorf throw out the first pitch at Wrigley if someone could guarantee them four Fall Classics during the next 58 years.

Pildes knows this. He grew up in Chicago. He used to go to Wrigley as a kid, sit through a Cubs loss, and then report to one side of the stadium at game's end. Then he'd pick a row and push the seats up all the way around the ballpark. "When you got to the other end, they'd give you a free pass to the next day's game," he says.

Pildes was 12 when the Cubs collapsed in '69. He was out of law school by the time the Cubs gagged in 1984. He was a professor of law at NYU when the Cubs exploded in 2003 like a tanker truck. Now he's sweating out this season. Believe me, Pildes knows a curse when he sees one.

His opponent is Alan Dershowitz, famed civil liberties attorney, Harvard law professor, and brilliant blowhard who can stir things up faster than a nor'easter. I fear Alan. He has geography (Yonkers? Gee, I'm sure there aren't any people in Yonkers who remember Bucky Dent.) on his side, but his Red Sox upbringing is a bit disingenuous. Yes, he lives in Boston, but he was born and raised in New York.

Pildes asked for a change of venue to, say, St. Louis, but his request was ignored. Still, he didn't think twice about accepting the made-for-TV case.

"When they called up and asked me to do it, I found it irresistible," he says. "It was a wonderful opportunity to relive all those moments of my memories of the Cubs from the '60s and '70s."

What moments? The Cubs sucked then. Of course, Pildes also enjoys pulling whiskers off kittens, inner-ear piercings, and pouring a cup of Starbucks down his pants.

To prepare for the case, Pildes enlisted the assistance of Pulitzer Prize-winning historian Jack Rakove. Rakove, also a Cubs enthusiast, did much of the research and discovered what we already knew: There might be something to this Curse of the Billy Goat. And if the Billy Goat isn't enough, there's always Steve Bartman as a curse security net.

"Of course, like everybody, as soon as Bartman interfered with the ball, you think this is it," he says. "And nobody thought they were going to win Game 7. It's kind of like the Red Sox when the ball went through Buckner's legs. Nobody thought they were going to win Game 7."

ESPN arranged the witness list for Pildes. Actor George Wendt, former Cubs Rick Sutcliffe and Phil Reagan, and NPR's Scott Simon will testify on behalf of the Cub Curse. I would have kept Sutcliffe and Simon, and invited Ron Santo and Sam Sianis. Then I would have begged Bartman to make a surprise appearance.

"He so wants not to have anything to do with this, which I think is a mistake for him," says Pildes. "I think it would be a relief for him. If he could come out and participate in things like this, and be able to have some fun with this and make light of some of this, I think it would be much easier for him in many, many ways. You get trapped in your own . . . whatever the emotions are: anger, self-hatred, a sense of loss. It's much better to deal with it in a public setting. But there was no chance he would do this."

Then I think Pildes is cooked. Truth goes only so far in a courtroom, especially with the clever Dershowitz playing to a jury much more aware of Red Sox history than of Cubs failures. You think the folks in Yonkers know the name Sianis? No, but they probably can recite, in one form or another, the supposed Curse of the Bambino.

Pildes hasn't been to Wrigley in nearly 15 years. He loves the place, but he also refers to it as a Garden of Eden, post fig leaf. But despite that knowledge, Pildes can't help himself. He sees the standings, he understands the legacy, and yet he says, "It's almost time to start fantasizing about a Red Sox-Cubs World Series."

This is the Cubs fan defined: a fatalist and optimist all at the same time.

Lawyers often advocate stances not necessarily their own. So, Counselor, thumbs up or down on a Cubs curse?

"It depends what moment you catch me in, I suppose," he says. "You ask me after the Bartman incident . . . those kind of things can make you a true believer. You ask me in my more rational, logical, lawyerlike moments, then I'm a rationalist—then I would say there are no such things. I'll believe in it less when they win the World Series."

Late, late this evening, thanks to a rain delay in the Yankees-Red Sox game (see, the Red Sox even screw with the Cubs' prime-time trial slot), Pildes makes his case to the jury.

The verdict arrives shortly after closing arguments.

Eleven to one, in favor of the Red Sox.

GAME 146

Saturday, September 18, 2004 . . . Reds 6, Cubs 5 . . . Great American Ball Park . . . Stuff: St. Louis clinches the division. So much for George Will's prediction of the Cubs bestriding the Central "like a colossus." Hard to crack wise on the Cardinals, though. They earned it—and the best record in baseball—fair and

square. . . . Wavin' Wendell Kim sends Mark Grudzielanek from second to
home on a single up the middle in the eighth. It's not a bad gamble, but the re-
sult is: Grudzielanek is easily tagged out. . . . Ron Santo suffers an atrial fibril-
lation episode, the result of taking the wrong medication. The doctors say he'll
be fine. Still, Santo will skip the Pittsburgh series. . . . Wild-card status: a half-
game behind San Francisco.

With the Cubs out of town in Cincinnati, Jim Oboikowitch and his bud-
dies take a much-needed R&R road trip to Knoxville for tonight's Florida-
Tennessee game. A school-record crowd of 109,061 squeezes into Neyland
Stadium, and Oboikowitch (and I) helps make UT attendance history.

The Vols win on a 50-yard field goal with six seconds remaining. The
Cubs lose after squandering chances to score in the eighth and ninth innings. Oboikowitch is bummed—not about the Tennessee game (he didn't
attend either school), but because his employer lost.

Oboikowitch is the Cubs' coordinator of special events and entertainment, which, on the team's marketing and broadcasting corporate ladder,
is listed as the 10th rung out of 11, just above the marketing secretaries. But
here's the thing: There are days—lots of them—when you would sell your
wife and kids to Bedouins for a chance to switch places with the 24-year-
old Oboikowitch.

Hey, isn't that Jim chatting up Julia Roberts? Hey, why is Jim talking to
Bill Murray—again? Hey, look, it's Matt Damon and Jim. Hey, that isn't re-
ally Jim with . . . Katie Holmes? Hey, what the heck are Michael Jordan and
Jim laughing about now?

As Cubs greeter, chaperone, and babysitter to the stars, Oboikowitch
isn't in it for the money but for the experience. Where else can you hang
with Kid Rock one day, Sharon and Ozzy the next?

You can't miss Oboikowitch ("O-boyk-O-which"). He's 6-7, 230-ish, is
unfailingly polite and professional, and always wears a long-sleeve shirt
and tie at games (Cubs rules). He also looks as if he could hip-check you
right out of the lane, which is what he did as a starter for Carthage College.
(Oboikowitch averaged 3.4 points, 4.2 rebounds for the 2002 team that
reached the NCAA Division III Final Four.)

During home games, Oboikowitch is often the guy who holds the hand
(figuratively, of course—though he'd like to make an exception with
young Katie) of those film stars, recording artists, celebrities, athletes,
coaches, broadcasters and journalists, high school champions, and spe-

cialty choices who are there to throw out the first pitch, sing the Seventh-Inning Stretch, or do both. And it isn't unusual for Oboikowitch to help arrange and deliver tickets to visiting celebs and dignitaries, or even escort them to their seats.

I ask Oboikowitch for his Top 10 chaperone moments. The results:

Honorable Mention

Jack Black ("He was crazy. He ended the Stretch with 'Let's drink some rum!' instead of 'Let's get some runs.'"), Vince Vaughn ("Really laid back and really witty. He was just a normal guy, never struck me as a celebrity."), Dwyane Wade, Kid Rock, Johnny Bench, Toby Keith, Russell Crowe, Tyson Chandler, and Jalen Rose.

10. Candace Parker, two-time national high school basketball player of the year, University of Tennessee signee (2004)

Oboikowitch remembers: "We presented her with a signed basketball by our players, and it was my job to escort her. Anyway, I was standing on the on-deck circle with her, and Bill Murray starts messing with her. He actually tried to talk her into going to UConn instead of Tennessee because his son goes there. Who would have ever thought Bill Murray knew who she was? Then he invited her into his suite to watch the game."

9. The *Ocean's Twelve* Cast (2004)

Oboikowitch remembers: "They were filming in and around Chicago during the spring. So it's the first week of the season and I'm sitting at my desk when the phone rings. It's Matt Damon's people calling to say Matt is on his way and can we get him seats. Before we even secure tickets for him, I go through our administration office and there he is, standing there with his girlfriend and a few other people. He was thrilled, like a kid in a candy shop.

"After we seat Matt, I walk back in and Andy Garcia is standing there wanting tickets. Luckily, we get Andy in. Then I turn around and Casey Affleck and someone else are trying to sneak down by Damon and Garcia. *Ocean's Twelve* was more like Ocean's 50.

"The next week, Joe Rios [Cubs manager of Special Events, Player Relations, Entertainment] and I went out to the *Ocean's Twelve* set to talk to them about singing the Stretch. The first person I met when I walked in was Julia Roberts. She was sitting on the stairs getting her makeup done, but she looked as good as ever."

8. Isiah Thomas and Mark Aguirre, former NBA stars (2004)

Oboikowitch remembers: "Both guys are from Chicago and finally made it back to Wrigley this season. We always show our guest singers a highlight tape of past guests to ease their nerves. After the tape, we had some time to kill and got into a conversation about the Bulls-Pistons rivalry during the late 1980s and early 1990s."

7. Bernie Mac, comedian, actor (2004)

Oboikowitch remembers: "He came to town for the Cubs-Sox series at Wrigley. He walks into the administration area [it's a lobby/office area located near the ticket windows], stands in the doorway, and pretends to be security. He's asking people for their IDs and tickets. Most of the people who go through that door are VIPs or families. They were shocked, even baffled, that we would have a security person there. Only about 1 in 10 of the people who went through recognized him. He had everyone in hysterics."

6. Shania Twain, country singer (2003)

Oboikowitch remembers: "I think the thing I will remember most about her is how little she was. She's like 5-3. All the players were hovering around her. No one had a problem with her coming into the clubhouse to meet the players."

5. Ozzy and Sharon Osbourne, rock star and talk-show host (2003)

Oboikowitch remembers: "This one will go down in history. I am not sure if any Seventh-Inning Stretch will get as much coverage as Ozzy and Sharon got in 2003.

"His singing was obviously awful, but even more memorable to me was his nonstop shaking. I'm sure he was sober, and he certainly wasn't acting, but I'm convinced he's done so much damage to himself over the years he'll never stop shaking.

"An underrated moment was Ozzy going down to the clubhouse after the Seventh-Inning Stretch. He had to see our trainer, and some clubhouse guys wanted pictures. So Ozzy was hanging out in the clubhouse as we're losing to the Dodgers. As the game was going on, players kept coming in to take pictures with him and have him sign stuff. We're trying to drag him to the door. The last thing we wanted was to be seen parading a celebrity in the clubhouse during the ninth inning of a close game."

4. Bill Murray, actor (2004)

Oboikowitch remembers: "He was here on Opening Day to throw out the first pitch and sing the Stretch. But all he wanted to do was warm up with Greg Maddux. Until he actually threw the first pitch over the backstop screen and was off the mound, I was convinced he was going to take off down the third-base line and ask Maddux to get in a crouch.

"He plays the crowd so well and he signs for everyone. At one point, I looked to see what he was signing. He'd write 'Merry Christmas' on one, then it would be 'Peace Be With You' on the next autograph. The man is awesome, but nuts. I got a feel for babysitting that day."

3. Katie Holmes, actress (2004)

Oboikowitch remembers: "It's my guess any guy my age had a crush on her. *Dawson's Creek* came out when we were in high school, and we followed her for years. She got more beautiful by the year. So my heart jumped when she called my cell phone and said she was here. That was a dream come true. Then she came back the next weekend and I spent a little more time with her. I told her I was going to New York, and she gave me advice on restaurants and even left her e-mail address if I had any other questions.

"Great. I have her e-mail address. Chris Klein has her as his wife. Not the same thing."

2. Ryne Sandberg, Cubs legendary second baseman (2003, 2004)

Oboikowitch remembers: "My childhood idol. I lived and died with every Sandberg at-bat as a kid [Oboikowitch is from suburban Libertyville]. I was always the tallest second baseman, because I refused to play anywhere else. I still bat second on my softball team in honor of him. To top it off, I now live with his stepson, B. R. Koehnemann, who works in the Cubs' media relations office. I've lived a dream by having a beer with Ryne Sandberg. But the first time I saw him in person was in the bathroom—not the place I would have expected."

1. Michael Jordan, no identification necessary (2003, 2004)

Oboikowitch remembers: "In my opinion, he's the greatest athlete ever and the best basketball player I will ever see. Just being in his presence is overwhelming. I escorted him and his family down to the clubhouse after one of the divisional series games in 2003. I looked at him and said, 'You ready?' and he said, 'Ready when you are.' I'll never forget it."

GAME 147

Sunday, September 19, 2004 ... Cubs 5, Reds 1 ... Great American Ball Park ... Cubs NL Central pennant flies: Second (82-65) ... Stat of the game: Down, 1-0, the Cubs tie the game in the eighth and score four more runs in the ninth off exhausted closer Danny Graves, who makes his 11,000th appearance this season.

Hey, everybody, it's Chip Caray of the Mouseketeers! He's the one with the perpetual Wal-Mart-greeter smile, the guy who makes Up with People look like Goths.

If you read enough of the letters to the editor ripping him in the *Tribune*, you'd think Caray ended every Cubs broadcast by belting out "The sun will come up to-morrow ..." He's a homer who dips every Cubs failing in powdered sugar—that's the gist of most of the viewer criticism.

But the Caray I'm getting to know isn't anything like the one-dimensional, talking head that too many viewers perceive him to be. Ron Burgundy types aren't clever enough to paste a mug shot of actor Jim Carrey over their own MLB-issued ID card photos and then see if any stadium security guard notices. (They don't. Caray has worn the doctored ID into 16 different stadiums and hasn't been stopped once.) And I'd like to know how someone supposedly so clueless could handle with such grace The Joe Carter Era (or Error, take your pick), The Players Whining About His Roy Oswalt Comments Era, and The Contract Renegotiations Era.

Yeah, OK, at first glance Caray looks like he's running for senior class president. He's 39 going on 17. But as Indiana Jones once said, "It's not the years, honey, it's the mileage." Caray has more mileage on his tires than you realize.

You think you know him because you spend three and a half hours listening to his play-by-play? You don't, because Caray figures you'd rather hear about the Cubs game than hear his life story. Sure, he'll drop in a University of Georgia reference now and then, but there's no mention of the heartbreaking events that truly shaped his life.

"I'm not the star, and never have been," he says during lunch at the team hotel. "The game is the star."

Ask Caray what career he would have pursued had he not become a broadcaster and you get, "Besides being a porn star?" This is his first instinct: to deflect with a one-liner, to bob a bit before deciding if the questions are worth the trouble.

"I thought about going to law school," he says. "I thought about going to medical school [Caray is a sucker for the *CSI* TV series]. My maternal grandfather was a dentist in St. Louis for 50 years and was a great, great man. He was a guy who taught me to be curious, to ask, to read, to stimulate your mind. Without question, he was the most caring, most kind, most giving person that I've ever encountered in my life."

You notice he didn't say his famous grandfather, Harry Caray. Or even his famous father, Skip Caray. Instead, a gentlemanly dentist by the name of Dr. Roy Osterkamp is the cornerstone of his personality.

"He died two years ago, on my birthday," says Caray. "I miss him every day."

Caray's parents split up when he was four. Dr. Osterkamp became his surrogate father.

"I remember my dad was driving a green Mercury convertible," he says. "We were in the front driveway of the house. My mom's parents were there. And my dad got into the car with his stuff, and I remember saying to my grandfather, 'Where's Daddy going?' And he said, 'He's going on a long road trip.'

"I remember my dad backing out, waving good-bye . . . he had tears in his eyes. I was crying. I didn't know why I was crying, but I was."

Caray and his mother moved from Atlanta to St. Louis a year later. They would shuttle between the two cities before finally settling on St. Louis, where Caray's life remained a daily challenge.

He was, in his own words, "the class geek in high school." He was tall but fat. He didn't play sports. By then his mother had become involved with another man, but it was a troubled relationship.

"The way I'd want this put is that it was an abusive situation and no kid should be exposed to that," says Caray, who at times was forced to physically protect his mother from her boyfriend.

Caray's mother later ended the relationship and married another man once her son had left to attend Georgia. By the time Caray was a junior, he weighed about 260 pounds. That's when he decided to reshape his body as well as his life.

Caray lost 75 pounds. He earned his journalism degree in 1987 and became a weekend sports anchor in Panama City, Florida, then Greensboro, North Carolina. He eventually joined his dad and the Atlanta Braves broadcasting team in 1991, then had stays with the Seattle Mariners and the Fox Network before accepting a second offer from the Cubs in 1998. The team had a TV-quality happy ending planned: Chip would work with his legendary grandfather, Harry, during home games.

Then Harry died.

Chip mourned his loss, but the truth is that Steve Stone and the late WGN producer Arne Harris knew Harry better than his own grandson. After all, Chip's parents were divorced, and Harry was on his third marriage. Chip grew up in St. Louis, and Harry lived in Chicago, Arizona, broadcast booths, and bars. Chip had just nudged past 30; Harry was nearly three times his age.

They were of different generations and, in many ways, were held together only by a common last name. They rarely saw each other more than twice a year.

"I'm not here to say we're the Brady Bunch, man," says Caray. "We had a different family. If you work on TV, people presume they know a lot more about you than they do. Sometimes the fantasy is better than the reality."

The reality is that Caray would love to have worked with Harry. Most of all, he would love to have known him better.

"It would have filled in a lot of blanks," he says.

As usual, Caray travels with an electric guitar and his iPod. His most prized musical possessions are a pair of Les Pauls, one of which features a photograph from a Caray Family Christmas card. That particular Les Paul hangs on a wall and has never been played.

Caray, who would love to front his own garage band, is a Rush disciple. He listens to "La Villa Strangiato" at least three times a day. He even has the song downloaded on his laptop. Another favorite is "Limelight," which should give you an idea what Caray thinks about celebrity.

Living on a lighted stage
Approaches the unreal

This hasn't been the most pleasant season of his Cubs broadcasting career. Then again, hardly a season has gone by where he hasn't been criticized for something. He's not Harry . . . he's too gee-whiz-ish . . . and the new criticism by the players: He's too complimentary of other teams' players.

"The most challenging thing about this particular job was, No. 1, replacing someone who's irreplaceable," he says. "No. 2, sharing the same name as Harry Caray. And No. 3, being thrust into a situation that until you've been there, until you have worked there, and until you have seen the fer-vent nature and love of this franchise by our fans . . . you can't get your arms around that 800-pound gorilla until you get in the cage with them. It's the most unique place I've ever worked."

Look, you could have paired Vin Scully with Joe Carter and it wouldn't have mattered. Carter is the guy who once asked booth guest Jim McMahon if he still kept in touch with former NFL commissioner Pete Rozelle. Never mind that Rozelle couldn't come to the phone these days because he was, uh, dead. And it was Carter who once observed that a young Cubs player had a nervous look, "kind of like a deer with headlights."

Caray never had a chance.

Steve Stone's return to the booth in 2003 made Caray better, just as it made Harry better years earlier. And so what if a few of the Cubs are peeved at Caray and Stone? Caray is only following the advice of Harry and Skip, who said, "Tell the truth. Always tell the truth."

Sometimes the truth hurts.

"As a broadcaster, personally speaking, I don't ever take credit, and I'm sure as heck not going to take blame for what takes place on the field," he says. "We are paid to evaluate a performance. If a player plays hard, if a player plays well, that's what I say. If a player plays poorly, we point that out and move on.

"I think it needs to be said that this isn't an all-too-unfamiliar occurrence in sports. What is uncommon is the fact that some of this laundry was aired to the media. And it was not aired by the broadcasters."

Caray and Stone fly on the team charter, stay in the team hotel, wear the team logo during some broadcasts. "But we are the media," says Caray. "We're not in the family."

Caray likes family, maybe because his was so fractured during parts of his life. He and his father have worked to rebuild their own relationship, to the point that Caray calls Skip "my hero." Now he waits to see if he'll remain in the Cubs family photo. His contract is up at season's end.

"They're talking, and I hope we come to an agreement," he says. "But until it's done, it's not done. I love being here. I love the fans. They've been great to me. I hope at the end of the day I'll be able to be here longer than my grandfather was."

Whatever happens, Caray says he'll remain a baseball broadcaster. "Again, I'm fully confident, barring some unforeseen circumstance, that it will be in Chicago," he says.

I hope so. The last thing I want to see is him pulling out of the Wrigley parking lot in a green Mercury.

GAMES 148, 149

Monday, September 20, 2004 . . . Cubs 5, Marlins 1; Marlins 5, Cubs 2 . . . Pro Player Stadium . . . Cubs NL Central pennant flies: Second (83-66) . . . Stat of the game: Go figure. The Cubs beat 17-game winner Carl Pavano in the opener (Mark Prior looks Fernando Lamas marvelous during his 7⅔-inning, nine-strikeout performance), but lose to David Weathers in the second game. Weathers, normally a reliever, makes his first start since 1998. . . . Stuff: In the Game 2 loss, Matt Clement lasts only 2⅓ innings, gives up five runs, and forces Dusty Baker to dig into the bullpen with four different relievers. . . . Wild-card status: a half-game behind San Francisco.

I don't make the one-day trip to Florida. Instead, I stay back and sift through pages and pages of player prospect scouting reports never before seen by anyone outside the Cubs organization. Yeah, I know: It sounds like a scene from *Nerd in a Library*, but you should see this stuff.

Not more than a block away from Wrigley is the Brown Lot parking structure, which is owned by the Cubs and used not only for cars but for the storage of decades' worth of invoices, register receipts, human resource files, inventory documents, concession stand statements, spreadsheets . . . and scouting reports.

Scott Nelson, a former assistant director of scouting who now oversees the Cubs' baseball operations, gives me the nickel tour of the place. It doesn't take long. Inside the enclosed street-level section of the building are three storage rooms filled with metal shelving units and cardboard box files. Air-conditioning? Forget it.

Nelson is the one who finds the two worn metal filing cabinets containing the thousands of handwritten or typed index cards and scouting sheets. He thumbs through a few of the reports, glances around the dust-filled, fluorescent-lighted room, and then makes his way to the garage door.

"Just lock up when you're done," he says.

This is the baseball equivalent of Moses saying, "When you're through with the two stone tablets, just store them behind that burning bush, will ya?"

I stay three hours. It's just me, a metal stool, Cubs scouts, and Lee Smith, Greg Maddux, Lou Brock, Barry Bonds, Mark McGwire, Glenn Beckert, Roger Clemens . . .

Barry Lamar Bonds's file contains 29 different Cubs scouting reports, the first one written in March 1982, when he was a 6-2, 170-pound senior at Serra High School in San Mateo, California.

"Last year Barry couldn't pull the ball; is now getting the bat around to where he is a marginal prospect."

Three months later another scout writes, "Natural ability impressive. Near complete player. Arm should improve to near average with maturity. Bat speed indicates hitting should improve."

Bonds is drafted out of high school by the San Francisco Giants but doesn't sign. Instead, he accepts a scholarship offer from Arizona State and spends the summer of 1983 playing for the Fairbanks Goldpanners in the Alaskan League.

An August 1983 report: "Possesses that combination of speed and power we are always looking for. Well below-average throwing arm will limit him to left-field or first base. I like him better at first base."

A November 1984 report: "Still undisciplined in behavior. May miss a curfew from time to time, but has the ability to play winning ball at all levels. Negotiations will not likely be easy, but is potential high draft [pick]."

A February 1985 report: "Lean, athletic body that will remain in good shape for a long time. Will fill in and gain total body strength with maturity. . . . I cannot see him getting to our selection in the draft [No. 22 in the 1985 draft] unless there is something seriously wrong."

Another February 1985 report (Bonds is now listed at 6-1, 185): "His ability is worth $100,000 [signing bonus], his effort [worth] $5,000."

Another February 1985 report: "B. Bonds is no longer a prospect in my book. He'd be more trouble than he's worth."

A March 1985 report: "Could become complete player if proper motivator is found. Will continue to improve with maturity. High draft with exciting tools."

Another March 1985 report: "Not an easy sign, and a potential pain. Undisciplined on and off the field, but so talented he can play winning ball and should mature eventually. Not a bad kid, just spoiled."

Another March 1985 report: "He has all the tools to be a superstar in the show."

Another March 1985 report: "He still has good physical ability (except arm), but he does not have the aptitude or attitude to be a player I would want selected by our ballclub."

A May 1985 report: "This player can be a superstar. Has all the tools we are looking for. Will play in Major Leagues quickly. Attitude might be only thing to hold him back."

The last report (May 24) before the June draft: "He's used to doing as he pleases."

Bonds was drafted No. 6 overall by the Pittsburgh Pirates. The Cubs selected outfielder Rafael Palmeiro.

The Cubs' scouts were right: He is a pain (to pitchers and sportswriters), and he did become a superstar, setting the single-season record for home runs in 2001 (73) and moving into third place on the all-time home run list in 2004.

Lee Smith is the Cubs' all-time leader in saves (180) and retired in 1997 as the Major League career leader in saves (478, for eight different teams).

A March 1975 report: "Worth $13,500. Intelligent. From large rural family. Likes to play. Desires education. Competes well. Has signed scholarship [for] basketball/baseball [at] Northwestern Louisiana."

Another April 1975 report: "Ten of the longest fingers I've seen. Pitchers fingers."

Another April 1975 report: "He should be pitching in the Major Leagues in 3 to 4 years. I feel sure he will be a first round choice. He should be one of the best pitchers in baseball in a few years."

A June report, this one from the legendary Buck O'Neil, shortly after Smith was selected in the second round of the 1975 draft: "Has all the tools to become top ML pitcher—take care of him, he is just a baby. Signed $28,000 cash bonus . . . Player is from one of the nicest families I've ever met."

Mark McGwire retired after the 2001 season with 583 home runs and, at the time, the single-season record for home runs (70, set in 1998). He was originally scouted at Damian High School in La Verne, California, as a pitcher.

A March 1981 report (in which his name is spelled "McGuire"): "Fastball lacks movement and velocity at this time to be effective Major League pitcher. . . . Size, pitching mechanics and projected pitches make him a fringe Major Leaguer."

Another March 1981 report: "This boy is big and still growing. . . . He looks like a big Chicago Bear tackle. This boy has a good delivery and good control for a high school boy. . . . He is a good prospect."

A May 1981 report: "Another player that will be a tough sign because the 'Big' schools in this area are going for this fellow in a big way."

McGwire, drafted in the eighth round as a pitcher by the Montreal Expos, accepted a scholarship from USC.

An August 1983 report: "Power hitter! Set new record for home runs at USC . . . Not a liability at first base."

A February 1984 report: "Worth $30,000. Most likely a first round selection in June. Pretty fine young man. Intelligent and easy to talk to . . . Has the potential to hit a lot of home runs."

Another February 1984 report: "Will see more of Mark in the days ahead, but from what I have seen to date I am not confident that he will hit for an average. I KNOW HE HAS GOOD POWER, but I am doubtful about his hitting good pitching."

A March 1984 report: "This report is to upgrade the value. I am basing this upgrading on the fact that he has demonstrated to me that his frequency of power is very good. Worth $60,000."

An April 1984 report from the same scout cited in the March report: "INCREASE IN VALUE. McGwire looks better each time I see him. . . . Worth $80,000."

Another April 1984 report: "Dollar value: $105,000 . . . It will surprise me if he gets to us in the draft."

A May 1984 report: "Cannot consider in first three for 6/84 selection . . . In this NCAA Regional I am thinking McGwire, despite bat power, may have difficulty vs. pitching other than college, and with wood bat, to hit the home runs in the numbers necessary."

McGwire was the No. 10 overall pick by the Oakland Athletics. The Cubs chose left-hander Drew Hall with the No. 3 pick.

Greg Maddux was selected in that same 1984 draft, but in the second round. His beige Cubs index card shows his signing bonus was $75,000 and that he earned $700 a month during his first season in minor league ball at Pikesville of the Appalachian League.

Shawon (or "Shawn," as it reads on his beige index card) Dunston, the No. 1 overall pick of the 1982 draft, received a $135,000 signing bonus and earned $600 a month during his first season of rookie ball in Sarasota.

Louis Clark Brock, signed by Buck O'Neil and Harry Hickman in 1960, signed for $12,000, but the club paid the bonus out in three $4,000 payments over three years. He earned $450 a month for St. Cloud in the Northern League before making his Cubs debut in September 1961. Under

Nationality, someone has typed *Negro*. Written neatly in longhand on the back of the index card are the saddest of words: *1964, 6-15, St. Louis—Brock, Toth & Spring for Broglio, Clemens and Shantz.*

Glenn Beckert's index card details his $8,000 bonus plan after being drafted by the Cubs from the Boston Red Sox in 1962. He spends most of 1963 as a minor league third baseman and all of 1964 as a shortstop. His minor league manager writes in 1964: "Has chance for Major Leagues, but not as third baseman. Could make it at shortstop or second base. Has trouble going to his right; no power. Improves with each game." Beckert made his big league debut in 1965—as the Cubs' starting second baseman. And that's where he stayed until his 1973 trade to the San Diego Padres.

Roger Clemens is a 300-game winner and no-brainer for the Hall of Fame. Of course, no Cubs scout was predicting that in 1982.

A June 1982 report: "Fastball is certain to reach above-average velocity prior to his entering the pro ranks. Has enough raw talent to be interesting prospect."

A February 1983 report: "I feel there is good talent here to work with. A few minor adjustments should produce a good Major League pitcher."

An April 1983 report: "Worth $45,000. Cannot consider for round 1."

Clemens was drafted by Boston with the No. 19 overall pick. The Cubs chose right-hander Jackie Davidson with the No. 6 selection.

Randy Johnson is another first-ballot Hall of Famer-in-waiting. But in 1981, when he was a 6-7, 180-pounder at Livermore (California) High School, who knew?

An August 1981 report: "Randy is very tall and has a skinny body and is rather frail looking, but he has good coordination for his size. . . . He has the tools to become a fine pitcher."

A June 1982 report: "Signability interview . . . Randy wants to sign. Parents think college is best . . . I discussed our entire program with them tonight. They seemed impressed."

Johnson was drafted by the Atlanta Braves in 1982, but instead signed a scholarship deal with USC.

A February 1985 report: "6 ft. 9 in. 225 LBS . . . Like his arm. Strong and agile for height. Hyper. Seems more confident and aggressive."

Another February 1985 report: "Dollar value: $55,000 . . . Believe this young man will be a first round pick come June. Has improved with each outing. Liked in high school, like more now."

A March 1985 report: "Very inconsistent. Had trouble with mound. Got rattled. Couldn't find the plate. Didn't miss much, but threw 11 straight balls.... Dropped $10,000."

An April 1985 report: "Delivery getting worse.... I just can't project this delivery and arm action to the big league level. May be prone to arm trouble and I question his ability to handle stressful situations on the mound."

Another April 1985 report: "Dollar value: $15,000 ... At 6-10, there is no one like him.... Would be a re-construction project."

The only May 1985 report: "Took him off last report, but would like to add him back on."

Johnson was chosen by Montreal in the second round of the draft (36th pick), three picks before Oakland selected a University of Missouri pitcher named Dave Otto. The Cubs, who earlier selected Palmeiro with the 22nd overall pick and right-hander Dave Masters with the 24th overall choice, didn't choose again until the 50th spot.

From a May 1992 *Player's Make-Up Inventory* report on Derek Jeter: "A super nice kid. Home-body type. Very smart. Wants to study medicine. Loves a challenge. Wants to be up in tough situations. Plays with fun. Teammates love him."

A May 1992 report by Scott Nelson himself: "This player will be complete. Like not only physical tools, but the way he plays the game. This guy is a ballplayer. Ball jumps off his bat. Has speed. Can throw and field. Nothing not to like."

The New York Yankees, picking sixth overall, selected Jeter. The Cubs, picking 11th, got right-hander Derek Wallace.

In three hours' time, I learn how inexact the art of scouting can be. It is part instinct, part gut feeling, part divining rod. These scouts are judged by time, which is the least understanding judge of all.

GAME 150

Tuesday, September 21, 2004 ... Cubs 5, Pirates 4 ... PNC Park ... Stuff: A plastic deer with a miniature Kyle Farnsworth jersey stretched across its back sits in the middle of the clubhouse. Since the "lucky" deer made its appear-

ance, the Cubs are 8-2. Yet the players will tell you they don't believe in the Curse of the Billy Goat. . . . Matt Clement, who hasn't made it out of the third inning in two of his last three starts and has one win in his last nine starts, just got bumped out of the rotation. Clement learns of his demotion from Daily Southtown *writer Jeff Vorva. . . . Cubs president Andy MacPhail, I, and several reporters are on the same flight from Pittsburgh to Chicago this morning. As we wait to board, MacPhail asks each of us if we think the Cubs will make the playoffs. The vote: a unanimous yes. MacPhail concurs.*

The Cubs don't have to be on the field for pregame stretching for another hour, so I swing by the locker of Todd Walker. Walker always is good for an honest answer, plus he's been through the kind of playoff races that put hair on your chest.

Thirteen games remain in the Cubs' regular season. They trail the Giants by a half-game. Every pitch, at-bat, throw, ground ball, fly ball, decision . . . everything means more as September sprints toward the postseason. These are sphincter-muscle moments, and some players handle the pressure better than others. At least, that's my theory.

Walker listens patiently as I blather on. He tries to help.

"The way you're supposed to hit is to be calm," he says. "Against Houston about a month ago, if I get a hit we win the game. I don't know, maybe I just tried too hard, but I didn't get it done. You put some pressure on yourself."

I look it up: In the August 28 game against the Astros at Wrigley, Walker struck out with the bases loaded in the bottom of the eighth. A hit likely would have won the game.

"People want to say that if you try harder you'll get in [the playoffs] for sure," he says. "If you care more, you'll win more. It doesn't work like that."

So how does it work?

"You just keep playing," Walker says. "The reality of it—and no one wants to hear this—is that it comes down to luck. There's three, four great teams trying to get in, and it comes down to how things break for you."

Luck? Has Walker seen the scouting report notebooks compiled by the advance scouts? They're thicker than the *Baseball Encyclopedia.* Has he watched Baker carefully construct a lineup card? Has he noticed Larry Rothschild meticulously prepare his pitchers? The entire sport revolves around tendencies, the law of averages, matchups, empirical baseball evidence. Luck? Please.

I return to the press box thinking a little less of Walker's baseball IQ.

Just for grins, I decide to test his theory. I'm going to chart luck during the course of the game.

Two hours and 52 minutes later, I can absolutely, positively tell you . . . Walker was right. And scarily so.

The Cubs shouldn't have won this game. And here's why:

First Inning
Something is going on with Kerry Wood. He walks leadoff man Jason Kendall. He walks Jack Wilson. He looks uncomfortable. What no one in the press box, PNC Park box seats, or Pirates' dugout knows is that Wood woke up this morning with a bad back. He spent much of the day in the trainer's room, and even as late as this afternoon, there was a possibility he might have to be scratched from the start.

But Wood decided to gut it out, though the early indications aren't encouraging. He can't find the strike zone, and Baker is screwed if Wood is unable to give him some quality innings. The bullpen is as vulnerable as a comb-over in a wind tunnel.

Wait—Wood strikes out Jason Bay, then Daryle Ward, then Craig Wilson. Crisis averted. The back is loosening up.

Second Inning
Or is it?

Wood gives up a leadoff double, then a single. Pirates on first and third. Tike Redman scores on a fielder's choice. Wood almost hits Pirates pitcher Josh Fogg in the chest during a sacrifice bunt. Kendall walks. But Wood coaxes a ground ball out of Jack Wilson to end the inning.

Fourth Inning
The Cubs tie the game, but it should have been more. With runners on first and second and one out, Sammy Sosa crushes a liner toward the right-field seats. The Gladiator does his signature home run bunny hop, jogs toward first, and then realizes the ball hasn't cleared the 21-foot-high scoreboard wall in right. It isn't until halfway to second that Sosa decides to sprint, but by then Craig Wilson throws to Jose Castillo, who throws to Jack Wilson, who applies the tag to our rally-killing hero.

Seventh Inning
The Cubs lead, 4-1. Wood is grinding. With his pitch count nearing 100, this will be his last inning.

The Pirates send former Cub Bobby Hill to the plate as a leadoff pinch hitter. He sends a sinking line drive toward center. Corey Patterson will play it as a single, catch it on one hop, and toss the ball to second. No problem.

What the . . . ?

Patterson races in, veers to his left at the last moment, and tries diving for a ball that Willie Mays in his prime would have missed by 10 feet. The ball skips past Patterson and toward the center-field wall. To Sosa's credit, he backs up the play and holds Hill to a triple. Doesn't matter. Hill scores on a groundout. The Cubs' lead is cut in half.

Ninth Inning

Closer LaTroy Hawkins enters the game. Hawkins hasn't given up a run in his last seven appearances, but this is his third consecutive day of work. The Cubs keep statistics on this sort of thing, and the numbers show a reliever's effectiveness is at its worst on Day 3 of consecutive outings.

Baker doesn't want to use Hawkins, but he doesn't have much of a choice. So naturally, the Pirates ding Hawkins for two hits, a walk, and the tying run.

Tenth Inning

Patterson leads off. He faces reliever Salomon Torres, who is making his 77th appearance this season, the most by a Pirates right-hander since Kent Tekulve made 76 in 1983.

But Torres is showing signs of wear. He has given up runs in his last two appearances. Of course, Patterson has only one hit in his last eight at-bats.

Patterson swings late and sends a high fly ball slicing toward the left-field line. Bay sprints toward the foul wall, slides, and watches the ball land fair by inches. Inches. Patterson has a double.

Neifi Perez sac-bunts him to third. Aramis Ramirez is intentionally walked. Moises Alou strikes out. Up steps Derrek Lee, who watches Torres carom a ball off Kendall's catcher's mitt and toward the Cubs' dugout. Patterson scores the go-ahead run.

In the bottom of the inning, the Cubs rely on Ryan Dempster, less than 13 months removed from Tommy John surgery, to close out the game. Dempster has exactly one career save and isn't accustomed to pitching in games that mean something in September.

"Usually, I'm making my flight arrangements to get home," he tells me later.

Dempster, fast becoming a favorite of his teammates and Baker, retires the side 1-2-3.

I check my scorebook for asterisks. There's Wood's stiff back, Sosa's massive brain cramp, Patterson's bonehead play. There's Baker's gamble on Hawkins, Patterson's 10th-inning double, Torres's wild pitch, Dempster's shutdown effort.

How do you explain any of it? You don't.

"Man, I'm getting gray," says Baker of the improbable win.

Afterward, some of the Cubs hit the postgame spread, grab a seat on the clubhouse couches, and watch wild-card leader San Francisco play Houston. Walker stops for a moment to look at the score.

"Well, you were right," I tell him.

"Yeah," he says, "we got lucky tonight."

GAME 151

Wednesday, September 22, 2004 . . . Cubs 1, Pirates 0 . . . PNC Park . . . Stuff: Sammy Sosa makes a spectacular diving catch in the bottom of the eighth to end a bases-loaded would-be rally. The Gladiator, perhaps smarting from the criticism of his premature bunny hop a night earlier, runs out a foul fly ball in the sixth. . . . Baseball beat reporters are not normal people. The Tribune's Paul Sullivan travels with a digital camera and keeps a collection of photos featuring him mock-kicking, choking, or beating big league mascots. Tonight he nearly shrieks with joy when he sees the Pirate Parrot mascot walk through the press box. . . . Wild-card status: a half-game behind San Francisco.

Mark Prior is fresh from throwing a pregame bullpen session. He has two Popeye-sized ice packs on his right shoulder and elbow. The timer clipped to the ice wraps is counting down from 15 minutes. So before the ice melts . . .

Q: *Is it possible to put your career in any sort of perspective yet?*
Prior: My rookie year I was on a team with 97 losses, with no expectations, and pitched OK, all right. I had decent numbers, but I felt like I could have pitched better at times.

Last year was a great year. A lot of things kind of fell into place for me.

And this year I dealt with new variables: being hurt, pitching, coming back from an injury, rehabbing, being thrown in the middle of the season without having the same preparation that everybody else gets in spring training. I think I now have a newfound respect for what spring training can be. Everybody starts off running in April, but I kind of started flat-footed. I had three rehab starts, but obviously A-ball and Triple-A hitters are a little bit different from facing Pujols, Rolen, and those guys.

Q: *Is there anything more terrifying to a pitcher than feeling a twinge in your arm or shoulder?*
Prior: Probably not, except for a ball coming back at your head. And actually, I've had a couple of those this year.

It's more the uncertainty. This game is tough as it is. But if you have one ounce of doubt about things physically . . . But once I got answers, they knew I was fine. And when I got answers the second time, they knew I was fine. But when the initial thing happens during the course of a game and you don't know the answers, your mind's just racing around out there. "Where am I at? Am I out for a year? Two years? OK, I'm not, but where does that leave me?"

Q: *You open up your* Chicago Tribune *one day and there it is: "The Prior Watch." What did you think?*
Prior: It was humorous at times. I think when it first started there was a picture of my feet. I don't even know they were my feet. But there was a picture, and at least they had the right tennis shoes. I read it a couple of times and guys would kind of harass me in a joking way. You kind of laugh about it.

But I guess it's part of the environment of Chicago. There's a lot of attention paid to us on the North Side. You just deal with it. I knew what I was getting into when I was drafted by Chicago, as far as the history.

Q: *During the season, a ballplayer is sort of shielded by a protective cocoon—*
Prior: I kind of like being in a cocoon. I stick to myself a lot, as far as not letting the public attention interfere with what my job is. I'm not some sort of recluse, but I know what I want to do, and I know what my job is. As far as getting ready for games, I don't let anything get in the way. But seeing something like the "Prior Watch," seeing the interest and how everybody felt when I went down, it was kind of shocking. Obviously, I knew I was a

big part of this team, but to see the fan reaction and how they were kind of bummed when I was hurt—it was like they genuinely cared about me getting back and helping the ballclub.

Q: *You've had to deal with the Chicago media in ways no previous Cubs or White Sox pitcher has had to. Your thoughts on what sort of media town Chicago is?*
Prior: I don't know what it's like in New York, what it's like in Boston. Nomar says it's nothing like Boston, where all they care about is New York and the Yankees. They dwell on the Yankees.

Here we don't dwell on a specific team, except maybe when it's the Cardinals and the series is going on. Here I think there's more focus on the history, The Curse, '84, '69. I think that's fine to a point—it's good to know history and to learn from it—but I don't think you need to dwell on it. Learn from your mistakes, but don't second-guess yourself.

Q: *Game 6 of the NLCS—The Bartman Game—is such a seminal moment in this franchise's history. You got the loss in that game. When were you able to move past what happened that night?*
Prior: Game 7.

But the first time I think I actually watched film of that game was when I pitched against [the Marlins] 10 days ago. That's the first time I've watched anything from that game.

I knew what happened that game. I could play that game over in my head if I wanted to. But when I look back on it, I wouldn't change anything that I did. I probably would have made the same pitches. Nine times out of 10, maybe I'm right, maybe I'm wrong. The fact is, they were a good team.

Some people made it sound as if we beat ourselves, as if New York beat themselves, that New York choked. No one ever really focused on the fact that Florida won.

Q: *It's also been said that Moises Alou's reaction after the Bartman incident had a trickle-down effect on you and the Cubs. Once and for all—did it?*
Prior: No. It's been asked. [When Alou couldn't catch the ball], I had a reaction of pointing [to the umpire] and saying, "Fan interference?" It's the same way I'd point if there was a check swing. It was a question more of "Can you get help?" That's the best way to compare it.

It was the ninth pitch of the at-bat. Maybe I tried to do a little too much on the last pitch and I walked him. But no, I don't think it affected me.

GAME 152

Thursday, September 23, 2004 . . . Cubs 6, Pirates 3 . . . PNC Park . . . Stat of the game: The Cubs have won 12 of their last 15 games and are 14-6 in September. . . . Stuff: Sammy Sosa meets the press. As usual, The Gladiator is good for the usual head-scratcher. Instead of saying he screwed up Tuesday night with his premature bunny hop and subsequent jog to second base, Sosa says he's not changing a thing. "For what? I've been doing The Hop for 14 years. You want me to change it now? Huh? This is my style." Sosa doesn't get it. The Hop is fine—just do it when you hit an actual home run, not a sure double off the wall that you jog into a single and an out.

The light-blue lineup card sits at the top of Greg Maddux's just-packed equipment bag, right next to a jockstrap and a white plastic protective cup. Dusty Baker made sure the little piece of history reached its proper owner.

In black ink Baker has printed a message on the official batting-order card.

Greg Maddux won Game #15 for 17th consecutive year, 6-3.

Baseball often overdoses on statistics, but Maddux's streak is one worth telling the grandkids about. Nobody, from Cy Young to Roger Clemens, has ever won 15 games for 17 straight seasons. Nobody has done it for 16 seasons.

I ask Paul Bako, who catches Maddux every fifth day, if there's a way to explain to Joe Fan just how difficult it is to win at least 15 games for nearly two decades.

"I don't think I can," he says. "For somebody who's not in the game, it's hard to put it in perspective. All I can say is it's really amazing. It's really unusual. It's really ridiculous, that's what it is."

Glendon Rusch finished 1-12 last season for Milwaukee. He knows how precious, and difficult, wins are in the big leagues.

"It's tough to comprehend what he's done," says Rusch. "In my opinion, he's a first-ballot, 100-percent-of-the-votes Hall of Famer."

A two-deep semicircle of reporters is waiting for Maddux when he returns from the shower. He's wearing a blue towel, but pulls on a black Nike golf shirt before facing the Minicams.

"OK," he says.

Someone asks what the 15/17 streak means to him.

"Well, you always have your goals, and it's always to win 20," Maddux says. "But one of the goals is to pitch 200 innings. If you can go out there and get your 200 innings, you got to be doing something right. Getting to 200 innings, to me personally, means more than the wins."

This one mattered. Maddux won his 15th (he's 8-3 since the All-Star break) and surpassed the 200-inning mark ($201\frac{2}{3}$). The Cubs climbed 20 games above .500 and would later leapfrog the Giants in the wild-card standings.

"So what are you going to do with the lineup card?" I ask after everyone has left.

"Whattaya mean?" he says.

I point to the card in his bag. "Oh," says Maddux, who didn't know the card had been delivered. He leans down and reads Baker's note.

"So?" I say.

"I'll probably put it up for auction on the Internet," he says.

Maddux is smiling. This card isn't going anywhere except his trophy case.

GAME 153

Friday, September 24, 2004 . . . Cubs 2, Mets 1 . . . Shea Stadium . . . Stat of the game: Glendon Rusch, starting in place of the banished Matt Clement, makes Dusty Baker look like a genius: six innings, one run, six hits, seven strikeouts. Then the bullpen pitches four scoreless innings. . . . The Curse in Reverse: The Marlins lose their fourth in a row. They're wild-card sushi, eight games behind the Cubs.

This is Hidemi Kittaka's third season in the States as the *Kyodo News*'s baseball correspondent. Kittaka is based in New York (the *News*'s offices are in Rockefeller Center) and helps cover the nearly dozen Japanese players in the big leagues.

Kittaka on Chicago, Wrigley, American baseball, Sammy Sosa, and Dusty Baker:

I've been to Wrigley four times. It's very nice. My first time at Wrigley Field was 1995, when [Hideo] Nomo made his debut for the Dodgers. I remember he struck out Sammy Sosa.

[Mets shortstop] Kaz Matsui was talking to us, and he said it has history to it and the atmosphere is really nice. It is the same way I feel. Everything is so different [at Wrigley], and yet it's so beautiful.

It's not the best place to work, but for baseball Wrigley is the best place. Wrigley and Fenway Park. That's the other one I like. The fans are great. They really get into it. But I guess the fans in Chicago are nicer to the players than the fans in Boston.

There is something similar to Wrigley in Japan. It's in the Osaka area, Koshien Stadium. That's where the Hanshin Tigers play. It's very old, and there's some ivy sticking outside the stadium. I think it was built at least 50 years ago. It has history.

Kingston Mines is my favorite place in Chicago. I like hearing blues. That's where [Masato] Yoshii, when he was with the Mets—he's back in Japan—liked to go.

It's obvious that there's better pitching, better hitting, more speed [in the MLB vs. Japanese baseball]. But the biggest difference is that it's more like dynamic. Here they'll challenge the outfielder, even if it's Mike Cameron or Sammy Sosa. Most of the outfielders here have good arms. In Japan, it's very cautious. A base hit to Ichiro, they don't challenge him in Japan. But they challenge him more here than they do in Japan.

Sosa is very well known in Japan. In Japan, people know [Barry] Bonds, [Mike] Piazza, and Sosa. There are Cubs fans. They root for the Cubs. The main reason is Sosa and Dusty Baker.

If it's 11:35 P.M. in Chicago, it's 1:35 P.M. the next day in Japan. But if it was all the same time zone, all the Japanese baseball teams would be bankrupt because all the fans would watch these guys on TV.

This year I'm covering Kaz Matsui. I was with the Yankees all season last year. I hope that someday a Japanese player plays for the Cubs.

GAME 154

Saturday, September 25, 2004 . . . Mets 4, Cubs 3 . . . Shea Stadium . . . Cubs NL Central pennant flies: Second (87-67) . . . Stat of the game: Sammy Sosa goes 0-for-5, strikes out four times, grounds into a double play, and strands eight runners. If he could, I think Dusty Baker would bat Sosa 10th in the lineup. . . . Stuff: If the Cubs miss the playoffs, this might be the devastating defeat that does it. Ahead, 3-0, with two on (thanks to two Ryan Dempster walks) and two outs in the bottom of the ninth, rookie Victor Diaz hits a two-strike LaTroy Hawkins pitch over the right-field fence to tie the game. The Mets, essentially fielding their Triple-A team, win it in the 11th when rookie Craig Brazell hits his first-ever big league dinger, this one off Kent Mercker. . . . Hawkins, making his sixth appearance in seven days, will catch most of the heat for the loss, but the Cubs' offense has scored three or fewer runs in four of its last six games. . . . Wild-card status: a half-game ahead of San Francisco.

You should have seen Victor Diaz Sr. and his wife jumping up and down on their living room sofa today. You'd jump, too, if your son just hit a three-run, game-tying homer with two outs and two strikes in the bottom of the ninth inning on national television.

No Cubs curse, huh? Then explain this:

Two weeks ago, Victor Diaz Jr., a minor league outfielder in the Mets organization, was back home in Chicago after completing the season at Triple-A Norfolk. He thought he was done for the year, and he wasn't happy about it.

Three of his Norfolk teammates—pitcher Matt Ginter, pitcher Tyler Yates, and first baseman Craig Brazell—had been called up to the big club on September 1. Diaz Jr., who was born in Santo Domingo, Dominican Republic, raised in Chicago, and graduated from Roberto Clemente High School, couldn't believe he'd been left behind. Nothing against Brazell, but he had a higher batting average, more home runs, and more RBI.

"We never think he going to be in the big leagues this year," says Victor Sr. "Then Ginter got an operation."

On September 10, Ginter was placed on the 60-day disabled list with bone chips in his right ankle. Diaz Jr. got his call.

"He was at my house that Friday," says Diaz Sr. "He flies out that day. He calls me the next day and says, 'I'm in the lineup. I'm batting sixth.' I say, 'Get ready.' He plays against Philadelphia. Goes 1-for-3."

So now Victor Jr. is on his collision course with Cubs destiny. Of course, we should have somehow seen this coming. After all, Victor Sr. played pro ball for seven years, five of them in, ta-da, the St. Louis Cardinals organization.

Victor Jr. didn't start today's game. It wasn't until there was one out in the top of the seventh that Mets manager Art Howe pulled Richard Hidalgo from right and replaced him with Victor on a double switch.

They call him "Little Manny" in New York, because he bears a resemblance to Boston slugger Manny Ramirez. Squattish-looking. Strong. Power to all fields. But really, he takes after his old man. Until the Mets turned him into an outfielder this season, Victor Jr. played second base, just like Pop.

Pop watched Victor Jr. in the eighth inning, when he pulled a Mark Prior two-strike pitch past Aramis Ramirez for a hit. Victor Sr. didn't like the swing. "Too much weight in the front," he says. "You got to stay a little bit at back. I'm his batting coach. He listens to me."

Then came the ninth inning. Hawkins replaced Dempster, who had replaced Prior.

Ball one . . . A called strike . . . A foul ball . . . A ball in the dirt.

Then . . . the shot heard 'round Shea, Cubs Nation, and the Diaz living room.

"I wanted him to make good contact, just a base hit," says Victor Sr. "When I see him hitting, I know the ball gone. I know the ball go. I know right away. When he put his head down, I know he got good wood.

"I jumped on the chair. Me and my wife. Very emotional. Hugging. Everything."

There have been no angry phone calls from local Cubs fans. To the contrary.

"No, no," says Victor Sr. "In the neighborhood, they are happy for him. He practiced all the time. He worked hard for that. That's not overnight. We put a lot of effort into that. Anyway, that's his job, right?"

Yes, but did he have to do it so well?

After the game, son called father. There was laughter, congratulations, and pride. Growing up, Victor Jr. wanted nothing more than to play for the Cubs and with his baseball hero, Sammy Sosa.

Now this: the Cubs done in by one of their own followers.

GAME 155

Sunday, September 26, 2004 ... Mets 3, Cubs 2 ... Shea Stadium ... Stat of the game: The Cubs go 8-4 on the road trip, but three of the four losses are one-run defeats. .... Stuff: With two outs, bases loaded in the fifth, and the Cubs down a run, Moises Alou gets jobbed when umpire Bill Miller rings him up on a 3-2 pitch that wasn't within a borough of the strike zone. Alou later tells reporters that some umpires are "definitely after me." If they are, Alou has only himself to blame for any ill will.

Even though the Cubs cling to a precarious half-game lead in the wild-card standings, they have to plan for the playoffs. That's why former Cubs general manager Ed Lynch, now a special assistant to GM Jim Hendry, has been in San Diego for the last six days scouting the Padres.

"They'll probably be eliminated," says Lynch of the Padres, "but ..."

The Padres are a bit of a postseason long shot, but who knows, right? They trail Los Angeles in the West by four and a half games, and the second-place Giants by two with six games left to play.

Lynch has taken his share of shots—some deserved, most not—for his nearly six-year tenure as Cubs GM. Anyway, Lynch fell on the Cubs sword shortly after the 2000 All-Star break, was reassigned as a special assistant, moved to Arizona, and scouts the major and minor leagues. I've got a soft spot for the lug, so I'm hoping he gets another GM chance one of these days.

In the meantime, he's assigned to the Padres playoff watch, which got a little help today as San Diego won its third in a row. Lynch's job: prepare a detailed scouting report for the Cubs should they somehow meet the Padres in the postseason.

"What you're trying to do, you're trying to predict what the team you're going to play is going to do in certain situations," says Lynch. "You're looking for tendencies. You want to know how to defend their hitters and how to attack their pitchers."

Lynch records an entire game on four different forms. He uses one sheet of paper for a pitching chart, one for each pitcher he sees, one for the team (its lineup, tendencies, right-handed and left-handed pitching), one for how to defense the Padres hitters.

"It's not brain surgery, but it's a lot of stuff," he says.

No tendency is too small to ignore. For example, Lynch noticed the other day that starter David Wells faced six right-handed Arizona Diamondback hitters and started each at-bat with a breaking ball. By the fifth inning, Wells had thrown first-pitch breaking balls to 11 D-Back righties.

Lynch, a former big league pitcher, also saw that second baseman Mark Loretta, when facing a right-hander in a breaking ball situation, tries to go the other way. And Lynch always pays attention to what a pitcher likes to throw in certain counts, and if the pattern changes depending if the batter is left-handed or right-handed. Why does it matter?

"Because it's amazing how true to form they get when guys make it to the postseason," Lynch says.

If/when the Padres are bounced, Lynch expects to move north to the Dodgers. That means he thinks the Cubs will hang on for a wild-card berth. The schedule certainly favors them. Why overthink it, right?

After all, it isn't brain surgery.

GAME 156

Monday, September 27, 2004 . . . Cubs 12, Reds 5 . . . Wrigley Field . . . Stat of the game: Carlos Zambrano wins his 16th game of the season. . . . Stuff: Matt Clement, persona non pitcher, is at his Pennsylvania home with his very pregnant wife. He's expected back soon, not that it matters. The Cubs have no plans to use him. . . . Kiss-of-death headline in today's Tribune *sports section: "Cubs Appear Playoff-Ready" . . . Kiss-of-death announcement by the Cubs: Playoff tickets will go on sale next Monday.*

Because she doesn't want to get pinched by the IRS, Gina asks that I use only her first name. That's fine, though I'm guessing the tax feds won't be tracking any Gina-generated offshore accounts in Bimini anytime soon.

Gina plays a *djembe*, sort of the Senegalese cousin to a bongo drum. She's staked out a regular postgame spot outside Gates K and J, which is where the Wrigley crowd empties out onto Waveland from the left-field bleachers and box seats on the first-base side of the stadium. CFD Engine Co. 78 is right across the street.

You can't miss the 31-year-old musician from Indiana. Today's Bohemian-flavored ensemble features purple Chuck Taylors, red socks, aquamarine pants, and a light cotton white shirt. A beaded string of miniature bells is wrapped around the socks, and a necklace of green beads and a gold Corona beer medal hang from her neck. Her blond dreadlocks are long and thick enough to use for batting practice.

The game finished more than an hour ago, but Gina keeps playing the $350 hand-carved drum as if someone is holding a Luger to her head. I don't know squat about *djembes*, but this one sound pretty good, much better than the five-gallon plastic cans the street drummers use on the Sheffield side of the stadium.

I lean against a newspaper vending machine and watch as the thinning crowd walks past Gina as she slaps the drum skin as if it owes her rent money. Hardly anyone stops to drop any cash into the black drum case that also serves as a collection basket. Sammy Sosa drives by in his Range Rover. The Gladiator doesn't wave.

Gina pounds out a steady, staccato beat, enough so that a sheen of perspiration forms on her forehead. Someone tosses a buck into the case. I reach into my pocket and count my remaining $1 bills. The four bucks die a hero's death and tumble into the darkness of the Remo case. What the hell, right? Gina needs a new pair of Chucks, and anyway, she's dying out here.

Or so I thought.

As Wrigley security workers pull shut the door on Gate J, Gina decides to call it quits. She places the drum on its side and uses it as a seat. Then she digs into the depths of the case and begins sorting.

I figure 20 bucks, tops. Instead, Gina unfolds and straightens dollar bill after dollar bill. Ten dollars . . . 20 . . . 30 . . . 40 . . . 50 . . . 60 . . . 70 . . .

I lose count. All I know is that I'm buying daughters Lara and Taylor *djembes* when I get home. Screw those college tuition payments.

"About $50, $60 is a typical day. But today was nice."

This isn't her full-time job. She works as a nanny in the Wrigleyville area, but that only pays the room and board. The *djembe* pays for most everything else.

"I moved to the community here, and some of the people are Ballhawks," says Gina. "They kept saying, 'Hey, man, come out to the Cubs games and you'll make money there.' So I just started doing that."

The city requires street performers to purchase a permit, but that guarantees nothing at Wrigley. There are at least two or three other drummers working the sidewalks outside the stadium. But Gina outplays them and outlasts them, sometimes playing nonstop 90 minutes or longer after the game.

"I've made $5 out here, which is usually when we get rained out," says Gina. "If it's raining, I can't play in the rain. And I've made as much as, well, one day last year I made more than $300."

Three Benjamins? Where do I sign up for lessons?

"That was unusual," she says. "I got picked up by some Republicans who had a lot of money to throw around."

Gina usually arrives at Wrigley by the fifth or sixth inning. She'll start playing during the seventh inning, later if the Cubs are winning. "If they're winning, people stay in their seats and they're not coming out," she says. "If they're losing, people will get tired of watching the game. That's when I'll start playing sooner."

That's the general *djembe* rule of thumb. But something changed during the 2003 NLCS. The business dynamic changed.

"Last year kind of ruined it for me when they tried to go to the World Series," she says. "Before that, if they would lose I would do better. If they won, I'd do all right. But when they were going for the Series and they lost, people would come out, and it was like the whole team had been gunned down. Now everybody has these expectations to win, so when they lose it's different."

GAME 157

Tuesday, September 28, 2004 . . . Reds 8, Cubs 3 . . . Wrigley Field . . . Stat of the game: Greg Maddux gives up four runs in the third and two more in the fifth, all on home runs. Game over. . . . Stuff: Ramon Martinez (groin) goes on the DL, allowing Neifi Perez to take his place on the Cubs' playoff roster—if there is a playoff roster. . . . The Cubs lose to Reds starter Josh Hancock (who?) and his 8.57 road ERA. . . . Wild-card status: tied with San Francisco, a half-game ahead of Houston.

Ashes to ashes, dust to Wrigley?

Earlier in the season, I saw someone linger near the outfield wall after a game. An usher shooed him along, but then the guy ran away long enough to lean across the basket and pour something onto the warning track. I didn't think much about it until I saw a woman in the bleachers do the same thing during batting practice a few days ago.

That wasn't Uncle Bob who's now part of the gravel mix, was it?

Afraid so. Some very deceased Cubs Nation residents are part of the Burial Confines, whether the Cubs organization likes it or not.

"I'll see it maybe three, four times a year," says Roger Baird, the head groundskeeper. "Ninety-nine percent of the time, it happens after a ballgame when people are exiting the stadium. They'll sneak down by the wall and toss something over it. We try to get a hose on it right away. If you get too much of that stuff on one area, it can kill your grass. It's something we learned over the years."

Baird has heard the sob stories. On occasion the crew will do a wink-wink thing and turn the other way while Aunt Beatrice is interred, so to speak. Other times people will sneak the ashes in during a paid tour of Wrigley. They'll pretend to admire the ivy and then casually mix in Dad.

"Most of the time, if we let them do it, we have them pour the ashes on the warning track. Then we drag it and hose it down. But it just shows how much loyalty our fans have to this organization and to this ballpark."

That's one way of looking at it. Either that, or they don't want to spring for mausoleum space or an urn at Pier One.

Then there are the families who buy caskets and want a Cubby-themed farewell.

"We do get a lot of heart-wrenching requests when somebody passes away and they want to be buried in a Cubs hat and/or they want to be buried with an autographed ball," says John McDonough, the Cubs' senior VP of marketing. "Or here's one I get a lot of requests for: the use of our logo on their tombstone. It's something that we generally grant."

Good, because it only makes sense that there be a link between the Cubs and the afterlife. After all, if you follow this franchise long enough, you die a little bit each day.

GAME 158

Wednesday, September 29, 2004 . . . Reds 4, Cubs 3 . . . Wrigley Field . . . Cubs NL Central pennant flies: Third (88-70) . . . Stat of the game: LaTroy

Hawkins blows his second consecutive save opportunity and does it again with two outs and two strikes in the bottom of the ninth. . . . Stuff: For the first time in franchise history, the Cubs go over the 3 million mark in attendance. And for what seems like the 3 millionth time, the Cubs also break hearts. The Cubs no longer control their own postseason destiny. Losses in four of their last five games, combined with four straight wins by Houston (and thanks, St. Louis, for rolling over like circus dogs in your three-game series against the Astros), now leave the Cubs in a horrible spot: one game remaining against the suddenly unbeatable Reds, followed by three games against the Braves, who would like nothing better than to avenge last season's NLDS series.

In a small booth on the fifth and final row of the Wrigley press box is a mounted steel device that has been party to Cubs misery and their infrequent successes since 1937. That's when the Holabird+Root/Hubertz Scoring System was installed at Wrigley, its main purpose in mechanical life to display balls, strikes, outs, hits, errors, and batters' jersey numbers on the ancient center-field scoreboard.

The box looks as if it were used in the control room of a Cold War missile silo. The keypad is rudimentary—a green button to enter something, a red button to clear it.

This is the booth where grounds crew member Rick Fuhs works during a game. He was hired at Wrigley in 1978, which means he started where every rookie starts: with a broom in his hands, seat rows to sweep, and garbage to bag after a game.

"You always found stuff," says Fuhs, 45. "We found a diamond ring. Gold coins. Wallets with cash. I always returned those kind of things. I was raised that way."

He later joined the grounds crew and eventually became responsible for caring for the home plate area. In 1989, he also became scoreboard operator.

It isn't much of an office. There's a tiny fan that spits out wisps of air. There's a Sony Watchman, a bag of peanuts, and a spare, red Sears polo shirt the grounds crew is required to wear when on the field. A pair of binoculars is within reaching distance.

The control box is old but efficient. Fuhs enters a number or letter, presses the green button, and it instantaneously activates the metal eyelids in the scoreboard. The relay time is actually faster than the computer system Wrigley operators use for the grandstand scoreboards.

Fuhs is one of four full-time groundskeepers (there are seven in all) who grew up in a three-block radius. They also grew to love the Cubs and, even more so, Wrigley Field.

"I was here in '84 when they lost to San Diego," he says. "The worst part about it is I was friends with Lee Smith and Leon Durham. Maybe people don't know this, but Smith was pitching with a bad shoulder. He pitched through a lot of pain."

And Game 7 of the NLCS?

"I really haven't gotten over that yet," he says. "When it was done, I hit the two Cancel buttons on the machine, put the cover over it, and I walked out of here."

The Cubs finish today a half-game behind streaking Houston. Fuhs, either in denial or too optimistic to notice the collapse, isn't giving up on his professional dream.

"I want to work a World Series and punch out that last out on the machine," he says. "That's my goal."

GAME 159

Thursday, September 30, 2004 . . . Reds 2, Cubs 1 . . . Wrigley Field . . . Cubs NL Central pennant flies: Third (88-71) . . . Stat of the game: The Cubs waste a nine-inning, one-run, 16-strikeout instructional video by Mark Prior. . . . Stuff: Got a knife and dab of butter? Go ahead and use it on the Cubs, because they're playoff toast. . . . Earlier in the day, Baker reveals that he occasionally seeks help from a lighted caricature of Harry Caray attached to a house that can be seen from the Cubs' dugout. "I'll say, 'C'mon, Harry, send us some stuff, man.'" Apparently, Harry isn't listening. . . . Baker and Steve Stone have an icy exchange on the Fox Sports Net postgame show. Then Stoney appears on WGN Radio tonight and goes Jack Nicholson on the Cubs: "You want the truth? You can't handle the truth. Let me tell you something, guys, the truth of this situation is [this is] an extremely talented bunch of guys who want to look at all directions except where they should really look, and kind of make excuses for what happened. . . . This team should have won the wild card by six, seven games. No doubt about it." Oh, boy . . . Wild-card status: one game behind Houston.

Mark Prior has already struck out eight Reds in just four innings by the time I knock on the door of Suite 32 on the mezzanine level. This is the suite used by general manager Jim Hendry, who doesn't have much to do in these post-trade-deadline/September call-up days other than to watch and hope for the best.

Chuck Wasserstrom, the team's director of baseball information, opens the door, waves me in, and then quickly joins Oneri Fleita, the Cubs director of player development, on the other side of the suite. The decor is Early Corporate, but the view belongs on a tourist brochure. The only thing missing is a Cubs lead; it's a scoreless game heading to the fifth.

Hendry leans against a counter in front of the suite windows, sips on a cup of coffee, and taps his hand as he watches Kearns strike out swinging against Prior. The sound of Hendry's 1991 College World Series ring (he coached Creighton to a third-place finish) striking the counter surface fills this half of the room.

The Cubs GM still hasn't fully recovered from the weekend in New York, when Chicago lost those two one-run games to the dreadful Mets. Now they've lost two out of three to a Reds team that begins today 29 games out of the NL Central lead.

"I'm usually the eternal optimist, enthusiastic," says Hendry. "Now things have gotten to be real tight. It's crunch time, and we're going to have to play great these last four games to get in. I mean, that was kind of a devastating one at Shea the other day. And then yesterday. Anybody can go back at the end of the year and say we should have won that game or this game, but the timing of the one in Shea and the one yesterday are a little tougher than normal."

Sometimes Hendry prefers to sit by himself in the suite. Other times, such as today, he welcomes the company. There isn't anyone in the Cubs' front office more affable than the 49-year-old Hendry, but that doesn't mean he takes losses well.

The wall phone to his immediate right went for an unexpected ride last season when he pulled it out of the jack and tossed it after a particularly gruesome Cubs defeat. But generally speaking, it usually takes Hendry about an hour to get over a loss.

"This time of year—I've got to be honest with you—it carries over a little bit more than an hour," he says. "I haven't done real well since Saturday. You start thinking what a shame it will be if we don't get in. I think we're good enough to get in. But let's give the other two guys credit, too. Houston and San Francisco have won a lot of games the last two months."

On some level, Hendry truly wants to give the Astros and Giants their proper due. But he can't help but do the what-if thing. What if the Cubs hadn't blown that 3-0 ninth-inning lead? Or if they had to lose that day, why couldn't it have been a conventional 5-1 defeat?

"I think what happens is that, the closer you get to the finish line, it's not sometimes the loss itself, but it's *how* you lost that lingers a little more than if it were May or June," he says.

Prior strikes out Anderson Machado to end the fifth inning, then strikes out the side in the sixth. The game remains scoreless until Sammy Sosa arrives at the plate with one out in the bottom of the sixth. Then The Gladiator cranks a solo homer over the left-field wall.

Hendry barely says a peep. "Ah, we're ahead," he says as the ball leaves Sosa's bat barrel.

A suite attendant pokes his head into the room. They're baking a fresh batch of cookies in the mezzanine-level kitchen. Is Hendry interested? Sure he is. After all, alcohol isn't allowed in the suite, so why not a sugar fix?

Hendry isn't in playing shape these days. He injured his knee before the season began and he still can't run on it. Occasional hourlong walks are what pass for exercise during this season.

He's a member at Ridgemoor Country Club in West Gunnison, but his schedule never allows for more than a few holes of golf at a time, or a quick session of beating range balls. His handicap, once near scratch, is now within viewing distance of double digits.

This GM gig exacts more of a toll than just ruining your golf game. Hendry has never been a big sleeper, but during the season he doesn't get more than four or five hours of shuteye a night. "And I slept a little less yesterday and Saturday," he says.

Earlier this year—and for reasons not entirely related to his job—Hendry's marriage ended. But it isn't uncommon to see him at Wrigley with his young daughter and son in tow.

"I've never been in anything but baseball, so I'm a little different," he says as the seventh inning begins. "Even if I were at high school or coaching at Creighton, I've always been kind of engulfed in it, maybe to a fault. I'm not proud of that. I'm way too one-dimensional. Every job I've had in baseball has been kind of a consuming thing for me. But I don't blame that for . . . I don't feel like I had a good marriage before I was a GM. But I have two wonderful children."

Hendry isn't some sort of sleep-on-the-office-couch kind of guy. He likes work. You often can find his car there on Saturdays and Sundays during

November and December. That's when, with the second-floor offices nearly deserted, he analyzes the board in his office that lists every big league roster. He assesses the list of available free agents. He examines the Cubs' minor league system and forms ideas for possible deals.

"I don't want people to think—" he says before stopping in midsentence as Kearns pulls a ball down the left-field line.

"Oh, no," says Hendry as the ball caroms off the foul pole for a game-tying home run in the seventh. "That's some kind of good player. There's the best player in the league having the worst year. Anyhow . . ."

Prior strikes out Darren Bragg to end the inning. He has 14 Ks so far.

I push my luck and ask Hendry if he'll have any regrets about any of his decisions should the Cubs fail to reach the postseason. Hendry runs down his list of biggies: loved the Greg Maddux signing, felt good about the roster depth, even liked the bullpen situation. But that was before the Cubs became a Blue Cross commercial.

"I guess my biggest regret would be I'd like to have seen what we'd look like without the quantity of injuries we had," he says. "But you expect injuries. You're going to get them. It's not 'Oh, poor me.' Houston had some tough injuries and overcame them. But what's surprising, we're sitting here September 30 and [Kerry] Wood, Prior, and [Matt] Clement are 23-25. So the flip side of that is we're lucky we're still in it."

I glance at the scoreboard. There's two out in the top of the eighth. Time to leave.

Hendry says I'm welcome to stay, but it's probably best I return to the press box. Smart move. I probably didn't want to be there in the 11th when the Cubs failed to get a two-out hit with bases loaded. And I definitely didn't want to be there in the 12th when the Reds scored on a two-out double and the Cubs stranded two runners to end the game.

As the Cubs drop a full game out of the wild-card chase, my thoughts and prayers go out to a certain inanimate object.

The wall phone.

OCTOBER

●●

GAME 160

Friday, October 1, 2004 . . . Braves 5, Cubs 4 . . . Wrigley Field . . . Cubs NL Central pennant flies: Third (88-72) . . . Stuff: Not much optimism among the regulars. "Today's the wake, tomorrow's the funeral," says a Wrigley usher a few hours before the game. . . . As the Braves take a 5-1 lead in the fifth, a fan pleads with first baseman Adam LaRoche, "You guys already clinched. Give us one, c'mon." . . . One Braves scout recently told a Cubs scout that Atlanta wants to eliminate Chicago from the playoff race. The reason: The Braves don't want to risk facing the underachieving Cubs in the NLDS. . . . Sign seen in stands: "Bluto 1978: It's never over. Ask Dean Wormer." Sorry, Blutarsky. It's over. . . . Michael Barrett is 0 for his last 16, Derrek Lee is 2 for his last 21, Corey Patterson is 9 for his last 56 . . . I do my customary postgame swing by the Bartman seat. Debrah Heiselman and Brad Martin, two University of Florida students here for the day (Martin skipped his Friday Elements of Advertising class to make the trip), pose in the seat. . . . The Optimism Award goes to the Cubs' PR staff, which continues to put the finishing touches on a playoff media guide. . . . Wild-card status: doomed.

The name tag on the security guard's shirt says "Bill." Bill is stationed outside the WGN-TV booth, presumably to protect Steve Stone from danger.

This is how off-the-charts comical this season has become. The Cubs have lost five consecutive games and seven out of eight, and the main topic of conversation today is . . . Stone?

Stone popped off Thursday, and he did so too smugly and too soon after an excruciating 2-1 loss to the Reds. His remarks on WGN Radio concerning the Cubs' season were mostly legitimate, but his timing (before today's loss, the Cubs still had a remote chance of squeezing into the playoffs) couldn't have been worse. And you needed a chain saw to cut the tension between Stoney and Baker on the Thursday postgame show.

About 9,000 reporters are waiting today for Stone to make his usual pregame appearance near the batting cage. He's a no-show. And partner Chip Caray flies solo on the *Leadoff Man* show, too. Hmmm.

Rumors are as thick as the outfield grass: Stone is meeting with management . . . He's going to get canned . . . He's not going to get canned.

Meanwhile, Cubs GM Jim Hendry doesn't need a name tag on his shirt. You can identify Hendry by the steam coming out of his ears. If he were any hotter, you could fry okra on his forehead.

"I think we went past constructive criticism on how the game was managed and I think it became personal," says Hendry of Stone's comments.

Baker is equally blunt about The Interview.

"It shocked me," he says. "A man can say what he wants to say. I don't understand it. I don't understand the timing of it. It's bad timing. If there is something personal, you need to talk about it with somebody instead of broadcasting it to everyone else. I don't know where he's coming from. I feel bad for my team, and sorry for him for even doing that."

Baker says this latest incident might force him to forgo postgame interviews with Stone next season—that is, if Stone is back next season. He also calls 2004 "the messiest year I've seen in my whole life."

Someone asks if it's possible for the two former friends to have a professional relationship.

"I'm not the one with the problem," Baker says. "It appears to me some of the problem went back to me defending my players when they said what they said about him. You got to ask him. This came out of his mouth, not mine."

Stone's mouth isn't available until later. Turns out he did have a little get-together with management.

"I had a very nice conversation with Dusty Baker," Stone says. "We talked, and Dusty and I are on the same page and we do want the same thing, and that is a world championship for the Chicago Cubs, which I think will be brought here. If not this year, then in the near future. Dusty expressed those feelings. I expressed the same feelings to him, and at the end of the day we both knew we were on the same page in that respect. He has his job to do, and I have my job to do."

But there will be no public softening of those Thursday comments.

"I regret nothing," says Stone.

Just to gauge crowd sentiment, I spend most of the game with the Wrigley crowd. The Cubs aren't going to like the poll results.

When pitcher Mike Hampton hits a two-run homer in the fourth, I hear a Cubs fan yell toward the Chicago dugout.

"Hey," he says, "it must have been Stone's fault!"

GAME 161

Saturday, October 2, 2004 . . . Braves 8, Cubs 6 . . . Wrigley Field . . . Stat of the game: The Cubs, losers of five consecutive games and seven of their last eight, are officially eliminated from the wild-card race. It's 96 years and counting without a World Series title. . . . Stuff: Moments after the Cubs are playoff contention history, the always subtle Fox Sports cues Paper Lace's song "The Night Chicago Died." . . . "This is sad, not to be in the playoff," says Carlos Zambrano. "I don't want to say it, [but it's] kind of like bad luck." Really? Big Z needs to meet Sam Sianis. . . . News flash: Chip Caray has a sweetheart offer to join the Braves broadcast team. Caray and the Cubs won't say a peep about it, which probably means he's gone. . . . Wild-card status: none.

What better way to begin Fan Appreciation Weekend than with another blown lead, one hit in the final four innings (oh, sure, now Antonio Alfonseca pitches lights out—for the Braves), and a playoff-ending defeat. The fans appreciate the effort so much that they save their best boos for the eighth inning, when the Cubs blow a 6-5 lead.

The Cubs are used to it—the blown leads and the boos.

"We deserve it," a Cubs coach tells me earlier this morning. "If the fans boo all day, we deserve it. This is the most frustrating season I've ever had. It was right there for us."

You don't need *CSI: Chicago* to analyze this homicide scene. In fact, the Miller Lite sign beyond the Wrigley right-field wall has it right. It reads: "Wrigleyville's Magic Number: 12 Ounces."

Anyway, here's chief medical examiner Dusty Baker to perform the autopsy.

[Choke?] Agh, that's what they always say. Did Florida choke? Did Philly choke? Does that mean everybody who doesn't win is a choker? I think that's just a word that people use when they don't have another word.

How would I describe it? Hey, it just didn't end right. These guys are running on fumes. Big-time fumes. We knew when we had to go to Florida to make up that doubleheader and you have 20-some days in a row, we knew it was going to be a tough period. Guys are running out of gas. Guys are trying, they're trying to win. I never had a team that was described as a choker, and I'm not going to have one now.

It's been my toughest [season]. I've had a lot more disappointing seasons than this one. It's just been the toughest from the beginning. You come to spring training and everything's fine. Then we lose Prior, then we lost Gonzalez . . . never had Remlinger from the beginning. And Borowski. And Grudzielanek. I'm trying to hang on, trying to put everything together on a daily basis, and we're not getting much appreciation for the job we were doing. All we got was criticism for what we weren't doing. Hey, man, these guys busted butt. They gave all they had.

And it was the hardest [season] just because of stuff: the stadium stuff we had to answer, the steroid stuff in spring training, the stuff with the media, the stuff with Stone. I had a feeling it was going to be a tough year before we got started.

Got up this morning, went to the gas station to get gas—and I haven't had a flat in 20 years—and I had a flat. I was like, "Oh, Lord, what is going on here?"

We have a good nucleus here. The thing I'm praying for next is that we stay healthy and don't have any mess. Not necessarily better luck, but better health. I always believe what Arnold Schwarzenegger says: "I'll be back." I believe that from the bottom of my heart.

I didn't have nothing to do with Stoney. At least, I didn't think I did. But I went to the players and said, "Hey, man, if you don't like a guy, or you don't like whatever, go to him or leave him alone." I did that. I did that on two or three occasions.

If you take away this last week . . . boy, this last week has been a nightmare.

How do you not [say] you've had a partial success out of this when you haven't had winning seasons back-to-back for 30 years? We've done something. We haven't done what we like, or whatever everybody expected, but we've done something. We're not failures. So what's the opposite of failures? You tell me. So I'll use the word "partial success." How's that?

[The 2003 record], I didn't expect that to come until Year 3. When we did it that quickly, it actually put more pressure on us to do more.

What you do is just regroup and get stronger. That's why I came here, to change [the Lovable Losers tag] permanently. I came here to win.

GAME 162

Sunday, October 3, 2004 . . . Cubs 10, Braves 8 . . . Wrigley Field . . . Cubs NL Central pennant flies: Third (89-73) . . . Stat of the game: The Cubs actually win one more game than their 2003 total, but still finish 16 games behind Central winner St. Louis and three games behind Houston, which clinches the wild-card berth today.

A day in the life (and death) of the 2004 Cubs, beginning at 9:29 A.M. and ending at 5:47 P.M.
Dusty Baker steers his black Chevy convertible (the flat tire of a day earlier has been patched) into the Wrigley parking lot. Son Darren, who was pulled from school because the Bakers thought the Cubs would make the playoffs, is with him. They walk into the clubhouse, where someone has written on the greaseboard "Expect to Win." Next to the greaseboard is another sign: "Tom Otis Hellmann and his staff hope we served you well."

Ah, yes, tip day for the clubbies.

I walk out to the dugout. Someone has left a *Sun-Times* on the wooden bench. The day's headline speaks to all Cubs fans: "Why Do They Keep Doing This to Us?" Good question.

The Miller Lite billboard on a Sheffield rooftop has already been swapped out for a new theme. "Go Bears!" it says. Cubs management is thrilled with that.

The clubhouse opens to the media at 9:50. The lineup card is already posted: no Sammy Sosa, which probably explains why he's a late arrival.

I make the rounds, first stopping at Matt Clement's locker. Clement is driving back to Pennsylvania immediately after the game to be with his pregnant wife. "If I can ever help you, let me know," says the classy Clement, who never once whined about his hard-luck 9-13 record or his late-season demotion to limbo.

Kent Mercker sits in a folding chair in front of his locker. The surprising source of rants against umpires, Steve Stone, and Chip Caray knows he's Cubs history. He gestures toward Greg Maddux, who is standing nearby. "How do you think he feels?" says Mercker. "He hasn't missed a playoff since, what, 1993?" Actually, it's 1992—Maddux's last season with the Cubs.

Nomar Garciaparra meets the press. Is it for the last time? Garciaparra is a free agent at game's end. "This is definitely a place I'll seriously consider," he says. "I love Wrigley. I love the city. I love the fans here."

Next up: Baker. It takes only a few minutes until someone asks about Sosa's absence from the lineup.

"He's just ailing," says Baker.

WSCR's George Ofman asks the question that matters: "Do you want him back [in 2005]?"

"Yeah," says Baker. "I'd want him back if . . . he's got to go to work this winter. Just get in tip-top, tip-top shape mentally and physically. It's a big year for him next year. So I assume he'll have a very good year, especially since it's his option year."

Baker says he expects to retain his entire coaching staff. He says he'd like for Corey Patterson to spend time in the off-season with former leadoff man extraordinaire Brett Butler. He says he'll consult with GM Jim Hendry about possible trades and acquisitions. "With my wish list," says Baker, "our payroll would be $200 million."

Most of all, Baker is bummed about the Cubs' cartwheel down the playoff stairs. He says he'll take the heat for the collapse, but: "One thing about it, I didn't get dumb overnight. It doesn't happen like that."

The Cubs begin to emerge from the dugout for pregame stretching. Still no Gladiator sighting.

Chip Caray arrives on the field and is instantly surrounded by reporters. He says he'll have something to announce after the game. Body-language-o-meter: He's out of here.

I notice Caray approach Moises Alou near the batting cage. They shake hands. I hear Alou say, "At least you had the balls to come down here."

Sosa finally walks into the clubhouse a few minutes after noon.

The wind is blowing straight out, which explains seven homers, including Jason Dubois's first big-league dinger (the substitute right fielder finishes with four RBI, and actually throws to—gasp!—cutoff men. Gladiator Who?) and Alou's career-high 39th.

Roger Baird's grounds crew, who split a playoff share in 2003, sings the Seventh-Inning Stretch, and at song's end the announced crowd of 38,420 (more like 30,000, with the empty seats) gives Steve Stone an ovation. He waves to the fans as if they were his royal subjects. They wave back. It's a lovefest.

Mercker gets booed off the field after giving up a homer to Dewayne Wise, the only batter he faces in the eighth.

Maddux gets his 16th win, tying him with Carlos Zambrano for the team lead. LaTroy Hawkins, who gets booed as he walks to the mound, pitches a scoreless ninth for his 25th save.

As the Cubs leave the field, several players toss their caps into the crowd. One fan holds up a sign that reads, "Championship or not, we still love our Cubs." Wrigley organist Gary Pressy plays "Our Day Will Come."

Afterward, Maddux, who didn't sign with the Cubs to finish third, says his 16th victory means zilch. In fact, he apologizes that the game took so long—a brisk 2:18.

"It just didn't feel right walking on the field today," he says. "It should have felt different. I know I'm embarrassed, but that's me."

Maddux then gives Wrigley a hug. "It's a place that makes baseball special." Asked what the 2005 Cubs need, he says, "Nothing. Nothing except a few extra wins."

A Tampa Bay Bucs game is on the clubhouse plasma. In the middle of the room, Alou gives what could be his farewell address. The Cubs hold a 2005 option on the 38-year-old outfielder, who led the team in homers, RBI (106), and umpire bitching.

"This is one of the best teams I've ever played on," says Alou. "For us to be out on October 3 . . . I didn't expect this."

Once the reporters disperse, Alou begins stuffing his belongings into an Iowa Cubs equipment bag. The *Daily Herald*'s Bruce Miles peels back and shakes Alou's hand.

"It was very nice dealing with you," he says. "I hope to see you back."

"I hope so, too," says Alou.

Garciaparra, wearing a Whittier Police T-shirt, sits in the players' lounge chowing down on the postgame spread. Aramis Ramirez, still in his uniform, sits in front of his locker with his head down. Kyle Farnsworth relaxes in a recliner and reads the Best Buy ads.

Dubois is still beaming about career homer No. 1. The fan who dug it out of the juniper bushes got a bat for the ball.

Hendry makes the rounds, shaking every player's hand and thanking them for their work. He can't shake Sosa's hand, because it turns out The Gladiator bolted hours ago. Sosa's Cubs jerseys, the ones with the *C*-for-captain logos on the elastic sleeves, hang from his locker. Hendry looks as if he wants to cut the fabric in very small pieces, preferably with Sosa in it.

"Even if he wasn't playing, obviously he should have been here with his teammates," says Hendry, seething.

A few minutes later, we're led into Baker's office for his reaction to the Sosa AWOL.

"This is a first for me," Baker says wearily.

The *Sun-Times*'s Mike Kiley reaches Sosa not long after leaving Baker's office. Sosa tells him he left the stadium during the seventh inning because he didn't want to talk to reporters (even though he had promised earlier in the day to do so). And then, in response to Baker's pregame comment about Sosa's return in 2005, Sosa says, "I'm tired of being blamed by Dusty Baker for all the failures of this club. I resent the inference that I'm not prepared. I live my life every minute every day to prepare for combat. No one has ever questioned my mental or physical preparation at any level."

No, but I question his grammar. And since when did Sosa start using agent-speak such as "resent the inference"? Unless, of course, his agent fed him those lines. And please—combat? It's baseball, not Hill 49.

Ever so slowly, the Cubs' clubhouse begins to thin out. Handshakes are exchanged. Checks are handed to Otis. Farnsworth walks out with a broken Maddux bat signed by the Hall of Famer himself.

I walk out to the players' parking lot, where one of the attendants tells me Sosa left 15 minutes after the game started. What? The Gladiator lied? Shocking.

Mark Prior walks over to the parking lot fence and signs autographs for 20 minutes. Hawkins comes out and is immediately greeted by jeers.

"Hey, LaTroy, I can do your job!" yells a fan.

"No, you can't!" says Hawkins before closing the door to his silver Beemer.

Baker and Darren are among the last to leave the Wrigley lot. Baker lowers the top on the SSR, then waves his right hand like a prom queen as he drives south on Clark.

I walk back to the nearly deserted Waveland side of Wrigley and take one last look at the center-field scoreboard. Maddux's No. 31 jersey number is still posted, along with the final score. The white W flag points toward nearby Lake Michigan.

I can't believe the season is finished. Seven days ago, the Cubs owned the wild-card lead. Now, like me, they're going home.

There is one last thing to do. I pull out my wallet and extract a folded wager ticket from the Palace Station Race & Sports book in Vegas. It reads: *To Win 2004 World Series. Cubs. $20.*

I tear that little sucker bet in half. Then, in a moment of perfect Cubs clarity, I'm struck by a single thought.

I wonder what kind of odds I can get on them for 2005?

EPILOGUE

....

As of January 30, 2005:

Dusty Baker spent his first October at home since 2001. . . . Greg Maddux's 16-11 2004 record was identical to his 2003 record, but his 4.02 ERA was the highest of his big league career. . . . Leo Mazzone and the Atlanta Braves won the NL East, but were eliminated in the NLDS. . . . The Mirage and Palace Station made lots of money on Cubs bets. . . . ESPN.com fantasy guru Eric Karabell finished second in his Bristol-based league, while Craig Nustadt and partner Glen Brown of the injury-plagued Vultures team finished 14th in the Chicago division of the National Fantasy Baseball Championship and didn't come close to winning the $100,000 overall prize.

Pat Hughes and Ron Santo completed the season without a single toupee fire in the booth. . . . Todd Walker re-signed with the Cubs. . . . Wayne Messmer was available for motivational-speaking engagements. His fee: $5,000 to $10,000, plus expenses. . . . Dave Davison remained the modern-day leader in Most Balls Caught by a Ballhawk. . . . Neither of Governor Rod Blagojevich's 2004 baseball wishes came true: a batting practice session and a Cubs World Series championship.

After paying a commission to the auction house, Dan Miller got about $5,000 for Sammy Sosa's career No. 513 home run ball. . . . Todd Jones signed with the Florida Marlins. . . . Billy Corgan wrote a book of poetry entitled *Blinking with Fists*. . . . Sergio Mitre finished the season 2-4 with a 6.61 ERA. . . . Kyle Farnsworth, who finished with a 4-5 record and 4.73 ERA, was expected to remain a Cub.

Chaplain Edwin Caraballo hoped to preach again at Wrigley. . . . Mark Grace wasn't offered the vacant Arizona Diamondbacks managerial job. . . . Paul Sullivan, hater of mascots, continued to mull over a possible move off the Cubs beat. . . . Gary Matthews was replaced by Gene Clines as hitting coach. . . . The Boston Red Sox swept the St. Louis Cardinals in the World Series. . . . Rick Hummel and Bernie Miklasz of the *Post-Dispatch* covered the collapse.

George Will had to find a new colossus. . . . Gary Hughes was wrong about the Anaheim Angels, but not much else. . . . John Tait was infected by The Curse; the Bears finished their season 5-11. . . . Dan and Cherina Felten were still happily married. . . . Paul Rathje returned to the Cubs in September.

Case No. 04CR-12777—the first-degree murder trial of Rodrigo Caballero, who is accused of killing Frank Hernandez Jr.—made its way to court October 21 and resumed January 4, 2005. . . . Denise Gawrych continued to get top dollar for Wrigley rentals. . . . Moises Alou signed a two-year deal with San Francisco. . . . A Sammy Sosa "At the Ballpark" ornament went for $3.99 on eBay. . . . Umpires' room attendant Jimmy Farrell promised to write luckier Ws on baseballs.

Mark Prior finished with a 6-4 record and the same ERA as Maddux. . . . Todd Hollandsworth's history of injuries meant the free agent would be offered a 2005 Cubs contract only as a last resort. . . . Dave Groeschner was fired, becoming the second Cubs trainer in as many years to be dismissed. Assistant trainer Sandy Krum also was fired and sued the Cubs. . . . Glendon Rusch, the only guy I saw tip the Wrigley car parkers (and he wasn't even driving that day), finished 6-2 with a 3.47 ERA and re-signed with the Cubs.

Chip Caray accepted the Atlanta Braves broadcasting job. . . . Steve Stone resigned the day after the World Series. . . . Wendell Kim was fired. . . . Wrigley Field maintenance crews began city-mandated repairs the day after the season. . . . Scott McClain returned home from Japan and is a free agent.

Tony Cooney awaited word on his application to mortuary science school. If he isn't accepted for the upcoming class, he'll return to the Wrigley players' parking lot, where his streak of no dings or accidents remains unchallenged. . . . John Stockstill started a new 2005 draft board. . . . Grant Johnson, the Cubs' top draft pick, was expected to begin the 2004 season in Single-A Peoria or Daytona. . . . The Cubs-commissioned DVD project by MLB's Robert Haddad was canceled. . . . Corey Patterson returned to Atlanta, presumably with Brett Butler's phone number.

Sammy Sosa, who was caught on security cameras leaving Wrigley long before the seventh inning of the October 3 finale, was fined one game's pay—$87,400 (he's appealing). . . . Jim Hendry traded Sosa to the Baltimore Orioles, pending The Gladiator passing a physical. . . . Ramon Martinez ended the season on the DL and wasn't offered a contract. . . . Michael Barrett had the best season of his career (.287, 16 homers, 65 RBI). . . . Eric Karros was hired by Fox for its pregame and postgame playoff shows.

Rey Ordonez retired—for now. . . . Ozzie Guillen and the White Sox finished 83-79 and out of the playoffs. . . . The White Sox hired a new ad agency. . . . Michael Wilbon signed a new contract with ESPN's *Pardon the Interruption* and swore off (and at) the Cubs—until 2005 spring training. . . . The Milwaukee Brewers drew 2,062,382 fans, 421,759 of which came from the 10 games played against the Cubs.

Kent Mercker's Cubs career lasted one eventful season. He signed with Cincinnati. . . . The Wrigley grounds crew winterized the field (took the wall pads off, dried out the rain tarp, raked leaves from the ivy branches, cut the grass until the first freeze). . . . The Second City's *Doors Open on the Right* ended in October. . . . Mark Grudzielanek (.307, 6 homers, 23 RBI) signed a one-year deal with the Cardinals. . . . Nomar Garciaparra, who was voted a full playoff share by the Red Sox, agreed to a one-year deal with the Cubs.

Matt Clement was offered arbitration, but signed with Boston. . . . Omar Minaya left the Expos to become the Mets' head of baseball operations. . . . Joe Borowski started counting the days until spring training. . . . Ryan Dempster's 2005 option was picked up. . . . Jim Riggleman and the L.A. Dodgers were eliminated in the NLDS. Riggleman became the St. Louis Cardinals' minor league coordinator.

New Era rep Tim Isaacson found a cold adult beverage the day the Cubs were eliminated from the playoff chase. . . . Kerry Wood, who finished with an 8-9 record and 3.72 ERA, had to endure his first-ever trade talk. . . . Jon Leicester, Sergio Mitre, Todd Wellemeyer, and Michael Wuertz would be invited to training camp to compete for an expected three job openings. . . . Lemon Tom Goodwin wasn't offered a Cubs contract. . . . Ron Santo was placed on the 2005 Hall of Fame Veterans Committee Ballot.

Lemon Paul Bako signed with the Dodgers. . . . Bill James was getting fitted for a World Series ring. . . . David Samson and the Marlins finished third in the NL East, with six fewer wins than the Cubs. . . . Nobody came close to hitting the Wrigley scoreboard. . . . John McDonough's marketing machine helped produce a club attendance record of 3,170,184. . . . Frank Maloney oversaw the distribution of playoff ticket refunds.

Jim Oboikowitch said Kid Rock almost got him fired, but never told me why. . . . In light of the Red Sox championship, Rick Pildes should ask for a mistrial and Alan Dershowitz should be disbarred. . . . ESPN.com conducted a poll listing the reasons for the Cubs' failure to reach the playoffs. Out of 108,635 respondees, 34.4 percent blamed injuries, 20.6 percent blamed The Curse, 18.5 percent blamed Baker, 17.3 percent blamed Sosa,

9.9 percent blame LaTroy Hawkins. . . . ESPN.com rated the Cubs the No. 1 cursed team in sports. . . . The new 2005 MLB schedule had a sense of humor: The Red Sox make their first-ever appearance at Wrigley June 10-12. The two teams haven't played each other since September 11, 1918, when Boston won its last World Series before the 2004 title.

Steve Bartman politely declined or ignored repeated requests to be interviewed for this book. He has yet to speak publicly about the Game 6 incident. Rumor had it that immediately following the 2003 NLCS his employer, a suburban-Chicago-based consulting firm, transferred Bartman to the company's London office. There also was water cooler talk at the company that he had taken a leave of absence or was considering attending law school. This much is for sure: The volume of post-NLCS e-mails and phone calls to the company's headquarters crashed the firm's Web site and overloaded the phone system. A companywide memo was distributed prohibiting anyone to speak with media members about Bartman. According to several employees I recently contacted at the firm, the well-liked Bartman has returned to the Chicago office, where he keeps a low profile and rarely, if ever, discusses the incident with coworkers. He has changed his hairstyle and glasses but, contrary to urban legend, hasn't undergone cosmetic surgery. Still, said a coworker, "people wouldn't recognize him." Added the coworker, "He's a good guy."